POLICE WORK WITH JUVENILES

and

The ADMINISTRATION of JUVENILE JUSTICE

Sixth Edition

POLICE WORK WITH JUVENILES
and
The ADMINISTRATION of JUVENILE JUSTICE

By

JOHN P. KENNEY, Ph.D.

Professor, Department of Criminal Justice
California State University at Long Beach

DAN G. PURSUIT, M.S.S.A.
Director Emeritus, Delinquency Control Institute
School of Public Administration
University of Southern California

DONALD E. FULLER, Ph.D.

Director, Delinquency Control Institute
University of Southern California

ROBERT F. BARRY, M.S., M.P.A.

Associate Director, Delinquency Control Institute
University of Southern California

CHARLES C THOMAS • PUBLISHER
Springfield • Illinois • U.S.A.

Published and Distributed Throughout the World by
CHARLES C THOMAS • PUBLISHER
2600 South First Street
Springfield, Illinois, 62717, U.S.A.

© *1982 by* CHARLES C THOMAS • PUBLISHER
ISBN 0-398-04670-0
Library of Congress Catalog Card Number: 82-732

Printed in the United States of America
CU-R-1

Library of Congress Cataloging in Publication Data
Main entry under title:

Police work with juveniles and the administration of
    juvenile justice.

    Rev. ed. of: Police work with juveniles and the
administration of juvenile justice / by John P.
Kenney, Dan G. Pursuit. 5th ed. 1975.
    Bibliography: p.
    Includes index.
    1. Police services for juveniles.   2. Juvenile
justice, Administration of.   I. Kenney, John Paul,
1920-   .   II. Kenney, John Paul, 1920-
Police work with juveniles and the administration of
juvenile justice.
HV8079.25.P64   1982   364.3'6'0973   82-732

This second edition of *POLICE WORK WITH JUVENILES AND THE ADMINISTRATION OF JUVENILE JUSTICE* is dedicated to our co-author, Dan G. Pursuit, Professor of Public Administration (Emeritus) at the University of Southern California. He has had a long and distinguished career in the field of juvenile justice education and research. As the director of the Delinquency Control Institute from 1948 to 1958 and associate director from 1958 to 1981, he guided the fortunes of several thousand police juvenile officers and juvenile justice workers from throughout the world. From 1958 to 1981, he directed the multifaceted research activities of the Youth Studies Center as its executive officer and professor of public administration.

Throughout his academic career at the University of Southern California, he taught numerous juvenile-justice courses and served as a juvenile-justice consultant to many federal, state, and local governmental agencies, universities, and private agencies.

He is a co-editor of *POLICE PROGRAMS FOR PREVENTING CRIME AND DELINQUENCY* and *JUVENILE JUSTICE MANAGEMENT* published by Charles C Thomas, Publisher and co-author of the monographs, *CALIFORNIA JUVENILE TRAFFIC STUDY and POLICE SERVICES TO JUVENILES*. He has also authored numerous articles on the subject of juvenile justice.

Professor Pursuit has made major contributions to the following professional associations: American Society of Public Administration; the International Association of Chiefs of Police; The International Juvenile Officers Association; The California Juvenile Officers Association; The California Peace Officers Association; The National Council on Crime and Delinquency; The California Probation, Parole and Correctional Association; The National Association of Social Workers; and The Creative Education Foundation.

Professor Pursuit retired in 1981, but his contributions to juvenile justice continue unabated.

Dan, we and your many friends throughout the world are proud of you!

J.P.K.
D.E.F.
R.J.B.

PREFACE

*P*OLICE WORK WITH JUVENILES AND THE ADMINIS-
TRATION OF JUVENILE JUSTICE makes a unique contribu-
tion to the juvenile-justice literature. It is a scholarly treatise on the
subject. However, it addresses the principal issues and concepts with
a practical orientation, making it an invaluable resource for both
students and practitioners.

Although the book highlights the police role and functions, the
interrelationships between community agencies, the courts, correctional agencies, and the police are emphasized. Each component of
the juvenile justice system is treated in a meaningful manner.

In this new sixth edition, we have broadened the scope of
theoretical and practical juvenile justice concepts and issues in order
to address more realistically current societal concerns and problems.
Legal rights and responsibilities of juveniles have been dramatically
changed by court decisions and legislative actions. Child abuse and
use of dangerous drugs and narcotics by juveniles are now recognized as very real problems, whereas only a few years ago they were
almost ignored. Labeling theory has modified our understanding of
delinquents and how they see themselves. In essence, we have
drafted a new approach to the study of juvenile justice.

The material in the book has been substantially reorganized, with
consolidation of some chapters and the addition of the new subject
matter. Considerable new material is presented in the chapters that
have been retained from previous editions. Complete new sections
are as follows: "Labeling Theory," "Police Discretion," "Forensic
Hypnosis," "Child Abuse," and "Sexual Exploitation of Children."

We acknowledge with sincere appreciation the contributions of
our many students who have critiqued previous editions and made
suggestions for change. We are especially grateful for the research

efforts of Jim Pass, Robert Kennedy, and Robert Ihrke.

J.P.K.
D.G.P.
D.E.F.
R.J.B.

CONTENTS

                                             Page

Preface vii

Chapter

1. INTRODUCTION 3
2. THE JUVENILE JUSTICE SYSTEM 10
3. THE LAW AND LEGAL PROCEEDINGS 37
4. LABELING THEORY 58
5. DELINQUENCY PREVENTION 81
6. SPECIAL PROBLEMS 90
7. VANDALISM AND JUVENILE GANGS 128
8. POLICIES AND THE EXERCISE OF DISCRETION 145
9. THE POLICE ROLE AND FUNCTIONS 165
10. POLICE ADMINISTRATIVE ORGANIZATION 175
11. POLICE OPERATIONS 199
12. INTERVIEWING 229
13. FORENSIC HYPNOSIS: ITS USES IN LAW ENFORCEMENT
   INTERVIEWS 256
14. JUVENILE COURT AND PROBATION SERVICES 264
15. STATE PROGRAMMING 270
16. REPORTS AND RECORDS PERTAINING TO JUVENILES 278
17. CHILD ABUSE AND NEGLECT 307
18. SEXUAL EXPLOITATION OF CHILDREN 326
19. PLANNING 346

Index 363

POLICE WORK WITH JUVENILES

and

The ADMINISTRATION of JUVENILE JUSTICE

Chapter 1

INTRODUCTION

A S we embark upon the 1980s society has turned pervasively hostile toward the juvenile offender. No longer viewed as "wayward youth," or errant troublemakers acting out the adverse effects of one-parent families, educational failure, and paucity of employment opportunity, society tends to view today's juvenile as a serious deviant. Used to perpetrate armed robbery in view of the lesser sanction in juvenile statutes, absorbed in the tumult of gang and criminal activity, increasingly involved in violence, and often in possession of a firearm, today's youth has seemingly entered the world of the young adult criminal at ages thought to be adolescence in prior times.

The clamor for action toward curtailing today's youthful offender is exploding in proposed statutory revisions around the country. Juvenile judges abhor the serious nature of offenses confronting them before the bench, reconciling themselves to the futility of acting in parental fashion by practicing legal "social work" in hopes of preventing further system penetration by most youthful offenders. In the urban centers of America most juvenile court judges are confronted by a parade of youthful recidivists whose offenses turn increasingly toward crimes against the person. District attorneys lament their need to bypass formal prosecution of early offenders in attending to recidivists whose records seem more similar to yesterday's long-time adult offender. Law enforcement, prosecutors, and judges alike fear the consequences of failure to confront the early offender who may well return at a later date with more ferocity than most care to condone. Perhaps most disturbing of all, this lugubrious description of today's juvenile offender occurs following an entire decade of intense and prolonged governmental spending directed toward the prevention and reduction of crime with substantial attention directed toward the juvenile. While certain successes did occur, most juvenile justice professionals seem somewhat hardened by the deterioration of their hopes for a "better" juvenile justice system. The challenge for the 1980s looms large, particularly in view of substantial cuts in governmental funding at all levels. If successes were few with massive governmental funding, the 1980s may require the support of private sources hitherto positioned somewhat on the sidelines.

POLICY TRENDS IN JUVENILE PROCESSING

Age of The Offender

The obvious trend among the states is to lower the upper age limit for juvenile court jurisdiction and to favor the transfer of juveniles in the 16–18-year age range to criminal court. Whereas in 1972, 66 percent of the states retained jurisdiction over juveniles until age 18, 25.5 percent of the states now have lowered their maximum age of jurisdiction to age 16 or lower.* It is argued that today's 16-year-old is a sophisticated offender whose potential for rehabilitation in the juvenile court has been already tested on several occasions. Secondly, there is a belief, supported by evidence, that youth of today are more violent than their predecessors, and that today's victim is equally vulnerable to the juvenile as to the adult offender. Finally, it is argued that modest juvenile sentences are no longer appropriate for offenses as serious as those committed by adults.

Juvenile Court Versus Criminal Court

With the exception of a jury trial, bail, and shorter sentences,

---

*Connecticut, New York, North Carolina, and Vermont retain jurisdiction until age fifteen.

juveniles share identical processing as adults. Some argue that, therefore, the distinction between the two courts should no longer exist. With the exception of juvenile judges, many judges fail to see the rationale for maintaining separate courts. While it is true that in re *Gault, Winship, Kent, Miranda,* and other landmark cases have eliminated the *parens patriae* doctrine in many juvenile courts, other advocates suggest that the younger offender needs the separate court. Accordingly, the new juvenile code in the state of Washington and a new felony statute in New York steer the serious offender to criminal court. In Washington, the younger offender receives the attention of the juvenile court.

It is argued that the juvenile court cannot now serve the best interests of the child and those of society by continuing to mingle the first-time offender with the serious recidivist. Those who fear penetration of the juvenile justice system are concerned with "labeling" juveniles under juvenile court jurisdiction. Those who urge retribution for serious offenders urge swift justice and stiffer sentences. Whether or not these two views can be reconciled in one court lies at the center of the debate.

Labeling

For some time advocates have argued the exacerbating effect of formally bringing a youth into the criminal justice system. By labeling a youth as a "delinquent," the premise is that the stigma that attaches makes delinquency a self-fulfilling prophecy. It is argued that the probability of becoming a delinquent is substantially increased by processing a youth through arrest, adjudication, and formal disposition, though empirical studies have not substantiated this premise as a truism. The first-time offender may, indeed, offend a second time. Once he repeats, the probability of reoffending does increase. However, it is not clear that delinquency is a function of formal processing. The Gluecks, in their studies, found a thin line between the offender formally charged and the offender who is not apprehended. The causes of delinquency appear to be complex and about which few authors are in total agreement. Certain youth brought formally into the criminal justice system will not reoffend; others will reoffend. For the most part, the criminal justice system has diverted the first-time offender. It is not clear that charging and adjudicating a juvenile will be more detrimental in the long run than diverting him. No one can assess the encouragement afforded the potentially dangerous delinquent by eluding formal processing. Similarly, few can accurately predict the probability that a particular offender will reoffend. Carried to the extreme, were it so that pre-delinquent traits can be accurately identified (and some argue that they can be), we would place certain children under protective custody very early in their lives. To date, the trend has been to separate delinquent youth from status offenders and adults, to divert most status offenders, and to divert most first-time offenders. Reoffenders are typically processed and sentenced. Violent and serious offenders are ultimately incarcerated. Crime continues despite the labels we attach. The actual causes of recidivism seem little affected by current processing. In fact, the filing and processing rate in juvenile courts has varied very little during the years 1957-76. While the rate has varied only from 57 percent to 69 percent, the number of juveniles processed has increased from 280,000 to 715,800.[1]

In comparing, however, those arrested under the age of 18 between 1968 and 1977, we find only a 16.8 percent increase in the total number of arrests (from 1,054,568 to 1,241,881). Naturally, arrest rates and recidivism are subject to substantial error. Self-reported crime rates would be much higher. It is not clear, however, that familiarization with the court process impedes or encourages crime. Whether or not incarceration acts in the same way is not clear. Since, however, society needs to be protected we find a trend toward lowering the processing age and increasing the sanctions. Since we tend to adhere to the theory of labeling, we seek to protect the younger, less sophisticated youth by processing them cautiously through the juvenile court.

Detention

Detention of juveniles has been an issue for some time. States have, by statute or in compliance with the Law Enforcement Assistance Administration (LEAA), eliminated status offenders from continued detention and have separated juvenile offenders from adults. It is argued that status offenders, juvenile delinquents, and adults are different enough in behavior, type of offense, and threat to others to differentiate in their detention. Accordingly, the trend toward detention is down. The last census of state and local juvenile detention facilities (1975) contrasted the juvenile population detained of 11,767 in 1971 to 11,089 in 1975, a 6 percent decrease! At the same time, the number of U.S. public detention centers increased from 305 in 1971 to 347 in 1975. Accordingly, during the years 1974-75 a slight increase in the juvenile population occurred (+ 1%). The substantial reduction in detention of status offenders during the latter years of LEAA would seem to continue the trend toward limiting the detention of juveniles.

Probation

As noted, the filing rates against juveniles have varied from 57 percent to 69 percent despite the increased processing of juveniles brought to the attention of the court. During the past ten years the courts, as well as law enforcement, have turned toward diversion techniques to avoid formal processing. While the concern for labeling was articulated, the primary impetus would seem to have been LEAAs substantial funding of diversion and pre-trial programs. Similarly, the courts turned toward probation whenever possible to avoid incarceration. In 1976, for example, the juvenile probation population in the United States amounted to 668,769, as opposed to those juveniles placed in long-term correctional facilities (34,255) in 1975 (1976 not available). Thus, about a twenty-to-one ratio exists between probation and incarceration. What generally is not clear is the impact of diversion upon later recidivism rates. The LEAA over the years has experienced severe difficulty in evaluating its diversion programs. It is clear that certain youth have entered diversion programs who would typically have been lectured and released prior to the program's existence. It was argued that these youths would benefit from pre-delinquent counseling. Naturally, this early offender responded more positively than the recidivist, and most diversion programs have reported successes. The absence of a control group, however, has often plagued these evaluations. To some extent, post-conviction programs, such as *New Pride* (Denver, Colorado), which has now been replicated, have earned greater support in view of the high predisposition toward delinquency among the client population and the substantial need for intensive psychological, educational, and experiential development.

Incarceration

Incarceration of juveniles in training schools, ranches, and group homes is affected by the availability of spaces (beds). During the years 1971-75, training school sites actually decreased while halfway houses and group homes increased.[2] Certainly advocates of child care have resisted additional construction of facilities. Some, such as Dr. Jerome Miller, argue for the closing of juvenile facilities. Nevertheless, since the court typically reserves such incarceration as a last resort, the continual flow of violent juveniles has placed pressure upon crowded youth facilities. Despite this pressure, the population in secure and semi-secure juvenile facilities decreased 24 percent from 1965 (34,242) to 1978 (26,000).[2] One would have to assume that, considering the increased referral of juveniles to the court, today's youth institution is receiving a larger proportion of serious juvenile offenders. Accordingly, probation and diversion programs would seem to have borne the brunt of most nonviolent offenders for the past several years. Naturally, some of the most violent youth offenders may have been placed in facilities accommodating the 18–25-year-old population.

The fact remains that today's juvenile correctional facilities exist primarily for the purpose of incapacitation: that is, removal from society. Rehabilitation for today's youthful reoffender, particularly one prone to violence, seems more hope than fact. California, in which the incarcerated juvenile population is slowly rising, reports the characteristics of its California Youth Authority population as follows: "Forty percent of the department's current population (1979) was committed for crimes of violence... murder, robbery or aggravated assault... *three times* the proportion of 10 years ago."[2]

"Another effect of the past decade's trend has been to increase the average age of youth authority wards in institutions. Ten years ago the average ward was 17. Today, the average ward is about 18.5 years, with their numbers almost evenly divided between those committed by juvenile and adult courts."[2] (California permits incarceration of youthful offenders, ages 16-21, in the youth authority.) At the same time, the length of stay for youthful offenders in California has increased from 10.9 months in 1977 to 13.2 months in 1980 (estimated). The fact remains that serious juvenile recidivists offer limited hope for rehabilitation. The California Youth Authority (CYA) reports a 45.6 percent failure rate for those youth released for two years following incarceration. The CYA counts nonfailure as success. Since some may go undetected, go on to adult institutions, or leave the jurisdiction, one would need to be cautious regarding success rates.[2]

REFERENCES

1. U.S. Department of Justice, Bureau of Justice Statistics, *Source Book of Criminal Justice Statistics*, 1980, Washington, D.C.: U.S. Government Printing Office, 1981.
2. Pearl S. West, The Youth Authority in 1980, *Youth Authority Quarterly*, Spring 1980.

Chapter 2

THE JUVENILE JUSTICE SYSTEM

B EFORE describing the current juvenile justice system it is appropriate to define the term *system* and comment on its present significance. "A system is a complex unit formed of many often diverse parts subject to a common plan or serving a common purpose."

The President's Crime Commission Report in 1967 stressed the need to apply the system approach to the criminal justice system and to the solution of our nation's crime and delinquency problems. Such a systems approach had been successful in solving large-scale industrial and business problems and needed to be applied to major social problems as well. The report pointed up the vast complexities of attempting to coordinate such diverse components as the police, courts, and corrections while attempting to attain the common purpose of crime prevention and control. In the past inadequate planning had resulted in the process being really a nonsystem rather than a well-integrated systematic operation.

It is essential to view the juvenile justice system as an integral part or subsystem of the total criminal justice system with the police assuming a major role because of its unique position at the beginning of the process.

Definition

A broad definition of the juvenile justice system is preferable to a narrow one, which usually includes only the police, courts and corrections. Other important elements also need to be included so that a more useful definition is as follows: "The juvenile justice system is the interrelationship between citizens, schools, community resources, police, courts, and corrections to prevent and control unlawful youth behavior, neglect, and abuse of juveniles." This more inclusive definition helps to emphasize the important role of citizens, schools, and other community resources which are so instrumental in preventing juvenile delinquency and keeping youth from entering the system through intervention.

It is also desirable to view the system in the light of the basic elements of any system input-processing-output-feedback. *Input* would represent unlawful behavior and other undesirable social conditions that bring matters to the attention of the police at the beginning of the system. Input can be limited through effective planning and coordination by lay and professional persons at the local level.

Processing would include activities and decisions by police; courts, prosecution and defense; and corrections (probation, institutions and parole). Each of these specialized components are considered subsystems of the total system. The ensuing description of the juvenile justice process will reveal the many key decision points in the system where youth can be diverted from the system or processed further into the system.

Output can be considered the behavior of juveniles following their diversion from various points in the system or behavior following final release on parole. Output might also include some jointly planned constructive social action to control undesirable community conditions which encourage unlawful behavior. It could also include new legislation resulting from joint planning.

Feedback can be considered the research data including the behavioral and other results of system processing and the use of that information to reinforce or modify various aspects of the total system. Without adequate feedback the system would continue in its disorganized, fragmented style.

The Juvenile Justice Process

The following discussion of the juvenile justice process will focus on the current complex processing of juvenile offenders starting from police contacts through parole.

Juveniles and the Law Enforcement Process

There is evidence that the police handling of juvenile offenders is more a function of informal police-community relations, the nature of the community, and its geographical location than observance of abstract principles of law enforcement. For example, it is has been found that the proportion of juveniles arrested who are referred to court depends on the type of community and the relationship of police and the public there. Rural communities, where there is apt to be a high degree of personal relationship between citizens and police, tend to have significantly fewer court referrals of arrested juveniles than do communities with a high degree of impersonality in contacts between police and public. In each case, police reflect their perception of community attitudes toward delinquency, exercising maximum discretion in homogeneous rural areas and less in urban areas where the population is heterogeneous and therefore perceptions of the citizenry are likewise varied.

Some empirical indices, however, show that even in high-density metropolitan settings police exercise considerable discretion. Most large police departments have specialized divisions for handling juveniles. Officers of these divisions often deal only with youths who are referred to them by patrol officers. Most police-juvenile arrests in the field, i.e. on the street, are made by patrol officers. It is up to the patrolman to decide whether or not to arrest a particular suspect and to refer him to the youth division for a potential referral to the court having jurisdiction over juvenile matters.

While most available research on juvenile justice tends to focus on events occurring after the police field encounter, a recent exploratory study of police control of juveniles in Boston, Chicago, and Washington, D.C., showed that only a small fraction of the legally liable juvenile suspects are arrested. A second significant finding corroborated earlier evidence that most police work with juveniles stems from citizen complaints. Of a total of 281 juvenile encounters studied, 72 percent were citizen-initiated. Only 28 percent were initiated by police on patrol. In view of this evidence, police work with juveniles should be regarded more as responding to citizen requests than as being initiated by police.

While discretion not to arrest in the field is vital to the successful and equitable operation of law enforcement, discretion to release is equally vital after a child has been arrested and brought to the police station. At the present time, police "station adjustments" (referral to community resources or other interdepartmental handling by police) occur in 45 percent to 50 percent of all juvenile contacts in the nation as a whole. A study of Washington, D.C., juvenile detention needs by the National Council on Crime and Delinquency found that exercise of police discretion resulted in court referral of only 50 percent of young persons who had been arrested. Finally, an analysis of national data on juvenile dispositions found that 46 percent to 50 percent of juveniles arrested were referred to the court, with considerable variations depending on community size and, to some extent, on geographical region.

In recent years, there has been a movement in some areas to guide and structure the exercise of police discretion. Departments have established written policies and review procedures to protect against discriminatory treatment and to make dispositions more appropriate. In addition, numerous police agencies are now engaging in formally organized diversion programs.

While some have criticized police discretionary and diversion policies as inappropriate to the police role, the trend today is clearly toward support of such policies. There is increasing recognition of the value of police authority to channel youths into community resources or other nonjudicial alternatives. Police should be allowed to exercise as much discretion in the use of informal disposition as the safety of the community permits. Jurisdictions that lack enabling legislation should seek to establish it in order to facilitate early police screening techniques and to develop criteria and programs for their use.

The judiciary often vests law enforcement agencies with responsibility for controlling admissions to detention centers when court or probation office services are not available. Police frequently have complete control of intake on weekends, during night hours, and on holidays — periods during which most detention decisions have to be made. Theoretically, the judiciary should specify the rules and regulations for control of detention admission, but few jurisdictions have exercised this judicial prerogative, most leaving intake control to police discretion.

The Juvenile Court Process

The juvenile court proceeding is a special statutory proceeding involving civil and criminal principles and specifically designed to determine what is in the best interests of the child brought before the court. Juveniles frequently come in contact with the courts for behavior that would not bring them before the law if they were adults. Offenses such as truancy, curfew violations, running away, teenage drinking, and smoking are cases in point. Dependency and neglect by parents can also bring a child into juvenile court jurisdiction.

The juvenile court's location in the judicial structure varies considerably among the states. It may be a division of the court of general jurisdiction, the probate court, or the family court system, or it may constitute a separate system. Depending on the case load, its judges may be assigned only to juvenile proceedings, or they may have additional functions. The location is less important than the purpose: to provide the court system that addresses delinquency with separate facilities and personnel to perform its special functions.

Two crucial issues in regard to juvenile court jurisdiction are the upper age limit of persons who may be brought before it (usually 16, 17, 18) and whether it has concurrent jursidiction with criminal courts. These two factors determine whether a juvenile court can waive its jurisdiction over some juveniles in favor of their being prosecuted as adults on criminal charges and, if so, at what age.

There may be constitutional problems in concurrent jurisdiction. After the juvenile court grants waiver and a juvenile is acquitted by a criminal court, the juvenile court should not be able to reassert jurisdiction on the basis of the same conduct.

Philosophy

Although today's juvenile court personnel have shed the naive expectations of early reformers, it is still true that the juvenile courts, more than other courts with criminal jurisdiction, are imbued with a rehabilitative orientation. Less emphasis is placed on punishing particular offenders to deter others, or on frightening particular offenders into abstaining from future offenses. More emphasis is placed on using scientific methods to change an offender's motivation so that he has alternative methods of satisfaction and no longer desires to commit criminal acts. Since the objective of juvenile proceedings is regarded as treatment rather than punishment, the power of the court has been defined in terms of the need for treatment rather than in terms of demonstrated dangerousness that justified punishment.

Procedure

Juvenile courts have traditionally used a more flexible procedure than their counterparts in the adult criminal justice system. This has meant that many of the procedural devices used in the adult process to guard against conviction of an innocent defendant have not been utilized in juvenile court. During the 1970s, however, decisional law has substantially narrowed procedural differences with adult courts. Since a juvenile court's proceeding results in treatment rather than punishment, the stringent procedural safeguards against unjustified punishment have been considered unnecessary. Moreover, treating has been viewed as requiring more flexibility than the procedures of the adult system permit. The philosophical objective of the juvenile courts, then, has provided both the need and the justification for use of more flexible procedures than are used in the adult system.

The difference in procedure — as well as the desire to set apart the juvenile system from the adult system — has resulted in the development of specialized terminology for the juvenile court system. The document upon which proceedings are brought does not charge delinquency, neglect, or dependency; it alleges it. The document is not an indictment or information, but a petition. The court, in determining whether the juvenile who is the subject of a petition is in fact delinquent, neglected, or dependent, does not convict, it adjudicates. The process of deciding what to do with a delinquent, neglected, or dependent juvenile is not sentencing, it is disposition.

Role of Intake Personnel

Though states typically have statutory provisions regarding the court intake process, there are wide variations with regard to intake procedures, criteria, and personnel. While smaller courts sometimes rely on "good primary screening" by police, schools, and other agencies and may have no intake personnel at all, most larger court systems have separate intake sections or departments with specially trained staff.

Practically all jurisdictions require that the decision to adjudicate be based on an intake report, but there are few indications as to who shall conduct the study. Some states have no specification at all; in others this responsibility is given to the court, and in still others the responsibility is given to probation officers.

There is considerable conflict whether referring a case for judicial hearing is in the best interests of the public and the child. Since individual statutes provide little guidance, the concept of "best interests" is so vague and inclusive that it may be conducive to subjective, arbitrary, or irrational choices in determination of whether to file a petition. In an effort to remedy the problem, clearer definitions of intake criteria are needed. Also needed is a closer analysis of the central figure in the process — the probation officer — and his role in the judicial system.

The probation officer may be charged with gathering and presenting evidence in an adjudicatory hearing and at the same time be expected to develop the child's confidence and cooperation. While states vary on views, statutes, and practices as to the degree to which a probation officer should assume responsibility in evidence gathering, he is usually asked to function in contradictory capacities. This situation should not be perpetuated.

Initial Screening

Children coming to the attention of the police and courts generally may be classified into two principal categories: those accused of committing acts that would be considered crimes if committed by adults, and those who are not accused of any offense. The latter category can be further differentiated into those who have broken certain rules applicable only to children — such as running away, truancy, curfew violations, and teenage drinking or smoking — and those who have violated neither laws nor rules but who are labeled for various reasons as "persons in need of supervision" (PINS), "minors in need of supervision" (MINS), "incorrigible and beyond control," or found to have been living in an "injurious environment" or in "situations dangerous to their morals or those of others."

Despite the obvious inequity of the situation, certain jurisdictions do not differentiate legally between delinquent and nondelinquent children. Even if great care were taken to provide separate legal categories by statute, it is doubtful that such differentiated labeling as PINS or MINS would be any less stigmatizing or injurious than being adjudicated delinquent, although several states have now statutorily separated the detention of status offenders from delinquents.

How often and how appropriately youngsters are screened out of the juvenile justice process will depend largely on whether suitable services and other options are actually available in the community. A major concern of those who favor retaining court jurisdiction over nondelinquent children is the need for "protective custody" in many cases in which delinquency is not at issue. This is particularly true in regard to runaways and other youth who are having problems in their relationships with their own families.

Prejudicial Dispositions

Informal Service

Analysis of existing legal provisions for informal adjustment yields a bewildering array of terms used to denote similar processes: informal adjustment, informal probation, informal disposition, informal supervision, unofficial probation, counsel and advice, and consent decree. The term *informal service* will be used here to denote any provisions for continuing efforts of the court to provide informal adjustment without the filing of a petition. The consent decree represents a more formalized order for casework supervision, which would be included as "informal service," because a formal determination of fact is not involved.

Informal Adjustment

Most jurisdictions empower intake staff to "adjust" at intake certain cases that in their judgment do not warrant official action by the court. Minor first offenses or trivial cases would be suitable for such informal disposition.

Little is known about the success or failure of informal adjustments, and no definite criteria are available for assessing the eligibility of youngsters. Most recommendations are rather vague and permit the probation officer considerable latitude. Seriousness of the act, prior police and court encounters, parental and child attitudes, and age of the child are commonly listed as factors for consideration. One analysis of the juvenile intake process indicates that more than half the juvenile cases in a sample of 170 handled on an informal basis were closed at intake, 17 percent were closed after a short period of informal handling, and 13 percent were placed on informal probation. Among the major reasons for case closure at intake were: family able to cope with the problem (20.4%); no further difficulties since referral (11.8%); child a nonresident (8%); and offense being minor (6.6%). An analysis of the major reasons for closing cases after a period of informal handling revealed that about half of them experienced no further difficulties. Petitions for formal court action were filed on the other half.

Informal Probation

Informal probation, another method of nonjudicial handling of juvenile cases coming to the attention of the court, permits informal supervision of young persons by probation officers who wish to reserve judgment regarding the necessity for filing a petition until after a child has had the opportunity for some informal treatment. There are several recognized advantages to this type of disposition.

1. It does not interrupt school or job attendance.
2. It avoids the stigma of a delinquent record and a delinquent reputation.
3. It does not reinforce antisocial tendencies, as formal adjudication has a tendency to do.
4. It is less costly than formal probation.

Informal probation may be differentiated from informal adjustment in that the former generally denotes some kind of brief "probationary period" during which the child must fulfill certain requirements, such as attending school or obeying his parents, while informal adjustment generally denotes an informal disposition without any probationary period.

Consent Decrees

A consent decree is a more formal order for casework supervision or treatment to be provided either by the court staff or another agency. It is approved by the judge with consent of the parents and child. The court does not make a formal determination of jurisdictional fact or a formal disposition.

The consent decree provides another method of disposition that can ease the case load of the court as well as provide an intermediate approach for cases too serious for informal handling but not grave enough for formal probation or institutionalization. This additional procedure serves to protect the public as well as the youngster and eliminates the stigma associated with findings of delinquency.

Constitutional Rights of Juveniles

Gault asserted a juvenile's right against self-incrimination and his right to counsel. In addition, the young person is entitled to the same warnings provided by the *Miranda* decision, 384 U.S. 436 (1966), for adults, i.e. a child in custody needs to be warned of his right to counsel and the right to remain silent while under questioning. Special care needs to be taken that the child understands these rights. Juveniles are under great pressure to cooperate when in custody, even after *Miranda* warnings, and they may need adult advice from unbiased sources. In addition, parental interests sometimes may be different from the child's so that their advice as to actual waiver for the child may not necessarily protect the child's rights. In view of these serious reservations, the Model Rules for Juvenile Courts, published by the National Council on Crime and Delinquency, recommend that all extrajudicial statements to peace and court officers not made in the presence of parents or counsel be rendered inadmissible in juvenile court. Decisional law has further limited the admission of a juvenile's confession or incriminating statements perhaps beyond that of criminal courts.

In the initial intake interview, when an intake officer decides whether or not to refer to the court for formal petition, the parents and the child should be allowed to answer questions without their statement being used as evidence in any formal adjudication that may result. This recommendation dovetails with those of the Model Rules for Juvenile Courts, extending them to intake services and the entire preadjudication disposition process. Only in this manner can the dispositional decision be made with adequate information. Thus, the juvenile can take advantage of the informal disposition possibilities, if offered, and yet not lose his right to remain silent if formal adjudication results.

Because a child's liberty is at stake, a child and his parents should have the right to counsel at each phase of the formal juvenile justice process, detention, adjudication, and disposition hearing. The right to counsel should be a nonwaiverable right. In the interest of an equitable and more uniform process, a juvenile taken into custody should be referred immediately to court intake services. Professionally trained personnel must again inform him of his rights in a version of *Miranda* that, it is hoped, he can understand. His parents, if not already present, should be notified immediately and informed of their child's rights. At this point, the intake worker would gather the information necessary to decide whether or not an informal disposition is desirable.

In all situations, the child and parents should be apprised of his options and the possible consequences of each. One option is formal disposition — the filing of a delinquency petition or equivalent court proceeding. The moment this option is chosen, counsel should be provided. If the alleged offense is such that informal disposition is possible, it is not likely that a formal hearing will be chosen.

Assuming the juvenile chooses the informal proceedings, he should be informed that he can, at any time, terminate such a disposition and request formal adjudication. The restraints placed on his freedom as a result of such disposition should be minimal, since no adjudication has actually occurred. Obviously, such dispositions can be used only where both parents and child are willing to cooperate.

As a general rule, formal proceedings appear appropriate where

1. accusations are in dispute, and, if borne out, court ordered disposition and treatment appear desirable;
2. detention or removal from the home is indicated;
3. the nature or gravity of the offense warrants official judicial

attention;

4. the juvenile or the parents request formal adjudication.

To avoid arbitrary decisions, general criteria should be specified by state statute, with authority being granted to intake personnel to set more specific criteria as experience dictates.

OVERVIEW OF CURRENT DETENTION PROBLEMS

Many agencies have advocated that detention be limited to alleged delinquent offenders who require secure custody for the protection of others. However, certain jurisdictions use detention not only for juveniles who have committed delinquent acts that would be considered crimes if committed by adults but also for children who have committed acts deemed by the court to be conducive to crime (truance, disobedience, incorrigibility and the like), who are frequently categorized as "persons in need of supervision" (PINS), or "minors in need of supervision" (MINS).

Although data on the extent of this problem are scarce, indications are that youth in the PINS group comprise a significant population in detention. This estimate does not include the number of children detained in jails or other holding facilities in areas not having detention centers. This situation is now increasingly recognized by correctional administrators, the judiciary, and behavioral scientists as detrimental to the goals of delinquency prevention and as a major obstacle in implementation of intake services planning.

Residential detention care should be a service exclusively for the court in its delinquency jurisdiction and should never be utilized for dependent or neglected children or those in need of supervision. Shelter care serves the court as needed, and it presents more options by providing access to a wide range of private and public child welfare services and family agencies.

Certain states have statutes permitting detention of juveniles in jail provided that they are segregated from the adult population; others do not keep juveniles in jails; while still others have statutory or administrative prohibitions against keeping juveniles in jails, but these prohibitions may be violated.

Very few detention homes even approach the recommended standards of providing recreation, education, group discussion, individual guidance, constructive work activities, and voluntary religious services. Few have education programs that are conducted by the public school system, as recommended by most standards.

Considering the known deleterious effects of incarcerating juveniles in jails and lockups, it is shocking that a substantial number of homes indicate that juveniles are placed into such facilities in their jurisdictions.

In summary, juvenile intake and detention practices throughout this country are characterized by great disparity or even an absence of service. The need to organize and integrate the multitide of programs and activities into a coherent and integrated whole is great, particularly if the goal of crime reduction is to be achieved. The prevailing concept of the detention center, with its overemphasis on secure custody and neglect of its other purported objectives (such as programs and guidance), is counterproductive.

The Question of Bail

Intake processes in many jurisdictions prior to *Gault* reflected indifference and perfunctory rubber-stamping of police decisions. While a number of jurisdictions have found the *Gault* guidelines reasonable and workable and have extended their application to the preadjudication stage, unacceptable practices still exist throughout the country. For example, in some instances court orders to detain juveniles still can be obtained by telephone calls. Further, individual states are divided on whether or not juveniles should be entitled to bail. Since *Gault*, however, juveniles are entitled to due process, and all safeguards should be provided through a formal hearing. Furthermore, in view of the recognized disruptive experience of detention, counsel should insist on a formal detention hearing.

The right to bail has plagued the adult criminal justice system for decades. Few have realized that the same issue is involved with the detention of juveniles. In view of the recognized inadequacies of the bail system as it is now generally practiced for adults, it would be more prudent in juvenile justice to pursue some of the new developments in the area of bail program alternatives such as release on own recognizance, or release to a third party, than to impose an essentially faulty and discriminatory system on the juvenile process.

Finally, in the interest of a fair and speedy process, detention hearings always should be separate from the adjudicatory and disposition hearings.

The Detention Hearing

Although there is considerable variation among states, there is consensus regarding the detrimental effects on children of undue delays in hearing. The Standard Juvenile and Family Court Act proposed by the National Council on Crime and Delinquency provides that children may not be held in a shelter or detention facility without a court order for more than forty-eight hours, excluding Sundays and holidays. California requires that a child admitted to detention must receive a hearing on the next judicial day after filing of a petition. Illinois has reduced this requirement to thirty-six hours.

In view of the consensus of most jurisdictions on the gravity of detention and the well-documented proof that long detention periods are unnecessary, detention hearings ordinarily should be afforded within twenty-four hours after a child is detained. The period should not exceed forty-eight hours without a court order.

Role of the Prosecutor and Defense Counsel

Two major cases decided by the U.S. Supreme Court, *in re* Gault 387 U.S. (1967) and *in re* Winship 397 U.S. 358 (1970), have greatly increased the role of both the prosecutor and defense counsel in juvenile court. In the *Gault* case the Court held that advance notice was required of the adjudication hearing; that the juvenile has the right to counsel; that he has the right of confrontation of witnesses and cross-examination; and that he be afforded the protection of the privilege against self-incrimination. In the *Winship* case the Court held that the burden of proof in delinquency proceedings must be proof beyond a reasonable doubt as in adult criminal cases. Formerly, proof had only to be the preponderance of the evidence.

The prosecutor's role in delinquency matters differs from his role in adult courts in that most juvenile cases come to his attention through the juvenile intake worker instead of by direct referral from police.

Under this arrangement, if the intake officer thinks the case should be referred to court, the prosecutor determines whether there is a legal basis on which to file a petition. If there is not, the child should be diverted from the system. There is also a developing movement to have petitions drawn by the prosecutors office on direct request from police rather than by juvenile court personnel.

Prosecutors now serve increasingly as legal representatives of the state to present evidence in the adjudication hearing supporting the allegation of delinquency.

Counsel

No single action holds more potential for achieving procedural justice for the child in the juvenile court than provision of counsel. The presence of an independent legal representative of the child, or of his parent, is the keystone of the whole structure of guarantees that a minimum system of procedural justice requires. The rights to confront one's accusers, to cross-examine witnesses, to present evidence and testimony of one's own, to be unaffected by prejudicial and unreliable evidence, to participate meaningfully in the dispositional decision, and to take an appeal have substantial meaning for the overwhelming majority of persons brought before the juvenile court only if they are provided with competent lawyers who can invoke those rights effectively. The most informal and well-intentioned of judicial proceedings are technical; few adults without legal training can influence or even understand them; certainly children cannot. Papers are drawn and charges expressed in legal language. Events follow one another in a manner that appears arbitrary and confusing to the uninitiated. Decisions, unexplained, appear too official to challenge. But with lawyers come records of proceedings; records make possible appeals, which, even if they do not occur, impart by their possibility a healthy atmosphere of accountability, i.e. cases in which facts are disputed and in which, therefore, rules of evidence, confrontation of witnesses, and other adversary procedures are called for. They deal with many cases involving conduct that can lead to incarceration or close supervision for long periods, and therefore, juveniles often need the same safeguards that are granted to adults. And in all cases children need advocates to speak for them and guard their interests, particularly when disposition decisions are made. It is the disposition stage at which the opportunity arises to offer individualized treatment plans and in which the danger inheres that the court's coercive power will be applied without adequate knowledge of the circumstances.

Since 1967 there has been a large increase in the size of public defender staffs to represent youth and their families who cannot afford private counsel. The number of private attorneys serving at reasonable fees set by the court has also increased in jurisdictions that do not provide public defender service.

Adjudication and Disposition

Perhaps the height of the juvenile court's procedural informality is its failure to differentiate clearly between the adjudication hearing, the purpose of which is to determine the truth of the allegations in the petition, and the disposition proceeding, at which the juvenile's background is considered in connection with deciding what to do with him. In many juvenile courts the two questions are dealt with in the same proceeding or are separated only in the minority of cases in which the petition's allegations are at issue. Even where adjudication and disposition are dealt with separately, the social reports, containing material about background and character that might make objective examination of the facts of the case difficult, are often given to the judge before adjudication. Practices vary on disclosure of social study information to the juvenile and his parents and lawyer, if he has one. To minimize the danger that adjudication will be affected by inappropriate considerations, social investigation reports should not be made known to the judge in advance of adjudication.

The Adjudication Hearing

Juvenile court adjudication hearings are now adversary in nature and similar in most respects to adult criminal court hearings with the participation of prosecutors and defense counsel. Hearings are however closed to the general public and, for the most part, there are no juries. Minutes of the proceedings are maintained by the court staff.

Hearings are usually before juvenile court judges, but other hearing officers who are lawyers such as commissioners or referees are often appointed in metropolitan counties.

Disposition Hearing

At this hearing, with prosecutor and counsel often present, the probation officer presents the detailed social study report on the juvenile and the total family situation. Included are the minor's response to the allegations and adjustments in the family, at school, and in the community. The study often includes reports by physicians, psychologists, or psychiatrists. The quality of these reports varies considerably because of the court's budget, education of the probation staff, and training and time pressures in large metropolitan areas.

The judge, commissioner, or referee hearing the matter has the following dispositions available when the court finds the minor to be a law violator:

1. He may place the juvenile on probation for a specific period of time (usually less than six months without adjudging him a ward of the court).
2. Adjudge the minor a ward of the court and place him on probation with or without special conditions to be met while under probation supervision.
3. Commit the minor to any special probation camp or other facility operated by the probation department.
4. Transfer legal custody to an appropriate agency or relative.
5. Commit the minor to the state department responsible for the operation of state training schools.

Probation Supervision

There is great variation in the quality of probation supervision or treatment after the juvenile court judge officially places juveniles under the court's supervision by probation staff.

Variations in services result from such factors as education of probation officers, training, size of case loads, and salaries. Educational requirements range from high school graduation to master's degree, although a college degree has been the standard for many years.

Some probation staffs combine investigation, court appearance, and supervision responsibilities, while others separate these functions, with some officers doing only social study investigations for disposition hearings, while other officers do only follow-up supervision or treatment.

Supervision case loads vary in size from a small number of 20 intensive cases to more than 150, even though professional associations have been urging standards of 50 for many years.

The basic treatment processes continues to be the social casework method in which the officer counsels with the juvenile and parents to help them understand their problems and change behavior patterns. More progressive departments are engaging in group supervision, team supervision with other specialists, and family therapy.

There is a strong trend toward a wider variety of community-based programs such as foster homes, group homes and probation camp programs. More innovative programs of collaboration with police are also developing in progressive departments through the use of funds from state criminal justice planning agencies.

Increasing numbers of states are granting subsidies to counties to encourage a higher quality of probation services and to develop more innovative diversion programs. Some few departments are adopting sophisticated methods of classification of offenders and providing specialized treatment for different types of delinquents.

State Institutional Care

State institutional care in training schools is still required for hard-core offenders and those who continue to violate laws while on probation. Because of the emphasis on diversion and community-based treatment, the population of state training schools has declined. This results in a larger percentage of high-risk or hard-core offenders in the institutions who tend to make poor adjustments when paroled.

Institutional Weaknesses

The failure of major juvenile and youth institutions to reduce crime is incontestable. Recidivism rates, imprecise as they may be, are notoriously high. The younger the person when entering an institution, the longer he is institutionalized, and the further he progresses into the criminal justice system, the greater his chance of failure. It is important to distinguish some basic reasons why institutional programs continuously have failed to reduce the commission of crime by those released.

Lack of clarity as to goals and objectives has had a marked influence on institutional programs. Programs in youth institutions have reflected a variety of objectives, many of which are conflicting. Both society and the other components of the criminal justice system have contributed to this confusion.

A judge may order a juvenile committed as an example to others or because there are no effective alternatives. The police officer, whose function is to provide community protection, may demand incarceration for the temporary protection it provides for the public. The public may be fearful and incensed at the seriousness of an offense and react by seeking retribution and punishment. To the offender, commitment means he has been banished from society.

Institutions do succeed in punishing, but they do not deter. They protect the community temporarily, but that protection does not last. They relieve the community of responsibility by removing the young offender, but they make successful reintegration unlikely. They change the committed offender, but the change is more likely to be negative than positive.

Another contributing factor to the failure of major youth institutions has been their closed nature. The geographic location of most institutions is incompatible with a mission of services delivery. Their remote locations make family visitation difficult and preclude the opportunity to utilize the variety of community services available in metropolitan areas. They have been staffed largely with local residents, who, unlike the young offenders, are predominantly white, provincial, and institutionally oriented.

Most existing institutions were built before the concept of community programming gained acceptance. They were built to last and most have outlasted the need for which they were established. For economic reasons, they were constructed to hold large numbers of people securely. Their structure has restricted the ability to change and strongly influenced the overall direction of institutional programming.

Many administrative policies and procedures in youth institutions also have contributed to their closed nature. The emphasis on security and control of so many people resulted in heavy restrictions on visiting, mail, phone calls, and participation with community residents in various activities and programs. For reasons that are now archaic, most institutions have been totally segregated by sex for both residents and staff.

All these factors have worked together to create an environment within the institution totally unlike that from which the population comes or to which it will return. The youths, often alienated already, who find themselves in such institutions, experience feelings of abandonment, hostility, and despair. Because many residents come from delinquent backgrounds, a delinquent subculture flourishes in the closed institution. This, in turn, reinforces administrative preoccupation with security and control.

Large institutions are dehumanizing. They foster an increased degree of dependency that is contrary to behavior expected in the community. They force youths to participate in activities of little interest or use to them. They foster resident-staff relationships that are superficial, transient, and meaningless. They try to change the young offender without knowing how to effect that change or how to determine whether it occurs.

With the shift in emphasis to changing behavior and reintegration, the major institution's role in the total criminal justice system must be reexamined. Changing that role from one of merely housing society's failures to one of sharing responsibility for their reintegration requires an attitude change by the corrections profession. The historical inclination to accept total responsibility for offenders and the resulting isolation are clearly counterproductive.

Juvenile Parole Organization

The National Survey of Corrections found tremendous shortcomings in juvenile aftercare programs. In some states young persons released from training schools were supervised by institutional staff. In others they were made the responsibility of local child welfare workers, who simply included these youngsters in their case loads of dependent or neglected children. In some states no organized program of juvenile parole supervision existed. Whether distinct juvenile correctional agencies should exist or whether such services should be carried out as a regular part of welfare services has been a matter of controversy for years.

The events of the last years have virtually ended that argument.

Distinct division and departments of juvenile correctional services are emerging. There is less agreement about whether such departments should be combined with agencies serving adult offenders. Yet it is widely agreed that separate program units should be maintained, even if adult and juvenile programs are combined in a single agency. Statewide juvenile correctional services embracing both institutions and field aftercare represent an established trend that should be supported.

Feedback in the Juvenile Justice System

This chapter's presentation of the current status of the juvenile justice system reveals a complex process of many separate city, county, and state agencies attempting to deal effectively with juvenile law violators. The past results have not been encouraging. The key decision points in the system where one agency interfaces with another, such as the police-probation relationship, provide not only occasions for greater collaboration but also for considerable conflict.

One of the most glaring weaknesses in the system is the lack of adequate feedback of the results of system processing and the use of that research data to modify the total process to attain more effective results.

The system will only improve with development of a much closer relationship among all the system components and interested lay leaders. Such organizations as a criminal justice coordinating council or a juvenile justice coordinating committee should be developed to build an effective system by making use of feedback to correct inadequacies.

NATIONAL STANDARDS

The past ten years has seen a proliferation of standards having to do with juvenile matters. These standards reflect the national and local dialogue with respect to juvenile delinquent offenders, status offenders, and child abuse. In addition, depending upon the makeup of the deliberating body, standards were formulated to create policy affecting the behavior of key groups such as law enforcement, the courts, probation, and corrections. For the most part, the key standards paid particular attention to the rights of juveniles (due process), the protection of status offenders, and concern for the abused child. With very few exceptions did the standards concern themselves with society's increasing fear of the violent, youthful offender. California did add language to its juvenile code (actually the Welfare and Institutions Code) that society had interests in its own protection. The state of Washington bifurcated its legislative interest by strengthening disposition of serious, youthful offenders, while protecting the less serious and status offenders.

The primary debate regarding policy toward juveniles emanates from two firmly held views: the first view being one group seeks to remove juveniles from the formal, adjudicative system, believing that such penetration "labels" the juvenile and makes recidivism more likely. This group prefers massive educational and social scientific remedies for delinquent or pre-delinquent youth whose behavior emanates from environmental and/or physiological causes. It is argued that delinquency, in its early stages, is potentially correctable and, even if not, should be given its chance for rehabilitation. Advocates suggest that some juveniles do not reoffend even when left entirely alone. Inclusion in the criminal justice system might infect some who now choose their own option of compliance with the law. Naturally this group points to the high probability of recidivism once a juvenile enters the system. The second group concerns itself with the serious, youthful offender. This group argues that all of the concern for early offenders simply mutes the concern for the wave of victimization by the serious offender. While this group acknowledges the excesses by the state in the *Gault* case, it argues that Gerald Gault's obscene phone call is not comparable to aggravated assault, robbery, and murder. This group argues that today's youthful offender has all of the protections of today's adult offender, coupled with lesser sentences. What is needed, says this group, is a greater willingness to incarcerate the youthful offender; not to rehabilitate, which is seen as long past possible, but rather to incapacitate. The group argues that only "corrective" sanctions will modify behavior of these offenders if anything will. Most professionals would find some wisdom in each view: attempt to rehabilitate the early offender, and incapacitate the serious offender. Nevertheless, this dilemma tends to be reflected in the standards and "weight" them in a particular direction. Naturally, advocates of the "protective school" and those of the "lock 'em up" school cite those statistics that surround the offender in which *they* have the greatest interest. The major views are contrasted most clearly when comparing the National Advisory Commission (NAC) standards with that of the IJA/ABA.*

Standards on Police and Juveniles: A comparison of the National Advisory Commission and the IJA/ABA

Organization for Work with Juveniles

Both standards advocate a separate police unit specifically trained to work with juveniles. The IJA/ABA extend this standard to the designation of at least one officer in small departments unable to form a juvenile unit, even though the officer may be assigned to additional duties such as patrol. The state of Illinois has made this a statutory requirement. While the standards agree on the importance of a juvenile unit or an officer, departments have increasingly chosen to reassign juvenile officers, as the effects of Proposition Thirteen-type legislation have caused budgetary cutbacks.

Policies Relating to Juveniles

Both standards emphasize the need for law enforcement to involve the lay public and community agencies in developing appropriate policies for working with juveniles, and both emphasize selecting "the least coercive" alternative in processing the juvenile. Naturally, limitations on law enforcement are posed by restrictive budgets, which may foreclose existing programs or prevent initiation of new ones; federal funds may be unavailable or in short supply; social service agencies may be unable to gain the confidence of law enforcement; community-wide cooperation may be quite limited; professionals and politicians may prefer a strategy of retribution; and the community may resist the establishment of neighborhood centers, particularly group homes or halfway houses.

Selecting Personnel for Work with Juveniles

Both standards emphasize the importance of appointing officers

---

*IJA/ABA refers to the Institute of Judicial Administration/American Bar Association Joint Commission on Juvenile Justice Standards.

to juvenile work who are well experienced in police work and who are possessing the desire and ability to work with juveniles. The IJA/ABA standards extend this reasoning to require the equivalent of graduation from college. Secondly, they grant preference to officers sharing the racial, ethnic, and social background of the youths with whom they will work. This standard is, naturally, affected by the composition of the department's sworn officers. Most departments are experiencing difficulty in recruiting sufficient numbers of minority officers. The Honolulu Police Department, perhaps an exception, closely matches the demography of its population.

Training for Juvenile Work

The IJA/ABA standards are quite brief in stressing the need for law enforcement to familiarize itself with dispositional alternatives. These standards would restrict decision-making authority during a probationary period. The NAC standards advocate a strong training component for juvenile officers, coupled with an annual, 40-hour update. Emphasis is directed toward interdisciplinary training, including temporary exchange of assignments with other police agencies. The NAC essentially sets out a required educational program directing the state law enforcement training commission to establish statewide juvenile officer standards. The NAC formula clearly follows the pattern of those states committing substantial funds to law enforcement training. California, which derives such funds from the penalty assessment emanating from moving violations, exemplifies this approach. The NAC standards stress the need for family, crisis, intervention techniques as well as furthering the understanding of ethnic, cultural, and minority relations. The NAC is suggesting a broadened role for law enforcement, one suggesting the multiple disciplines impinging upon today's officer. In a sense, the officer is seen as a "broker" of alternative community resources that extends beyond his control function. The IJA/ABA standards, by contrast, imply caution in releasing the new juvenile officer to decision making. Understanding is best gained by exposing the officer to agency roles and practice.

Investigations and Taking into Custody

The essential difference between the two standards centers upon

the role of the juvenile officer or investigator. The NAC standards
envision a broad role in which the investigator acts as follows:

1. Determines underlying causes of law violation to assist in the
   rehabilitation process.
2. Safeguards the constitutional rights of juveniles.
3. Is sensitive to and respects the personal dignity of both juveniles and adults.
4. Takes appropriate action in responding to family disturbance
   calls.
5. Secures emergency medical treatment.
6. Enforces all moving traffic violations involving juveniles.
7. Provides for the safety of children attending school.
8. Provides protection for children whose health or safety is en-
   dangered.

In contrast, the IJA/ABA standards seek to narrow or limit the
role of law enforcement by stressing the need for the juvenile officer
to intercede in the decision-making process as soon as the patrol
officer's contact accelerates beyond initial and informal handling.
The IJA/ABA standards show concern for deliberate decision making and priority for the least restrictive dispositional alternative as
follows:

1. Juvenile codes should *narrowly limit police authority* to utilize the
   formal, juvenile justice process.
2. Authority emphasis should be given to the use of *summons in lieu
   of arrest*.
3. A juvenile *cannot be detained*, even temporarily, in adult detention facilities.
4. Juveniles should receive the *same safeguards* available to adults
   in the criminal justice system.
5. Greater constitutional safeguards are needed because of the
   vulnerability of juveniles.
6. Juveniles should *not be permitted to waive constitutional rights*.
7. Where constitutional guidelines are absent, *guidance to law enforcement* should be provided either legislatively or administratively by court rules or police policies.
8. *Juvenile officers should take charge* of all cases that go beyond an
   initial and informal handling.
9. Members of the uniformed patrol should employ the *least coer-*

cive measures of control.

10. Every patrol unit should contain *at least one officer to whom juvenile cases will be assigned* to the fullest extent possible.
11. Cases in which further work is necessary should be *transferred to juvenile officers.*

Discretionary Authority and Alternative Dispositions

For the most part, the standards agree with respect to dispositional alternatives: seek the least restrictive alternative for the less serious offender, and protect the juvenile's constitutional rights during the processing stage. The earlier dichotomy exists with respect to discretion: the NAC standards emphasize the need for police agency policy, whereas the IJA/ABA standards prefer narrow limits upon police discretion. The latter standards point to the need for protecting immunity of police authority to civil liability, particularly emphasizing a preference for the use of a summons in lieu of arrest. Both standards agree that juveniles should be separated from adults at all times in detention facilities. The question of the charging process is avoided in the NAC standards. The IJA/ABA standards assert the need for prosecutorial review for appropriateness "under the surrounding circumstances. If a trend exists it would appear to lie in the direction of enhanced prosecutorial authority to file a petition with or without appeal by the probation department.[4]

Coordinations with Agencies and Delinquency Prevention

The NAC standards stress a comprehensive role for law enforcement in providing "leadership" toward the development of interagency and community programs dealing with juvenile problems. This role would enhance the social service or "broker of services" role of law enforcement. It expands the need for law enforcement to be involved in delinquency prevention. By contrast, the IJA/ABA standards stress the need for law enforcement to collaborate *with* outside sources. Moreover, law enforcement officers are directed to be "accountable" both to police administrators and "to the public" in carrying out their responsibilities. Monitoring and control of the police function is advocated by suggesting community "involvement" in police programs and strengthened by "administrative sanctions and procedures and remedies for citizens whenever warranted."

SUMMARY

The NAC standards envision an expanded, enlightened role by law enforcement in juvenile matters, anchored particularly in a juvenile bureau and developed by trained, expert juvenile officers. It is believed that this approach will aid the prevention of delinquency, protect the constitutional rights of juveniles, divert the less serious juvenile offenders in the most appropriate manner and provide essential leadership to the criminal justice system.

The ABA/IJA standards argue in favor of restricting police discretion; ensuring constitutional rights through statutes, guidelines and policy directives; and lessening the likelihood of discretionary abuse through outside agency and citizen involvement in the development of juvenile programs and the review of police actions. This strategy centers upon a "checks-and-balances" foundation rather than upon an "enlightened police leadership."

REFERENCES

1. President's Commission on Law Enforcement and Administration of Justice: *The Challenge of Crime in a Free Society.* Washington, D.C., U.S. Government Printing Office, 1967, pp. 261-264.
2. Coffey, Alan R.: *Juvenile Justice as a System.* Englewood Cliffs, Prentice-Hall, 1974, p. 43.
3. U.S. Department of Justice, Office of Juvenile Justice and Delinquency Prevention: *Standards for the Administration of Juvenile Justice: Report of the National Advisory Committee for Juvenile Justice and Delinquency Prevention.* Washington, D.C., U.S. Government Printing Office, 1980.
4. H. Ted Rubin: Retain the juvenile court? Legislative developments, reform directions, and the call for abolition. In H. Ted Rubin (Ed.): *Juveniles in Justice: A Book of Readings.* Santa Monica, Goodyear, 1980.

Chapter 3

THE LAW AND LEGAL PROCEEDINGS

L AW and legal proceedings come into play in controlling the conduct of members of society when less formal methods of social control have failed. There are many of these less formal methods. Of primary importance is the control exercised by family. Schools are another source of social control essentially nonlegal in nature, as are the church, the neighborhood, the private club, and the work setting. The combined effect of all of these institutions on life in the U.S.A. is extremely strong. Their influence is enough to persuade and allow most of us to live in a way that prevents all but occasional conflict with the rest of society.

When these influences fail to bring about the minimum amount of conformity that society requires as necessary for all of us to have a maximum of freedom, it is necessary to bring legal controls into action. When one of us asks our legal structure to come to his personal aid to settle conflict with another individual or group, it is the civil or private law part of the structure to which he addresses his appeal. When the wrong that has been done is one which is as much a threat to all of society as it is to him as an individual, he appeals to the public law; usually the criminal law. The criminal law then proceeds against the alleged violator in a dual manner, acting in a capacity

37

representative of all society against the defendant not only as a person but also as a representative of all who would destroy our way of life by refusing to abide by the necessary rules. These rules are created by the legislatures, administered by the executive branch of government including police agencies, and enforced by the courts. This is the traditional role of the criminal law. The institution of probation and parole and the use of treatment and training techniques as incorporated into our modern prison systems are an attempt to weave rehabilitation into the punishment process. However, basic emphasis in criminal procedure remains on deterrence through punishment.

Through a slow evolutionary process, a realization has developed not only among professional correction personnel but also among lay persons that children who engage in antisocial conduct present a different problem to society than do adults similarly engaged. After several centuries of trial, it was evident that the criminal law approach was not doing the job with children. Government first reacted to this growing public conviction by providing separate institutions for child offenders. A house of refuge for children was established in New York City in 1825. Massachusetts opened the first such state institution in 1847. By 1875 most of the other states had followed suit. Since the actual chronology in an individual case of adjudicated juvenile delinquency goes from police to court to institution, this first showing of governmental concern was with the last step in the processing of a case. It did nothing to make apprehension and trial consistent with efforts toward rehabilitation.

Awareness that imprisonment, even enlightened imprisonment, could not do much to make better citizens of young persons who ran afoul of the law led to the establishment in Illinois in 1899 of the first juvenile court. The Cook County Juvenile Court was not actually a new court but a branch of the trial court of general jurisdiction, the Cook County Circuit Court. This court was a source of governmental help for juveniles, not merely an arena for public punishment and revenge in the hope of some measure of general deterrence.

In recognition of the immaturity and the potential of young people, a philosophy has developed, for the most part, that labels the antisocial acts of children as behavior problems rather than as criminal behavior. But despite the fact that the machinery for dealing with juvenile delinquency is basically protective in nature and aimed at rehabilitation, the fact remains that it is sometimes necessary to deprive children of their liberty and parents of the companionship of their children at home. Because these are important rights, many of the safeguards afforded the adult person charged with crime must be observed for the protection of the child, of his family, and of the community. The machinery for deciding when these rights shall be abrogated is centered largely in the juvenile court or, where separate juvenile courts do not exist as such, in their counterparts.

Justice for juveniles in the United States has traditionally encompassed care, concern, treatment, training and rehabilitation. Juveniles have been treated as children who are not deemed to be entirely responsible for their actions and when subjected to humane rehabilitation programs, may become useful members of society. The juvenile justice system has focused upon directing children away from a life of delinquency and crime toward becoming productive members of society. Punishment and retribution has legally been "reserved" for adults. By protecting juveniles from the stigma of criminality it has been presumed that they are more easily assimilated into society following proper treatment and rehabilitation for their indiscretions.[2]

The "law and order" era of the 1960s brought with it increasing legal sanctions against adult criminals as crime increased, especially crimes of violence. The 1970s became an era of increasing violent juvenile crime and with it a public outcry that juveniles were "getting away with murder" and a clamor for a "get tough" policy. This moved state legislatures to rethink the juvenile justice philosophy that had prevailed for seven decades. The purpose of juvenile justice acts were altered by the addition of language that calls for the protection of society from *criminal behavior* by juveniles, a purpose that legislatures apparently consider as important as the originally expressed purpose of protecting the juveniles from the results of their criminal acts.[2] The era also brought about changes in laws relating to status offenses, i.e. incorrigibility, runaway and truancy, and redefinitions of ages for which youthful offenders may be charged as adults.

Effective January 1, 1977, the California legislature added a new subdivision to the Welfare and Institutions Code, which reads: "The purpose of this chapter also includes the protection of the public from the consequences of criminal activity, and to such purpose probation officers, peace officers and juvenile courts shall take into account such protection of the public in their determination under this chapter." The state of Washington left little room for ambiguity in the purpose clause of its new Juvenile Justice Act of 1977: "It is the...intent of the legislature that youth...be held accountable for their offenses.... It shall be the purpose of this chapter to protect the citizenry from criminal behavior...[to] make the juvenile offender accountable for his or her criminal behavior, [and to] provide for punishment commensurate with the age, crime and criminal history of the juvenile offender." And the state of Virginia followed suit by including in its law the purpose of "protect(ing) the community against acts of its citizens which are harmful to others and to reduce the incidence of delinquent behavior."[6]

Other changes that are being made include modification of the "civil" nature of juvenile court proceedings by changing "respondents" to "defendants" and substitution of the word "juvenile" for "child."[6] These modifications, along with the purpose changes, reflect the tenor of the times to hold young people accountable for their behavior.

The New York legislature was the most responsive to the hysteria of the era in the modification of its statutes relating to young offenders.[3] In an extraordinary session in July 1978, it decreed that cases against thirteen-, fourteen-, and fifteen-year-olds accused of a long list of offenses *must* be initiated in adult criminal courts. The law transferred original jurisdiction over the offenses designated as felonies in the Juvenile Justice Reform Act of 1976 to the adult criminal courts. Penalties for the offenses were increased for fourteen- and fifteen-year-olds if they were referred from the criminal court to the juvenile court for processing.

The New York statute charged the prosecuting attorneys to make the determination of whether the juveniles are to be tried in the adult or juvenile courts. Judges in the criminal courts may refer juveniles to the juvenile court with the consent of the prosecuting attorney "in the interest of justice."

Unfortunately, the changes in the New York laws resulted in incarceration inequities for juveniles. In a number of situations juveniles charged with lesser offenses and processed in the family court may be incarcerated for longer periods in juvenile institutions than their counterparts charged with major crimes.

California has also made a number of substantive changes in its juvenile laws as codified in the Welfare and Institutions Code. These changes reflect the numerous appellate court decisions that extended to juveniles many of the rights enjoyed by adults and in a large measure reflect a response to public hysteria over the increased violence of juvenile behavior.

As was indicated previously, effective January 1, 1977, the California legislature for the first time acknowledged that the purposes of the juvenile court law should include protection of the public from criminal conduct of minors, and that minors must assume a sense of responsibility for their own acts. It further made a clear distinction between status offenders (e.g. runaways, incorrigibles, curfew violators and law violators and defined quite different procedures for the handling of each type of offender. In essence, the legislation recognized that status offenders are generally children exhibiting personal and parental conflict as opposed to behavior that would be a criminal act if committed by an adult.

If a juvenile is arrested for a crime the law provides that the probation officer retains authority to investigate the necessity of a petition. However, if the decision is made to commence court proceedings the determination to file is made by a prosecuting attorney. The prosecuting attorney is required to specify whether the offense is deemed to be a felony or a misdemeanor. If the case goes to court the juvenile is entitled to be represented by an attorney, and the prosecuting attorney is required to represent the state.

The law did not modify existing provisions that permit a probation officer to supervise a juvenile up to six months with parents consent if he believes the minor is within the jurisdiction of the juvenile court, or if he believes the minor will "soon be within the jurisdiction." The probation officer retains the right to file a formal petition at any time.

Procedures and conditions for transferring juveniles to adult courts for prosecution were spelled out in the law. Existing juvenile court law provided that the juvenile court has jurisdiction of persons under eighteen years of age who are charged with the commission of a public offense. Revisions made in 1975 provided a due process to the criminal court for sixteen- and seventeen-year old minors that the juvenile court finds unfit. In these "fitness" hearings, the juvenile court judge must consider the following criteria: (a) degree of criminal sophistication, (b) whether the minor can be rehabilitated, (c) previous delinquent history, (d) success of previous attempts to rehabilitate the minor, and (e) circumstances and gravity of the offense. Existing law and practice provide for the court's consideration of prior offenses and the gravity of the alleged offense in determining whether to certify the minor to the adult court. Existing law also places the burden of proving a minor "unfit" on the petitioner.

The law shifted the burden of proof to the minor to prove his/her fitness for juvenile court by adding a "rebutable presumption" if the minor is charged with any of the following eleven offenses:

1. Murder.
2. Arson of an inhabited building.
3. Robbery while armed with a dangerous or deadly weapon.
4. Rape with force or violence or threat of great bodily harm.
5. Kidnapping for ransom.
6. Kidnapping with bodily harm.
7. Kidnapping for purpose of robbery.
8. Assault with intent to murder or attempted murder.
9. Assault with a firearm or destructive device.
10. Assault by any means of force likely to produce great bodily injury.
11. Discharge of a firearm into an inhabited or occupied building.

In transferring juveniles to the criminal courts the juvenile court must utilize established criteria set forth in the law and must set forth the reasons in its court order.

The law restricted confinement of a juvenile in an institution to a period of time not to exceed the maximum term of imprisonment that would apply to an adult for a specified crime. Prior to passage of the law, a minor could be confined until his/her twenty-first birthday. Physical confinement was defined in the law as placement in a county camp, ranch, or school or any youth authority facility.

The laws also expressed legislative intent that by January 1979 at least one-half of the juvenile court work load will be handled by judges as opposed to referees or commissioners.

POLICE AUTHORITY IN JUVENILE CASES

Even prior to the advent of juvenile court statutes, children of tender age were given special consideration under the doctrines of the criminal law. In our legal system, children under the age of seven have been freed from criminal liability for acts that would be criminal if committed by older persons. A few states made this floor on criminal liability a year or two higher. This policy is based on the belief that children of these ages are not sufficiently mature to be able to understand the organization of society and the seriousness of their antisocial acts. This has meant that police agencies could not initiate proceedings against such children when they transgressed but were required to leave them with their families for education and control.

Special protection was also given to children who had reached their seventh but not their fourteenth birthdays. These children were prosecuted just as were adults, except that the state was required to prove in every case that the child was sufficiently mature to have understood the social disruption which his conduct was capable of creating. In cases in which the child had reached his fourteenth birthday, capacity rather than incapacity for mature judgment was presumed, and the children were prosecuted just as were adults.

Whether modern juvenile court laws have altered the exemption from criminal liability that was extended to children under seven or the presumption against capacity to commit crimes extended to those from seven to fourteen by the common law is not clear. Most state juvenile court laws are similar to the Standard Juvenile Court Act, which gives the court jurisdiction over " . . . any child who is alleged to have violated any federal, state, or local law or municipal ordinance." When such an allegation is made on the basis for juvenile court jurisdiction, it has been held that evidence must be offered tending to show the existence of every element of the offense, including "criminal" intent. In view of these decisions, it is certainly possible that there must also be a showing of sufficient legal maturity to establish responsibility for violation of law. If violation of the criminal law, as distinguished from the child or parent's general course of conduct, is used as the determinant of the court's jurisdiction, then all elements of criminal procedure should apply. Halfway measures just do not suffice.

Adoption of this view would eliminate the necessity of a juvenile court judge's having to face the ludicrous decision of whether to commit a four-, five-, or six-year-old "delinquent" to an institution. Extreme cases involving children of this age would almost always involve dependency or neglect and could be handled on that basis. It is just as difficult to envisage four-year-old delinquents as it is four-year-old criminals.

Changes in the law of criminal responsibility of children that have been made by the juvenile court laws of the United States are generally of the five following types:

1. Absolute substitution of jurisdiction of the juvenile court for criminal liability for children up to a specific age, usually sixteen, with possible exceptions for certain types of crimes, usually (a) felonies which are punishable by death or life imprisonment, or (b) some other larger, defined group of felonies, and (c) traffic offenses (which are crimes in most but not all jurisdictions).

2. Primary substitution of juvenile court jurisdiction for criminal liability for an additional narrow age group, usually sixteen- and seventeen-year-olds but sometimes including fifteen-year-olds, but with a provision that the juvenile court may transfer the cases of these children to the regular criminal court if defined felony-type offenses are involved and if it appears that the child cannot benefit from the services available to the juvenile court.

3. Primary substitution of juvenile court jurisdiction for that of criminal courts for youths eighteen, nineteen, and twenty who are alleged to have committed offenses while under eighteen, with the same transfer prerogative in the juvenile court as outlined in 2 above.

4. Establishment of juvenile court jurisdiction over acts of children defined as acts of delinquency would not be violations of the criminal law if committed by adults.

5. Substitution of juvenile court jurisdiction for exclusive parental control over children up to a certain age, usually eighteen, whose parents do not make minimal provision for their welfare either because of neglect or inability to do so.

One result of these laws is that the juvenile courts have jurisdiction over juveniles in situations where the criminal courts would not have jurisdiction over adults. Most juvenile court laws also contain statements to the effect that juvenile court actions are not criminal. The purpose of these provisions is to assure that the juveniles who come before them will not suffer from the stigma of criminal conviction. Although these statutes do not specifically so state, they have been interpreted by the appellate courts as making the juvenile court actions civil actions. These cases have usually involved a question of whether criminal or civil procedure should apply in the juvenile court in an instance where the law establishing the court did not specify a procedure to be followed, for example, on appeal.

Unlike the usual civil case, the rights involved in these cases are not ordinarily property rights. They are personal rights — rights and freedoms that are deemed fundamental under our system of law — the right of a child to live with his family in a community of their choice, the right of the parents to the unrestricted care, custody, and control of their child.

In the past the courts have pointed out that the state should not be able to intervene merely because it disagrees with the parent as to the best method of child rearing. Nor should it be permitted to take children from the parents merely because a public official believes that the child can be better cared for and trained as a ward of the state. Both social policy and the law require that the primary responsibility for child rearing be left to parents, and only when conditions in the family seriously affect the health and welfare of the child or when his conduct is dangerous to the community or to himself should authoritative action be taken by the state.

Doing something for a child and family also entails doing something to a child or family which they may have the right to reject. This does not mean that help should be denied. All appropriate procedures should be used to provide help to children and handicapped families experiencing problems. Nor does it mean that offenses by young persons should be excused or condoned. Society should be protected, and young people should be held responsible commensurate with their degree of maturity. It does not mean that fair practices which meet the requirements of due process must be devised to determine when, how, and under what conditions the state can authoritatively enter a family situation. These apply no less to the police than they do to the courts.

Because they are a new kind of court designed for a special purpose, juvenile courts need not be either civil or criminal. It has been pointed out that they possess some of the characteristics of both. The fact that these courts are unique, however, means that they must also be given a unique law of procedure. Some of this procedure might be analogous to criminal procedure in establishing safeguards for those within its jurisdiction, and other procedures might be analogous to civil procedure. Much of the difficulty arising from this ambiguity as to the procedure to be followed in juvenile courts stems from attempts to measure the procedure used in a particular court by constitutional standards. Decisions in these cases are pointing out that there are constitutional rights in both criminal and civil proceedings, although these rights may differ. The problem appears to be to define what procedures are required for fundamental fairness to juveniles in juvenile court proceedings.

The changes that juvenile court laws have made in application of the law of criminal procedure do raise questions regarding police authority in some cases involving juveniles. Police agencies have as their basic function the protection of lives and property. They deal with actions against persons and property that are made criminal by statute. These statutes speak in terms of all persons who violate them. As a result, they apply to juveniles as well as to adults. Once it has been established that a juvenile is the violator, an alternate procedure may be required, but up to that point, the legal structure for police operation is the same as with an adult, although the special aptitude, training, and experience of a juvenile officer will make for more effective handling of some cases.

But juvenile court laws also envisage action by the police in situations where it would not be authorized in the case of similar conduct by an adult. These are cases that do not involve violation of law. The Standard Juvenile Court Act and some actual juvenile court laws contain grants of authority to the police to act in such cases, but many do not. In such states, the authority of the police must be inferred from general provisions. This is frequently referred to as the Doctrine of Protective Custody. The legal basis for a police officer taking a child, or any other person who has not violated the law, into custody against that person's will without making an arrest is nebulous, however. Most of the writers merely say that this power "of course" exists, without any discussion or citation of authority.

The authority is clear where the person agrees to cooperate, or at least may easily be made clear by statute. It is not so clear where the person, child or otherwise, does not agree that he needs the benevolent assistance of the state. To meet this situation, statutory authority is definitely required. Section 16(c) of the Standard Juvenile Court Act accomplishes this purpose. Every juvenile court act should have such a section.

Another question of police authority under juvenile court laws arises in connection with service of the process of the court. Although the wisdom of so doing has been challenged, appellate courts have almost uniformly characterized juvenile courts as civil courts. This means that their process is civil process. For historical reasons, many municipal police agencies are forbidden to serve civil process. Yet these police agencies are expected to serve juvenile court process. Every state should do as some have done and make special provision for the service of the process of the juvenile court. Section 14 of the Standard Juvenile Court Act so provides.

Police Discretion not to Exercise Their Authority in Juvenile Cases

Use of police discretion not to invoke the criminal process has been characterized as resulting in low-visibility decisions in the administration of justice. The term *low-visibility decision* is used to refer to decisions by public officials about which information is not readily available to the public for consideration and criticism. This characterization does not result in an argument that police should exercise no discretion but is an assertion that police discretion should be guided by written policy statements of the police administrator, the public prosecutor, or the legislature, as recorded in public documents, and that the exercise of discretion should be reported in a systematic way. Only in this manner, it is argued, can the public evaluate the effectiveness of its criminal laws.

This is equally true of the use of police discretion in cases of juvenile delinquency. Exercise of such discretion is necessary to effectuate individualized handling based on the principle that, in the usual case, the home is the best place for the rearing of a child. As in the case of criminal law enforcement, guidelines for the police in these cases can be established by the police administrator or by the legislature.

Legal Complications in Police Investigations and Taking into Custody in Cases Involving Juveniles

Police officers rely heavily on the cooperation of the citizenry in their work toward the solution of crimes. In many instances, it is possible to proceed in an investigation without obtaining a search warrant or without making an arrest because the citizens involved consented to waive their constitutional right to these procedures. When asked by police to assist in clearing up a reasonable suspicion that has arisen about their possible connection with an offense, most citizens will agree to cooperate. They may even allow the police to search their homes, offices, or automobiles without search warrants and often agree to accompany the police to the station to talk over an apparently incriminating situation. When voluntarily consent is thus given, the police do not need court process or other legal authority because these have been waived by the citizen in giving his consent. These informal procedures result in great saving of time for both the police and the citizens involved and are certainly to be encouraged.

The reason behind the legality of these procedures with adults is that the constitutional safeguards regarding arrest and search and seizure are being waived by a mature person who understands what he is doing. This is also true with some young persons, but probably not with all. In considering whether consent of a young person of juvenile court age in such a situation is truly a voluntary consent, the courts have considered the immaturity of the child as one of the factors to be weighed. For example, in discussing whether statements made by a child are voluntary, the courts have said that the age of the child along with the hour at which he was questioned, the duration of the questioning, whether he was given food and allowed enough rest during the period of questioning, whether he was allowed to seek the advice of his parents or of a lawyer, and the apparent overall attitude of the police toward his rights were all important factors to be considered. In view of the immaturity of many young persons of juvenile court age, serious consideration should be given to allowing the parents to be present during the questioning. The overall test is whether the young person has been treated with fundamental fairness.

This means that police officers must decide in each case whether a child is sufficiently mature and sophisticated to really know what he is doing when he gives consent to be taken to the police station or be questioned, or to be searched without being taken into custody, or arrested on the basis of probable cause. Factors to be considered by the police in making this decision in addition to the age of the child are his apparent intelligence and all around maturity, his experience or lack of experience in such situations involving the police, the seriousness of the violation that he is suspected of having committed, and the extent of the continuing danger to society in the situation. Even when the police decide that the child is mature enough to make these decisions for himself, every effort should be made to notify his parents at the earliest possible moment so that they can furnish their support and advice. The basic test of the legality of such procedures with children of juvenile court age is whether the proceedings show fundamental fairness to the child and due consideration for the child's rights, along with the right of society to be free of violations of law.

Because this concept of fundamental fairness is given somewhat different substance in different jurisdictions, every police administrator should seek the counsel of this legal advisor as to what the law probably is in his jurisdiction before he sets policy as to questioning, searching, and taking juveniles to the police station with or without taking them into custody or arresting them.

Because of a belief that the problem of a child is also a problem of his family and that a child should have the right to the advice and support of his family when he is in trouble, it is recommended that children who are going to be questioned about alleged violations of law be approached through their families if at all possible. This would not affect routine questioning of juveniles in the neighborhood when all persons found there, both adults and juveniles, are being interviewed not as possible suspects but on the chance that they may have some information that may be helpful to the police. It would not affect unsolicited admissions and confessions made to police officers by juveniles. It would affect the questioning of juveniles suspected of violations of law, whether before or after the evidence amounted to probable cause, in cases in which the police had not yet decided to refer the case to court. Whenever possible, juveniles should be interviewed in such cases in their homes after a discussion of the case with their parents. If the parents prefer, the questioning could occur at some other suitable place. In any case, the child should have the significance of his statement explained. The child and his parent should also be told whether the contact with the police amounts to an arrest or taking into custody.

Significance of the Miranda Decision

Police work with juveniles as well as with adults was significantly affected by the U.S. Supreme Court decision in the *Miranda* case (Miranda v. Arizona 1966, 384-U.S. 436). The court ruled that if a suspect is in custody or if he is deprived of freedom of action in any way, he must be advised of the following:

1. He has a right to remain silent.
2. If he gives up this right to remain silent, anything he says can and will be used as evidence against him in court.
3. He has the right to consult with an attorney and to have that attorney present during the interrogation by the police.
4. If he is unable to afford an attorney, he is entitled to have an attorney appointed to represent him during the course of the interrogation, free of charge.

State legislatures have amended their juvenile court laws to include these requirements by police officers when taking juveniles into temporary custody.

Admissibility of Juvenile Admissions and Confessions

When investigating the kind of alleged violation of law by a juvenile that may be waived to criminal court if this is allowed by the law of the jurisdiction, police officers should keep in mind that the law as to admissibility of confessions and admissions is stiffer in the criminal courts than it generally is in juvenile courts. A recent case in the United States Court of Appeals for the District of Columbia held that statements made to police by a juvenile during a period when the juvenile court was considering whether to waive jurisdiction could not be admitted in the district court after waiver had in fact occurred. The court held that "It would offend these principles [of fundamental fairness] to allow admissions made by the child in the noncriminal and nonpunitive setting of juvenile court procedures to be used later for the purpose of securing his criminal conviction and punishment." It has also been held that such statements, when later repudiated by the juvenile, will not be considered trustworthy even in the juvenile court (Harling v. United States 295 F. 2d 161 (1961). These court decisions emphasize that police should not rely too much on statements of juveniles for establishing jurisdiction of the juvenile court or for conviction after waiver to criminal court.

Taking Juveniles into Custody

Regardless of the desirability of leaving a juvenile with his parents, there will be occasions in which he/she must be taken into that physical custody. This is another police operation that has been affected in different ways in different jurisdictions by the different statutes passed along with the juvenile court laws. The result in many jurisdictions has been ambiguity in the law, which makes it unclear just what the duties and responsibilities of the police are.

When a police officer has decided that there is a basis for juvenile court jurisdiction over a child, that circumstances indicate that the child is in need of the help of the court, and that the child should immediately be taken into custody for transfer to the court, police then must carry out the procedures necessary to accomplish this result. Since the primary reason for taking the child into custody is to obtain the help of the court for the child, he/she should then be taken to the court as soon as possible. The term *court* is used here to include the probation office and the detention facility of the court. The exact place where transfer of control over the child will take place, whether in the courtroom, at the probation office, or at the detention home, should be established by court policy. This is the duty of every juvenile court judge.

The Gault Decision

Another major decision affecting the rights of juveniles was made by the U.S. Supreme Court on May 15, 1967, in the case of Gerald Gault (*in re* Gault 387, U.S.1 [1967]). The Supreme Court for the first time considered the constitutional rights of children in juvenile courts.[4]

The Case of the "Lewd and Indecent" Phone Call

Gerald and another boy were taken into custody in the morning of June 8, 1964, by the Sheriff of Gila County, Arizona. The police were acting upon a verbal complaint from a Mrs. Cook, a neighbor of the boys, that she received a lewd and indecent phone call. Both of Gerald's parents were at work that morning, and no notice of the police action was left at their home. Gerald's mother learned of his being taken to the Children's Detention House only after Gerald's older brother went to look for him at the home of the other boy. At the detention home, the mother and brother were told "why Jerry was there," and that a hearing would be held the next day at three o'clock.

A petition praying for a hearing was filed on June 9 by an Officer Flagg, which recited that "said minor is under the age of 18 years and in need of protection of this honorable court, [and that] said minor is a delinquent minor." The petition was not served on the Gaults and they first saw it two months later.

On June 9, a hearing was held in the chambers of Juvenile Judge McGhee with Gerald, his mother, his brother, and the probation officers being present. No formal or informal record of this hearing was made. Judge McGhee questioned Gerald about the telephone calls without advising him of a right to counsel or a privilege against self-incrimination. There is conflicting testimony as to Gerald's answers. Both Officer Flagg and Judge McGhee stated that Gerald admitted making at least one of the indecent remarks, while Mrs. Gault recalled that her son only admitted dialing Mrs. Cook's number.

Gerald was released from the detention home without explanation on either the 11th or the 12th (again the memories of Mrs. Gault and Officer Flagg conflict) pending further hearings; a hearing was held before Judge McGhee on June 15. Mrs. Gault asked that Mrs. Cook be present but was told by the judge that "she didn't have to be present." Neither the Gaults nor Officer Flagg remembered any admission by Gerald at this proceeding of making the indecent remarks, though the judge did remember Gerald's admitting some of the less serious statements. At the conclusion of the hearing, Gerald was committed as a juvenile delinquent to the State Industrial School "for the period of his minority [6 years] unless sooner discharged by due process of law."

No appeal was permitted under Arizona law in juvenile cases. Gerald filed a writ of habeas corpus with the Supreme Court of Arizona, which was referred to the Superior Court for hearing. Among other matters, Judge McGhee testified that he acted under a section of the Arizona Code that defines a "delinquent child" as one who (in the judge's words) is "habitually involved in immoral matters." The basis for the judge's conclusion seemed to be a referral made two years earlier concerning Gerald when the boy allegedly had "stolen" a baseball glove and "lied to the police department about it." No petition or hearing apparently resulted from this "referral." The judge testified that Gerald had violated the section of the Arizona Criminal Code which provides that a person who "in the presence of or hearing of any woman or child...uses vulgar, abusive or obscene language, is guilty of a misdemeanor...." The penalty for an adult convicted under this section is a fine of five to fifty dollars or imprisonment for not more than two months.

The Superior Court dismissed the habeas corpus petition, and Gerald sought review in the Arizona Supreme Court on many due process grounds. The Arizona Supreme Court affirmed the dismissal of the petition.

The appellants, in their appeal to the United States Supreme Court, did not raise all of the issues brought before the Supreme Court of Arizona. The appeal was based on the argument that the Juvenile Code of Arizona is invalid because, contrary to the due process clause of the Fourteenth Amendment, the juvenile is taken from the custody of his parents and committed to a state institution pursuant to proceedings where the juvenile court has virtually unlimited discretion and in which the following basic rights are denied: notice of the charges, right of counsel, right to confrontation and cross-examination, privilege against self-incrimination, right to a transcript of the proceeding, and right to appellate review.

The *Gault* decision was handed down May 15, 1967, a little over five months after its oral argument was heard by the Supreme Court. Mr. Justice Fortas wrote the opinion for the majority, which was, in effect, eight to one.

The legal precedents handed down by the *Gault* decision are neither numerous nor complex. At any proceeding where a child may be committed to a state institution, that child and his parent or guardian must be given notice in writing of the specific charges against the child sufficiently in advance of the proceedings to permit adequate preparation. The child and his parent must be notified of the child's right to be represented by counsel, and if financial considerations so require, counsel must be appointed for them. The child and his parents or guardian must be advised of the child's right to remain silent. Admission or confessions obtained from the child without the presence of counsel must undergo the greatest scrutiny in order to insure reliability. In the absence of a valid confession, no finding of "delinquency" and no order of commitment of the child for any length of time may be upheld unless such finding is supported by confrontation and sworn testimony of witnesses available for cross-examination.

Right to Counsel

In Lewis v. State (1972, Indiana, 288 NE2d 138), a seventeen-year-old boy was picked up at his home and taken to a police station for questioning concerning a homicide investigation. The youth was given the Miranda warnings, and after stating that he understood them, he signed a waiver. After a brief period of interrogation the youth gave a confession and was subsequently convicted of first-degree murder. Prior to the confession the defendant did not speak to either his parents or an attorney. On appeal the conviction was reversed. The court held that a juvenile's statement or confession cannot be used against him unless both he and his parents or guardian are informed of his right to an attorney and to remain silent. A child must also be given an opportunity to consult with his parents, guardian, or attorney in deciding whether he wishes to waive such rights.[1]

Burden of Proof

Juvenile proceedings have, in the past, been governed by the rule of preponderance of evidence in proving the issues of its cases. This standard of proof was based on the theory that juvenile proceedings, unlike adult criminal proceedings requiring issues to be proved beyond a reasonable doubt, were civil in nature and therefore should be governed by civil rules of procedure.

In 1970 the United States Supreme Court rejected this theory and required the application of the adult criminal standard of proof beyond a reasonable doubt to juvenile cases. The new criminal standard was to apply at least in those juvenile cases where a possibility existed that the juvenile proceeding might result in a loss of liberty for the minor. In the case of *in re* Winship, 397 U.S. 358, the application of the reasonable doubt standard to such juvenile proceedings was based on the reasoning of the *Gault* case that rejected the use of what it called the "'civil' label of convenience which had attached to juvenile proceedings." (*In re* Gault, 1967, 387 U.S. 1, p. 50) the court in Winship continued...

"We make clear in that (*Gault*) decision that civil labels and good intentions do not themselves obviate the need for criminal due process safeguards in the juvenile courts..." (pp. 365-366).[4]

It may be argued that such a change in the standard of proof is more academic than substantive in terms of the affect on juvenile procedures. The magistrate now says that he is satisfied that the allegations have been proved or have failed to be proven by a reasonable doubt rather than by a preponderance of the evidence. This is sufficient to satisfy the new requirements under *Winship*. More importantly, however, the *Winship* case represented another weight on equalizing the juvenile proceedings with adult criminal proceedings. As we shall see below, this equalizing process may have been substantially modified by the attitude represented by the court in deciding later cases.

Right to Jury Trial

If the requisites of due process apply to juvenile proceedings when the minor's liberty is at stake, then according to *Gault* the juvenile is entitled to the right against self-incrimination, the right to counsel, the right of confrontation and cross-examination, and the right to notice. Furthermore, as we have seen under the decision of in re *Winship*, the minor is entitled to have the issues proved beyond a reasonable doubt. A little over a year after the *Winship* case was decided, the issue of the right to a jury trial reached the United States Supreme Court in the case of McKeiver v. Pennsylvania, (1971, 403 U.S., 528). By this time the law enforcement agencies, legislatures, and courts were well aware of the direction taken by the U.S. Supreme Court, and the question was raised how far would the court go in equalizing juvenile procedures to that of adult criminal procedures. A partial answer came in *McKeiver* where the court refused to extend the similarity to the issue of jury trials. In holding that due process requirements do not compel jury trials in juvenile proceedings, the court said: "We are reluctant to disallow the states to experiment further and to seek in new and different ways the elusive answers to the problems of the young, and we feel that we would be impeding that experimentation by imposing the jury trial."

And so, a signal was given to the states that the transformation of juvenile procedures into adult criminal proceedings need not be complete. Indeed, the policy that now seemed to govern was that of "wait and see." The court now was taking a closer look at the conversion process and appeared to be proceeding on a case-by-case, issue-by-issue basis. It was certainly not a foregone conclusion that differences in the juvenile court procedure from those of the criminal court would soon be eliminated.[5]

Parole Revocation Hearings

Late in June of 1972, the United States Supreme Court decided

the case of Morrissey v. Brewer (1972, 408 U.S., 471). The facts of
the case typified the standard practices regarding the revocation of
parole as it then existed in approximately twenty states where no
hearings were held to determine the necessity for the revocation of
parole.

The two petitioners in *Morrissey* were originally sentenced for a
term in an Iowa penitentiary for forgery. About a year thereafter
each was released on parole only to be returned approximately six
months later for having committed alleged violations of parole. They
were never offered the opportunity to a hearing or to know, question, or challenge the facts or allegations that were the basis of the
alleged violations. Under these circumstances, the petitioners claimed they were deprived of their right of liberty without due process
under the Fourteenth Amendment of the Constitution.

The Court agreed in declaring that the termination of liberty of
the parolee inflicts a "grievous loss." It, therefore, was seen as within
the protection of the Fourteenth Amendment, and this called for
some orderly process, informal as it may be. The Court then attempted to lay down guidelines establishing minimum standards of
due process in the conduct of revocation of parole hearings which the
Court held were required before a parolee could suffer the termination of his parole status for alleged violations. As the court stated:

> They include: (a) written notice of this claimed violations of parole;
> (b) disclosure to the parolee of evidence against him; (c) opportunity to
> be heard in person and to present witnesses and documentary evidence;
> (d) the right to confront and cross-examine adverse witnesses (unless the
> hearing officer specifically finds good cause for not allowing confrontation
> (e) neutral and detached hearing body such as a traditional parole board,
> members of which need not be judicial officers or lawyers; and (f) a written
> statement by the fact finders as to the evidence relied on and reasons for
> revoking parole (408 U.S., p. 489).

Although the above requirements were stated in the content of
the Court's opinion explaining the necessity of a revocation hearing,
the Court also required substantially the same conditions at a
preliminary hearing conducted before the revocation hearing and
shortly after the arrest of the parolee. The preliminary hearing, the
Court said, should be "conducted at or reasonably near the place of
the alleged parole violation or arrest and as promptly as convenient
after the arrest while information is fresh and sources are avail-

able. . . to determine whether there is probable cause or reasonable ground to believe that the arrested parolee has committed acts that would constitute a violation of parole conditions (408 U.S., p. 485).

It should be noted further that *Morrissey* did not require that the preliminary hearing be conducted by a parole board member. The decision requires only that it be conducted by some person "other than the one initially dealing with the case" and specifically permitted the use of another parole officer for such purposes.

The Court conspicuously refused then to decide the issue of the right to counsel at such hearings. However, in the later case of *Gagnon* v. *Scarpelli* the Court held that there was no constitutional requirement of counsel but instead that the need for counsel should be made on the basis of the facts and circumstances of each case, the administering agency using its discretion accordingly.

By implementing constitutional safeguards of due process to parole revocation hearings, the Court has taken another step in granting the parolee a more significant distinction as a free person entitled to a more favored position under the consitutional protections than the incarcerated prisoner. Recognizing as a practical matter the distinction in life-style if not in the mere exercise of liberty and its consequent expectations, *Morrissey* initiates the process of maximum standards designed to protect the status of the parolee from unreasonable or unwarranted termination of his liberty.[5]

REFERENCES

1. Bailey, F. Lee and Rothblatt, Henry B .: *Handling Narcotic and Drug Cases*. Rochester, New York: The Lawyers Co-operative Publishing Co., 1973.
2. Bay, Kathleen Ford: Juvenile justice in California: changing concepts? *American Journal of Criminal Law, 7*(2):171-191, 1979.
3. Thorpe, Mara T.: Juvenile justice reform. *Trial, 15*(1):27-30.
4. Neigher, Alan: The Gault decision: due process and the juvenile courts. *Federal Probation, 31*(4), December, 1967.
5. Paulsen, Monrad G. and Whitebread, Charles H.: *Juvenile Law and Procedure*. Reno, Nevada: National Council of Juvenile Court Judges, 1974.
6. Sussman, Alan: Changes in juvenile law and procedure. *Criminal Law Review Bulletin, 15*(4):311-342, 1978.

Chapter 4

LABELING THEORY

I N recent years, the labeling perspective has made major contributions to deviance theory. The labeling perspective came into being because observers noticed that what they were seeing was more a product of the social definitions that were imposed upon the juvenile "delinquent" by others than it was a product of any characterological defects and socialization failures that may have occurred.[20]

Labeling theory emphasizes the important consequences to those who are sanctioned by official agencies and significant people.[3] The act itself is not as important as the reaction to it. Labeling theory does not focus on how deviant behavior originates but on how deviance is perpetuated.

By emphasizing the label, the problems caused by social reactions that attach stigmas to individuals and the later negative effects that these types of attachments will have are made more obvious. The kind of deviance will depend on the type of label that society places on the person in the ideal situation. Although labeling theory may apply to a variety of deviantly labeled roles such as delinquent,

---

We are indebted to Jim Pass, M.S. in Criminal Justice, for the research and preparation of this chapter.

homosexual, prostitute, and insane, this chapter deals with the deviance of so-called juvenile delinquents.

Before discussing labeling theory in greater detail, it is appropriate to briefly mention its history. When talking about labeling theory, it must be realized that there is no strong or integrated school of thought that exists. Labeling is basically a loosely organized group of theorists not committed to the school to any high degree.[6] Many feel they are mislabeled as labelists, but they don't disavow it completely, either.

The labeling theory has developed from the more general social-psychological theory of symbolic interactionism. Before there was any thought of a labeling theory, many sociologists and criminologists were writing about similar processes.

Charles Cooley's concept of "looking-glass self," formulated in 1902, has been a strong foundation for sociological thinking almost since its conception and was the first reference of significance to the labeling process. Cooley's theory basically states that people come to see themselves as they imagine they are defined by others. He realized that perhaps deviants were not "bad" inherently.[4]

It was back in 1912 when Gabriel Tarde published his observation that the criminal is created by the way society treats his actions.[24] Walter Lippman talked about "pictures in our minds" (stereotypes) in 1922.

Frank Tannenbaum was the first labeling theorist to apply the theory to juvenile delinquency. He believed that separating the natures of nondelinquents and delinquents is an error, because there is no initial difference. There are no physiological or psychological inferiorities in the delinquent's makeup.

Tannenbaum published an extremely important work that helped to give what would become the labeling perspective a sense of direction. He stated in part that

> the person becomes the thing he is described as being. Nor does it seem to matter whether the valuation is made by those who would punish or those who would reform. In either case the emphasis is upon the conduct that is disapproved of. . . . Their very enthusiasm defeats their aim. The harder they work to reform the evil, the greater the evil grows under their hands. The persistent suggestion, with whatever good intentions, works mischief, because it leads to bring out the bad behavior it would suppress. The way out is through a refusal to dramatize the evil.[23]

He set forth the proposition of the existence of a very powerful social process, but it was not quickly noticed. Gove argues that Tannenbaum presented a theory but presented no evidence to support it.[12] It was this lack of evidence that caused Tannenbaum's theory to be ignored until the works of Lemert in 1951 and Becker in 1963 made the labeling theory too important to set aside any longer.

Retrogressing for a moment, Emile Durkheim did some similar work at the same time as Tannenbaum. But although Durkheim had also shown the importance of the social audience's response to the actor's deviant act in 1938, deviance of any sort was persistently seen as a property either of individual actors or of defective social arrangements for the communication and inculcation of prevailing conduct norms.

Edwin Lemert made the distinction between primary and secondary deviance in his 1951 publication entitled *Social Pathology*. Primary evidence is the original act that is detected and defined as deviant by others. Actually, primary delinquency can continue until it is reacted to by society. Secondary deviance is more important and is an adaptation to the societal reaction to primary deviation in terms of social roles, social identity, and processes in fixing a person in a deviant category.[18]

Now, almost all labeling theorists make the fundamental distinction between primary and secondary deviance. From this point on, secondary deviance will be narrowed in scope to mean secondary delinquency. According to Lemert secondary delinquency is delinquent behavior, or social roles based upon it, which becomes a means of defense, attack, or adaptation to the overt and covert probblems created by the societal reaction to primary delinquency.

To labeling theorists, delinquency is not the quality of an act, but is the interaction between the actor and the respondents of the act. Even though they do not focus on primary delinquency, they have offered four explanations for its commission, which are (1) a person may belong to a minority or subculture whose values and ways of behaving may lead to violations of the rules of the dominant group; (2) he or she may have conflicting responsibilities, and the adequate performance of one role may produce violations in a second role; (3) he or she may violate rules for personal gain, usually with the expectation that he or she will not get caught; or (4) he or she may be simply unaware of the rules and violate them unintentionally.[12] Since the labeling process begins after the juvenile is caught in a delinquent act, secondary delinquency is the product of the labeling process.

The labeling perspective, as a recognized school of thought, actually came about quite unintentionally in the writings of Howard Becker in 1963. Like other symbolic interactionists before him, Becker explained the existence of delinquency in terms of delinquent self-definitions. He mentioned the terms *label* and *labeling* sparingly, but others picked up on it, and now Howard Becker is regarded as the founder of labeling theory.

Howard Becker has, in fact, been very narrow in his explanation of delinquency after primary delinquency has been detected. The delinquent is one to whom that label has been successfully applied; delinquent behavior is behavior that people so label. Becker has made a distinction between rule-breaking, in which the individual is not necessarily labeled because he broke a rule or law, and delinquency, in which the label is attached even though it may be a mistake.[1]

The major criticism of Becker refers to his overstatements of the effects of labeling. Using Becker's definition, acts can be identified as delinquent only in reference to the reaction to them through labeling by society and its agents of social control. There is no doubt, according to his critics, that the effects of labeling by society can be great on certain juvenile delinquents, but the effects are not as generalized or universal as Becker has claimed.

Hidden delinquency is when delinquent acts occur without society's officials being aware of them. Precisely because a significant amount of hidden delinquency is not labeled by official agents of social control, and does not show up in the official statistics, makes the labeling process weak in accounting for the majority of delinquency. This rather large percentage of delinquents is recognized by the labelists, but they are not dealt with until after they are detected and labeled.

Problems and inconsistencies such as these have hurt labeling theory. Many sociologists, criminal justice experts, and criminologists have abandoned the labeling perspective before it has even become twenty years old in its formal state. Research methodology has been a weak point for labeling. Qualitative methodology, especially participant observation in different forms, is almost exclusively used. Descriptive methods have been criticized by Richard

Ward, who said, "A major fault of the labeling theory, at least in my opinion, is its dependence upon subjective criteria."[39]

For labeling theory to revive itself, it appears certain that objective, quantitative methods have to be employed. Labeling must prove it can stand up to all the scrutiny that critics can dish out. It is not enough to ignore criticism and advocate labeling without substantial proof. Labeling can survive if research becomes more legitimate.

Dynamics of the Labeling Process

Clarence Schrag has identified nine characteristics of the labeling process:

1. No act is intrinsically criminal [delinquent] but is made so by the law.
2. Criminal [delinquent] definitions are enforced in the interest of powerful groups by their representatives, including the police.
3. A person does not become a criminal [delinquent] by violating the law, but by the labeling process by which authorities confer this status upon him.
4. Dichotomizing people into criminal [delinquent] and non-criminal [nondelinquent] categories is contrary to common sense and empirical evidence.
5. Only a few persons are caught in violation of the law, while many may be equally guilty.
6. While the sanctions used in law enforcement are directed against the total person and not only the criminal [delinquent] act, the severity and consequences of the penalties vary according to the characteristics of the offender.
7. Criminal [delinquent] sanctions also vary according to other characteristics of the offender, such as minority groups, transients, the poorly educated, residents of deteriorated urban areas, and other factors.
8. Criminal [juvenile] justice is based on a stereotyped concept of the criminal [delinquent] as a willful wrongdoer who is morally bad and deserves condemnation.
9. Once labeled as a criminal [delinquent], it is difficult for an offender to "live down" the label and restore himself to respected status in the community.[22]

Most labeling theorists would basically agree with these nine principles. The most important variable in studying delinquency is not the individual actor, but the social audience, because it does the labeling. In fact, the delinquent is seen by most labelists as a victim of the labeling process: "Labelists view [delinquency]...as a product or outcome of the interaction betwen the individual who performs the [delinquent] act and the labeling person. Thus, the labeling theory approach to the analysis of [delinquent] behavior typically stresses the importance of the impact of societal reaction on the [delinquent] person rather than focusing upon his psychological or sociological characteristics."[37]

American society depends on labels if it is to run smoothly, even if the labels are unfair or inaccurate. Put another way, the labeling process in human groups, whether for good or ill, remains a fixed feature for a species extraordinarily dependent on symbolic modes of communication.[21] Social control is an important function of our society, and labeling is the process whereby delinquency is identified and treated accordingly.

Hans Toch has stated that "classifying people in life is a grim business which channelizes destinies and determines fate. A man becomes a category, is processed as a category, plays his assigned role, and lives up to the implications"[38] Juvenile delinquency is seen as a normal product of our society. Evidence suggests that juveniles, under certain conditions, become involved in a cycle of events in which certain youths among them are singled out and forced into the symbolic fringes of the group, where they become heretics and outcasts.[20]

Most social scientists treat juvenile delinquency as a scientific concept and have therefore had problems in explaining why it occurs. The labeling theory does not put such a rigid definition on juvenile delinquency, because it recognizes that delinquency is a natural phenomenon that is conferred upon a juvenile by other people.

It is the children who are most easily influenced by labels placed upon them. Most of them, luckily, are positive labels. The negative label leads to later events (once it attaches) that become future delinquency. Lemert believes that social control leads to delinquency instead of the reverse, as many believe.

The power of the law does not affect most juveniles even when they are technically "delinquent." There are basically three types of delinquency: (1) undetected delinquency, (2) detected, unsanctioned delinquency, and (3) sanctioned delinquency. Undetected delinquency, is considered to be primary delinquency and will probably be labeled if it persists. Detected, unsanctioned delinquency is also primary delinquency in most cases and is really only tolerated. There are some acts that are not serious enough to place a stigma on a juvenile. Such juveniles may be dealt with on an unofficial level, so that a negative label will not hurt them too much. Sanctioned delinquency is detected and labeled behavior and thus is susceptible to becoming secondary delinquency.

The law does regularly define delinquency. The more the range of official values is restricted, the fewer the types of legitimate roles that are available.[21] New laws invent new types of delinquent roles. There is a greater chance of delinquent behavior occurring in America as legal restrictions increase and become more complex.

Delinquency is conduct that is generally believed to require the attention of social control agencies; it is conduct that something should be done about. Elements of conflict must be included in any discussion of labeling. The outcome of the labeling process is dependent upon the complex effects of the many confrontations that take place between those with the power to label and those who are potential victims of their applications. Others must know of the delinquent act, and there must be reaction to that act by formal agencies of social control.[3] Conforming members of society identify, interpret, and react to behavior according to its form. Of course, delinquent behavior is reacted to negatively in most instances.

The labeling process not only affects the juvenile who is labeled delinquent, but the ones doing the labeling as well. The labeled individual acts differently as the result of the negative tag placed on him, and the officials doing the labeling act different because they must deal with him in some way. A police officer, therefore, cannot justify calling an act delinquent unless he also refers to those who gave him the authority by legally categorizing the act as well.

Edwin Schur has divided the reacting audience to an act of delinquency into three types. The types of audiences are the society at large, the immediate and significant others (who often encourage delinquency), and official agents of control.[19] Labeling cannot be understood very well if one looks at the audience as a whole, since labeling theory appears inconsistent. This is because each audience type or segment reacts differently to the same situation, although each audience type is pretty consistent when looked at separately.

Labeling theory, in general, places most of its attention on the formal or official agency categorizing. But labeling is more inaccurate, unfair, and destructive when it is done by a huge impersonal bureaucracy such as the juvenile justice system than if done by a small group on a more personal level.[21] Formal labels are the most effective in producing an increase or a persistence in delinquent behavior because they represent a more generalized stigma and have greater labeling implications than most informal expressions of disapproval.

If there is any doubt, Gove suggests that the juvenile justice system tends to label the guilty innocent, because incorrectly labeling a child delinquent is a potentially costly mistake.[12] This is not to say that labeling mistakes do not occur, because they do from time to time, but the point is that the official agencies seem to recognize the possible consequences of the labeling process.

As mentioned earlier, Tannenbaum wrote about "the dramatization of evil" in 1938, saying that informal agents of social control often impose negative labels on those who are disruptive or even destructive of normal social routines before the formal agents of social control do their official damage.[21] The labeling process, then, occurs before formal agents of control come into the picture in a good number of cases.

False public accusations are not made with the same precaution as formal accusations, and the former can even be more damaging to the juvenile in some cases. Mistaken complaints made to the police, for example, may cause the formal agents of the juvenile justice system to continue the mistaken identity based on the informal agents' initial labeling error. However, there is a greater chance of accurate labeling when the youth's referent others are involved.

The labeling theory accounts not only for the patterns of delinquency and the social-psychological process of becoming delinquent, but also for the role of the juvenile justice system in delinquency.[18] The most crucial step in creating a stable pattern of delinquency is probably the continuous encountering of others who catch and publicly label the juvenile.

Labeling a juvenile as a delinquent may result in a self-fulfilling prophecy. The term *self-fulfilling prophecy* was coined by Robert Merton in 1957. It is set into motion once a juvenile is stigmatized by a label of delinquency, because others perceive and respond to him as a delinquent. Acting in the manner that one believes is expected of oneself is carrying out the self-fulfilling prophecy.

Once a juvenile is labeled as a delinquent he no longer enjoys all of the freedoms that other juveniles do. Frederic Faust has recognized that the "consequences of a delinquent label include informal sanctions following from social stigma (such as differential consideration and treatment by neighbors, teachers, or prospective employers); formal sanctions when adjudication follows identification (such as corrective intervention through probation, mandatory involvement in specialized treatment programs, or commitment to state training facilities); and, as pointed out by Reckless, Dinitz, and others, considerable loss of self-esteem."[29] Such a juvenile is often still in the social community but is no longer considered a legitimate part of it.

Before he is labelled, however, the juvenile who commits occasional delinquent acts rationalizes his behavior as "kicks" and convinces himself that such infrequent behavior is normal and fits legitimately into the legal system. This is rarely true for the juvenile who has committed serious crimes, because in such a situation rationalization is harder to justify, and the delinquent label will attach itself much easier. A serious offender's behavior is easier to spot and poses an immediate threat to the community, so quick action is taken.

Since the average youth does not commit a serious offense, his rationalizations will continue to satisfy his conscience until he is formally labeled. At such time, if the pressure is persistent enough, the juvenile will start to internalize the negative conceptions of himself that others have supplied him with. These internalizations gradually replace the once adequate rationalizations. Primary delinquency at this stage is behavior that is recognized as bad. It should be mentioned, though, that in some cases the labeling of one act as delinquent does not lead to secondary delinquency and may cause the juvenile to behave himself so as to avoid the consequences.

Labeling becomes more reinforced as the youth goes through the various levels of the juvenile justice system. Police officers are generally recognized as the most influential labeling authorities, but they are certainly not the only ones. "Ironically, the juvenile court—largely created by social reformers who sought to curb the early stigmatization of youth in trouble—is a major arena for labeling processes for the social, and to a considerable degree, organizational production of deviants."[19] The experience of being negatively labeled is a significant factor in the socialization of the young.

The juvenile court judge must be careful of the decisions that he makes, because the labels that are dispensed are additionally subjected to social forces, and secondary delinquency is made more likely to develop. The social definition is especially important because of its impact on the individual's definition of self.[9] Juveniles, like all people, act in terms of their self-identity, so the definition of *self* is instrumental in determining behavior.[18] Once a juvenile's behavior is defined or labeled as delinquent (especially by a judge), the definitional or labeling pressures that are leveled against him have personal identity implications. Labeling often sets in motion a process that tends to shape the individual into the image that people have of him or her.

Thus, a juvenile who has been labeled delinquent is more likely to commit acts that are consistent with his externally defined identity than a youth who has not been so labeled. During the labeling process the juvenile faces problems in the course of his regular social interaction that he took for granted before.[9] Labeling theory is based on the creation of delinquent identities through the process of symbolic interaction in which juvenile justice authorities can be a dominant force.[9]

Despite the strong insistence of labelists that labeling creates secondary (internalized) delinquency, others maintain that "no study has conclusively shown that agencies of social control 'create' delinquency. However, one might argue that varying delinquency rates and social control actions do tend to set the 'standards' for delinquency."[39] The debate will ultimately be resolved with future accumulation and analysis of empirical studies.

Most theories about juvenile delinquency see social norms as rigid, unchangeable guidelines that everyone must follow in life. Any type of dysfunction is of the person himself or of social adaptation. This was generally the thinking before labeling theory was formed in an organized manner. Labelists, however, have come to recognize categorizing juveniles as "good" or "bad" or "nondelinquent" or "delinquent" based on strict stereotypes as unrealistic.

One unfortunate consequence in societal reaction caused by labeling a juvenile as delinquent is that he is from that point on considered to be potentially dangerous often without regard to how harmless an act was committed. Thus, community reaction is often negative even to the most harmless delinquent.

Another related societal reaction from labeling a youth as delinquent is that others show signs of anger toward him.[20] Their anger usually manifests itself in negative or punitive reactions. As stated earlier, the juvenile justice system was set up to "help" America's youth so they do not become "bad people," but by trying to do this their labeling creates unforeseen consequences.

It follows, then, that the labeling perspective rejects the notion of a simple dichotomy. Labelists recognize that society is a diverse structure. There are many cultural diversities, especially in urban societies. Labeling theorists have replaced the assumption that society is characterized by a consensus over norms and values with the assumption of pluralistic value systems.[21] It is not possible to tell based on one act of delinquency the character of an individual. John Kitsuse wrote that the forms of behavior alone do not separate delinquents from nondelinquents, but it is the responsibility of a society's officials to make such a distinction.[31]

Nearly all juveniles commit delinquent acts, but only a small percentage are singled out and subjected to the labeling process. The majority do not see themselves as delinquents when there is no pressure on them. Those juveniles who are not caught violating the law are never stigmatized formally and therefore never develop a negative self-image. Police and other juvenile justice officials do not have the resources to catch all juvenile offenders, and many researchers have concluded that those not caught have a better chance of not rejecting society and committing secondary delinquency.

A false label at the outset can be as damaging or more so than a correct label, since the labeling theory does not dwell on primary delinquency. It does recognize the significance of primary delinquency, as previously stated, since it is because of primary delinquency that the labeling process is set into motion. Some secondary delinquency is caused by labels meant as reinforcement from peers, some from negative labels by informal organizations, some from negative labels by formal agencies, and some by various combinations of the former three sources.

The labeling position on secondary delinquency is not clear about the specific social-psychological processes that occur between apprehension and labeling, and the internalization of a delinquent identity.[3] Some delinquents see labeling as a helpful intervention that straightens them out (this is rare); others see it as only a temporary reaction; and still others see it as permanent punishment (at least in their eyes).

Labeling is viewed as being a powerful and dynamic force, but just because a juvenile is labeled as delinquent, and there is societal reaction to that label, does not automatically lead to a progression toward secondary delinquency.

A great bulk of labeling research has involved the police. Scott Briar and Irving Piliavin concluded in a 1966 study of 66 police encounters with juveniles that the outcome of police discretion depends, to a great degree, on "cues which emerged from the interaction between the officer and the youth, cues from which the officer inferred the youth's character."[39]

Their findings are generally still true today. The juvenile's style of dress, hair length (to a lesser degree), demeanor, and other characteristics can be important factors in determining how a juvenile will be treated. Passing the appearance and attitude tests leads to a favorable outcomes in most instances; thus, the labeling process will not be employed.

Low status members of the community tend to be singled out more than those members with average or high status rankings. Furthermore, inaccurate labels seem to affect different class youths in different ways as Wodarski, Feldman, and Pedi have found in their study: "...when the behavioral referents are vague, ill-defined, or undifferentiated, lower-class boys, in particular, may be unduly susceptible to accepting the dysfunctional labels imputed to them by others. In contrast, middle-class boys may be more able to resist inaccurate imputations of deviance, even when the requisite behavioral referents are relatively ambiguous in nature."[40] Juveniles may find it harder to fight a public delinquent stigma, because they have fewer resources, and their low socioeconomic status has caused the labeling process to work against them in other forms. It may simply be that these youths are exposed to more opportunities to allow the self-fulfilling prophecy to take effect.

In other words, the labeling process leads to secondary delinquency, and since the disadvantaged are singled out and labeled more often than average juveniles, they come to commit more delinquent acts.[18] Although juveniles in the lower socioeconomic classes and in minority groups are no more likely to commit delinquent acts than those falling into the mainstream society, they are much more likely to be labeled as delinquents.

So it is clear that labeling is not a random process that is applied to all juveniles who break the law. There is a lot of discretion on which individuals are officially labeled based on such factors as social class, occupation of parents, racial and ethnic background, age, past record of delinquency, and the resources available to apprehend or deal with delinquents.[3] It is evident that discretionary practices in the labeling process occur at all levels of the juvenile justice system.

Police officers have been given considerable discretion in apprehending youths, and it has been observed that certain youths, particularly from minority racial and ethnic groups or those dressed in "tough" styles, were treated more severely than others for comparable offenses.[10] Police discretion is critical in the prevention or initiation of a delinquent career. The ideal situation for treating all the encountered juveniles fairly according to the act they commit is unfortunately not possible because of individual discretion. Generally, then, the poor and the minority youths are products of the labeling process most often.[3]

Juvenile delinquents, though still often young, are often viewed as morally inferior compared to the average juvenile. Labeling a youth as a juvenile delinquent implies that he is somehow different than everyone else in all aspects of his personality. This is because the labeling approach regards stereotyping as a central component of the social process of which delinquency is created.[2] A youth is often treated by others based on his master (or overriding) status, i.e. delinquent.

Generalizing in this manner about a juvenile tends to be done by those who feel true compassion toward him as well as by those who do not know or do not like him. The latter two groups of labelers include those whom the labeling theory focuses upon, but the former group often provides reinforcement that aids the labeling process.

A newly defined delinquent will receive a quite different reaction than he did before the label was applied to him. He is usually treated as a stereotype of a juvenile delinquent rather than as an individual. It can hardly be doubted that labeling theory's emphasis on the effect of stereotypic categorizing on the behavior of young law violators has had a large impact.[21]

This impersonal treatment often causes resentment from the youth toward the "establishment" and contributes to the self-fulfilling prophecy. Juveniles eventually define themselves in terms of the societal stereotypes defining their delinquency. Police officers (the most common official labelers), through labeling, put pressure on the juvenile and his significant others, often causing subsequent internalization of negative attitudes and values. This process will slowly change the old dominant behavior traits into the stereotyped delinquent traits.

Erving Goffman refers to the label of "delinquent" as a stigma and to the process by which a person is discredited as stigmatization, as the terms have been used throughout this discussion.[11] The labeling process separates the stigmatized juveniles from those not stigmatized and puts each type of label together. Stigmatization sometimes serves as a catalytic agent that initiates delinquent careers.[10] The labeling process produces effects that actually reinforces delinquent behavior and creates a "reputation" among the juvenile's delinquent and nondelinquent peers.

Because the newly labeled delinquent is separated symbolically (at least) from the nondelinquents, they are forced to associate with other established delinquents, especially when society regards the delinquent act as serious. A delinquent role is reinforced by others who participate in the same kinds of delinquent behavior. When many juveniles are labeled as delinquent, they band together because of their common fate.

Lemert explains the problems juveniles have in overcoming the labeling processes' pressures: "When the teacher uses the tag "bad boy" or "mischief maker" or other invidious terms, hostility and resentment are excited in the boy, and he may feel that he is blocked in playing the role expected of him. Thereafter, there may be a strong temptation to assume his role in the class as defined by the teacher, particularly when he discovers that there are rewards as well as penalties deriving from such a role."[15] This classroom situation applies to all societal levels and relationships, of course.

When pressures become too great and rewards seem appealing, labeled delinquents gather to form a subculture or join an existing one. A common type of subculture is the delinquent gang. Every subculture, by definition, has norms and values different from the dominant society. These different norms and values are often opposed to the dominant ones. Gang members may commit offenses as secondary delinquents and thus are not regarded as "delinquents" in their own eyes.[3] Membership in the delinquent gang gives each member a sense of belonging and gives his life a new sense of legitimacy.

Primary delinquency in a gang means that the members accept the dominant norms and values but still defy the authorities that enforce them. Usually, such members have not been publicly labeled. These gangs do not constitute a subculture.

The secondary deviant, however, develops a delinquent role that involves greater participation in the gang, the acquisition of more knowledge and rationalizations for the behavior, and skill in avoiding detection and arrest.[3] The stigma of the label that is placed on a certain delinquent in a subculture is minimized by the other members who participate in the same activities. By the time a juvenile falls into the delinquent, self-fulfilling prophecy pattern, he feels that he has failed in the dominant world, so the subcultural world seems easier to live in.

But even the juvenile not involved in any subculture finds it hard to regain a respected status in the community. Labeling is most effective when a youth is in role confusion during his identity crisis stage because it gives him a temporary identity. It is always possible to fight the stigma, but it is often extremely difficult. Becker has said, essentially, that the power to label people delinquent is the power to determine their fate. Although such a statement is a bit strong, it puts across the seriousness of the labeling process.

Once a juvenile has adopted a delinquent self-image, he has experienced a degrading and frequently irreversible socialization process.[12] In American society, the delinquent status overrides all others in importance; it is the major identification source.[9,12] A labeled delinquent is seen as a delinquent, no matter what other skills the juvenile may have, to an overwhelming degree.

Labeling theory alone is usually not influential enough to turn a juvenile into a career criminal, but it is influential enough in many cases to turn a juvenile into a juvenile delinquent through its processes and consequences. By the time a juvenile enters his early twenties, the labeling process tends to lose its effects and wears off to a considerable degree.

Juvenile delinquents do not become career criminals in the majority of cases, because their true developing self is buried under the newer reactional interpretations of others caused by the labeling process. The juvenile's true self develops to some degree in opposition to his temporary labeled self and resurfaces later in his life when he is about to enter adulthood.

Societal pressures of the most frequent kind help to force the delinquent's true self to resurface. The majority of societal pressures are meant to be those other than the negative, labeling-process pressures. A main pressure is to obtain money. If a delinquent does not become a career criminal he has to get a job or go to school to get a better job in the future. These types of needs and other new responsibilities usually cause the delinquent to conform to the dominant society's norms and values, and he becomes, essentially, a law-abiding citizen.

It may even be said that the labeling process works in opposite ways when the juvenile reaches his early twenties. Instead of applying delinquent or criminal labels to these juveniles, those stressing conformity are applied, so a second chance is given. As David Madza and others have proposed, signification (the attachment of a stigma by formal control agents) may be neutralized by the older juvenile's strengthening character. Recognition of this may justify allowing delinquents to receive a second chance.[16]

Diversion and Labeling

To paraphrase an earlier quote of Tannenbaum's, it does not seem to make much difference whether a juvenile is evaluated by those involved in punishment or rehabilitation, since any talk about delinquent behavior tends to increase that behavior instead of suppressing it. Although it is better not to talk about it if it can be helped, this is rarely possible within the juvenile justice system or society in general.

"While 'protection of society' and action in the 'best interests' of children through 'individualized treatment' are worthy objectives, the adverse effects of this system on labeled delinquent youth are considerable."[29] The system in its present state is not personalized enough despite the claims of its officials.

An example of the impersonal nature of the juvenile justice

system's operation is reflected in its evaluation procedures. Probation reports, for example, develop stereotypic words, phrases, and writing styles in describing people and events through the authorities who produce them. Everyone tends to be treated similarly. Labels put in juvenile justice records stick because they are made by "experts."[38] It must be recognized that community members can have positive impact on the problems that the juvenile justice system is experiencing.

After a juvenile's self-image has been significantly damaged, it is not enough to simply remove the label. It seems likely that negative labels, once attached, can best be countered by applying positive labels, which instill confidence and self-worth. Labeling theory implications have contributed to the current treatment programs, but not without heated debate.

Using labeling applications, new diversion programs are being developed. The major aim of these programs is to divert those who are seen as being in trouble with the law away from official juvenile court processing and its consequences when it is practical.[21] It is best to circumvent the juvenile justice system when it will best benefit the youngster. Lemert recognized how formal institutions manufacture deviance when, in 1967, he stated: "I have come to believe that the reverse idea, i.e. social control leads to deviance, is equally tenable and the potentially richer premise for studying deviance in modern society."[39] This type of reinforcement often leads to recidivism, and its form is often that of secondary delinquency.

Tannenbaum put it very well when he wrote: "The process of making the criminal [delinquent], is a process of tagging, defining, identifying, segregating, describing, emphasizing, making conscious and self-conscious; it becomes the very traits that are complained of. . . ."[19] Based on the extensive work of labelers since Tannenbaum, it would seem prudent to develop alternatives to juvenile justice institutions, yet a growing number of criminologists and sociologists seem to be questioning the general principles of labeling theory.

Those who oppose diversion programs point out that the juvenile justice system was formed in order to divert youths from the adult system at the end of the nineteenth century.[35] It seems useless to them to attempt another schism when the effects of the labeling process are unconvincing.

Three other basic underlying concerns causing many to oppose diversionary programs are "(1) the concept of diversion is dangerously ambiguous; (2) the goals of these programs may be unattainable; and (3) diversionary efforts may be incompatible with concepts of due process and fundamental fairness."[26] In regard to the first objection, it is felt that the concept of diversion is different to different people, since there is diversion within the juvenile justice system and diversion outside of the system. Outside diversion programs are frowned upon, because it is felt by some that "the juvenile justice system is already in the business of diverting young offenders from adjudication and institutional treatment."[26] In fact, much delinquency is detected but unsanctioned.

It is argued that the goals of diversionary programs, i.e. eliminating the stigma caused by a delinquent label and restoring a respectable status for the juvenile, are most likely beyond the reach of "nonprofessional" community members. Furthermore, it is believed that inconclusive studies have shown that a continuous labeling process does not appear to encourage delinquency.[33]

There is a strong opposition against removing the juvenile, even the status offender, from the jurisdiction of the juvenile court, because it is felt that this method of dealing with juveniles will encourage rather than prevent delinquency.[30] There is a certain fear of losing control of the juvenile's welfare: "Placing properly adjudicated delinquents in these programs may be a commendable alternative to incarceration, but it would be a serious step backward to permit diversionary placement without legal safeguards which assure that the community has a sound basis for any intervention at all."[26] Any placement of youths in a diversionary program that takes place outside of the legal process is believed by many opponents to be a violation of the Due Process Clause in the Fourteenth Amendment of the United States Constitution.

Guarna provides a good summary of the position opposing the labeling dynamics and the diversionary programs that they logically lead to for purposes of rehabilitation: "In conclusion, organizations and interested citizens who constantly are playing verbal games with the juvenile court terminology are not really helping those children who are in dire need of assistance. What they ought to be doing is working with the juvenile court to stimulate the creation of necessary programs for children who come into the system. In this manner, the juvenile court will not be the Court of Last Resort but will continue to be the *best resort.*"[30]

Proponents of the labeling perspective and diversion believe that stigmatization brought about by public, formal authorities is much more severe than informal labeling dynamics. The former situation, which is a conflict relationship between formal agents of social control and juveniles labeled as delinquent, is more likely to lead to at least the beginning of a self-fulfilling prophecy.[21] Faust has pointed out that the National Council on Crime and Delinquency has stated that "once brought into the juvenile court process these children—whether labeled status offenders or delinquents—become stigmatized."[29]

Labels, whether applied formally or informally, should be explained to the juvenile being labeled so that it is understood what is meant. Label usage has to be more fair. Treatment will be less likely to reinforce delinquency if the possible consequences are known and guarded against. The labeling process tends to be more positive when the labeler is respected and trusted. The important thing is to neutralize negative labels so that conforming behavior becomes more likely.

SUMMARY

Labeling theory is a valuable perspective in understanding the perpetration of delinquency after a juvenile is caught and labeled. Even when taking into account the various flaws and inconsistencies of the proposed effects of the labeling process, it cannot be ignored that labeling does have many negative influences on a significant number of juveniles. The juvenile justice system, to make matters worse, is structured in such a way as to incorporate the problems of labeling at most of its levels.

Labeling is limited in explaining initial (primary) delinquency, but by linking it to other symbolic interactionist theories, such as Sutherland's differential association, all phases of delinquency can be better understood. Labeling theory must not be segregated from other explanations that propound the same or similar processes simply because "label" and "labeling" (and other terminology) are not used in the explanations and descriptions.

Police first officially label a juvenile in a negative fashion when an arrest is made. The labeling process involves more labelers as the youth moves through the juvenile justice system. The general assumption is that a juvenile has a better chance of committing secondary delinquency as he moves through the system, because his label appears to be more justified to him as other officials reinforce the face validity of the label.

Once the juvenile finds himself in a delinquent role, he will act the way he believes is expected of him, usually using the stereotype of his category of delinquent as his model. Such a labeled juvenile will stay a delinquent as long as there is enough reinforcement to outweigh the social pressures to reform. There is always cognitive dissonance between the two forces of the juvenile's parents and society trying to keep him "good," and peer group pressure and the labeling process forcing him to turn "bad."

Career delinquency brought about by the self-fulfilling prophecy usually lasts until a juvenile's early twenties. The delinquent role is terminated, and the role of law-abiding citizen (to some degree) takes over. There are, however, some juveniles who cannot make this transition, and these persons often become career criminals.

Labeling theory explains why those who are on the margins of society, such as minorities and the poor, are most likely to become juvenile delinquents. Unlike most of the other social science theories, the labeling perspective does not attribute a large significance of deliquency causation to social structure characteristics.

Critics of the labeling school of thought argue that too much attention is placed on those people — private and professional — who do the labeling and not enough is devoted to the delinquents themselves and their actions.

It is also stated that the labeling process is too deterministic. However, it is not advocated by labelists that the juvenile being labeled is a passive object that is categorized and given a function for life. The juvenile, to the contrary, must internalize the concept of delinquent and accept this societal definition before a delinquent role is acted out.

This is not to say that the labeling theory does not have its problems. One problem is that labelers tend to view the interaction between labelers and those labeled as a one-way relationship. This is not determinism, because the youth makes internal decisions. It is certainly plausible that labeling is a two-way process with each label affecting both persons and stimulating interaction.

Today, labeling theory seems to have been largely abandoned, as many former labeling supporters have moved beyond labeling and into radical criminology. The labeling theory, to revive, must get away from its oversimplifications and involve the complexities of reality. Labeling has received so little attention lately partly because of its narrow concentration on the effects of labelers and its refusal to address all aspects of life. Labeling analysts have stressed how the labeling process reinforces behavior in most cases but have shied away from addressing those situations in which the same process may have deterrent effects on delinquent behavior. Research has not conclusively proven that the labeling process fosters secondary delinquency, but it has apparently shown that the outcomes may be in the forms of reinforcement and deterrence. Negative and positive outcomes must be looked for in empirical studies.

Finally, there is a problem with labeling research in that it tends to be only qualitative (descriptive) in design. Participant observation in its various forms is used, and no advantage is taken of the statistical resources that are widely available. Current research efforts must be bolstered by quantitative methods for the labeling theory to survive.

REFERENCES

Books

1. Becker, Howard S.: *Outsiders: Studies in the Sociology of Deviance.* New York: Macmillan and Company, 1963, pp. 18, 22.
2. Bliss, Dennis, C.: *The Effects of the Juvenile Justice System on Self-Concepts.* San Francisco: R & E Associates, Inc., 1977, p. 14.
3. Clinard, Marshall B.: *Sociology of Deviant Behavior.* New York, Chicago, San Francisco, Atlanta, Dallas, Montreal, Toronto, London, Sydney: Holt, Rinehart and Winston, Inc., 1974.
4. Cooley, Charles H.: *Human Nature and the Social Order.* New York: Scribner's, 1902.
5. Davis, Nanette, J.: *Sociological Constructions of Deviance: Perspectives and Issues in the Field.* Dubuque, Iowa: William C. Brown Company Publishers, 1975.
6. Downes, David, and Rock, Paul (Eds.): *Deviant Interpretations.* New York: Barnes & Noble Books, 1979, p. 87.
7. Empey, LaMar T. *American Delinquency: Its Meaning and Construction.* Homewood, Illinois: The Dorsey Press, 1978.

8. Ericson, Richard V.: *Criminal Reactions: The Labelling Perspective.* Westmead, Farnborough, Hants., England: Saxon House, D.C. Heath, Ltd., 1975, pp. 18, 100.

9. Farrel, Ronald A., and Swigert, Victoria L. (Eds.): *Social Deviance.* Philadelphia, New York, and Toronto: J.B. Lippincott Company, 1975, pp. 4, 377.

10 Fox, Vernon: *Introduction to Criminology.* Englewood Cliffs, New Jersey: Prentice-Hall, Inc., 1976, pp. 145, 147.

11. Goffman, Erving: *Stigma: Notes on the Management of Spoiled Identity.* Englewood Cliffs, New Jersey: Prentice-Hall, Inc., 1963, p. 15.

12. Gove, Walter R. (Ed.): *The Labeling of Deviance: Evaluating a Perspective.* Beverly Hills and London: Sage Publications, 1980, pp. 3, 4, 6, 7, 187, 191.

13. Hawkins, Richard, and Tiedeman, Gary: *The Creation of Deviance: Interpersonal and Organizational Determinants.* Columbus, Ohio: Charles E. Merrill Publishing Company, 1975.

14. Krohn, Marvin D., and Akers, Ronald L. (Eds.): *Crime, Law, and Sanctions.* Beverly Hills and London: Sage Publications, 1978.

15. Lemert, Edwin M.: *Social Pathology: A Systematic Approach to the Theory of Sociopathic Behavior.* New York: McGraw-Hill Co., 1951, p. 75.

16. Matza, David: *Delinquency and Drift.* New York, John Wiley and Sons, 1964, p. 37.

17. Merton, Robert: *Social Theory and Social Structure,* 2nd Ed. Glencoe, Illinois: The Free Press, 1957.

18. Sanders, William B.: *Juvenile Delinquency.* New York: Praeger Publishers, 1976, pp. 52, 54.

19. Schur, Edwin M.: *Labeling Deviant Behavior: Its Sociological Implications.* New York: Harper & Row, 1971, pp. 10, 87, 186.

20. Scott, Robert A., and Douglas, Jack D. (Eds.): *Theoretical Perspectives on Deviance.* New York and London: Basic Books, Inc., 1972, pp. 10, 16.

21. Short, James F., Jr. (Ed.): *Delinquency, Crime, and Society.* Chicago and London: The University of Chicago Press, 1976, pp. 239, 241-2, 244-6.

22. Schrag, Clarence: *Crime and Justice—American Style.* Washington, D.C.: United States Government Printing Office, 1971, p. 25

23. Tannenbaum, Frank: *Crime and the Community.* Boston: Ginn and Co., 1938, pp. 19, 20.

24. Tarde, Gabriel: *Penal Philosophy.* Translated by Rapelje Howell. Boston: Little, Brown and Company, 1912.

Periodicals

25. Briar, Scott, and Piliavin, Irving: Police encounters with juveniles. In Diallombardo, R. (Ed.): *Juvenile Delinquency: A Book of Readings.* New York: John Wiley and Sons, 1966.

26. Bullington, Bruce, Sprowls, James, Katkin, Daniel, and Philips, Mark: A critique of diversionary juvenile justice. *Crime and Delinquency, 24*(1):59-71, 1978.

80 *Police Work With Juveniles*

27. Chiricos, T. G., Jackson, P. D., and Waldo, G. P.: Inequality in the imposition of a criminal label. *Social Problems, 19:*553-572, 1972.
28. Ericson, Richard V.: Social distance and reaction to criminality. *The British Journal of Criminology, 17*(1):16-29, 1977.
29. Faust, Frederic L.: Delinquency labeling: Its consequences and implications. *Crime and Delinquency, 19:*41-48, 1973.
30. Guarna, Anthony A.: Status offenders belong in juvenile court. *Juvenile Justice, 28*(4):35-37, 1977.
31. Kitsuse, John: Social reactions to deviance: Problems of theory and method. *Social Problems, 9*(Winter):247-256, 1962.
32. Klein, Malcohm: Labeling, deterrence, and recidivism: A study of police dispositions of juvenile offenders. *Social Problems, 22*(2):292-303, 1974.
33. Martin, Christopher A.: Status offenders and the juvenile court system: Where do they belong? *Juvenile Justice, 28*(1):7-17, 1977.
34. Newman, Graeme R.: Acts, actors, and reactions to deviance. *Sociology and Social Research, 58*(4):434-440, 1974.
35. Padon, Edward: Here we go again—The child savers. *Juvenile Justice, 28*(1):41-45, 1977.
36. Shawyer, Lois; and Sanders, Bruce: A look at four critical premises in correctional views. *Crime and Delinquency, 23*(4):427-435, 1977.
37. Thorsell, Bernard A., and Klemke, Lloyd W.: The labeling process: Reinforcement and deterrent. *Law and Society Review, 6:*393-403, 1972.
38. Toch, Hans: The care and feeding of typologies and labels. *Federal Probation, 34:*15-19, 1970.
39. Ward, Richard H.: The labeling theory: A critical analysis. *Criminology, 9:*269, 283, 449, 1971.
40. Wodarski, John S., Feldman, Ronald A., and Pedi, Stephan J.: Labeling by self and others: The comparison of behavior among "anti-social" and "pro-social" children in an open community agency. *Criminal Justice and Behavior, 2*(3):258-275, 1975.

Chapter 5

DELINQUENCY PREVENTION

URING the 1970s many observers of the criminal justice system opined that court referral of a juvenile came too late. By the time formal processing occurred the youth was well known to law enforcement, having appeared several times prior on department "contact cards." Earlier intervention, it was hoped, might attenuate the pre-delinquent process, if not avert it. For the most part, law enforcement had a dichotomous set of alternatives: (1) lecture and release or (2) refer to court. Referral to court typically materialized after several "lecture and releases" seemed unproductive. In frustration, law enforcement referred the juvenile to juvenile court hoping for formal sanction. Often the court, viewing the juvenile for the first time, lectured and released. Acting very much as law enforcement, the court might not take formal action until more informal approaches seemed to fail. Consequently, the adjudicated juvenile was an individual well known to the court, as well as to law enforcement. What then might transpire if some action, formal or informal, were taken at the first or early contact with law enforcement or the court? Would not this intervention act as a preventive device?

For some ten years we have experimented with various forms of diversion. It was hoped that diverting a youth from the system

81

would avoid the labeling stigma. It was hoped that diversion would impress upon the youth the need for modifying his behavior or face subsequent formal processing. It was hoped that a rehabilitative approach would, at the very least, act upon the behavioral symptoms, thus making recidivism unlikely. It was hoped that role models, often important components of diversion programs, would suggest alternate life-styles and future directional paths.

For some time, critics argued that diverted youth were simply those whose prior disposition would have been "lecture and release." They argued that the Law Enforcement Assistance Administration's massive funding was being utilized to enlarge the net of the criminal justice system by adding youth to the system. This, it was argued, would simply expose more youth to the potential of labeling and make more likely the prospect of additional pre-delinquent careers finding their genesis. Moreover, they said, local politicans and community leaders were exhorting the virtues of such programs to political advantage. Project funds were being channeled to constituent groups and to neighborhood leaders. Anyway, presumably, transfer of community problems back to the community made sense, particularly in view of establishment failures. Thus, said the critics, the prospect that any juvenile would be deterred from crime was based upon pure chance. Those odds, it was argued, always existed before the arrival of LEAA. Many youths released to their parents by law enforcement were never heard from again. Why now involve them in the "system" when they might seek their own solutions—hopefully productive ones? For the first time, however, we intervened formally at an earlier stage for many juveniles, thus testing, to some extent, the premise that early intervention might deter further penetration into the juvenile justice system.

Still other critics positioned themselves on the "nonbelieving" side of a different ilk. This group was not fearful of the "widening net" theory, since early intervention was seen as a potential deterrent. If a juvenile or two became enamored of the criminal justice system and reoffended, this group presumed that such an outcome was likely anyway with such a youth. From this group's standpoint labeling did not cause aberrant behavior—it became an *ex post facto* identity. Many youth turned away from crime despite the potential tarnish of labeling. It was better, said this group, to intervene and *attempt* to deter, rather than *assume* that intervention by itself would initiate a delinquent career. This group, however, objected to the prevailing strategy.

Many diversion programs sought to direct the youth toward a community program not only to avoid labeling, but to introduce a community intervention posture. It was argued that diversion should exclude the criminal justice agencies from the action or rehabilitative phase. If the criminal justice agencies diverted youth to offices within the official establishment such as law enforcement or probation, it was theorized that youth would fail to respond, that behavioral change would be largely cosmetic to avoid further sanction, and labeling would occur. The "nonbelievers," however, envisioned conceptual problems emanating precisely from this community emphasis. In the first place, some questioned whether certain neighborhood leaders would simply condone the referred youth's alleged behavior and assist the youth in learning how to avoid further contact with the criminal justice system while continuing hostile activity. Second, it was feared that few sanctions, if any, would occur, and the presumed impact of informal sanctions, to compensate for the avoidance of labeling, would be lost. Finally, it was doubted that many community leaders would become effective program managers and that their real intent was political power.

Apparently, after ten years of LEAA, those who now admit they were enthusiastic about the program must have been an ill-advised "fringe" occupying a middle position that argued for proceeeding—if for no other reason that there was little to lose and much to gain. Besides, federal dollars began arriving in heady quantities. Probably not since a wartime mobilization effort did so much energy, manpower, and enthusiasm coalesce as it did in the 1970s toward the reduction and prevention of crime. In some respects, the most exciting phenomenon was the convocation of committees, councils, and commissions consisting of politicians, bureaucrats, the public, academia, and officials from law enforcement, the courts, and corrections. Many remembered the days of John F. Kennedy in which, for better or worse, commentators remarked about the descent of so much brainpower on Washington. Some mused in those days that if a national government composed of such academic lustre could not solve society's problems there might be little hope for ordinary men and women in the future. As history suggests, however, progress is not solely dependent upon intelligence quotients. Painfully, apparently, we observe progress occurring in curious mixtures of intelligence, determination, political acumen, and perhaps even luck. Such, seemingly, was the fate of LEAA's ten years.

It is true that excesses occurred during the LEAA era. In addition to misappropriation of funds, one might question the expenditure of millions of dollars toward the reduction of crime only to enter the 1980s with crime rates at precipitous levels and the "fear of crime" exceeding even the probability of a criminal act occurring. Was nothing successful? Was nothing learned? Observers of this era are analyzing the period, and it is presumed that insights, evaluations, and critiques are in process. A full treatment of the LEAA period is not the intent of this chapter. Of those projects listed as "exemplary projects," we find a handful that have earned the approval of professionals as well as the likelihood of continued funding. Scholarly inquiry will need to explore the effectiveness of LEAA strategies that seemingly produced this handful of exemplary projects. It is possible that nothing would have occurred without this massive programming, though this is for scholars to evaluate. For our purposes, what may be learned from those projects that have survived and which continue their existence? Or, in the alternative, what are we reasonably certain failed to reap sufficient benefit?

DETERRENCE

Researchers and policy makers anguish over what deters crime. Factors such as the law, probability of apprehension, and fear of sanction are explored for possible insights. Two central perspectives to this inquiry are helpful in organizing the discussion. First, one might question to what extent the criminal justice system is capable of deterring crime at all. A negative answer would question the deterrent effect of any criminal legislation, decisional law, penal sanction, or fear of apprehension. Such a view would suggest that most Americans do not enter into criminal behavior for motivations that have little to do with the formal structures of the criminal justice system. One might call this a "middle class" perception of turning toward crime. This group identifies with the establishment, earns its living from it, supports it politically, and fears absolutely nothing when capital punishment is discussed, debated, or accepted as an appropriate sanction for specified cases of homicide now or ever. If a neighbor, of the same persuasion, murders his wife with a hunting rifle, the cause of such a tragedy is psychological and impulsive: self-control failed the neighbor. He was hardly perusing the capital punishment cases in his mind as he grasped for his rifle. Thus, this group sees no deterrent effect of formal sanction on anyone holding the same persuasion as they. This is not to say that such a group would not espouse strict criminal sanctions for persons violating the law, because such persons have no intent of violating the law, nor do they even know a close acquaintance who has been convicted of a crime. While they do not believe that formal sanctions deter crime, they assume that those who do must pay the penalty. If prevention of further crime occurs, society has gained a side benefit.

A second group believes that deterrence is affected by formal sanctions but that its effect is incremental. This group believes that capital punishment will deter precisely because its marginal effect over life imprisonment is significant enough to have a deterrent effect. Similarly, this group believes in increasing law enforcement's ability to apprehend, since it assumes that crime, for the most part, is committed by persons who do weigh the costs and benefits. In this group's opinion, crime is committed precisely, since criminals find the odds of success substantial and the odds of apprehension minimal. Similarly, this group believes that criminals are well aware of the frailties of court processing and the unlikelihood of penal sanctions materializing. Both groups, it should be borne in mind, are generalizing from their own perspectives of the criminal justice system. About that which actually deters we know very little.

If all of the drug addicts in the United States were, in some way, maintained by the government, we would experience a drop in burglaries and robberies. We know this from self-reported studies involving addicts who were maintained on treatment programs and who reported a drastic reduction in their daily crime activity. Since not all drug users are in such programs and since such users may still commit one criminal act each day, as opposed to ten in the absence of the program, society questions the impact or even the propriety of such programs. We are further aware of strategies achieving limited degrees of success, such as team policing, saturation patrols, and air support. Such strategies either suppress crime for certain time periods or displace it to other locales. Essentially, a prevention strategy must consider either dealing with the symptom or dealing with the causes. While our knowledge of symptoms has substantial gaps, our knowledge of causes seems powerless to answer policy questions. We seem, in the United States, to be about as close to understanding why crime exists as Europeans are to explain the existence of terrorism in their countries. Multiple theories do exist, but their utility in establishing crime prevention policy is problematical. It is instructive to know that some offenders are children of one-parent families, that welfare payments constitute the sole family income, and that no marketable employment skill exists in the family. Crime prevention policy cannot address those factors, since, for some reason, many children do not turn toward crime despite the existence of identical conditions, and second, elimination of one-parent families, poverty, and nonemployables is beyond the scope of crime prevention strategy. Thus, dealing with causes, particularly theoretical causes, does not seem likely to emerge as crime prevention policy. If dealing with symptoms simply displaces crime and dealing with causes is an impossibility, the potential for crime prevention seems limited.

Existing crime prevention programs center largely upon reducing either the opportunity to commit a crime or, at least, reducing the attractiveness of committing the act. For example, marking one's own valuables with indelible identification may reduce the prospect of fencing the stolen items; installation of deadbolt locks and alarm systems may provide a sufficient obstacle to dissuade the attempted burglar; canine escorts, mace, and other weapons carried in one's hands may impede the easy purse snatch; and a neighborhood watch program may create a set of eyes and ears that the potential intruder will begrudgingly elect not to test, though such measures do not deal with the symptomatic behavior of the offender, but rather with the crime. As such, it can only lessen the expectation of a successful crime rather than modify the behavior of the offender. It deals with the power of suggestion rather than with the criminal's life-style. It deters the offender at that instant and in those circumstances, but does not deter in a general sense. The offender does not recant his intent to commit a criminal act—he simply seeks another opportunity. Metal detectors at American airports have, for the most part, dissuaded hijackers from consummating their plans. The crime of hijacking has at least been controlled, if not entirely eliminated. However, the potential hijackers have, no doubt, channeled their energies elsewhere toward the perpetration of some other crime. Similar strategies for the control or prevention of narcotics importation have suffered, since the task of detecting such traffic has defied most standard techniques. This is not to say that such detection devices are impossible to develop in the future. If a criminal, however, was considering prevention devices as a deterrent, he would calculate his odds on a successful narcotics delivery as substantially higher than a hijacked aircraft.

The dilemma for prevention strategies is whether or not to allocate resources toward crime or toward criminals. Allocation toward crime seems merely to reroute the offender toward another objective. Concentration on the criminal or potential offender seems costly and necessarily limited to those few whom the system can directly influence. It is unlikely that all potential crimes can be made improbable or that all potential offenders can be deterred. The unifying rationale, however, seems to be that in each case (if either were to succeed), it is the offender or potential offender who elects to commit the crime, since he calculates the odds to be not in his favor or, alternatively, he modifies his behavior because of an intervention strategy or program that offers him a way out or a viable alternative to criminal activity. He comes to the same conclusion in both thought processes, but for seemingly different reasons. Perhaps prevention must concentrate on convincing the proposed offender that crime is not all easy pickings and big payoffs. Prevention must create conditions in which the potential offender elects out of the crime system rather than electing to stay in. For this to happen either crime will need to become substantially more difficult than it is now or the advantage to avoiding crime must increase, or both.

INTERVENTION STRATEGIES

While it is possible to influence some lives through an "officer friendly" program, this intervention essentially comports with the prior discussion. We attempt to influence youth, either by role model or suggestion, that advantages accrue to avoiding crime. Many youthful offenders, however, act in concert with group norms, which may involve unlawful activity in the community between groups, or, conceivably, within groups. The prevention of gang activity, for example, must cope with cohesion within accepted enforceable norms. Gang behavior stresses solidarity; defense of one's possessions, family, and friends; and reprisals against trespassing rival gangs. Gang members may persist in such behavior either from feelings of fear and self-defense or from ego rewards provided by group reinforcement, or both. Intervention with the juvenile who accepts group norms will be less likely to have effect when that youth is advised of the probabilities of incarceration and removal from society. Mentally, the group member may accept this as part of the apprenticeship for group acceptance.

There remain two directions worthy of consideration as regards the continuing volume of crime and the difficulties in curbing crime inherent in a free society. The first is based upon the premise that law enforcement cannot succeed with crime prevention acting alone.

Law enforcement requires the cooperation of the public. The public has not viewed its responsibility as one of crime prevention. Americans do not view themselves as extensions of the police power. The power of the state, or perhaps the good of society, is distant from the average American. While Americans have occasionally turned toward vigilantism when perceiving a void in law enforcement, their respect for police power, as opposed to individual police officers, has perhaps reflected a populist sentiment for protection of one's own rights. This protection of one's own privacy and independence has precluded most Americans from becoming "involved" in the apparent violation of laws, mores, rules, and regulations. Americans may prefer not to participate in such violations *themselves*, and to become the eyes and ears of police power or government authority has not seemed particularly "American." Few Americans seem comfortable with making a citizen's arrest, as this is the responsibility of police.

Today's citizen perceives the pervasive presence of crime whether in the city or in the rural communities. It is estimated that one-third of the American households have been affected by criminal acts; in many cases, more than once. With no indication that this trend will decline the criminal justice system seems poised for voluntary cooperation from its citizens. The extreme interest in self-defense measures seems destined to reach a peak in which the citizen realizes the limitations posed upon effective self-defense against the violent offender. Indiscriminate violent acts have raised the national level of consciousness to a "fear level" that transcends, to some extent, the actual probability of becoming a victim. In reality, however, the young, the elderly, and even fit adults are limited, with known technology, in defending against the skilled, violent offender who acts by surprise with a loaded handgun held against the victim's head. This converging of realization of vulnerability with the need for public cooperation seems likely to produce a number of cooperative ventures perhaps unknown in the past.

We are familiar with neighborhood watch programs, networks of CB and ham radio operators, anonymous witness programs, and police reserve programs. Enlisting civilians in the crime fight poses a major opportunity for extending the prevention arm of law enforcement at a time when national and state legislatures attempt to create an arsenal of statutes designed to assist the professional police officer and criminal justice official. Without public support, however, even existing statutes bear a heavy burden. Decisional law emanating from the nation's courts, with some exceptions, creates a framework within which detection, apprehension, and adjudication of offenders must comport with constitutional safeguards. Though some relief may occur, the greatest number of successes occur in those cases utilizing reliable witnesses, effective investigation, and vigorous prosecution. During each of these processes the public can play an important role. Participation may well be essential. In effect, the courts are saying that weak cases will not be bolstered by stronger laws.

On a second front, law enforcement is turning toward the addition of nonpeace officers even within its own ranks. The trend toward civilianizing police power may be as important as broadening the role of the police officer. Forced to become social worker, counselor, lawyer, paramedic, and crime fighter, the police officer is likely to retain the primary responsibility for application of deadly force given the implausibility of civilians exercising effective self-defense. Allocation of civilians to prevention, detection, and even investigation may expand the effectiveness of police power while maintaining constitutional and statutory safeguards.

Chapter 6

SPECIAL PROBLEMS

N ARCOTICS, dangerous drugs, alcohol, sex crimes, suicides, and violence pose special problems for law enforcement. Studies are limited as they pertain to the police role in coping with some of these serious problems; however, knowledge about them is increasing, and concerted action in some communities is pointing the way toward at least partial solutions. The purpose of this chapter is to identify various features of the problems and some approaches that are being made toward the solution.

NARCOTICS AND DANGEROUS DRUGS[1,2]

In the past decade the United States has experienced a national health crisis that has crossed all strata of society, i.e. drug abuse. It has also contributed substantially to our crime problem, accounting for countless thousands of crimes (particularly against property) costing millions of dollars. It has been estimated that over half of our population under eighteen years of age have used illegal drugs, and they are posing an increased problem for law enforcement agencies. The drug traffic has found its way down to the junior high school and even the elementary levels. A large percent of the total arrests of juveniles is related to illegal drug and alcohol use.

Drug use is not a new phenomena. Some five thousand years before the the birth of Christ, people of what is now Iraq recorded the earliest known information about narcotics. The Greek physician Hippocrates, in the fourth century B.C., recommended white poppy juices for a variety of illnesses (opium is obtained from the poppy). The Spaniards, while conquering and exploring Latin America, noted that the natives were stimulated by chewing the coca leaf, from which cocaine later derived its name. Marijuana has been known to man for over 5000 years. Very early in Chinese history it was used to relieve pain during surgery.

But no one seems to have sounded an impressive alarm about the improper handling of the useful narcotic drug until 1729 when Yung Cheng, a Chinese emperor, issued the first edict prohibiting opium smoking. Apart from the Catholic Church's prohibition of peyote consumption by the American Indians, this appears to be the earliest general official regulatory measure directed against narcotics. The imports of opium into China had developed into a big business as addiction became widespread. The Chinese addicts paid little or no attention to their emperor's command.

Subsequent emperors issued many edicts prohibiting the use and importation of opium, but because of the inability of the government to enforce these measures they were generally ignored, and a large fraction of China's annual earnings were siphoned off by the opium importers. In 1839, the Chinese emperor appointed an energetic administrator, Commissioner Lin, in charge of Canton. Lin demanded the surrender of all opium stored in Western ships and held in warehouses in compliance with Chinese law. To insure compliance, he forcibly detained all westerners in Canton. As the opium was surrendered the detained Europeans were released.

This new and bold approach was a blow to Western profits, as well as prestige, and resulted in a good deal of tension, particularly between the British and the Chinese. Certain drunken sailors, British or American, or both, became involved in a brawl that resulted in the death of a Chinese. The Chinese demanded the surrender of British seamen thought to have been involved, and the British refused. This precipitated the struggle known as the "Opium War" (1840 to 1842). Following the war, in which the Chinese were defeated, the importation of opium was resumed, and Chinese domestic production mounted until, in 1906, the annual Chinese production was estimated at 44 million pounds of opium, with 7 million pounds coming into the country from India.

In America, a trickle of narcotics started coming to our shores even before the founding of the republic. In the latter part of the nineteenth century the volume began to swell and the problems of addiction began to increase. In 1853, the hypodermic needle was invented by Dr. Alexander Wood of Edinburgh. The injection method of using morphine was thought to be free from addiction, as the drugs would not reach the stomach and so create an appetite. For a while patients were encouraged to buy this new device and apply the morphine on a do-it-yourself basis.

By the time the American Civil War ended in 1865 many thousands of soliders had received numerous injections to relieve their suffering from wounds and sickness. So many of those treated became addicts that morphinism came to be known as the "army disease."

With the growth of advertising, which in those days promoted patent medicines containing narcotics, many persons who took such medicine became dependent upon it. Later they often found out about the specific narcotic ingredient and started using that. The passage and enforcement of the Pure Food and Drug Act in 1906 helped to relieve this particular situation.

In 1874, diacetylmorphine, or what we now know as heroin, was developed in England. There was little interest in this drug until about 1890, at which time it was reported as a more effective remedy for illnesses that had previously been treated with codeine or morphine. In response to the favorable reports and the increasing interest of the medical profession, the Bayer Company of Elberfeld, Germany started production of heroin commercially in 1898. Within four or five years scientists became doubtful of the value of heroin as a cure for morphinism. An increasing number of heroin addiction cases were being reported and they seemed much more difficult than those of morphine.

It took the medical profession a long time to fully appreciate the dangers of heroin addiction. The underworld, however, quickly appreciated this new drug. Since it could be taken in snuff it appealed even to those who were repelled by the use of the hypodermic needle. It might be added, however, that those who became addicted to heroin usually were soon converted to the injection method and eventually to the intravenous method, becoming "mainliners."

Because of the increasing number of addicts, the public and Congress became aroused and the Harrison Narcotic Act was passed in 1914. Subsequently the Bureau of Narcotic Enforcement was created in 1930 under the Treasury Department to administer both the legal and illicit use of narcotics. The bureau's activities were moved to the Department of Justice in 1971, and in 1973 following considerable expansion of its responsibilities it reorganized as the Drug Enforcement Administration.

Since the late 1950s as the drug problem became more acute, more states became active in narcotic and dangerous drug enforcement. An increasing number of states have created state agencies to assist local agencies in the enforcement. The problem has become so widespread that most local police agencies give some attention to the enforcement, control, and education.

Narcotic Drugs

The narcotic drugs include some of the most valuable medicines known to man as well as the most abused. The term *sleep narcotic* originally referred to opium and the drugs made from opium such as heroin, codeine, and morphine. Opium is obtained from the opium poppy; morphine and codeine are extracted from opium, and heroin is chemically made from morphine. Medical science has subsequently synthesized drugs, called opiates, which have properties similar to heroin, codeine, or morphine. These drugs are classified as narcotic drugs.

Federal law classifies the coca leaf and a chemical derived from it, cocaine, as narcotics, but these drugs are stimulants, and medical science does not consider them narcotics.

Marijuana (Marihuana)

Marijuana is a greenish or brownish tobaccolike material consisting of leaves, flowers, small stems, and seed(s) of the plant, *Cannabis sativa* L. The plant grows throughout the world, especially in Jamaica, Mexico, Africa, India, and the Middle East. It also grows in the United States. Its leaves, stems, and flowers are dried into a grasslike form which is rolled into a homemade cigarette. It has the strong odor of fresh cut alfalfa hay. It is smoked in cigarettes, and it is often referred to as "pot," "tea," "weed," "stuff," "reefers," or "sticks."

Marijuana produces unpredictable actions varying from one cigarette to another. Often there is a complete loss of time and space, along with a loss of inhibitions. It may develop a psychological dependence although it is not considered addictive.

Stimulants

These are drugs that stimulate the central nervous system. The most widely known stimulant is caffeine, an ingredient of coffee, tea, cola, and other beverages. Since the effects of caffeine are relatively mild, its usage is socially acceptable and not an abuse problem. The synthetic stimulants such as the amphetamines, methylphenidate, phenmetrazine and other closely related drugs are more potent and can be abused. Cocaine is often abused in combination with other drugs. The stimulants produce excitation, increased activity, and an ability to go without sleep for extended periods of time.

Depressants (Sedatives-Hypnotics)

This group includes the barbiturates; the most widely abused among the depressants, glutethimide and meprobamate. They depress the central nervous system and are prescribed in small doses to reduce restlessness, emotional tension, and to induce sleep. The appearance of drunkenness without an alcoholic breath may indicate excessive use of depressant drugs.

Barbiturates are known to drug users as "barbs," "candy," "goof-balls," "sleeping pills," or "peanuts." Specific types are often named after their color or shape.

Hallucinogens

Hallucinogens are drugs that distort the user's perception of objective reality. They produce illusions involving various senses and if taken in large doses can produce hallucinations. The drugs are chemicals that have been extracted from plants or have been synthesized in laboratories. Illicit laboratories produce hallucinogens in the form of capsules, tablets, powder, or liquids, while peddlers and users will utilize many methods to transport or hide the drugs.

The hallucinogens include LSD-25 (lysergic acid diethylamide), mescaline (peyote), psilocybin and psilocyn, DMT, DET (dethyl-tryptamine), DOM and PCP (phencyclidine).

Glossary of Slang Terms for Drugs

Amphetamines	Beans, Bennies, Black Beauties, Black Mollies, Copilots, Crank, Crossroads, Crystal, Dexies, Double Cross, Meth, Minibennies, Pep Pills, Speed, Rosas, Roses, Thrusters, Truck Drivers, Uppers, Wake-ups, Whites
Barbiturates	Barbs, Blockbusters, Bluebirds, Blue Devils, Blues, Christmas Trees, Downers, Green Dragons, Mexican Reds, Nebbies, Nimbies, Pajaro Rojo, Pink Ladies, Pinks, Rainbows, Red and Blues, Redbirds, Red Devils, Reds, Sleeping Pills, Stumblers, Yellow Jackets, Yellows
Cocaine	Blow, C, Coca, Coke, Flake, Girl, Heaven Dust, Lady, Mujer, Nose Candy, Paradise, Perico, Polvo Blanco, Rock, Snow, White
Hashish	Goma de Mota, Hash, Soles
Heroin	Big H, Boy, Brown, Brown Sugar, Caballo, Chiva, Crap, Estuffa, H, Heroina, Hombre, Horse, Junk, Mexican Mud, Polvo, Scag, Smack, Stuff, Thing
LSD	Acid, Blotter Acid, California Sunshine, Haze, Microdots, Paper Acid, Purple Haze, Sunshine, Wedges, Window Pane
Marihuana	Acapulco Gold, Cannabis, Colombian, Ganja, Grass, Griffa, Hemp, Herb, J, Jay, Joint, Mary Jane, Mota, Mutah, Panama Red, Pot, Reefer, Sativa, Smoke, Stick, Tea, Weed, Yerba
Peyote	Buttons, Cactus, Mesc, Mescal, Mescal Buttons
Methaqualone	Quaalude, Quads, Quas, Soapers, Sopes, Sopor
Morphine	Cube, First Line, Goma, Morf, Morfina, Morpho,

                      Morphy, Mud
Phencyclidine   Angel Dust, Crystal, Cyclone, Hog, PCP, Peace
                   Pill, Rocket Fuel, Supergrass, TIC TAC

Alcohol

The easy availability of alcohol has led to general widespread use by juveniles. The effects of alcohol are well known, and the problem is evident in almost every community.

Most state laws make it unlawful for minors to buy alcoholic beverages. Some state laws make it unlawful for minors to consume alcoholic beverages. Unfortunately, there are other state laws that do not make it illegal for juveniles to use alcoholic beverages, therefore, complicating the problem of enforcement of its use. Regardless of the law, however, juveniles still obtain and use alcoholic beverages in almost every community of the United States. The police are confronted with an almost insurmountable task of controlling its use.

THE DRUG ABUSER

Although much is known about the effects of drugs with abuse potential, the user himself remains an enigma. Slum conditions, easy access to drugs, peddlers, and organized crime have been blamed for the problem. While any of these factors may contribute, no single cause nor single set of conditions clearly leads to drug dependency, for it occurs in all social and economic classes.

The key to the riddle may well lie within the abuser and any one of many sets or conditions. Drug dependency cannot develop without a chemical agent. Yet, while millions are exposed to drugs by reason of medical need, relatively few of these people turn to a life of drugs. It is true that in metropolitan areas there are invariably found groups of "hard-core" users, and a large proportion of the young persons who use drugs are in the ghetto areas. Even though drugs may be available on street corners in metropolitan areas, only a small percentage of individuals exposed join the ranks of abusers.

For the most part, hard-core addicts suffer from certain types of emotional instability that may or may not have been apparent prior to initial drug abuse experience. Occasional cases may have a background (often undiagnosed) of psychiatric disorders. Some psychiatrists have said that addicts have an inherent inability to develop meaningful interpersonal relationships. Others have said that addicts are persons who are unwilling to face the responsibility of maturity. Adolescent addicts may have suffered childhood deprivation or overprotectiveness, or they simply may not be able to cope with the physical and emotional changes accompanying this period. It is significant that many addicts have their first drug experience in their teens.

The transition from childhood to adulthood is seldom smooth, and many individuals are not emotionally equipped to meet the demands they face. The early and middle teens bring a loosening of family ties, a diminution of parental authority, increasing responsibility, and sexual maturing. Beset with anxiety, frustration, fear of failure, inner conflicts, and doubts, the adolescent may find that amphetamines and marijuana promote conversation and sociability; barbiturates relieve anxiety; hallucinogens heighten sensations; and narcotics provide relief and escape. Drug abuse may provide the entry into an "in group" or be a way of affirming independence by defying authority and convention.

In general, drug abusers fall into four main groups. The first group employs drugs for a specific or "situational" purpose. Examples: the student who uses amphetamines to keep awake at exam time; the housewife who uses antiobesity pills for additional energy to get through household chores; the salesman who uses amphetamines to keep awake while driving all night to an early morning appointment. Such individuals may or may not exhibit psychological dependence.

The second group consists of "spree" users, usually of college or high school age. Drugs are used for "kicks" or just the experience. There may be some degree of psychological dependence but little or no physical dependence because of the sporadic and mixed pattern of use. Some spree users may only try drugs once or twice and decide there are better things in life. Drug sprees constitute a defiance of convention, an adventurous daring experience, or a means of having fun. Unlike hard-core abusers, who often pursue their habits alone or in pairs, spree users usually take drugs in groups or at social functions.

The third group is the hard-core addict. His activities revolve almost entirely around drug experience and securing supplies. He exhibits strong psychological dependence on the drug, often reinforced by physical dependence when certain drugs are being used. Typically, the hard-core addict began drug abuse on a spree basis. He has been on drugs for some time and presently feels that he cannot function without drug support.

A new type of drug abuser emerged in the 1960s that makes up the fourth group—the "hippies." These drug users tend to believe that the systems of today are either antiquated or wrong, and that a new way of life should be found. Drugs are an integral part of the hippie life, and they could be considered the same as the hard-core abusers. The major difference is that most hippies do not come from the slum areas, but from middle or upper-middle income families, and their educational level is far above that of the ghetto dweller.

Obviously, there is much overlapping of these groups, and a spree or situational user may deteriorate to the hard-core group or become enmeshed in the hippie philosophy. The transition occurs when the interaction between drug effects and a personality causes a loss of control over drug use. To the user, the drug becomes a means of solving or avoiding life's problems.

Slum sections of large metropolitan areas still account for the largest number of known heroin abusers. But frustration, immaturity, and emotional deprivation are not peculiar to depressed neighborhoods, and the misuse of a variety of drugs by middle and upper economic class individuals is being recognized with increasing frequency. Drug dependence is not discriminating. A drug, an individual, an environment which predisposes use, and a personality deficiency are the key factors in drug dependence development.

Problems of Abuser Identification

Although drug abuse in its various forms can produce identifiable effects, almost all such manifestations are, at their onset, identical to those produced by conditions having nothing whatever to do with drug abuse.

Many people use legitimate drugs in accordance with physicians' instructions—but without the knowledge of their associates. For example, such disorders as epilepsy, diabetes, or asthma may require maintenance drug therapy that will produce low-level side effects.

Or, a person might be drowsy from ingesting a nonprescription product—such as an antihistamine.

A clue to the possibility of drug abuse comes with persistence of symptoms that might otherwise appear "routine." When tablets, capsules, or other forms of drugs are found on a person suspected of being an abuser, they are not necessarily narcotics or some other dangerous drug.

There are no instant tests for identification of most drugs. The only way many drugs can be identified is through a series of complicated laboratory procedures performed by a trained technician. Simple visual inspection cannot be relied upon for drug identification. Many potent drugs that are misused are identical in appearance to relatively harmless drugs—many of which may be readily obtained without a prescription.

Although it is difficult to recognize drug abusers, many potential hard-core addicts can be rehabilitated if their involvement in drug abuse is spotted in its early stages...when professional help can be brought to bear on the problem in an effective manner.

Common Symptoms of Drug Abuse

Not all drug abuse related character changes appear detrimental, at least in the initial stages. For example, a usually bored sleepy person may, while using amphetamine, be more alert and thereby improve performance. A nervous, high-strung individual may, on barbiturates, be more cooperative and easier to manage. What must be looked for, consequently, are not simply changes for the worse, but any sudden changes in behavioral expressions that become usual for an individual. The causal factor may be drug abuse.

Signs that may suggest drug abuse include sudden and dramatic changes in discipline and job performance. Drug abusers may also display unusual degrees of activity or inactivity, as well as sudden and irrational flare-ups involving strong emotion or temper. Significant changes for the worse in personal appearance may be cause for concern, for very often a drug abuser becomes indifferent to his appearance and health habits.

There are other, more specific signs that should arouse suspicions, especially if more than one is exhibited by a single person. Among them are furtive behavior regarding actions and possessions (fear of discovery), sunglasses worn at inappropriate times and places (to hide dilated or constricted pupils), and long-sleeve garments worn constantly, even on hot days (to hide needle marks). Of course, association with known drug abusers is a sign of potential trouble.

Because of the expense of supporting a drug habit, the abuser may be observed trying to borrow money from a number of individuals. If this fails, he will not be reluctant to steal items easily converted to cash, such as cameras, radios, or jewelry. And if his habit is severe enough, forcing him to use drugs while on duty, he may be found, at odd times, in places such as closets or storage rooms.

In addition to these behavioral clues, which are common to most drug abusers, each form of abuse generally has specific manifestations that help identify those engaged in it, which follows next.

The Glue Sniffer

The glue or solvent sniffer usually retains the odor of the substance he is inhaling on his breath and clothes. Irritation of the mucuous membranes in the mouth and nose may result in excessive nasal secretions. Redness and watering of the eyes are commonly observed. The user may appear intoxicated or lack muscular control and may complain of double vision, ringing in the ears, vivid dreams, and even hallucinations. Drowsiness, stupor, and unconsciousness may follow excessive use of the substances.

Discovery of plastic or paper bags and rags or handkerchiefs containing dried plastic cement is a telltale sign that glue-sniffing is being practiced.

The Depressant Abuser

The abuser of a depressant drug, such as the barbiturates and certain tranquilizers, exhibits most of the symptoms of alcohol intoxication with one important exception: there is no odor of alcohol on his breath. Persons taking depressants may stagger or stumble, and the depressant abuser frequently falls into a deep sleep. In general, the depressant abuser lacks interest in activity, is drowsy, and may appear to be disoriented.

The Stimulant Abuser

The behavior of the abuser of stimulants, such as amphetamine and related drugs, is characterized by excessive activity. The stimulant abuser is irritable, argumentative, appears extremely nervous, and has difficulty sitting. In some cases, the pupils of his eyes will be dilated even in a brightly lit place.

Amphetamine has a drying effect on the mucous membranes of the mouth and nose with resultant bad breath that is unidentifiable as to specific odor such as onion, garlic, alcohol, etc. Because of the dryness of mouth, the amphetamine abuser licks his lips to keep them moist. This often results in chapped and reddened lips, which, in severe cases, may be cracked and raw.

Other observable effects: dryness of the mucous membrane in the nose, causing the abuser to rub and scratch his nose vigorously and frequently to relieve the itching sensation; incessant talking about any subject at hand; and often, chainsmoking.

Finally, the person who is abusing stimulant drugs often goes for long periods of time without sleeping or eating and usually cannot resist letting others know about it.

The Narcotic Abuser

A drug abuser deeply under the influence of narcotics usually appears lethargic, drowsy ("on the nod"), or displays symptoms of deep intoxication. Pupils of the eye are often constricted and fail to respond to light.

Some individuals may drink paregoric or cough medicines containing narcotics. The medicinal odor of these preparations is often detectable on the breath.

Other "beginner" narcotic abusers inhale narcotic drugs such as heroin in powder form. Sometimes, traces of this white powder can be seen around the nostrils. Constant inhaling of narcotic drugs makes nostrils red and raw.

For maximal effect, narcotics usually are injected directly into a vein. The most common site of the injection is the inner surface of the arm at the elbow. After repeated injections, scar tissue ("tracks") develops along the course of such veins. Because of the easy identification of these marks, such narcotic abusers usually wear long sleeves at odd times. Females sometimes use makeup to cover marks. Some males get tatooed at injection sites. Associated with the injection of any drugs under unsterile conditions is the hazard of transmitting malaria and other tropical diseases, hepatitis, and blood poisoning.

The presence of equipment ("works" or "outfit") used in injecting narcotics is another way to spot the narcotic abuser. Since anyone injecting drugs must keep his equipment handy, it may be found on his person or hidden nearby in a locker, washroom, or some place where temporary privacy may be found. The characteristic instruments and accessories are a bent spoon or bottle cap, small ball of cotton, syringe or eyedropper, and a hypodermic needle. All are used in the injection process: The spoon or cap holds the narcotic in a little water for heating over a match or lighter, and the cotton acts as a filter as the narcotic is drawn through the needle into the syringe or eyedropper.

The small ball of cotton ("satch cotton") is usually kept after use because it retains a small amount of narcotic that can be extracted if the abuser is unable to obtain additional drugs. The bent spoon or bottle cap used to heat the narcotic is easily identifiable because it becomes blackened by the heating process.

The Hallucinogen Abuser

It is highly unlikely that persons who use hallucinogenic drugs (such as LSD) will do so while at work or in a similar environment except that of a recreational time period. Such drugs are usually used in a group situation under special conditions designed to enhance their effect. Persons under the influence of hallucinogens usually sit or recline quietly in a dream or trancelike state. However, the effect of such drugs is not always euphoric. On occasion, users become fearful and experience a degree of terror that may cause them to attempt to escape from the group.

Hallucinogenic drugs are usually taken orally. They are found as tablets, capsules, or liquids. Users put drops of the liquid in beverages, on sugar cubes, crackers, or even on small paper wads or cloth. It is important to remember that the effects of LSD may recur days—or even months—after the drug has been taken.

The Marijuana Abuser

While marijuana is pharmacologically a hallucinogen, its wide-spread use warrants separate discussion.

The user of marijuana ("pot") is unlikely to be recognized unless he is heavily under the influence at that time. In the early stages of the drug effect, when the drug acts as a stimulant, the user may be very animated and appear almost hysterical. Loud and rapid talking with great bursts of laughter are common at this stage. In the later stages of the drug effect, the user may seem in a stupor or sleepy.

Marijuana smokers may also be identified by their possession of such cigarettes often called "sticks," "reefers," or "joints." A marijuana cigarette is rolled in cigarette paper. Smaller than a regular cigarette, with the paper twisted or tucked in on both ends, the marijuana cigarette often contains seeds and stems and is greener in color than regular tobacco, but may also be gold or dark brown.

Another clue to the presence of "reefers" is the way in which they are often smoked. Typically, such smoking occurs in a group situation. But because of the rapid burning and harshness of the marijuana cigarette, it is generally passed rapidly, after one or two puffs, to another person. The smoke is deeply inhaled and held in the lungs as long as possible. The cigarette is often cupped in the palms of both hands when inhaling to save all the smoke possible. An additional clue to marijuana use is its odor. Similar to that of burnt rope, the odor is readily noticeable on the breath and clothing.

Drug Abuse Prevention Programming

The National Advisory Commission on Criminal Justice Standards and Goals in its *Community Crime Prevention Report*[3] presents a comprehensive discussion of drug abuse prevention. It addresses prevention activities related to both juveniles and adults, however, for the purposes of this book we will deal with material pertinent to youth. For the development of a comprehensive community drug abuse prevention program the reader is referred to the report.

The commission recommends for drug abuse prevention the following:

1. The roles of educating and informing youth about drugs

should be assumed by parents and teachers in the early stages of a child's life. It is from these sources that a child should first learn about drugs. Information should be presented without scare techniques or undue emphasis on the authoritarian approach. Parental efforts at drug education should be encouraged before a child enters school, and teachers should receive special training in drug prevention education techniques.

2. Peer group influence and leadership also should be part of drug prevention efforts. Such influence could come from youth who have tried drugs and stopped; these youths have the credibility that comes from firsthand experience. They must first be trained to insure that they do not distort their educational efforts toward youth by issuing the kind of double messages described previously.

3. Professional organizations of pharmacists and physicians should educate patients and the general public on drug abuse prevention efforts and should encourage responsible use of drugs. The educational efforts of these organizations should be encouraged to include factual, timely information on current trends in the abuse of drugs and prescription substances.

4. Materials on preventing drug abuse should focus not only on drugs and their effects but also on the person involved in such abuse. That person, particularly a young one, should be helped to develop problem-solving skills.

5. Young people should be provided with alternatives to drugs. The more active and demanding an alternative, the more likely it is to interfere with the drug abuser's life-style. Among such activities are sports, directed-play activities, skill training, and hobbies, where there is the possibility of continued improvement in performance.

Although there are multiple approaches to drug prevention, previous program efforts have been largely negated by a lack of understanding of the problem, confusion over causes and effects of drug use, and confusion that existed in the mass media drug abuse prevention programming. However, new strategies are emerging that deal with personality development and the influence of family and peers. These methods are fundamental in nature and reflect the understanding that approaches are required that do not focus simply on drugs and drug effects, as follows:[4]

Specifically, drug abuse experts now recognize that it is often necessary to equip youngsters to deal more effectively with life, so they will not resort to dysfunctional drug use. The burden for accomplishing this rests primarily with families and schools. There is need, therefore, to focus on increasing parental child-rearing effectiveness through various kinds of counseling. Where parents themselves have problems, these should be addressed as early as possible, before youngsters have begun school or, better yet, before the child is born.

Similarly, there is need for schools to develop family life curricula that are not focused on drugs alone. The emphasis here should be on enhancing self-understanding, intrafamily relationships, and the role of the family in society. If schools deal with these subjects from the earliest grades, drug use and abuse would become just one more area to be understood and thereby would be stripped of its more sensational aspects.

Educational emphasis would be placed where it belongs, i.e. on the development of at least three essential kinds of skills: (1) intrapersonal skills, or the child's awareness of personal feelings and the ability to deal with them; (2) interpersonal skills, that is, the ability to relate to others and communicate effectively with them; and (3) coping skills, that is, the ability to solve problems without the need to fall back on alternatives such as dysfunctional drug use.

None of these steps can be carried forward easily, but it is clear that they must be pursued. Fortunately, there are a number of programs, designed for use in high schools, colleges, and the general community, that attempt to achieve similar results and are more easily implemented. These lean heavily on the use of peers or specially trained coordinators and staff who can relate to young people on a confidential basis.

The peer group approach requires that selected students be trained in drug abuse prevention work in a way that will enable them to influence their fellow students. Where trained coordinators are utilized, they, too, must be able to maintain rapport with the student body. Rap sessions conducted by counselors after regular school hours provide an opportunity to deal with a wide range of subjects. Staff availability for one-to-one counseling on a drop-in basis is also essential.

Outside the school itself, other groups have sprung up in a

number of locations. These bring parents, youngsters, and trained counselors together in an effort to create a counterdrug culture, foster mutual understanding between youngsters and adults, and develop alternate activities. Such organizations go a long way toward developing rational perspectives. They also encourage adults to increase their awareness of their own behavior and thus become better role models for their children.

SEX OFFENSES

Sex offenses by and against both juveniles and adults pose a serious problem for the criminal justice system. Although the number of such offenses comprise a relatively small percentage of cases processed by the police and other criminal justice agencies, an outraged public reaction, particularly for offenses against children, becomes a dominant factor in assessing the importance of such cases. The subject is so broad and has so many ramifications that we shall present only some basic information concerning sex offenses and some suggestions for dealing with the problem.

The Problem of the Sex Offender[5]

A sex offender is anyone who breaks a law relating to sex behavior. Various cultures have differed in regard to sex laws and customs. The ancient Egyptians had incest in the royal families, as did the Incas. The Greeks made a cult of homosexuality.

Our own sex laws have been greatly influenced by the ancient Jewish and early Christian codes. Today the statutes within our states vary widely. No states permit parent-child or brother-sister incest, but there is no agreement about legal sex relations between other close relatives. Homosexual relations are subjected to a wide variation of laws covering sodomy and other defined illicit acts, and a number of states have special sex laws. Throughout history, all cultures have enforced sex laws and taboos. It is a mistake to think that primitive cultures have the fewest restrictions; often they have the most.

People vary in their opinion as to what constitutes normal or abnormal sexual behavior; hence we find various definitions of normal sex behavior. By some, normal sex behavior is thought of as ideal sex behavior; by others it is thought of as average behavior of the entire population. Still others might approach it from the standpoint of health, defining normal sex behavior as behavior that is healthy. And finally, there is the legal definition that any sex behavior forbidden by law is abnormal sex behavior.

Much confusion in thinking results from a lack of understanding about these fundamental concepts. For example, ideal sex behavior may mean to one religious group heterosexual relations within marriage; to another religious group it may mean only heterosexual relations for procreation within marriage. It is doubtful if physicians, including psychiatrists and biologists, would all agree as to what is healthy sex behavior. Finally, the variation in laws among the different states indicate that the legal approach is subject to the same confusion of thinking.

Despite the complexity and confusion in sexual mores, there has been some progress in the understanding and approach of this most difficult problem. The studies by Kinsey in the Institute of Sex Research in the late 1940s added enormously to our knowledge about sex.[6] Research continues, but change takes place slowly, particularly in the areas of legislation and enforcement.

It is apparent that general concern about sex crimes is focused primarily on sex crimes against small children and sex crimes of violence, with homosexuality causing a variable amount of concern.

It is important to keep in mind that sex is only one aspect of the personality and that sex cannot be completely isolated and studied apart from the rest of the personality. The methods of psychiatry have much to offer in studying the total personality. It is perhaps wise to discuss briefly some of the more common types of sex offenses.

Exhibitionism

From the standpoint of arrests and convictions exhibitionism is number one in frequency. The vast majority of exhibitionists are relatively harmless offenders; mostly they are public nuisances and sources of embarrassments, but there is a frequent and repetitious character that is worth noting. Exhibitionists are usually men, although now and then a rare case of female exhibitionism is reported.

The biological basis for exhibitionism appears to be the tendency of male animals to strut and show off before the females, although in the higher apes there has been reported some exhibitionism of the genitals on the part of the female as an invitation to the male to carry out sexual intercourse. In human beings exhibitionism can be regarded as a normal part of sexual foreplay. In exhibitionism, in some way or other, the emphasis is displaced, and sexual exposure becomes of maximum or sole importance to the individual. It is an obsessive-compulsive type of neurotic behavior for which psychoanalysis has offered specific interpretations. The urge to expose is closely associated with voyeurism — the wish to look as well as to be looked at — and tends to appear repeatedly in the same individual. The risk and danger of arrest seem to add spice to the desire to see and to be seen.

Exhibitionism and voyeurism are not dangerous unless they occur along with more serious types of sex behavior. It should be stated explicitly that persons convicted of serious sex crimes do not commonly begin with voyeurism and exhibitionism and work up to crimes of violence and murder. Sex offenders have the same tendency as do other criminals to stick to similar types of offenses. It is well known that burglars seldom become forgers, and vice versa. Such criminals stick to a particular type of criminal behavior; the same is largely true of sex offenders.

Homosexuality

The problem of homosexuality is extremely complex and opinions vary as to its importance in antisocial sex behavior. American culture has given little attention to female homosexuality and has been overconcerned with male homosexual relations. There are many variations in homosexual behavior. One group is normally heterosexual but resorts to homosexual behavior when a partner (of the opposite sex) is not available. Another group of individuals is ambisexual and regularly indulges in both heterosexual and homosexual relations and does not seek one form of sex behavior to the exclusion of the other. A third group desires only partners of their own sex. They can be divided into two groups: one group, the smaller, regard themselves as females and often ask for castrative operations. There is a record of two males, both of whom asked for complete castration, including amputation of the penis, construction of an artificial vagina, and the administration of female hormones. There are two cases of females who have requested a panhysterectomy and the amputation of their breasts, together with the giving of male sex hormones, in the hope that in some way the clitoris may finally develop into a penis. Male homosexuals of this type are called "queens" and seem to differ markedly from the main group of homosexuals who are more nearly like the average man. Here we have an extremely interesting field for further investigation.

Viewpoints as to the causes of homosexuality vary, with resulting differences in opinion as to the chances for successful treatment.

Freud felt that homosexuality is a disorder in psychological development. In each case of homosexuality, at any point, the development could have taken a different turn if the situation had been different. However, because of many conditioning experiences, the condition of homosexuality became fixed and the chances for cure small.

It is of interest that some of our officials in Washington have the naive idea that excluding homosexuals from government service will do away with the problem of foreign spies securing secret information. Homosexuals are no more open to seduction than are heterosexuals, and history is full of accounts of beautiful female spies who have secured imporant secrets from other governments by their heterosexual seductions. We find that some rulers in the past have tried to make their positions safe by surrounding themselves with eunuchs, but even this device did not prevent the rulers from betrayal at times. In view of the high incidence of some type of homosexual indulgence in American males as reported by Kinsey, there would seem to be little or no chance of keeping our government offices free of overt homosexuals. If one wishes to add the group of latent homosexuals, it is obvious that we are witnessing some of the wish fulfillment thinking, disassociated from reality, that we see in our schizophrenic patients.

The facts are that the majority of homosexuals are no particular menace to society. A small number of them, like those who are heterosexual, will attempt to seduce or sexually assault others or try to initiate sex relations with small children. They are undesirable persons in the community.

Society is entitled to protect itself against such individuals whether they are homosexual or heterosexual. Homosexual seduction of children is just as important as heterosexual seduction and perhaps even more serious in its effects. Society must and should guard against it rigidly. Certain dangerous acts do occur. Some overt homosexuals, in their hunt for partners, may be attracted to latent ones who greatly fear any homosexual expression.[6] Relations of this kind often end in atrocities which may be against children and youths. Homosexuality has been deleted as a classification of a mental illness by vote of the members of the American Psychiatric Association.

Fetishism

Ordinarily the perversion of fetishism is harmless. There are occasions, however, where it appears to be the beginning of a more serious type of sex abnormality in which murder and mutilation may occur.

It is not well understood in what situations fantasy passes over into action. In the well-known Chicago case, Heirens at age nine used female underclothing as a fetish.[7] Later, the act of *breaking through a window* to obtain feminine garments excited him greatly and often resulted in orgasm. By the age of seventeen he had committed twenty-five burglaries, one robbery, one assault to murder and three murders, including a kidnapping. During these crimes the least noise might set him off, and he might kill. To Eissler[8] it is incredible that parents, teachers, and priests did not suspect the many rich gifts, clearly beyond the youth's means, and that they ignored other signs. Heirens' wall daubing, "For heaven's sake, catch me before I kill more, I cannot control myself," Eissler considers a genuine plea for help.

Sex Offenses Against Young Children

Sex offenders of young children are a very serious social problem. In a very few cases the sexual attack on the child may be based on some superstition, as, for example, the idea that intercourse with a virgin, preferably a child under seven, cures venereal disease. In the majority of cases, however, the men are over forty years of age. A large percentage of them are impotent, either relatively or absolutely. In many of these cases it appears that the individual feels inadequate to approach a full-grown woman but is able to get more or less vicarious sexual pleasure through some kind of sex play with the small child. In homosexual acts with small children this may not be the case. In many of the older men involved in sex offenses toward little girls, it appears that the behavior is the evidence of an early senile or organic brain change, in which the ordinary controls and inhibitions are becoming lost. A great many of these men have had unblemished reputations so that these offenses could not have been anticipated.

The harmful effects of such sexual relations to the child victim have been at times exaggerated. Bender and Blau's[9] excellent study at Bellevue Hospital of sixteen children, aged five to twelve, who had sex relations with adults showed less fear and guilt in the children than expected. The immediate harmful effect was mainly interference with the child's education and other juvenile interests. The child's greater than usual preoccupation with sex hindered school advancement. For later effects these writers cite Rasmussen's Danish study of fifty-four women who had been child victims of convicted sex offenders. Only eight had serious emotional abnormalities in adult life and, in these, the early sexual trauma was not judged as an important factor.

Incest, more common than generally thought, is most frequent between father and daughter and between brother and sister. It is extremely rare between mother and son. Many reports stress such socioeconomic factors as very large families and bad living quarters as important causes.

A study of sex crimes against children can achieve no adequate, complete understanding without a thorough psychiatric study of the child and the child's family, as well as a full study of the offender. Dr. Karl Bowman[5] suggests first that often the most harmful effect of sex offenses to the child is the attitude of the family and associates; second, the question whether the crime is 100 percent the fault of the offender or whether in a considerable number of cases the child may have contributed more or less to the situation and may have some degree of responsibility for what occurs. Often children do not resist but even invite or initiate sex relations. In statutory rape, the sexually delinquent minor girl may be a more important psychiatric problem than the nonpsychotic male offender.

Murder

Observers estimate that genuine sex murder is rare. Homosexual panic may lead to sudden homicidal assault, or assaults on children by adults may end in murder. Psychiatrists have noted that some passive, effeminate boys may try to assert themselves by criminally aggressive behavor. Superficial investigation often intensifies these impulses and may lead to murder. Sex cases involving forceful rape or death after sexual relations is not, per se, a sexual offense, but primarily a crime of forceful assault or of murder.

Miscellany

Other sex offenses include sex relations with a corpse and bestiality. Some males and more than half of the boys raised on farms have some type of sexual contact with animals. Frequencies vary from once or twice in a lifetime to several times a week for some years. The incidence is very high in some western areas. Legal codes usually rate these acts as sodomy; the penalties vary. This over-valuation of animals may have some connection with the fanaticism of antivivisection. It is possible that the same forces which cause antivivisectionists to attempt to stop medical progress and allow diseased children to die, rather than subject a few animals to laboratory investigation, likewise motivate the high penalties for bestiality. Much opinion revolves around religious belief.

There are a number of types of heterosexual relations forbidden in many states, even if the couple is married and both are willing partners in the act. Such behavior is without effect on the rest of society and is even recommended as a part of the foreplay in most of the standard books regarding sex relations in marriage.

Treatment

All treatment must start with a thorough psychiatric study of the offender and, in many cases, of the victim. Sexual psychopathy is but one aspect of the whole personality, and any type of treatment must take into account the total personality. At the present time it must be admitted that the results of treatment are, on the whole, un-satisfactory. There is great need of developing better and simpler techniques. If mere detention is society's main protection against the offender, then imprisonment is more efficient than hospitalization, as some criminologists have noted.

Attempts should be made to determine exactly what cases require institutionalization. Certain cases of fetishism, some of the aggressive, seductive homosexuals, and sex offenders against children who show either the extreme compulsive, repetitive type of behavior or early signs of organic brain disease, should be segregated for the protection of society.

If one is interested in trying to help the offender to establish a more normal sex life, it is obvious that the ordinary imprisonment will not serve the purpose; particularly this is true in regard to homosexuality. Segregating a male homosexual for months or years in a prison where he will see only other men and where he will be often isolated with a group of other homosexuals can hardly result in anything but reinforcement of the homosexual tendencies.

In general, one may divide the methods of treatment into psychologic methods and physiologic methods. To those who feel that sex deviations are brought about according to Freud's ideas, an orthodox psychoanalysis may seem the best and, in fact, the only possible way of treating the patient successfully. Granting the most extreme claims of any of the Freudians, even assuming that they could cure every patient and increasing the number of psychoanalysis tenfold, one would find that even if the psychoanalysts devoted themselves exclusively to these problems the cures would be so few in number that the whole problem would be relatively unchanged.

Various types of short techniques and group psychotherapy have been tried by many with some varying results. One might sum it up by saying that all the standard techniques of psychotherapy have been used in the treatment of sex offenders without a very impressive result. We have a second group who feel that the approach should be primarily physiologic and who have reported results of treatment by hormonal injections, castration, convulsive shock therapy, and brain operations such as lobotomy. A variable degree of success is claimed by those reporting these types of treatment, but is disputed by most investigators.

Another point of special interest to the psychiatrist is to try to determine why one individual indulges in sex fantasies but does not carry them out in actual behavior, whereas in another individual the fantasies break through into overt acts. This may be closely linked up with the fact that the normal individual has a rich fantasy life, but never confuses fantasies with reality; whereas in certain mental disorders, particularly in schizophrenia, one often sees the fantasies breaking through with all the forces of reality and the patient living out his fantasy life as if it were real. Determining what factors cause the difference between fantasy and overt behavior might be of great value in helping to solve this problem.

Conclusion

From this brief presentation it is clear that the whole problem of the sex offender is a most complicated one and involves many fields. All attempts at better diagnosis, treatment, and prevention will require many years of cooperative research by scientists from many different fields. There is no one overall way of attacking the problem. Rather one must attack individual facets. It is possible to pose a series of specific questions to which there is reason to believe that we can get specific answers. By setting up more and more of these researches that will attack limited phases of the problem and by securing answers to such phases, we can hope eventually to be able to throw these answers together and by combining them obtain a solution to this problem.

Prevention and Control of Sex Offenses

There are no panaceas for the control and prevention of sex offenses and offenders. Criminal justice agencies are intimately involved in dealing with both offenders and offenses with the police bearing the major responsibility for investigation of offenses and the detection and arrest of offenders. The courts bear the awesome responsibility of determining guilt or innocence and prescribing penalties and treatment and rehabilitation programs. The correctional agencies are responsible for the incarceration, treatment, and rehabilitation of offenders not referred to some other agency. A collective responsibility pertains for the criminal justice agencies and other public and private agencies for both control and prevention.

Elements of an effective prevention and control program include considerable cooperation between the criminal justice, mental health, educational, and other community agencies for the purposes of detection, control, education, and public and community relations. As has been indicated, sex offenses and offenders result in highly charged public reactions and responses; thus it is incumbent upon the criminal justice agencies to develop comprehensive programs, particularly for the protection of young people.

The police are the responsible agency for investigation of offenses and the detection and arrest of offenders. In order to meet their obligations the police may enhance their effectiveness by the following:

- Establish special detail(s) to deal with sex offenses. A single detail may deal with both adult and juvenile cases or two details may be established.
- Maintain a "known" sex offender file that includes photographs and fingerprints of known offenders supplied by mental institutions and correctional agencies.
- Develop a cooperative working relationship with probation and parole agencies for the purpose of exercising control and supervision over known offenders in the community.
- Keep current addresses of known or suspected offenders insofar as may be feasible.
- Maintain uniformed field officers and juvenile patrol details as a matter of routine; constantly alert for activities and situations that lead to the commission of sex offenses.
- Provide special policing, as deemed necessary, for locations and situations that are susceptible to the commission of sex offenses.
- Develop a close working relationship with mental health and social service agencies responsible for dealing with sex offenders.
- Work closely with schools, recreational agencies, youth organizations, and other community agencies whose clientele may be victimized.
- Emphasize prevention by means of positive prevention and educational programs, not necessarily implemented by the police, but perhaps initiated and supported by them.

The courts, both juvenile and adult, bear a major responsibility for dealing with sex offenders. The courts' decisions, demeanor, and general response to community pressures do condition, to a great extent, how sex offenses and offenders will be handled in a community. The courts are well advised to:

- Make known their posture to the community for dealing with sex offenders, particularly as they pertain to offenses against juveniles and the handling of juvenile offenders and victims.
- Become actively involved in community efforts to control and prevent sex offenses. The "prestige" of the courts may make or break such efforts.
- Develop a positive program for dealing with violators of probation and make known the position to the public and particularly to the police probation departments, and the prosecuting agencies.

Correctional agencies, probation, parole, and institutions, both adult and juvenile, provide the incarceration, treatment, and rehabilitation component for the dealing with sex offenders. As far as the criminal justice system is concerned, correctional agencies may fulfill their prevention and control functions in a number of ways. Some of the ways are as follows:

- Provide reasonably adequate psychiatric care in institutions and on an outpatient basis.
- Provide appropriate training for counselors, probation and parole officers, and institutional personnel to deal with sex offenders.
- Develop programs for treatment and rehabilitation that utilizes available mental health and social services.
- Cooperate with the police by providing information on offenders released in a community, and develop relationships that may facilitate treatment and control rather than create a negative control environment.
- Participate in community programs designed to control and prevent sex offenses and activities of sex offenders.
- Participate in the preparation and implementation of community relations and educational programs which are designed to protect potential victims and identify potential offenders.

It must be recognized, however, that the criminal justice agencies are only limited components of a community system for the handling of sex offenses and offenders. Sex offenses often go unreported for various reasons, but mainly because people do not want to become "involved" or are unaware that "what is going on" may have serious consequences. Also, it must be recognized that many sex offenders are ejected from the criminal justice processes, beginning with the police, at any stage of the processing. Referrals may be made to any of a number of counselling, social service, psychological, or psychiatric programs for various and sundry reasons. At any state of the processing, sex offenders may be dealt out of the criminal justice system because it may be determined that an offense was between consenting individuals and thus has no consequent impact upon society, or it may be between two consenting juveniles, which can best be handled by the families of the involved.

A recognition that dealing with sex offenses and the behavior of sex offenders are highly emotionally charged responsibilities of criminal justice agencies is a prerequisite to the development of roles and functional activities. Cooperation and coordination of efforts is a must. But, coordination and cooperation with all community, mental health, social service, educational, and other public and private agencies dealing with sex offenses and offenders is essential for dealing with the problems presented.

School and PTA Help to Prevent Sex Offenses

The police can work closely with school officials to protect the children of the community from sex offenders. Certain precautionary procedures can be drilled into the children in the same manner that safety measures in respect to traffic are made a part of the school curriculum. As an example of one means whereby children can be taught to avoid the pitfalls into which a sex offender might lead them, we can cite is the use of comic booklets prepared by several police departments. These pamphlets are directed to the child and, by means of cartoons, attempt to teach the lesson that a child should not accept money, candy, or gifts from a stranger; that a child should not get into an automobile with a stranger; and that a child should not go any place with a stranger. Schools can distribute such pamphlets to children, as well as other material, and can devote instruction to the subject.

The police consistently work closely with the parent-teachers organizations in school systems. The PTA has been a forerunner in the development and dissemination of information for parents dealing with the subject of sex offenses and offenders; ideas that have been developed and utilized follow.

The most important responsibility of parents lies in trying to prevent sex crimes by educating and informing our children of the dangers of the sex offender (just as we caution against touching flame or petting a strange dog), by supervising their activities more conscientiously, and by accompanying young children to playgrounds, parks, theatres, skating rinks, dancing academies, dance halls, and beaches.

Caution your children:

1. To keep away from strangers in automobiles, especially if they ask directions or offer a ride.
2. To secure license number, kind of car, and description of driver if an offense is attempted.
3. Not to go away from school, playground, or movie with a stranger.
4. To refuse candy, cookies, money, or other gifts from strangers.
5. Not to allow a stranger to lift her dress up or fondle her.
6. Not to allow anyone to fuss with her clothes.
7. Not to enter a stranger's home, room, workshop, or shop alone.
8. To report any untoward incidents to parents, teacher, or police *as soon as possible*.
9. To report to an usher immediately if anyone attempts an offense in a theatre.
10. Always to play out in the open; not to go into alleys or secluded sections of parks or playgrounds.

To reinforce our cautioning, we should, as parents, take the following precautions:

1. Meet little children to bring them home without delay from school.
2. Do not allow young children to go unaccompanied by an adult to shows, skating rinks, playgrounds, and so forth. You can take turns with your neighbors in providing chaperonage.
3. See that school and city playgrounds are well supervised.
4. Become acquainted with your child's recreation supervisors, youth group leaders, and teachers.

5. Do not allow your child to go off with a youth leader without the rest of the group.
6. Know your "baby-sitters."
7. If you see suspicious behavior, watch long enough to be sure that you can identify the person with certainty, then report to the police immediately.

Remember that all school children may be menaced, boys as well as girls. Boys are almost exclusively the victims of homosexuals, the initial contact most commonly being made by picking up hitch-hikers, or in motion picture theatres, or in rest rooms. High school girls sometimes have tragic experiences with "blind dates."

As parents of teenagers, try to carry out the following suggestions:

1. Know the friends with whom your son or daughter goes out. Do not allow your daughter to go out on a "blind date."
2. Know *where* your children are and *what* they are doing.
3. Check occasionally on the truth of their statements.
4. See that your children obey the curfew laws and other protective ordinances.
5. Make sure that responsible adults will be present at dances or parties to which your child is invited. (This includes hay rides!)
6. Stay at home when your child gives a party—"supervise without snoopervising."
7. Warn your child against hitchhiking. In the event of an unfortunate happening, advise him to secure the license number of the car, its make and color, and to get a description of the person, then report it to the police *at once*.

Your interest in your child's activities need not be suspicious or severe. If you establish confidence between him and you when he is quite young, the channels of communication will be held open during his entire childhood and youth, and he will realize that your solicitude and precautions stem from your love for him.

JUVENILE SUICIDE

Each year in the United States more than five thousand young people, age twenty-four and under, commit suicide. It is suspected that these official figures are an understatement and that the actual numbers are, in fact, much higher. For 15-24-year olds, suicide is now the third leading cause of death, exceeded only by accident and homicides. Among white males, suicide is the second leading cause of death. Prior to 1965, the suicide rates in the United States and in much of the world increased directly with age. In the late sixties, the suicide rate among young people began increasing. Suicide rates now generally increase rapidly in the teen years, reaching a peak sometime in the twenties, taper off and drop slightly in the thirties and forties, and then go up again higher in the sixties and seventies. The very young, fourteen years and under, showed a dramatic rise during this period of about 150 percent. The suicide rate for males in the United States in the 14-25 age group was four times higher than the rate for females, and the suicide rate for whites was consistently higher than that of blacks and other non-whites. This is in contrast to earlier data showing suicide rates among young females rapidly approaching that of males, while suicide rates of young blacks being as high or higher than white youths. It would appear that more recent data suggest that it was a short-lived phenomenon of the early seventies and suicide rates of young females and non-whites are again lower.

Suicide attempters and threateners represent a considerably larger group in terms of total members. For example, the total number of committed suicides in the United States, age twenty-four and under, is probably in the neighborhood of five thousand. The ratio of attempts to commit appears to be much higher for young people than for older people. For people in general and those in the older age group, the ratio is somewhere in the neighborhood of from five or ten to one; for adolescents it may be as high as twenty-five or fifty to one. It is possible that there are as many as fifty thousand suicide attempters in the United States each year under the age of twenty-five. In addition, there are large numbers of people who never attempt suicide but think about it and talk about it. The ratio here is unknown, but it is safe to say that each year in the United States for this age population somewhere in the neighborhood of a million or more children move in and out of suicidal crisis, thoughts, ideations, and episodes.

We do know that white males commit suicide two to three times as often as females. In the area of attempted suicide, the sex ratio is reversed. Many more adolescent girls attempt suicide than boys.

With increased suicide deaths come increased suicide attempts. There are more youngsters thinking, obsessing, and worrying about suicide than ever before. Authorities suggest that up to 10 percent of the youngsters in any public school classroom may be considered at some risk for suicide. Police have observed that many suicidal youngsters abuse alcohol and drugs and become involved in criminal activities as a defense against their unhappiness and depression. The increase in these kinds of youngsters who become suicidal may, in part, account for some of the increase in suicide from the early sixties to the early and middle seventies.

Much of the behavior among young people is a flight away from emotional commitment or depth of feelings. Many women students are determined not to be overwhelmed by experience, but in the search for the antidote to emotion they often find that they have killed their power to care deeply for anyone. Working at making life not matter may be intended simply to remove the depressions, the hurts, and the angers that afflict, leaving only the better emotions; yet the habit of detachment, once acquired, leads inevitably to a general numbing in the face of all experience.

Analysis of the Increase of Suicide Among Youth

The problem that behavioral scientists, who are interested in the youth culture and self-destructive behavior, are faced with is to try to understand various trends among young people and various factors in the youth culture that contribute to an increase in self-destructive behavior. A number of complex variables may have contributed to the increase of youth suicide in the last fifteen to twenty years. The population explosion of the late forties and early fifties may relate to the youth suicide phenomenon. Children born between 1950 and 1955 passed through their teens and early twenties during the period that the suicide rate was rising most rapidly. The population of this age group was higher than it had ever been before and was certainly out of proportion to other age groups in size. It's possible that an overcrowding phenomenon occurred in this generation that resulted in too many young people wanting too many things that were not available, contributing to an increased feeling of anonymity and alienation.

The post-war baby boom, which weakened family ties and accelerated a breakdown in family relationships, resulted in a greater problem of emotional identity among youth and a trend towards greater isolation.

A number of other factors of importance have been discussed by a variety of authorities:

1. The previous history of suicide attempts or threat were significant in determining the outcome of current suicidal behavior.
2. Depression characterized by sleep disturbance, eating disturbance, trouble with concentration, and tiring easily are frequently identified as important factors.
3. A disturbed relationship with parents was considered crucial, as was frequent quarreling and actual physical assaultive behavior between parents and children. Family alcoholism was another factor mentioned, as was loss or threatened loss of a parent or a love relationship, withdrawal and isolation, accompanied by poor interrelationships were among the most frequently mentioned social characteristics related to youth suicide.

Some Psychodynamic Observations

Children who commit suicide find that their efforts to express their feelings of unhappiness, frustration, or failure are totally unacceptable to their parents. Such feelings are ignored or denied or are met by defensive hostility. Such a response often drives the child into further isolation, reinforced by the feeling that something is terribly wrong with him.

Certain specific, clear-cut differences have been found between the committed-suicide group and the other groups of suicidal adolescents. Greater frequency of psychiatric hospitalization, combined with a higher rating of emotional disturbance and fewer prior suicide attempts, marked the history.

There is some evidence that the adolescent who commits suicide has a greater predisposition toward self-destruction and therefore requires less overt stress than his colleagues to initiate the suicide act. This evidence was confirmed in some degree by the fact that the loss or threatened loss of a loved one operated less often as the precipitating stress or "trigger" among those in the committed-suicide group than it did on the attempts of those in the suicidal groups. Stress was reported to be higher among persons who attempted suicide. The reaction was to communicate their suicidal intent openly, i.e. verbally or behaviorally, in order to let others know of the psychologic pain that they were experiencing and thus, ultimately, to reduce the stress that they were feeling.

How we can better understand the factors associated with these suicides and better understand the cause for the increase is the subject of the remainder of this chapter.

Categories of Youth Suicide

Suicide Among the Very Young

In the 10–14-year age group, the actual numbers of suicide are low in comparison to older age groups. The rate has jumped by 33 percent from 1968 to 1976 (National Center for Health Statistics). It is suggested that the process of being "learning disabled" may bring with it such extreme feelings of loss of self-esteem as to place rather young children in an at-risk category for suicide.

The Loner

This personality type begins to emerge at age fourteen or fifteen and has been described as fitting a clear-cut symptom pattern. Characteristics associated with this kind of person center around loneliness, isolation, lack of friends, and poor interpersonal communication with peers and parents. Most often, youngsters who are described as "loners" come from intact families, though it appears that these parents have difficulty with their image of themselves as parents and are constantly concerned about making mistakes and not being good parents. They interpret the child's complaints about problems, unhappiness, or general life difficulties as a statement of their lack of competence and, therefore, in a defensive gesture, will often insist to the child that he really is not unhappy and has nothing to complain about. In these families, the child usually learns at an early age that what he thinks of himself and what his parents think of him are different and he begins to distrust his own thoughts and feelings. His solution is often to not communicate his unhappy thoughts and feelings to anyone. This builds up in the later teens to, finally, a youngster with a potential high-suicide risk.

Acting Out Depression

Suicidal thoughts and attempts are most common in this group. The number of youngsters that fit this category appear to have begun increasing in the early seventies. Although there still may be more white males in this group, there are a larger proportion of ethnic groups and females than in the aforementioned categories. These youngsters are characterized primarily by behaviors that are seen by others as illegal, dangerous, disruptive, harmful, or hostile. The major symptoms represented by people in this category are that of drug and alcohol abuse, running away, petty crimes (e.g. shoplifting and joyriding), assaultive behaviors (frequently with members of one's own family), and occasionally serious violence. Psychodynamically, most often these youngsters experience in their early teens surges of depressive feelings that they are unable to understand, explain, or cope with. They often experience and interpret these feelings as painful boredom, and, frequently, through role models in their nuclear or extended families, they decide that the most effective way to cope with these feelings is through some form of action. The action, which often includes substance abuse, typically helps them get through the most difficult part. They keep doing it as long as it works. However, often these people get in trouble, particularly with the authorities. The authorities tend to treat them as delinquents rather than depressed youngsters, which adds to their sense of despair. These children often come from broken homes, where chaos, inconsistency, and substance abuse is not uncommon. Learning to use alcohol and drugs as a solution to their problems is very frequently something that comes directly from a parent or older sibling.

The Psychotic Suicide

This category of youth suicide is somewhat smaller in numbers than the others. These youngsters are very difficult to work with, psychologically. The symptom picture often includes delusions, hallucinations, and, occasionally, direct messages from voices to kill oneself. Much of the fantasy and some of the behavior of these youngsters would be considered violent and bizarre. The suicidal behavior itself is often bizarre.

These youngsters most often come from single-parent families, i.e. at least families in which only one parent is psychologically present. Sometimes, the parents are grossly psychotic, alcoholic, or both; sometimes, the behavior patterns are quite varied and they resemble other categories of suicidal youngsters. But the decision to place the youngster in the particular category of the psychotic suicide is determined by the bizarre symptoms combined with suicidal behavior.

The Crisis Suicide

Youngsters who evidence suicidal behaviors and symptoms who fit into the crisis category probably represent less than 15 percent of all suicidal youngsters. The major findings among these kinds of patients is that there is an apparently normal pre-morbid personality, no history of severe emotional trauma, and a reasonably stable family pattern.

The typical pattern is that an adolescent reaches a point in his life where he becomes aware of, or has inflicted upon him, sudden traumatic changes. The changes may include the loss of a loved one or the loss (or threatened loss) of status in school through academic or athletic failure. Subsequently, the youngster undergoes sudden and dramatic changes in behavior that may include loss of interest in things that were previously important, sudden hostile and aggressive behaviors in a previously placed youngster, and signs of confusion and disorganization. There is typically an inability to concentrate and, frequently, a series of classical depressive symptoms.

Suicidal Behavior as a Communication

This final category focuses on a rather large number of suicide attempters and threateners, for whom communication is a major factor in their suicidal behavior. It is a much less frequent category when examining suicide death. In these cases, the person becomes suicidal when more common avenues of expression of frustrated feelings become blocked, interrupted, and stymied. This is not to say that the young suicidal person who is communicating through suicidal behavior is doing so in a calm, rational manner. The experience of the person is usually one of desperation, unhappiness, and great upset. But the lethality of the behavior is almost always low. The ultimate purpose of the behavior seems to clear the way to open up and break through the barriers, so that the significant others will know how desperate or how unhappy he feels. This represents the classical "cry for help." This suicidal youngster does not necessarily have a history of severe disturbance or prior suicidal episodes, although they may be present.

The foregoing is an attempt to look at youth suicide from different points of view. The goal is to make more efficient police officers. Identifying a suicidal youngster and then connecting him with appropriate treatment and rehabilitation programs represents a major way of saving lives. Law enforcement officers must be aware and alert to identify possible suicidal juveniles.

REFERENCES

1. Drug Enforcement Administration, U.S. Department of Justice: *Fact Sheets.* Washington, D.C., U.S. Government Printing Office, 1980 (Excerpts)
2. Bureau of Narcotic Enforcement, California Department of Justice: *The Narcotic Problem: A Brief Study,* 3rd ed. Sacramento, California, 1964. (Excerpts) See also Williams, John B. (Ed.): *Narcotics.* Dubuque, Wm. C. Brown, 1963. Also, *What You Should Know About Drugs and Narcotics.* The Associated Press, 1969.
3. National Advisory Commission on Criminal Justice Standards and Goals: *Community Crime Prevention.* Washington, D.C., U.S. Government Printing Office, 1973.
4. Nowlis, H.: *Drugs on the College Campus.* Doubleday, Anchor, 1969.
5. Bowman, Karl M.: Report of Karl M. Bowman, Medical Superintendent of the Langley Porter Clinic, *Progress Report to the Legislature 1951 Regular Session.* January 1951, pp. 149-158, as taken from The Menas S. Gregory Lecture, given at New York University, Bellevue Medical Center, College of Medicine, January 24, 1951.
6. Ploscowe, M.: Sexual patterns and the law. In Deutsch, A. (Ed.): *Sex Habits of American Men.* New York, Prentice-Hall, 1948.
7. Eissler, R.: Scapegoats of society. In Eissler, K.R. (Ed.): *Searchlights on Delinquency.* New York, International Universities Press, 1949.
8. Kennedy, F. et al: A study of William Heirens. *Am J Psychiatr, 104:*113, 1947.
9. Blender, L. and Blau, A.: Reaction of children to sexual relations with adults. *Am J Orthopsychiatr, 7:*500, 1937.
10. Kobetz, Richard W.: Juvenile vandalism: The billion dollar prank. *The Police Chief,* June, 1973.

11. Klein, Malcolm, W.: *Street Gangs and Street Workers*. Englewood Cliffs, N.J., Prentice-Hall, Inc., 1971. The material used appeared in POLICE WORK WITH JUVENILES AND THE ADMINISTRATION OF JUSTICE, 4th Edition, 1970, with permission of the author, referenced as follows: Klein, Malcolm W.: Juvenile Gangs: Facts, Fiction, and New Directions. -In Process. See also Klein, Malcolm W.: Juvenile gangs, police and detached workers; Controversies about intervention. The Social Service Review, 39 (No. 2), June, 1965.

Chapter 7

VANDALISM AND JUVENILE GANGS

J UVENILE vandalism is one of the most costly offenses confronting the police and society today. It is costly in the sense
that it leads to an estimated billion dollar plus annual property
loss and that it leads to an irreparable damage to individuals in
human relations and delinquency records for a countless number of
juveniles. At best we seem ill equipped to cope with the problem. It
seems to be a problem endemic to human nature. "Who among us
shall dare to cast the first stone to correct the situation without some
measure of guilt?" Perhaps that is the reason our endeavors are so inadequate.

Kobetz defines vandalism as *the deliberate defacement, mutilation, or
destruction of private or public property.* [1] These acts include such widely
diversified offenses as throwing rocks from freeways and railroad
overpasses, spraying graffiti on walls, ripping up shrubbery and
flower beds, stealing traffic signs, ripping aerials off cars, slashing
tires, putting sugar in gasoline tanks, and devastating school rooms.
The list is endless, and no individual, business, public agency, or industry is immune from attacks of vandalism.

The predominant vandal is a young person, the "kid" in the
neighborhood in which you and I live. Thus, vandalism is a very

real problem in all communities, the ghetto and the affluent neighborhood alike. The fact that the problem cuts across all strata of society is probably one of the reasons that it has been played down as a major delinquency problem and why the police have given only *ad hoc* attention to it. It is a subject much talked about, but little in the way of concerted effort is expended to solve it.

The "why" for vandalism is a mystery. Psychologists and psychiatrists provide only *ad hoc* answers, and all too frequently there seems to be no answer.

What can be done? Control of vandalism is a community responsibility involving parents, civic groups, schools, churches, businesses, industries, and the criminal justice agencies. A coordinated approach is essential — one that brings together for the planning and development of a comprehensive program that involves all concerned elements of a community. Anything less is self-defeating, for a program initiated by one or a limited number of community elements is doomed to failure because the problem is all-encompassing.

The police are the one criminal justice agency most involved with the vandalism problem. They receive the complaints, investigate the cases, and occasionally arrest perpetrators. The courts and other criminal justice agencies are involved after the fact and deal only with those who are apprehended and inputted by the police into the system. The police, to be effective, are confronted with the need to initiate control and prevention activities, as well as investigate and apprehend offenders.

What can the police do? Basic field police practices provide the obvious approach to physical control:

- Increased police patrol in areas where vandalism occurs most frequently.
- Invoke curfew ordinances.
- Use special details to concentrate on vandalized properties such as schools, parks, subways, developments, shopping centers, and travel stations.
- Assist schools, businesses, industries, home owners, and public agencies in planning the protection of their properties.

There are no surefire approaches, but a combination of these suggested can help.

The police, however, should not limit their approaches to physical controls. Public relations and educational programs can also contribute to the control and prevention of vandalism. Some suggestions follow:

- Related to physical control is the sponsoring of educational programs for all concerned citizens, business and industry officials, civic groups, school officials, and others who are victimized by vandalism.
- More importantly, the need is to reach the young people who are the "vandals." The police can initiate educational and public relations programs in schools and in a multitude of youth-serving agencies. The communication media can contribute much by presenting stories dealing with the problems and possible solutions based upon police releases.
- The police can solicit the cooperation and involvement of youth in a number of prevention and control programs. Police sponsored youth groups, such as a Police Youth Service Corporation, can be extremely helpful in controlling vandalism.
- Citizen involvement in specialized programs such as Operation Crime Stop, Citizen Block Watch, and Neighborhood Patrols can do much to curb vandalism. The police may or may not be involved in initiating such programs.

CURRENT TRENDS IN VANDALISM

Interesting information was presented at the Fourth Annual Workshop on Crime, Violence, and Discipline in the Schools, on March 6, 1980, in Los Angeles, California.

A recent nationwide random sampling of more than two thousand from among America's over 2 million teachers, by the National Education Association, revealed:

- 75 percent said discipline problems impaired their effectiveness to teach.
- 50 percent believe that their schools have not done enough to support these teachers with discipline problems.
- 5 percent reported that they were physically assaulted by a student during the 1978-79 school year, which statistically means that over 110,000 teachers were physically assaulted during that

school year, or over one in twenty of our teachers.

- Of those teachers physically assaulted, more than 11,000 needed medical attention for their injuries. Another 9,000 required medical attention for emotional trauma.
- 10 percent of the physical attacks were serious enough to cause a teacher to miss two days or more of school, thus approximately 22,000 days of instructional time was lost.
- 90 percent of these assaults were reported to school administrators, but only 50 percent of the reporting teachers were satisfied with the responses by the administrators.
- 11 percent were at least occasionally concerned that they may be physically attacked at school by a student.
- Whether they fear it or not, roughly 12 percent of California's high school teachers are annually threatened with physical harm.

School vandalism is also on the increase. The Administrative Services Attendance and Welfare 1979-80 Bulletin of the Los Angeles Superintendent of Schools revealed:

School Year 1978–1979

- Reported assaults increased 37 percent, from 2,428 to 3,317.
- Property loss increased 56 percent, from $5.5 to $8.6 million.
- Arsons increased 58 percent with a dollar loss of $3.8 million.

However, the truly remarkable magnitude of crime in Los Angeles schools emerges when the six-year period from school years 1973-74 through 1978-79 are cumulated. During that six-year period there were:

- 15,341 reported assaults.
- 1,666 arsons
- 17,507 thefts
- 111,624 vandalisms
- 31,203 burglaries
- 177,341 reported crimes

Not counting medical expenses to schools or to assault victims, the fiscal losses to crime during that six-year period are staggering:

- $9.4 million for arson

- $2.2 million for theft
- $17.3 million for vandalism
- $5.9 million for burglary
  For a fiscal total of:
- $34.9 million

While these figures are outrageous they still do not include:

- $9 million for a security force
- Fire and burglary costs
- Chain link fence costs
- Insurance costs

Altogether, it is probable that more than $100 million has been lost to crime and violence in Los Angeles schools since the end of 1972. This trend is undoubtedly reflected by a number of school districts throughout the United States.

The crime committed most often in the schools is vandalism, and it is also the most costly such crime. Therefore, a more detailed analysis of school vandalism should be of interest.

In 1979 the Center for Juvenile Delinquency Prevention, South West Texas State University, in San Marcos, Texas, released a report entitled "Vandalism."

Vandalism is deliberate property damage. In 455 A.D. the Vandals, a fierce Germanic tribe, overran Europe and sacked Rome, destroying all in their wake. Their name was the root of the word *vandalism*.

The following surveys are estimates of school vandalism in the United States:

- 1978 a total of $600 million in damage
- $3 million in school bus seats each year
- Enough arson to account for 40 percent of all vandalism costs each year
- At the end of the 1973 school year the average cost of damages from vandalism was estimated at $63,031 per school district

A typical school's chance of being

- vandalized in a month are greater than one in four, and the average cost of each act is $81.
- burglarized in a month are greater than one in ten, and the average cost of each act is almost $200.

These figures do not relate the hidden costs of school vandalism:

- Increased insurance rates
- Costs for security guards
- Fencing
- Instrusion and fire detection
- Special lighting
- Emergency communications equipment
- Vandal-resistant windows

Then there are the enormous social costs. The impact of dollar cans of spray paint to cover a wall with racial epithets or abuse words can destroy student morale, disrupt intergroup relations, undermine the administration, and cause riots, strife, and gang fights, and even close the school.

The following are some techniques that have made some schools less vulnerable to vandals. These are especially effective against problems occurring during nonschool hours:

- Occupy the school
- Watch the school
- Control access to the school
- Design or modify the school with vandalism in mind
- Revise the curriculum
- Change administrative policy and organizational structure
- Involve the students
- Involve the parents
- Involve the community

Violence and vandalism in our schools touches each citizen in America. All efforts must be made to attack this problem by combined community efforts.

JUVENILE GANGS

In many metropolitan areas police have had serious problems with juvenile gangs, particularly in the disadvantaged sections of cities. With the current social unrest in the nation, these gang problems continue to mount. More research on gangs has been conducted since 1960 than in all previous years, and the results should be helpful to police in developing effective programs to cope with gang behavior.

Results of a comprehensive study of youth gangs by Dr. Malcolm W. Klein of the University of Southern California provides a comprehensive picture of the character and nature of juvenile gangs.[2]

Gang Structure

The structural properties of the gang, using the term *structure* rather loosely, can be described by reference to five variables: size, age, sex, level of involvement, and cohesiveness. Most gangs, when judged on the variables, do not fit the stereotyped picture provided by the media or the police.

Size

Many gangs consist of from ten to around thirty members, similar in age and generally all male. Such a gang may exist for a few months or perhaps a year but seldom lasts long enough to develop a tradition. These "spontaneous" gangs may be the most numerous type, but usually represent only a minor threat to public safety. Others, variously called traditional, vertical, or area gangs, may include an active membership of between 30 and 100 boys (and sometimes girls) at any one time, and up to 150 to 200 over a period of several years.

Age

As with other adolescents, gang members affiliate with age peers. Since gang membership may range from the early teens to the early twenties, this means that the large traditional gang actually consists of three or four age-graded subgroups. The youngest and oldest subgroups are the smallest in size, while the sixteen- and seventeen-year-olds are the most numerous. While some subgroup has its own identity ("Senior Victors," "Junior Victors," and so forth), each also identifies with the overall structure that we will therefore refer to as a *gang cluster.*

Sex

While the smaller, spontaneous gangs are typically all male, traditional gang clusters often include one or two auxiliary groups of girls. These are separate, rather than coeducational, subgroups and exist more through mutual toleration than collaboration.

Level of Involvement

Not all gang members are equally involved in the activities of the group. A rough distinction can be made between *core* members and *fringe* members. Core members are more frequent participants in group activities, more visible with other members, and develop more serious police records than do fringe members. Additionally, core members (who may comprise up to 50% of the total membership) are likely to be somewhat more aggressive and more deficient in personal skills and achievements. However, these patterns are by no means pure. There are core members with no police records who are indistinguishable from nongang neighborhood peers; there are fringe members who are in constant trouble and seem to have absolutely nothing going for them.

In addition to the core–fringe breakdown, one can distinguish between clique and nonclique members. Most clique members are also core members, but a number of core members may not belong to identifiable cliques. Fringe members are seldom to be found in cliques, although dyads and triads are not uncommon.

Cohesiveness

Subgroup and clique membership, and to a lesser extent, core and fringe status, are shifting phenomena in the traditional gang. The relationship between the members is dynamic rather than static. This fact, plus the constant turnover in membership due to maturation, changes in residence, incarceration, and changes in school or job status prevents the development of a truly cohesive group. The large numbers of youngsters involved also work against cohesiveness. Thus, despite the popular image, the fact of gang life is that the traditional gang is a loose, unstable confederation of friendship groups held together more by the pressures of the environment than by any internal bonds, including delinquent values.

Gang Leadership

Three major myths seem to exist about leadership in the gang.

The first is that leadership is clearly defined. Our observations do not support this statement. Rather, gang leadership is best seen as *functional* and distributed, i.e. leadership varies according to the activity in question and is a group function that can be and is assumed by numerous boys in different settings and at different times. Unless popularity is equated with leadership, it cannot be said that a few leaders can be distinguished from a host of followers.

A second myth has it that gang leadership is psychopathic or sociopathic. It is true, in our experience, that gang membership can be expected to include boys who are seriously disturbed emotionally. However, they seldom exert leadership or do so only among a small number of members and only on infrequent occasions. Ordinarily, the obvious threat of a disturbed boy is recognized by his peers who avoid becoming entangled in his web of intrigue and violence. It is far more common for the influential gang member to be characterized by his "cool," by his style, or by his ability to bring benefit to the group.

Finally, there is the notion that gang leaders are the older members of the group, who consequently are able to entice the younger boys into various escapades. It is true that leadership is age-related, but not in this sense. Our previous comments on gang structure provide the clue here—leadership is primarily *age-graded*. In each subgroup one finds influence of one member over another far more often than across subgroups. The older boy has less influence on the younger than does another younger member. This is in the nature of adolescence. It is less true of status or prestige, but these variables are not the same as leadership. Many older boys are far more admired than followed.

Offense Patterns

What kinds of offenses do gang members commit, so far as one can judge by official records (police, court, probation)? Analyses of the records reveal several findings that, if not surprising, nevertheless refute some common assumptions.

Offense Frequencies

It is commonly thought that gang offenses consist primarily of assaults or of vandalism. Neither is true. Combining offenses into some gross categories it appears that thefts (excluding auto theft) are the most common charges, accounting for as much as a quarter of the total. Next came the various "juvenile status" offenses, those that can only be charged against minors. Examples include runaway, truancy, curfew violations, and possession of alcohol.

Auto theft, including joyriding, is the next most common, followed in fourth place by assaults of all kinds, which account for less than one in eight charges. Vandalism, drug use, traffic, and sex offenses are each even less common. Of course, this refers to official charges rather than behavioral acts. Still, the picture is far less frightening than is often supposed.

Offense Patterns

It is often supposed that gang members, much in the fashion of adult criminals, follow certain patterns of delinquent behavior; some specialize in thefts, others in sex delinquency, still others are primarily fighters, while others are primarily involved with liquor and drugs. Once again, the available data fail to support such an assertion. Rather, gang boys are arrested for a wide range of infractions. It's as if the penal code represented a cafeteria of choices, and each boy wandered down the aisle to stop first before the runaway counter, then the assault tray, and so on through the average of five or six "selections."

It has also been suggested that gangs, as groups, exhibit distinctive overall offense patterns; some are conflict gangs, others theft gangs, and others retreatist (drugs and alcohol). Mirroring the lack of pattern among individuals, our Los Angeles gangs are relatively indistinguishable by type of delinquency orientation. Further, of six published studies of gangs both here and abroad only one has reported finding the suggested intergang patterning. We must conclude at this point that the behavior of the boys and the reactions of the official agencies interact in such a way as to support the cafeteria hypothesis.

Offense Seriousness

The mainstay of delinquency prevention programs is the dictum to "get 'em while they're young." Several reasons for this are given: younger boys are more changeable; impact in the early years will prevent an accumulation of offenses; and impact in the early years will prevent the progression to the more serious offenses.

We have no argument with the first two rationales, but, so far as gang delinquency is concerned, the third is questionable. Our data demonstrate clearly that as boys get into more trouble, they do not, on the average, get into more serious trouble. The average seriousness of first offenses charged against gang members is not greater or less than the average seriousness of the second, fifth, tenth, or even fifteenth offense (limiting ourselves to offenses charged prior to the eighteenth birthday). It is true that later offenses are committed after shorter time spans, but this seems to be unrelated to the qualitative seriousness of the charge.

Gang Values and Attitudes

How differently do gang members look at life? How alienated are they from the dominant values of society? To what extent are they participants in a separate "subculture" with its own code of ethics? Questions like these have piqued the imagination of criminologists for a long time, but only recently has evidence begun to point to answers, however tentative.

For instance, such phrases as "honor among thieves" and "the code of the gang" represents the core of the general public's mythology about gang life. Recent research has indicated that, while "the code" exists, it is more verbal than behavioral. In a group setting, gang boys do indeed verbalize and reinforce a code of in-group loyalty reminiscent of *The Three Musketeers*. But in individual conversations and in times of personal threat they will often abandon the code in the interests of their own well-being. If gang members were aware of the extent to which each is willing to "fink" on the other, one of the main internal bonds of cohesion would be broken.

Even more generally, however, present research observations indicate that the separate value system attributed to the gang has been vastly overrated. Many of these boys are just as interested in the middle-class values of material gains and status, security, and personal achievement as their nongang peers. The major difference is that they accord higher legitimacy to values that support delinquency. In this sense, their value repertoire is similar to, but broader than, that of other youngsters. They can justify to themselves a wider range of activities. Despite their often-stated antagonism toward "the establishment" and the insensitivity of the white middle class, they would like nothing more than to share in the benefits of the "square" life. The major question is really whether or not they are able to reap these benefits before their own illegal behaviors divorce them from the means to achieve the benefits. But make no mistake about it, these boys are for the most part just as square as the rest of us.

Gang Girls

The gang girl may either be a "camp follower," attached with a few friends to individuals in the boys' gang, or part of a more formal girls' group having an auxiliary relationship to the boys' organization. The girls' group seems to consist first of siblings and girlfriends of the boys but soon expands through the recruitment of friends to develop as a separate friendship group. Far less delinquent than the boys, with records more commonly consisting of sex and "juvenile status" offenses, the girls seldom maintain their own group structure after dissolution of the boys' group. The independent girl gang is a rarity.

The most common fiction relating to gang girls is that they are intimately involved in the male gang's delinquency, fighting side by side, instigating gang fights by spreading rumors between rival gangs, and acting as weapons carriers for the boys. Occasionally, these patterns can in fact be observed, but again they seem to represent the exceptional situation. Interviews and observations with both boys and girls indicate that, more often than not, the presence of the girls serves to prevent or postpone delinquent episodes of a serious nature. Among other reasons given is the distrust of girls as witnesses; the boys have a stereotype that girls have loose tongues and will tell all with little hesitancy.

This fear is reflected in the results of interviews of detained gang members who admitted to female participation in the planning of only 2 percent of the incidents. Female participation in the actual events occurred in 11 percent of the cases (sex offenses are obviously omitted from these data—it takes two to tango). In almost all of the latter cases, the girls were usually present as observers, seldom as actors. Interestingly, however, data indicated that those incidents in which girls are present tend to involve more serious offenses, including assaults. Presumably, the presence of the girls brings out the masculinity of their male companions.

Perhaps most important is the fact that the majority of the boys do care about the girls' reactions to their arrest and do avoid serious trouble in the presence of the girls. It is our distinct impression that these girls represent a positive deterrent to male gang delinquency. With proper counseling, they could be employed as direct preventive agents. As a colleague stated, "After six years, we've decided we're in favor of girls!"

Group Work with Gangs

Action programs for dealing with gang delinquency have traditionally fallen along a continuum from "harassment" to "transformation." The harassment approach has seen the group, per se, as the root of the problem. Thus, the group structure became the target of negative intervention. If the leaders can be eliminated, the group will dissolve. Breaking up group activities, prohibiting the formation of "clubs," and other repressive techniques were designed to eliminate the problem.

But the harassment approach has suffered from several drawbacks. It has never been proven effective, and it may have caused an *increase* in gang cohesiveness through the provision of a common enemy: the harasser. It has not provided activities alternative to gang participation. It has increased resentment toward and isolation from "respectable" society.

The transformation approach has also concentrated on the group but has seen the structure of the group as a positive force. The attempt has been to take the "natural" group—the gang—and transform it into a prosocial organization through the provision of club meetings, outings, competitive sports, and the like. This approach, too, has its problems. It takes several years to bring about the transformation, by which time (a) the majority of boys mature out of the gang in any case, and (b) younger boys have now attained gang status. Group programming inadvertently works against positive gains since it increases gang cohesiveness and attracts new members.

The assumption of working with the "natural" group is rather questionable. The traditional gang, with 100 or more members, can only be called natural by a strenuous exercise of the imagination. It is, rather, a caricature of "natural" youth groups, and working with caricatures as if they were realistic portraits leads to strange distortions of effort and impact. Three empirically evaluated studies of the transformation approach done in Boston, Chicago, and Los Angeles have yielded discouraging findings. One showed only minor impact, while two provided evidence of negative impact—an increase in gang delinquency associated with the programs.

A brief summary of these transformation programs yields at least the following suggestions:

1. The ability of a worker to transform delinquent attitudes or values of either individuals in the gang or the gang as a whole is severely limited.
2. The effect of group programming for gangs may very well be to increase gang cohesiveness and increase gang recruitment.
3. The ability of these programs to reduce deliquency rates is severely limited, since these are a function of a complex tangle of environmental and personal factors not under the control of the programs.
4. Since detached workers are faced with a "case load" of up to 100 youngsters, measurable impact can only be attained by (a) augmenting resources available to them and/or (b) providing an intervention model that would increase the efficiency of their effort.

It seems clear at this point that the potential of the group work approach to gangs has not been adequately tapped. One reason is that programs have been based in part on such false assumptions as those discussed in this paper. It takes time to evaluate such assumptions, and data derived from prior action and research programs now permit us to redirect current strategies.

Another reason has been the relative absence of intervention approaches based on either sound theory or tight conceptual models that could guarantee a consistent application of action steps. Finally, too little attention has been paid to the inclusion of research procedures capable of evaluating the stronger and weaker facets of the group approach. We have been flying by the seat of our pants instead of by instruments, with the result that upon landing we seldom know where we have been or where we should go next.

Some guidelines for detached work operations can now be suggested. Derived primarily from the experience of past projects, they are not "sure bets." Still, by combining them into an overall package, it should be possible to develop a model approach worthy of being mounted and evaluated in the field.

1. We must move from detached worker programs to detached teamwork programs. The detached worker would restrict his activities primarily to individual and family counseling in the street and home settings. A second worker would concern himself with the development of jobs, remedial aid, welfare procedures, and the like that can act as alternatives to gang participation. The major collaborative effort between the two workers should revolve around the choice of the youth to be served and making the service connection. One or two worker aides should also be enlisted. These would be young men from the neighborhood who can serve as "listening posts" for the workers, provide greater coverage of the street scene, and follow up on the service placements of each boy.

2. Group programming efforts should be abandoned. This includes club formations and meetings, outings, dances, team sports, and all planned events that are specifically designed for a given gang. Such events merely reinforce gang identification and cohesion and give the worker a "crutch" that, while useful to him, inadvertently defeats his avowed purpose.

3. A method for "targetting in" on certain members of the gang is required. With a large number of gang members as clients, the worker tends to spend most of his time with selected leaders, boys who stay close to him, boys professing and having special needs (critical or intense), boys who show an interest in reforming, and so on. The difficulty here is in the reliance on clinical judgment and insight. A more rational basis for targetting is required both for the sake of efficiency and so that each worker's style is not so individualistic that a generalizable approach cannot be developed. Examples of appropriate "target" members might be as follows:

   a. *Clique leaders*, from whom positive impact might spread to other clique members.

b. *Cohesiveness builders*, boys who by their actions or statements serve to reinforce or build the gang image and structure.

c. *Potential or actual recruits*, who might have leaned away prior to active participation in the gang, e.g. younger brothers of active members.

d. *Low-participant fringe members*, whose weaker ties to the group can be more easily counterbalanced by alternative activities.

4. Similarly, community organization efforts should be submitted to a "targetting analysis." Analysis of community organization efforts tied to detached worker programs suggest that they are often too diffuse and too indirectly connected to the requirements of the gang problem. Attendance at community council meetings, PTA meetings, and recreational development affairs are all fine and good for general purposes, but they have little to do with the direct amelioration of gang problems. More to the point might be local employer groups, indigenous big brother organizations, and minority protest groups. These, at least, have the potential for attaching gang members directly to alternative participation patterns.

5. For gangs that are in immediate contact with rival gangs, coordinated relationships with detached worker teams assigned to the rivals must be established. There may be no greater source of gang cohesivensss than the real or assumed threat of the rival gang. To work only with one gang while its surrounding antagonists go unserviced is to invite frustration and failure. Thus, an *area* program rather than a block or neighborhood program is required.

The overall guideline being suggested here is that we stop treating gangs as if they were imbued with some inherent potential for growth that merely requires adult direction. Rather, we must recognize that, in the very special nature of the gang, there is a great potential for damage, not only to society but, even more, to the gang membership itself. Repressive attempts to "break up" the gang will only provide self-justification for its existence and for further self-damage. Programs banking on "transforming" the gang have proven themselves totally inadequate. With the recent appearance of new data on the nature of gangs and the evaluation of past intervention efforts, we should now be able to mount more realistic programs to serve the needs of the gang members and of society at one and the same time.

Police Relationships with Gangs

It must be recognized that no organization can hope to eliminate gangs completely, but the following police approaches can be helpful in minimizing gang problems:

1. Maintain firm but fair relationships with gang members to avoid giving them a reason to hate police more than they already do.
2. Keep detailed files on gangs, listing known members, leaders, nicknames, areas they consider their "turf," descriptions of jackets or insignias, special characteristics, and so forth.
3. Operate a good intelligence system to alert the department regarding pending "rumbles" or other planned unlawful conduct and have organized plans to intervene.
4. Some large departments have found it more expedient to organize special gang details to assume major responsibility for work with gangs.
5. Maintain cooperative relationships with detached workers (street workers) or other agency specialists dealing with gangs.

Written policies describing respective roles can help to build constructive relationships as can periodic meetings for discussion of mutual problems.

REFERENCES

1. Kobetz, Richard W.: Juvenile vandalism: The billion dollar prank. *The Police Chief*, June, 1973.
2. Klein, Malcolm W.: *Street Gangs and Street Workers*. Englewood Cliffs, N.J., Prentice-Hall Inc., 1971. The material used appeared in POLICE WORK WITH JUVENILES AND THE ADMINISTRATION OF JUSTICE, 4th Edition, 1970, with permission of the author, referenced as follows: Klein, Malcolm W.: Juvenile Gangs: Facts, Fiction, and New Directions. –In Process. See also Klein, Malcolm W.: Juvenile gangs, police and detached workers; Controversies about intervention. The Social Service Review, 39 (No. 2), June 1965.

Chapter 8

POLICIES AND THE EXERCISE
OF DISCRETION

THE responsibility for maintenance of order in society rests with the federal, state, and local police agencies. These agencies have been created by statute with the exception of the office of the county sheriff, which in most states is a constitutional office. The agencies have the powers and duties conferred upon them by law. Although much of the substance of statutes comes from the common law, the authority of the agencies is not changed.

Since most police work with juveniles is performed by municipal and county police agencies, the authority for the agency's operation emanates from delegated powers by the state. Practically all laws referring to juveniles are state laws; thus, the local police agencies are governed by legislative policy guidelines laid down by the state government.

There is no comprehensive code for the police handling of juveniles, thus police agencies have established their own practices by the evolution of custom. The practices vary considerably from jurisdiction to jurisdiction, but through the years a more standardized approach to police work with juveniles has emerged. The primary emphasis is to prevent crime and to create an environment in which orderly living may proceed. Acting as agents of the people, the police are responsible for assuring people that they can go about the ordinary way of living without disruption. In order to do this, it is important that they create the impression of "omnipresence" in order to eliminate opportunities for commission of crime and to reduce the desire on the part of persons who may be inclined to commit violations of the law or customs in the community. Police help people in trouble and, being the principal governmental agency available for twenty-four-hour service, answer emergency calls for help, and aid people in the normal routine of their work. They also help other governmental agencies in the performance of service to the public.

As agents of the people, the police are entitled to the full support of the public they serve. Excessive demands should not be made of them, nor should they be expected to provide services that may normally be better provided through other means or other agencies. The public should expect the police to treat all people equally and with fairness. Situations that compromise the effectiveness of the police operation should not be permitted.

The coalescing of the legal requirements, the wishes, and demands of the public and the evolved administration and governing body's prescriptions for activities provide the basis for the policies governing a police department. Policies manifest or clarify philosophies, values, objectives, goals, and ideals for the department and in essence are the rules for action. Such rules as are established for the purpose of framing, guiding, or directing the department's activities, including decision making, intend to provide stability, consistency, uniformity, and continuity in operations. Policy is one and at the same time both flexible and stable, and dynamic and static, and is the result of an equilibrium of many forces and originates as much in agreement as in command. Policies become formalized when they are written and officially approved and are then a firm commitment. Unwritten policies exist but by their very nature leave fuzzy direction for courses of action.

Formulation and formalizing of policy is at best a "muddling through" process, since it is impossible for man to separate his environment, emotions, values, and personality from facts and empirical data. However, police departments are experiencing an increasing need to face the issue and prepare policy guidelines. The increasing complexity of society, and its attendant demands upon the police, calls for clarification of the "rules of the game" to protect and guide the police in their operations and the public in their expectations.

A particular need is for guidelines to assist the officer in his decision-making role for the exercise of discretionary judgment in dealing with people. Decisions to arrest or not to arrest an individual who has violated a law involves a considerable element of personal judgment on the part of an officer. On the one hand an officer is guided in his activities by organizational policies, and on the other hand in fulfilling his functions as a peace officer he is solely responsible for his decisions with respect to the enforcement of laws. The development of guidelines for the exercise of discretion is a function of not only the department but the legislature and the courts.

THE EXERCISE OF DISCRETION

Most professionals agree that police officers possess the widest discretion in the criminal justice system. The police officer decides, for the most part, who will be brought into the formal system and for which violation of the law. Few would argue that law enforcement should enforce every law violation or take every offender into custody. Nevertheless, if labeling is to become a factor, if diversion is to occur, if the youth is to be referred to court for formal processing, the process will commence with law enforcement.

Despite the importance of law enforcement in initiating formal action against juveniles, the decision to take them into custody is a complex one. The nature of the offense is important. If the offense is relatively minor the officer may decide the value of taking the child into custody would be less than to provide a warning or a "lecture and release." To some extent the officer considers the likelihood that such an offense will result in referral to juvenile court. However, the juvenile may be either well-known to law enforcement, or this may be the first contact. Presumably, this information will be known to the field officer. For this to occur, however, field officers need the support of a good records system and accurate and timely information support. Naturally, if offender information is available, the field officer may then consider whatever prior behavior the youth has exhibited. Thus, the officer may now consider both the severity of the offense and the repetitive behavior of the youth. Finally, the officer must be well versed in the laws of arrest and, in particular, in the rules of search and seizure. Decisional law, by implication, has extended to juveniles the same rights of search and seizure as to adults. *Miranda* rights, particularly with respect to remaining silent, may be even more strict. Taking a confession from a juvenile in the absence of an adult will be perilous at best.

Perhaps as important as the structural factors or severity of offense, prior behavior of offender, and the statutory and case law is the behavioral aspect. In some respects the "law of the situation" is as potentially determinative as the events preceding the decision to take into custody unfold. More specifically, the exhibited behavior of the suspect, and perhaps co-suspects, the actions of witnesses, and perhaps bystanders, as well as the behavior of the field officer and partner may be critical. Today's juvenile, often unlike his predecessors, may be more defiant of public authority, more indignant at the "stop and frisk," more rebellious if already known to law enforcement, and more willing to question what appears to be selective law enforcement. Today's police officer, while certainly familiar with societal conflict, may view hostile behavior as pathological behavior, may be concerned at the increased possession of weapons, and may feel that removal of the youth or youths from the scene is warranted by the escalation of the crime scene even if the evidence has yet to be dispassionately sorted out. Should the suspect(s) resist arrest, the police officer will undoubtedly take the youths into custody, bearing in mind the potential for additional, possibly even deadly, force erupting. Often the amount of time to sort out all of these factors is short. The field officer has the reponsibilty for reaching crucial decisions that may well be reviewed, second-guessed, and evaluated at a later time by persons removed from the scene. Obviously, the preparation and training of the field officer is essential.

Certain parts of a particular city or county may receive what appears to be "aggressive patrolling" in view of high incidences of crimes for those areas. While such concentration of manpower may seem justified and even called for by local citizens, the probability of stopping juvenile suspects at a higher rate than in other locales may occur. Certain citizens may view this higher propensity for stopping "their" youth as discriminatory, inconsistent, and perhaps unequal protection. Law enforcement must weigh such a policy against the obvious dictates of constitutional protections. Field officers, in such instances, often steer a delicate path through stopping for probable cause and stopping for investigation. This particular aspect of stopping suspects has often aroused certain groups in the population and, in certain instances, has created a continuing hostility toward the presence of law enforcement in a particular locality. Other citizens, however, may interpret such a charge of bias as an insensitivity to the problems within that community. These citizens may then charge law enforcement with a *failure* to enforce the law when citizen reports receive minimal or no law enforcement response. Accordingly, law enforcement carries a heavy burden in such communities of responding to a high volume of citizen complaints, usually with limited manpower, while allocating most of its energies to crime control in a portion of the city suspicious of the priorities assigned by the department. Thus, the combination of those who claim insensitivity toward the victims may coalesce with those alleging insensitivity toward the defendants creating special problems for the police handling of juveniles.

For a number of years police departments ameliorated the "law of the situation" by creating juvenile units to which juveniles were referred for formal processing. The juvenile bureau was designed to provide consistency in filing a formal complaint against juveniles without becoming directly involved in street events leading to the arrest. Presumably the juvenile unit officer would exercise dispassionate judgment within the confines of the police station and removed from the emotion of the street. In addition, the juvenile unit had prior contact records as well as court information depending upon the police-juvenile court system of information exchange. In this model of juvenile operations the field officer would relinquish some judgment to the juvenile unit, thus being less certain, *in the field*, of the probable outcome of taking the youth into custody. Nevertheless, the juvenile unit depended upon field officers to make "good arrests," and, to the extent that consistency varied in view of the large number of patrol officers, juvenile units turned their attention to formulating rules and procedures for the guidance of field officers. Naturally, investigations were also the responsibility of the juvenile officer, which, it was presumed, followed from attempting to standardize the handling of juveniles. Thus, whatever enthusiasm a field officer might have for making a "good arrest" of a juvenile might be tempered by the subsequent presentation of facts to the juvenile officer, who might elect to lecture and release the youth. Similarly, the field officer, after awaiting the booking decision, may then be required to transport the youth to the nearest juvenile hall. Depending upon the distance, the field officer and partner may be absent from patrol for a minimum of two hours. While such a process was designed for efficiency, the field officer may react in horror once he is cognizant of apprehending a juvenile. He may lament the greater discretion existing in apprehending an adult. Nevertheless, where juvenile units exist, one finds many dedicated police officers whose attempts to interpret the changing case law provide essential links to the field officers attempting to *implement* the law carefully, but confidently.

It should be borne in mind that the juvenile unit performs an additional function, possibly exceeding anyone's earlier expectations. By removing the alleged offender from the street, and, in many cases, by summoning the youth's parents or responsible adults to the station, the juvenile officer on duty consistently performs a level of social work of amazing quality. In many instances the conflict between the juvenile and society has been played out on numerous occasions at home. The juvenile officer finds some satisfaction in his ability to initiate dialogue between parent and child in which each may derive some support that had been consistently lacking. Often, parents have a misguided view of the responsibility of law enforcement to "correct" the behavior of an errant son or daughter. Just as often, a juvenile will fail to accept the pleadings of a parent who seemingly "mistrusts" or "doubts" the veracity of the youth. An experienced juvenile officer often becomes expert, perhaps in a nontherapeutic way, in creating a communications flow between adult and child that may, at the very least, ameliorate the immediate symptomatic behavior. This opportunity for police "social work" may be challenged by many while still providing a practical, if somewhat unorthodox, tool in the police handling of juveniles. To some extent, juvenile units have adopted this function in the absence of alternative resources and perhaps, in frustration at the futility in referring juveniles for formal processing when a sea of more serious offenders stands in line for court hearings.

With the unfolding of state propositions limiting government income and spending, police departments have experienced tightened budgets causing unfilled vacancies in an era of rising costs. As departments have been unable to fill vacancies, the mere staffing of patrol assignments has created pressure on manpower not previously assigned to patrol. During this period, departments have questioned the advisability of maintaining special juvenile units at the expense of depleted patrol divisons. Forced to choose between maintaining a separate juvenile investigations unit and combining this unit with adult investigators organized by crime, such as burglary, homicide, vice and narcotics and robbery, departments are reluctantly yielding their juvenile officers to either patrol or a combined juvenile and adult investigations unit. Naturally, this strategy receives warm approval from city and county budget officers who applaud the apparent economies of scale. No one knows for certain, however, what the *system* loss might be. What impact will the reassignment of juvenile officers have upon the quantity and quality of crime prevention? We do not know this, so we centralize, using fewer officers while maintaining patrol levels in the face of increased juvenile crime.

Variety of Police Responses

Law enforcement has certain options in responding to an alleged juvenile offender. It may utilize a *citation, summons*, or an *order* to take a youth into custody. As manpower pressures mount, however, and juvenile units are disbanded, substantial energy will be addressed toward those juveniles for whom probable cause exists. While the 1970s experienced substantial interest in *diversion*, law enforcement has become somewhat suspect of this strategy in the absence of a viable, consistent, productive diversion agency. In fact, such diversion agencies are suffering similar budget constraints at a time when law enforcement has grown somewhat weary of inconsistent and apparent unproductive diversion programs. Faced with substantial numbers of serious offenders and lacking, in many cases, a viable juvenile unit, departments have either reduced their diversion activities or established in-house diversion programs, which may amount to mini-preprobation programs. If an offender avoids further law violations the diversion officer will have achieved an apparent "success." Some departments have added a civilian or non-peace officer to sort out these cases and maintain a law enforcement diversion program. While national standards have cautioned against this approach, law enforcement has increasingly done so in frustration, rationalizing that such activity may represent a "last ditch" attempt at routing less violent offenders away from further penetration into the criminal justice system. While law enforcement counselors may be viewed by some as an anomaly, there seems little patience remaining for further experimentation with outside programs that continue to experience funding hardships and, in some cases, estranged relationships with law enforcement. Increased emphasis on due process requirements causes such in-house programs to be viewed by reformers as extralegal proceedings and which have no place in the criminal justice system. As juvenile units disband, the future of in-house diversion programs may be subjected to continuing scrutiny not only by outsiders, but by department planners and administrators. The increasing transformation of juvenile matters to the adult criminal court model promises to narrow the experimental options of juvenile specialists and reconstruct the treatment of juveniles toward the due process model.

Crime control may well take its toll on delinquency prevention as the community and public officials urge greater efforts toward detection, apprehension, and prosecution of serious juvenile offenders. The early intervention approach may well yield to the formal sanction, which is most likely to occur at such time as the offender seems unable or unlikely to benefit from warning, in-house diversion, or lecture and release. Naturally, among departments these responses will vary substantially. Offenders in major metropolitan areas will mount the greatest challenge for formal processing. Perhaps only smaller departments will retain the strategy of community programming in the hopes that such efforts will deter further penetration of the system. With increasing juvenile gang activity, particularly in metropolitan areas, law enforcement seems more and more concerned with strategies that may interrupt, deter, and interdict entire patterns of crime and groups of offenders while enjoying fewer resources with which to deal with the individual offender. In fact, the greatest challenge of the 1980s may be to what extent other components of the criminal justice system, as well as other public components such as the schools, social serving agencies, and the public, may need to assist law enforcement in mounting a stronger system approach to the prevention and reduction of crime. Crime control, it would seem, has focused the attention of law enforcement in such a way that it drains much of its energy, manpower, and available funding.

Circumscribing Discretion

Since there exists much more latitude for the exercise of discretion by the police with juveniles than for adults, assurance must be provided that the rights of all persons irrespective of age must be protected. As discussed in Chapter 3, court decisions and legislation have substantially narrowed the gap between what *may* happen to juveniles and what *must* happen to adults. This calls for the juvenile court to formally recognize and clarify its expectations of the police. Likewise, police administrators should formally develop guidelines covering the exercise of discretion by all officers investigating cases involving juveniles.

A General Philosophy*

To be effective, policies should be developed within a framework of a general philosophy for the department. The lack of a general philosophy formally expressed as a mission statement to guide both routine and planned-change activities probably contributes most to the ambivalence in the administration of the police function. This means that most departments have not addressed the reason for their being, nor the principles essential for the conduct of the organization. Policies that are made or perceived to exist are often in conflict with performance. For example, a police executive may be committed to a strong crime and delinquency prevention posture for the department when in fact law enforcement is the major emphasis. Policies that are made are oriented toward crime control and deficient in a crime and delinquency orientation because they lack a philosophical construct in which to fit them, thus policy conflict is evident.

A general philosophy is particularly significant for the introduction of change or innovation, because the police executive must have a clear perspective of what he desires and why before he can effectively communicate the rationale to his employees. If employees lack understanding, their support and enthusiasm can be significantly impaired. A general philosophy is also necessary to assess the impact of change on the total organization and to prevent conflict. For example, increased emphasis on community service planning and

---

*Louis A Mayo, "Innovation Factors in the Role of the Police Chief Executive." Unpublished doctoral dissertation, The American University, Washington, D.C., 1981.

citizen involvement is in direct conflict with a performance evaluation system that emphasizes arrest productivity.

Preparation of a mission statement and policies is best achieved if
there is participation of a representative cross section of citizens in
the process. This is important to assure that the departmental operation reflects the policing needs and expectations of the citizens, as
well as the legal requirements. In order to assist a department in the
formulation of its mission and policy statements, considerable attention has been given by the authors in selecting guidelines. It is a
difficult and time-consuming process, and regular reviews and up-
dating should take place.

Preparation of a mission statement involves the articulation of
key concepts that set forth the desired role and functions of the police
department in the community. The principal concepts that need to
be addressed include crime control, crime prevention, service,
humane treatment, protection of individual rights, security, law enforcement, and protection of property and persons. In essence, the
mission statement articulates the goals for the department, which
are values to be achieved.

A general goal that a department may adopt could be Achievement of Excellence in the Maintenance of Ordered Liberty. This
goal reflects quality of service desired and incorporates the concepts
of order and liberty which are important values in our democratic
society.

GENERAL POLICIES

General policies that may be adopted serve to operationalize the
mission and goal statements. They circumscribe in definitive terms
the role and responsibilities of the police and set forth for the citizens
of the city and the personnel of the department what it is the police
shall do and what the citizens may expect. Some general policy
statements follow:

1. The police shall enforce in a reasonable and prudent manner
   all federal, state, and local laws and ordinances relating to the
   control of crime and regulation of conduct.
2. The police shall treat all persons with dignity and respect and
   in accordance with the dictates of the federal and state constitutions, amplified by judicial decisions as related to in-

dividual civil liberties and civil rights.

3. The police shall take such action as may be necessary and operate in such a manner as to assure the citizens of the city that orderly activities of the community may proceed without disruption from criminal and irresponsible elements.

4. The efforts of the police department shall be so directed as to help in the creation of an environment in the community that will prevent the occurrence of asocial and antisocial behavior.

5. The police shall be responsible for the protection of life and property from criminal attack and in emergency situations when the welfare of the community is threatened.

6. The police shall cooperate with and assist citizens of the community and units of the city, county, state, and federal government with such problems in such situations as customs and traditions dictate, in matters of both criminal and noncriminal natures.

7. The police shall treat all persons equally and with fairness, irrespective of race, ethnic group, creed, or societal status.

Specific Guidelines

More specifically, the following outline sets forth the characteristics and guidelines for operations.

I. Field Operations
  A. Patrol
    1. Purposes
      a. To control crime
      b. To eliminate actual or suspected opportunity for wrongdoing
      c. To regulate conduct
      d. To create an environment of security and stability in the community
      e. To provide services
      f. To prevent crime
    2. Activities
      a. Roving surveillance
      b. Called-for services
      c. Inspections

3. Guidelines
   a.' The patrol personnel shall act as eyes and ears for the police administrator.
   b. The patrol personnel shall maintain continuous and conspicuous operation.
   c. The patrol personnel shall constantly be available to supply complete area coverage for accomplishment of the police purpose and to perform such tasks so as to perpetuate this purpose. This means appropriate action when crime is committed in the presence of the officer and the appropriate processing of all requests for services, whether criminal or noncriminal.
   d. The patrol personnel shall be responsible for all activities in the field, except those that interfere with the performance of regular duties and those that are performed by specialists.
   e. Patrol personnel shall be responsible for complete investigation of all cases, including preservation of evidence and making arrests, except in those cases that interfere with the performance of regular duties and those that require the attention of specialists.
   f. One-officer patrol automobile operation shall be maintained on a twenty-four-hour basis, except as special assignments may require additional personnel strength.
   g. Two or more patrol personnel shall be assigned to answer all calls for service wherein the nature of the situation is not readily ascertainable from the complainant and a danger may exist.
   h. Patrol personnel shall request assistance when making an arrest or inspecting suspicious situations or circumstances.
   i. Inspections shall be regularly made of all business and industrial establishments during hours not regularly occupied.
B. Traffic Control
   1. Purposes
      To keep order on the streets and highways and to make

their use safe and expeditious.
  2. Activities
     a. Enforcement of traffic laws.
     b. Control of the flow of automobile and pedestrian traffic through means of direction.
     c. Investigation of traffic accidents.
     d. Perform such traffic educational and engineering duties as essential for advancing objectives of traffic control programs.
  3. Guidelines
     a. Patrol personnel shall be responsible for enforcement of all moving traffic violations, regulation of the movement of traffic, and investigation of accidents.
     b. Planning for traffic control activities shall be a staff function under the direction of the commander of field operation.
     c. Parking control activities shall be performed by the field operations unit by special assignment.
     d. Field procedures will be so designed as to give the impression of officer "omnipresence" for the purpose of prevention.
     e. The principles of selective enforcement and visible patrol shall prevail.
     f. All injury and fatal traffic accidents shall be investigated.
II. Investigative Functions
  1. Purposes
     a. To make a critical search for truth and information relative to all criminal and noncriminal cases.
     b. To gather facts and data on criminal cases in order to effect their proper dispositions.
  2. Activities
     a. Coordinate the processing of all cases.
     b. Gather and collate information on criminal activities.
     c. Make follow-up or complete investigation of criminal cases.

   d. Apprehend all violators and recover all property.
3. Guidelines
   a. Detectives shall aid and assist patrol officers in making investigations when required.
   b. Detectives shall be responsible for the follow-up investigation of all criminal cases that cannot be completed effectively and efficiently by patrol officers.
   c. Detectives shall have responsibility for the complete investigation of all criminal cases that require technical attention such as frauds, forgeries, and extortions.
   d. The detective unit shall be responsible for gathering and collating information on all criminal activities within the city and for making it available for departmental-wide use.
   e. Detectives shall apprehend offenders and recover property when such is not accomplished by the patrol officer.
   f. Detectives shall assist in the investigation of all complex cases such as safe burglaries, homicides, and forcible rapes.

III. Vice and Substance Control
   1. Purposes
      To enforce laws concerned with the regulation of gambling, narcotics, liquor, and certain illegal sexual activities.
   2. Activities
      a. Gather and collate information on vice activities.
      b. Coordinate the work of the department with other law enforcement agencies responsible for specific aspects of vice control.
      c. Apprehend violators of laws concerning vice activities.
   3. Guidelines
      a. Insofar as is feasible, absolute repression of vice conditions shall prevail.
      b. Every possible effort shall be made toward identifying persons at "higher levels" of vice operations

and in gathering evidence to prove their operations.

   c. All officers shall take action in vice cases coming to their attention.

   d. Procedures shall be established for the disbursement of undercover funds that will assure secrecy and at the same time protect those who disburse funds.

   e. Undercover operators and informants shall be used to gather evidence of vice operations only under carefully controlled conditions in conformance with legal requirements and with the approval of the responsible commanding officer.

   f. Continuous coordination and cooperation shall be maintained with other law enforcement agencies responsible for control of vice conditions.

IV. Juvenile Control and Prevention

  1. Purposes

    a. To aid in the correction of those factors or conditions which predispose or precipitate people's activities to antisocial behavior.

    b. To make appropriate dispositions of juveniles to prevent them from committing future law violations.

  2. Activities

    a. Exercise control over the conduct of juveniles who engage in asocial or antisocial behavior and conditions conducive to such behavior.

    b. Appropriately process juveniles who engage in asocial or antisocial acts for the purpose of preventing recurrence of such behavior.

    c. Coordinate police operations and cooperate with community agencies concerned with the prevention of crime.

    d. Make appropriate police disposition of all individuals known to have committed an unlawful or delinquent act.

    e. Assist the chief of police in the formulation and implementation of overall departmental policy for dealing with juveniles.

    f. Make follow-up investigations on specified types of

cases.

   g. Review all reports dealing with police contacts with juveniles.

3. Guidelines

   a. Juvenile officers shall cooperate and coordinate with community agencies for the purpose of preventing crime and delinquency.

   b. Juvenile officers shall make follow-up investigations of specified cases involving juveniles in which at the time of the complaint a juvenile is presumed to be involved. Cases include bicycle theft, domestic relations cases, and law violations on school properties.

   c. Juvenile officers shall assist officers of other units in the investigation of juveniles involved in cases in order to objectively make appropriate dispositions.

   d. Juvenile officers shall make final disposition of all juveniles apprehended or otherwise involved in cases.

4. Role of Police in Intake and Detention

Each juvenile court jurisdiction immediately should take the leadership in working out with local police agencies policies and procedures governing the discretionary diversion authority of police officers and separating police officers from the detention decision in dealing with juveniles.

   a. Police agencies should establish written guidelines to support police discretionary authority, at the point of first contact as well as at the police station, to divert juveniles to alternative community-based programs and human resource agencies outside the juvenile justice system, when the safety of the community is not jeopardized. Disposition may include (a) release on the basis of unfounded charges, (b) referral to parents (warning and release), (c) referral to social agencies, (d) referral to juvenile court intake services.

   b. Police should not have discretionary authority to make detention decisions. This responsibility rests with the court, which should assume control over admissions on a twenty-four-hour basis.

When police have taken custody of a minor, and prior to disposition under paragraph (b) above, the following guidelines should be observed.

(1) Under the provisions of *Gault* and *Miranda*, police should first warn juveniles of their right to counsel and the right to remain silent while under custodial questioning

(2) The second act after apprehending a minor should be the notification of his parents.

(3) Extrajudicial statements to police or court officers not made in the presence of parents or counsel should be inadmissible in court.

(4) Juveniles should normally not be fingerprinted or photographed or otherwise routed through the usual adult booking process.

(5) Juvenile records should be maintained physically separate from adult case records.

V. Sustaining Functions
   1. Purposes
     To facilitate operations of the program activities.
   2. Activities
     a. Records
     b. Communications
     c. Custody
     d. Laboratory services
     e. Maintenance of equipment and facilities
     f. Identification
   3. Guidelines
     a. Records and communications activities shall be integrated and centralized physically and functionally.
     b. Records of all police actions taken shall be made.
     c. Records shall serve to control offense classification and completeness of investigation.
     d. Records shall be available and shall be used to aid in all police operations.
     e. Use of records by departmental personnel shall be controlled to avoid damage to records.
     f. Only bona fide agencies or persons other than de-

partmental personnel shall have access to departmental records for reference purposes.

g. Prompt and efficient processing of all calls to the
department shall be made.

h. All persons in custody shall be treated fairly and
humanely.

i. Facilities and equipment shall be maintained in good
order at all times.

j. Criminalistics work for the department shall be performed by a competent criminalistic laboratory, with
the department performing only diagnostic preliminary laboratory processing.

k. All adults arrested and detained shall be photographed and fingerprinted.

VI. Administrative Functions

1. Purposes
To provide for effective administration, management,
and organization of the department.

2. Activities
a. Policy making
b. Direction
c. Planning
d. Personnel management
e. Budget
f. Public relations
g. Supply

3. Guidelines
a. All policies shall be consonant with achievement of
the objectives of the department.
b. Direction of the department shall be for the purpose
of achievement of maximum coordination and control.
c. Planning shall be carried on for the purpose of coping
effectively with tactical and strategic problems.
d. The department shall endeavor to obtain the highest
caliber of personnel possible.
e. Insofar as is feasible, a performance budgeting program shall be maintained.
f. The highest quality supplies and equipment shall be
obtained consonant with the needs of the department.

External Factors Affecting Policy Decisions

State laws place major responsiblity for the rehabilitation and treatment of delinquent youth upon the courts and probation departments. The laws and policies governing these agencies must be carefully understood before deciding upon the entrance of the police agency into any kind of adjustment or treatment program. Such activities by the police department are, in a great measure, delegated by the probation department and the juvenile court. Furthermore, the juvenile court and the probation department are often given the responsibility by law for initiation of delinquency prevention programs. It is therefore important that the police department gear its prevention activities to those of the juvenile court and probation department.

Services provided for youth by other community agencies should be carefully scrutinized by the police department before embarking upon any comprehensive crime prevention or juvenile control program. It is incumbent upon the schools to provide education and training for youth, the churches to give spiritual guidance, and the group work agencies and recreation departments to provide leisure-time activities. The police department must be co-partners with these agencies in the development of a comprehensive delinquency prevention program. Those agencies' programs should not be overlooked in establishing departmental policies. There have been occasions when police departments have had to lead the way in developing such services, but once established, it behooves the police department to shift such responsibilities to the proper agencies whenever possible, thus avoiding criticism by suggesting that the department is busying itself with expensive sidelines.

All public and private social agencies are important to the success of a police department's work with youth. For the purpose of referral, a thorough knowledge of the services provided by these agencies should be known to the police. Departmental activities, if any, in the field of rehabilitation and adjustment should be predicated on what these agencies are able to provide in the way of services.

In any community there are certain political pressures that the department must endure. These political pressures should not be allowed to interfere with successful prosecution of the comprehensive deliquency prevention and juvenile control program. Assignment of personnel should be on the basis of merit rather than on the basis of political pressure. Programs undertaken should conform to the needs of the community rather than pressures exerted for ulterior reasons.

Community groups interested in the police work with juveniles are invaluable to the success of the work. They are able to assist a chief of police in the development of worthwhile prevention programs and, in many instances, can aid in the creation of a juvenile unit and in staffing it properly. Occasionally, a community group may be misinformed as to the function and purpose of a juvenile unit. Such groups may pressure for an unusual type of juvenile program, such as participation of lay persons in the making of dispositions, or for assignment of more officers to the unit than are needed. To avoid illogical pressures, a department should take positive steps to assure understanding of departmental problems by the public and community groups leading to support of proper policies and programs.

Chapter 9

THE POLICE ROLE AND FUNCTIONS

POLICE work with juveniles is a function of the institutionalized role of the police in our modern democratic society. Although that role is not clearly defined, nor easily understood, there are a number of characteristics that stand out. Generally, law enforcement is emphasized by both the police and the public they serve. The police are independent of the court system and are heavily involved in the performance of social service and social welfare functions. In addition, the police are involved in the broad functions of keeping the peace, crime prevention, aiding in the creation of an environment of security and stability, and the *protection of the innocent and civil liberties*, as well as apprehension of the guilty. Society is concerned that the processes of living should proceed with a minimum of disruption and, to this end, it has given the police a major responsibility for the maintenance of ordered liberty.

Performance of the law enforcement function is an enigma in our society. On the one hand it relates to reported offenses and their investigation, and identified offenders and their release without arrest, or the invocation of the arrest process that inputs offenders into the criminal or juvenile justice processes.

By the exercise of discretion in accepting and formally processing a reported offense, the police determine the volume of crime and delinquency. And by the exercise of discretion the police determine whether an offender will be arrested and inputted into the criminal justice processes, arrested and released without official judicial action, arrested and referred to a nonjudicial or noncorrectional agency for processing, or released outright without any formal action other than the temporary detaining of the offender either in the field or in the police station.

By the exercise of discretion the police are in the awesome position of determining the parameters of crime and criminality in our society; yes, in our communities.[2] By virtue of this discretionary decision making position, the police are not really bound by the rule of law.

Related to the law enforcement function is that of the keeping of the peace. Much police work has to do with the resolution of problem situations between individuals and the maintenance of orderly relationships between individuals and groups. Often, offenses occur, but the police see fit to ignore the offense in the interest of justice and peace such as in family disturbances. Or offenses may be a potential but are not committed due to the presence of the police, such as at athletic events, parades, and other gatherings of crowds. The invocation of the law enforcement processes are always feasible.

A concomitant of the law enforcement and the peacekeeping functions is the exercise of force by the police. In fact, a *raison d'etre* for police is to legitimitize the use of responsive force.[1] The use of force or the threat of its use is intimately involved in the invocation of the arrest process and the keeping of the peace.

Egon Bittner suggests that "...the role of the police is best understood as a mechanism for the distribution of nonnegotiable coercive force employed in accordance with the dictates of an intuitive grasp of situational exigencies...." He made this statement based on observations of what the public seems to expect of the police. In essence it describes the range of activities that the police actually engage in and the theme that actually unifies all of the activities. By "nonnegotiably coercive" he posits a situation when a police officer decides that force is necessary, then, within the boundaries of the situation, the officer is not accountable to anyone, nor is he required to brook the arguments or opposition of anyone who might object to it. He sets this position forth not as a legal but as a practical rule.[1]

Since the police as an institution are independent of the courts, the judiciary cannot exercise a "superior" control over the actions of the police. The courts may and have provided definitive guidelines for police procedures in the investigation of offenses and the processing of offenders, and the police normally comply. However, the principal sanction that the courts have over the police is their refusal to permit prosecution or the hearing of a case, thereby "embarrassing" the police for their improper or incomplete actions. The police provide the principal flow of business for the criminal and the juvenile courts; thus, the relationship is one of interdependence and maintenance of mutual respect, or the administration of justice falters badly.[1] As a matter of fact, the *distance* maintained between the courts and the police pose a major threat to the administration of criminal and juvenile justice in the United States.

The social service and social welfare functions of the police have persistently been ignored or at best tolerated as legitimate functions of the police. However, as early as the first quarter of the twentieth century, the late August Vollmer as chief of police of Berkeley, California, posited that the police officer in the field was a criminologist, and that the police department is a "social agency" with a responsibility for resolving social situations at the community level. In fact, he went so far as to employ a trained social worker in 1928 to head the department's juvenile program. These functions are gaining credence as more social scientists address the subject of police work and diversion and other social welfare oriented programs are being initiated and accepted by police agencies.

The crime prevention role of the police is still clouded by lack of definition and understanding of program content and orientation. The subject is often confused with crime repression, which refers to short-term efforts to reduce specific crimes or crime in general in a specific area. Actually, the police have two concerns: first, there is the prevention of crime and secondly the prevention of criminality. It seems to follow that prevention of crime results from long-term efforts of the police in all activities oriented toward crime repression and crime control. Prevention of criminality is one of a community effort, with the police working closely with the judiciary and correctional agencies in rehabilitation and treatment programs and with community agencies in efforts to redirect individuals' efforts and activities away from criminal and delinquent behavior.

A secure and stable environment is much sought after by most people. The flight from the inner city to suburbia in a large part reflects a desire for such on the part of many people. The elderly are extremely concerned about the neighborhood in which they live. Businesses and industries seek out stable communities, and more and more "closed" developments, fenced or walled in with guards at a gate, are appearing. The police are becoming increasingly involved with efforts oriented toward the creation of secure and stable environments. Examples include a major industry that moved into a large city only after it was assured that the city would improve its police department as a means of creating a more desirable environment in which its people could live and work. And there is the case of the purse snatching from an elderly lady in a section of a large city in which many elderly persons lived. The clamor was such that the department had to saturate the area with police officers for an extended period of time, although the chances of a repeat offense were deemed rather remote.

There are no more important responsibilities of the police than the protection of civil liberties and the innocent. Individuals are frequently falsely accused of offenses, either maliciously or by mistaken identification, and occasionally are found guilty. Police investigations should always be thorough and complete in order to minimize such possibilities. Similarly, the protection of civil liberties, such as the right to freedom of speech, often involves the police. The police may not agree with the Communist or the Fascist speaking in the public park but are obligated to assure the individuals their right to speak even though the speaker and what he is saying may be anathema to the officers.

In summary, the role of the police in our modern democratic society revolves around the maintenance of ordered liberty. Society is concerned that the processes of living may go forward with a minimum of disruption and thus has given the police the responsibility for dealing with disruptive persons — persons whose behavior pose threats to the welfare, the property, and physical well-being of the members of society. In addition, the police are responsible for protecting the freedom and civil rights of individuals insofar as may be feasible.

Maintenance of order is achieved by police undertaking the two major sets of activities. The first are those activities that are coercive in nature. They include enforcement of criminal, traffic, juvenile, and regulatory laws, the keeping of the peace, and intelligence gathering. Secondly are those activities which are noncoercive in nature. They include social service, crime prevention, establishment of an environment of security and stability, and provision of service and protection of personal liberties and civil rights.

COERCIVE ACTIVITIES

Performance of the law enforcement functions is focused principally on the offense of law violation. In the majority of cases the police do not know whether an adult or juvenile may be involved; thus police activities are the same in all cases up to the point where an arrest has been made or an individual is taken into custody. With respect to juveniles, the difference comes when a juvenile is taken into custody. However, from a practical standpoint the police take the same action against a juvenile as they do against an adult. It is the action that follows the taking into custody that differs. Furthermore, the police are more prone to exercise their discretionary authority with juveniles than with adults. If there is a reasonable alternative to enforcement, that alternative will more usually be chosen. The younger the juvenile the more likely enforcement action will not be taken.

Keeping of the peace covers a broad category of activities, many of which could result in enforcement action, but usually do not. The family fight, the noisy party, young people congregated on street corners, and the barroom brawl are examples in which keeping of the peace is more important than enforcing the law. Also, police presence is usually required at certain kinds of social gatherings, primarily for the purpose of maintaining order. A considerable amount of such activities involve juveniles.

With respect to intelligence gathering, the police are concerned with organized criminal activity, subversive plotting, and potential criminal or antisocial behavior. The purpose of the police activity is to be forewarned of potential trouble.

NONCOERCIVE ACTIVITIES

The time has come for the police to formally recognize that they perform a social service function. Society is becoming increasingly welfare-oriented, and the police are becoming increasingly involved in human relations. Increasing demands are being made of the police to get involved in community affairs, and there is an increased emphasis on police work with juveniles to avoid referral to the juvenile court and to refer more cases to social agencies within the community.

Although the police do not perform social casework, nor do they engage in welfare activities in the traditional sense, they do counsel and advise people and, in particular, juveniles. They often counsel juveniles and their parents and deal with school counselors, religious leaders, and social workers; they work closely with community agencies, such as coordinating councils, schools, churches, civic groups, youth agencies, and other community organizations, for the purpose of reducing delinquent behavior and creating a healthy community environment. Without such activities on the part of the police the criminal justice system could become overwhelmed and the work of many community agencies less effective. Furthermore, common sense dictates that justice can be better served short of invocation of the arrest or taking into custody processes.

It is within the performance of the service function that the police direct much of their attention toward juveniles. Patrol officers in the field as well as the juvenile officers devote much time in counseling and guidance, interviewing, and the making of dispositions short of enforcement action. In addition, both groups of officers are increasingly involved in community activities. The uniformed officers meet with youths at schools, on playgrounds, and in gang and other group settings supplemental to the traditional work of the juvenile officers in meeting with community groups.

Crime prevention has long been considered a principal function of the police. Traditionally, police crime prevention activities have been focused on police work with juveniles and in some mystic fashion directed toward eliminating a desire to commit crime. Neither seem to satisfactorily explain the crime prevention function. More realistically, the crime prevention function encompasses the dispositions of individuals made by the police, with every disposition decision theoretically having as its objective prevention of the individuals from committing future offenses. Secondly, all field activities and relations with people are on a long-term basis pointed toward creation of an environment in the community that in essence *prevents* people from committing crimes. (Short-term objectives are to *deter* people from committing crimes.) These two general functions of crime prevention are not inconsistent with traditional police work with juveniles or for that matter with adults. They simply and more precisely describe what the police are doing and provide a reasonable theoretical rationale for the work.

With respect to disposition decisions the police have the alternative in most cases to invoke or not to invoke the arrest or taking into custody processes. The presumption is that in the exercise of discretion the police do what is best for the individual and society, and for the individual the theoretical expectation is that he will not commit further offenses. This applies whether the disposition results in "curbstone" counseling or the taking into custody with subsequent imposition of an institutional sentence by the court.

Establishment of an environment of security and stability serves the function of minimizing threats of disruption and disorder and providing people with a feeling of security that their homes and persons will not be threatened by criminal attack. This is accomplished by uniformed patrol and general police activity, which instills a sense of security in people's minds.

The police also provide a multitude of other services, including the delivering of babies, escorting monies, aiding the sick, the hungry and the disturbed, and finding lost children and recovering lost property. Basically, such services are provided because the police for the most part are the one single governmental agency available at all times to provide such services. Provision of such services may or may not be directly related to maintenance of order, but they often are. In many situations if the service is not provided, trouble and misbehavior on the part of the concerned people results. Also, the concerned people may be exposed to criminal attacks if they are not helped, or for example, the initial presumption in the cases of lost children must of necessity be that they may be victims of criminal attack. How much and how far the police go in performance of the service function depends on the community requirements and availability of other agencies to perform some of the services.

The police perform no more important function than that of protecting personal liberties and civil rights. A major concern of the police must be that individuals are not falsely accused of crimes and that when they are suspects in criminal cases that their constitutional and legal rights are protected. Likewise, the rights of free assembly and free speech must be protected. Conflicts often occur when individuals and groups disagree, and the police are often asked to intervene. Often there has been no overt violation of law and, when there is, it is often better to resolve the situation without invocation of the arrest or taking into custody processes. Such protection applies equally to both juveniles and adults.

ROLE WITH JUVENILES

The police have an important contribution to make to the welfare of youth. They are in a strategic position to discover many youths who are actually or potentially delinquent and to see conditions in the community likely to promote delinquency long before other agencies have knowledge either of the children or the conditions. The way the police use this knowledge in their contacts with children and in their relations with the rest of the community may help to determine the future attitude of young people toward the law.

Their knowledge, or lack of knowledge, of the community's social resources and how to use them may afford or deny some children the opportunity or impetus necessary for wholesome development. The alertness with which they recognize promiscuous activities and demoralizing influences in streets, parks, bus stations, dance halls, skating rinks, motion picture houses, hotels, nightclubs, restaurants, and taverns, and the vigor with which they enforce the laws and regulations provided for dealing with them plays an important part in determining whether the community is a good one in which to bring up children.

Work with delinquents and children in danger of becoming delinquent should be based on understanding of motivations and social situations. There is no single answer to what the determining factors are, and there is consequently no single approach that works with all boys and girls. The only common element in all good work is the police officer's clear realization that he is acting as an officer of the law (that is, with authority) and that as the law's representative it is his duty in a democracy to treat every citizen, child as well as adult, with consideration and respect. Over and above this, he must use his judgment case by case in deciding how he can represent law and authority and yet avoid actions such as shaming or intimidating that will cause any vigorous youth to rebel further.

The police have been given a major responsibility in working with youth. They are in the unique position of dealing with most boys and girls whose behavior is in direct conflict with legally required behavior of members of society. The evolution of these responsibilities finds the police concerned with control and prevention of delinquent behavior of juveniles.

The Control Function

The term *control* acknowledges the existence of unlawful behavior and the need to take action. Unlawful behavior of youth includes all types of activity in which laws and ordinances are violated and such other activity that may bring a youth before the juvenile court. Undesirable conditions refer to community hazards and broad community problems harmful to youth.

Control is accomplished in three major ways by the police:

1. Investigation of individual cases involving youth and conditions causing antisocial activities.
2. Providing a constructive disposition for individual cases and conditions through departmental action, diversion to other agencies, or to the juvenile court.
3. Providing overall effective police operations that reduce the opportunity for commission of law violations and maintaining cooperative relations with other components of the juvenile justice system.

The Prevention Function

Prevention implies the keeping of unlawful behavior from occurring originally or keeping unlawful behavior to a minimum and thus avoiding police intervention.

The prevention phase is accomplished by the following:

1. Influencing youth, parents, and the general public to meet the basic needs of youth, to conform to all laws and regulations made for their protection, and to make maximum use of community resources.
2. Participation in community organization planning with other

agencies and citizens to improve the total community.

3. Providing overall effective police operations that contribute to the creation of a community environment that reduces the desire on the part of individuals to commit unlawful acts.

The major portion of this book describes how police and other criminal justice agencies may effectively meet their broad responsibilities to youth. Many of the techniques and methods discussed may be applicable for police working with adults. Crime prevention responsibilities of police agencies are as important in the adult field in accomplishing overall police objectives as for youth. Similarly, utilization of community resources and agencies should not be overlooked in the adult field.

REFERENCES

1. Bittner, Egon: *The Functions of the Police in Modern Society*. Chevy Chase, Md., National Institute of Mental Health, 1970.
2. LaFave, Wayne R.: *Arrest: The Decision to Take a Suspect into Custody*. Boston, Little and Brown, 1965.

Chapter 10

POLICE ADMINISTRATIVE ORGANIZATION

THE changing nature of police organization has introduced a number of new dimensions for consideration in organizing for juvenile control. Operational personnel are becoming increasingly involved in the decision-making process influencing organizational relationships. There has been a recognition that the informal social behavior of personnel substantially influences relationships and modifies formal expected behavior. Functional specialization is being challenged, as is strict adherence to the concepts of hierarchy that emphasizes superior-subordinate relationships and the concepts of organization expressed in the so-called "principles" of organization. The recent melding together of formal and informal concepts of organization has provided a whole new theoretical basis for organization that more realistically describes relationships. The emerging police organization is based more on a team approach.

The continued persistence of the police to maintain the military-bureaucratic form of organization deemphasizes the importance of the one-to-one relationship, policeman-citizen, which generally pertains in police work. The emphasis on rules and regulations, internal controls, obedience to superiors, and all the other "virtues" of a military organization run counter to professionalization of the police service, which by its very nature requires a high degree of the use of professional discretionary methods for crime control and peacekeeping. Adherence to the military-bureaucratic model continues to be of value for police reform in the elimination of political and venal corruption that persists in many departments.

However, continued improvement in personnel standards and adoption of administrative practices that emphasize participative management may achieve internal control without a heavy emphasis on rules and regulations and military style super-subordinate relationships. All this suggests that changes are taking place.

Organization is not something fixed and unchanging. Neither are all organizations the same. Organizations reflect the nature and character of the people in it and their perceptions of the mission, goals and objectives, and operations.

The more traditional approaches to police organization have considerable merit and will continue to be with us for some time. The police are going through a transition period toward adoption of the emerging theories of organization. To accomodate to the transition period both the traditional concepts of police organization and emerging trends will be presented. Both proceed from a determination of departmental policies and functions. Organization for juvenile control is based on these determinations. Since there is such a wide variation in sizes of departments, several approaches will be discussed.

THE TRADITIONAL ORGANIZATION

In very small departments of from one to fifteen personnel, there is little problem in organization. Every officer has to be able to perform almost all police functions, and specialization is usually impracticable. It is desirable where possible for the chief of police to assign responsibility to one officer for coordinating departmental juvenile activities and to devote more time to work with juveniles than to other assignments. The chief himself may assume that responsibility along with his other duties. The latter is common practice in many jurisdictions.

Departments with a personnel of fifteen officers or more can specialize for juvenile control and crime prevention. Assignment of at least one officer for full-time duty is warranted, although that officer may be given additional responsibilities, including traffic safety and specialized adult investigations.

There is no question that a department with fifty or more peace officer personnel should establish a juvenile unit. Work load involving juveniles will have increased to a point where two or more officers will be needed for case investigations, dispositions, prevention endeavors, and coordination with community agencies. The officer in charge of the unit should be of sufficient rank to assure that the unit has a status equal to that of other specialized units of the agency.

Good criteria to follow in the establishment of a separate juvenile unit should be a demonstrated need for more effective utilization of departmental manpower. No other test has meaning. Need may be established in a number of ways, such as the following:

1. Inability of regular investigators to clear cases involving juveniles.
2. Juvenile case processing removes patrolmen from their beats for extended periods of time.
3. Community insistence upon police involvement in non-police youth programs.
4. Desirability of assigning a juvenile officer to present cases in court.
5. The extent to which the department is required to provide social background data to the juvenile court.

Specialization within the juvenile unit should follow a demonstrated need for more effective utilization of manpower. Overspecialization should be avoided. However, if some specialization is deemed necessary, it should follow functional lines. Details or subunits that may be created are as follows, and some may be combined:

Investigation	Traffic Safety/Bicycle
Patrol and Inspections	Detention
Coordination, Disposition and Referral	Special Events
Felony or Adult Investigation	Records

The following are schematic plans for the organization of small- and medium-sized departments. Organization of larger departments follow these basic plans, subfunctions being elevated to divisional and bureau status.

CHART 1

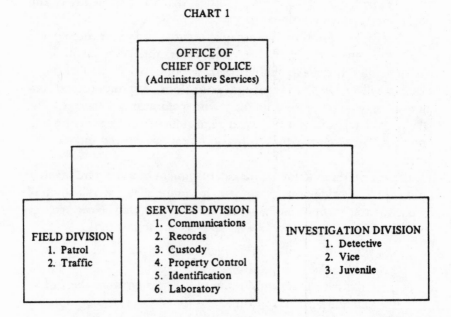

THE EMERGING PATTERNS OF ORGANIZATION

Police organizations are changing. The impact of the human relations approach on organization based upon a recognition of the importance of the socio-psychological behavior of man has modified the traditional approaches. Stringent adherence to the so-called principles of organization emphasizing hierarchy, command, and superior-subordinate relationships no longer reflects the real world of organization. Organization, in fact, is the relationships that exist between members of the agency. The human relations approach has treated the relationships as a reflection of informal organization, that which exists alongside of the formal organization as reflected in the traditional approaches, but influencing operations because it does reflect relationships.

The more recent theories of organization have brought a melding together of formal and informal organization that reflects organization as it really exists. The emphasis is on capitalizing on the capabilities of all personnel in the policy-making and decision-making processes and delegation of major responsibility for operations to the operating level personnel. The command approach to management and supervision is modified by participation of all personnel in the processes.

These changes that are taking place often lead to a more humanistic and understanding approach by police personnel in dealing with all citizens. Since most departments experience turnover in personnel, new employees, which reflect in many respects current community values, infuse these values into the police/decision-making processes, thus bringing about changes in operations and police/citizen relationships. Police/juvenile relationships are often improved, because it is young people who are most often in the forefront of changing societal values.

Team policing introduces a system whereby the field officers who are regularly in touch with juveniles are in a continuous position to influence the policy decision-making processes to reflect current community values and their impact on human behavior. The give and take in the policy/decision-making processes required of management personnel assures recognition of changes taking place. Management by administrative *fiat* no longer pertains.

The team policing model that follows is described in detail because it emphasizes the most advanced means of achieving coordination and cooperation within an organization. It stresses the need to recognize human values as the key to effective operations of an agency. Features of the model may be incorporated into traditional organizations, and the model may serve as an invaluable tool for evaluating key management approaches in a traditional organization.

The model provides a means by which all programs may be integrated, thus a juvenile program is perceived as having equal importance with all other programs. From a practical standpoint, juveniles are involved in a large proportion of police activities, thus all personnel become more attuned to addressing all facets of the juvenile program.

However, it should be emphasized that there is no "best" approach to organization. Good personnel will make for an effective organization irrespective of structure. The team policing model requires quality personnel or it won't work!

CHART 2

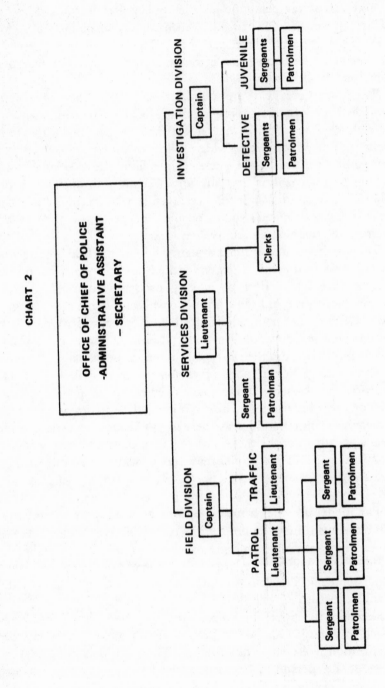

Team Policing Organization Model

Team policing is not new. In essence, most of our smaller police agencies use a team approach in that all officers including the chief of police or sheriff are involved in practically all activities and must work closely together. The late August Vollmer in designing his organization for the Berkeley, California, Police Department made his field officers responsible for all activities on their beats and designated his detective, juvenile, and traffic specialists as support personnel to aid and assist each officer, in team fashion, as the needs arose. And almost every agency has assembled teams to deal with special situations or events such as a major investigation or a narcotics raid.

More recently, however, the approaches to team policing are of a different nature. Significant organizational changes have taken place, and teams have been formalized and made an integral part of agency organizations. They vary from a basic operational field patrol team to a complex assemblage of teams for administration and management purposes as well as operational purposes.

First, a look at the field operational team resticted to patrol. The agency is otherwise organized in the traditional manner. In the simplest approach, a team of officers is assigned to a given area with full responsibility to perform the normal duties of patrol and, in addition, to develop a greater involvement in the community by participating in citizens/group meetings and visiting people in their homes and businesses. The team provides twenty-four-hour coverage for the area, and officers are assigned on a reasonably permanent basis.

Another operational team approach is to assign a patrol sergeant and from six to ten officers or deputies to a given area during their tour of duty. The sergeant has flexibility in the assignment of personnel and methods of operation. An entire city or station/precinct area will be policed by several teams, each team with the usual responsibilities for responding to calls and repressing crime. Responsibility for policing the entire area of assignment rests with the team as a whole, rather than each unit having responsibility for a designated area or beat. This approach could be expanded by giving a lieutenant watch-commander full authority to deploy the teams on a watch in varying area and operational patterns.

CHART 3

TEAM POLICING MODEL

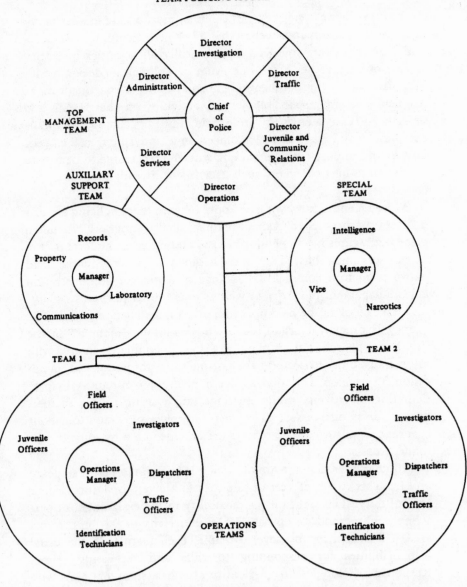

A third patrol operational team approach is to assign a lieutenant two or more sergeants and a sufficient number of officers to a designated area of a city or station/precinct, with full responsibility for policing the area twenty-four hours a day, seven days a week, 365 days a year. The team has responsibility for determining deployment and hours of assignment, as well as freedom in determining methods of operation.

Expansion of the patrol operational teams on either a shift or area basis to include detectives, juvenile officers, clerks and/or identification technicians is feasible. In essence, this provides the team a capability to perform the total field policing functions with support from specialty units as an agency determines is required. For the most part, the team will have the capability to handle most situations and incidents that arise with flexibility for deployment and assignment of personnel and methods of operation.

Creation of the teams previously described requires a commitment from management that it is in fact delegating to the operations team flexibility and full authority to operate as teams within the guidelines established. There is also the requirement that there be a reasonable permanency of assignment of personnel to the teams. *Planning* and *training* are two additional components essential if the team approach is to be effective.

The auxiliary support and intelligence teams perform functions that are not really amenable for incorporation into the operations teams. The latter have principal responsibility for the primary program activities of the department. The auxiliary support team provides essential services for all other departmental activities. The special team is both operational, in that it makes investigations, and supportive, in that it provides essential intelligence for management decision making and planning for some emergency operations.

The top management team consists of the chief of police and the top command personnel of a department. The command personnel will not have the traditional command responsibility but will bring to the team the "expertise" of their functional specialty, which will be utilized in planning, directing, coordinating and controlling an integrated operation. In essence, the team will be constituted as a "board of directors" with a collegial responsibility for overall management of the affairs of the department.

The chief of police is the "chairman" of the top management team. He may be perceived as the hub of the circle surrounded by other team members. His function is to provide leadership for the team as well as the department as a whole. The "buck" stops with him, but more importantly he is responsible for creating a management environment in which the top management team members may tackle and resolve major departmental issues. It is up to him to provide a proper balance in the resolution of issues to assure that no one program is overemphasized and that the operation of the department proceeds in a reasonably smooth fashion.

The other members of the top management team will be responsible for designated program areas for which their background of education and experience reasonably provide them with an expertise. Using the orthodox organization's command officers as examples, the commander of the investigation division would bring to the team expertise in investigation and juvenile programs; the commander of the operations division, expertise in patrol and traffic programs; the commander of the services division, expertise in records and property management, communications, and custody; and the head of the management services division, expertise in personnel, training, planning, and budget. Each in a sense would become the "director" of their individual program area. One director, more than likely the expert in operations in a medium-sized department, would become "director of operations" with responsibility for coordinating and directing the work of the operations teams. Departmental size would dictate the number of personnel for each team. Necessary support personnel would be provided to perform "staff" work.

How would the team function? Each member of the team would be responsible for inputting into the planning and policy decision-making process the program requirements for his area of expertise. Each input would be evaluated by the team as a whole, vis-à-vis all other inputs. The ultimate team decision with respect to each input would assure that implementation provides for a balanced operation. It is presupposed that there is a continuous flow of information on all operations and activities to the top management team. If conflicts arise the chief of police would have the final decision-making responsibility.

Although the director of operations would have primary responsibility for coordinating and directing operational teams, all other directors would engage in a continuous process of monitoring the operation of their program areas. This would be done by review of information and by inspections. Basically, the top management "circle" would revolve for the purposes of a continuous evaluation and integration of all programs to assure a proper balance in operations.

The responsibility of the basic operational team under one concept would consist of the performance of substantially all program activities essential for fulfilling the police role in the community and achieving departmental goals and objectives. In effect, each team will be self-contained with respect to performing all operational functions. The field operational personnel will consist of generalist patrolmen capable of performing the basic traditional field tasks, including traffic enforcement and accident investigation. Personnel traditionally performing investigation duties, including juvenile, will become an integral part of the field team. Thus, the field personnel will have the capability to handle all routine operations and major investigations. Preplanning calls for development of a case assignment system whereby the expertise of the most capable officer on duty will be assigned to handle each case. Routine cases will be handled by the generalist officer. The officer in charge of each case will, in effect, supervise the investigation of that case.

One may ask, "What about supervision?" The team approach suggests that basic supervision will be accomplished through a system of peer control. However, the model suggests that a "lead officer" approach could be used to supplant the traditional first-line supervisor, which calls for a clearly defined superior/subordinate relationship. A clear delineation of the superior/subordinate relationship does not appear necessary when all personnel become a collegial body equally responsible for the success or failure of operations. Furthermore, careful preplanning of relationships in which all personnel participate in the decision-making process can eliminate confusion and tension situations. In addition, a system can be preplanned for meeting emergency situations requiring precise leadership and supervision.

The team policing organizational model is based on a phenomena of accepting the premise that all personnel have a contribution to make to the policy and operational decision-making processes. It presupposes that all personnel have a major contribution to make to the operation of the department, are capable and willing to make that contribution, and that there will be acceptance of the contribution. It is a continuing process whereby involvement of all personnel takes place, a continuous input of ideas, suggestions and constructive criticism is fostered, and new ideas and concepts are ingested into the system.

Management personnel assume responsibility for broad policy making, planning of operational activities, and for dealing with substantive issues regarding personnel, operations, budget, and unusual situations and community relations. Operational personnel become concerned with routine day-to-day operations and implementation of broad policy guidelines laid down by the management team.

Team policing suggests that all personnel will be removed from a nice neat "box" that prescribes jobs, tasks, and duties. All personnel will be perceived as having a major contribution to make to the success of the organization, and capabilities will be maximized. It is recognition that each person in the organization has talent, develops an expertise, has a basic know-how and a quality of leadership, and an ability to contribute to the total operation of the department. Capitalizing on the talents of all persons in the organization is the key to success.

The team policing organization model is a drastic breach with tradition. However, it does provide a model that may reduce the rigidity and the tension-building features of current approaches to organization. It provides a means for involving the "new breed" of police officer, who brings to the department talents and potential capabilities superior to his predecessor.

It makes possible a continuous input of ideas and observations about the community, the operations, and agency relationships that have been severely restricted and which are becoming extremely vital for meeting the dynamic and changing demands of society on the police. Admittedly, many problems are posed in changing over to adoption of the model. Serious questioning of many current practices must take place and a number of "myths" challenged. However, the end result may be a viable, meaningful and dynamic organization.

Juvenile Teams

Team policing by a juvenile division is feasible. The division may decentralize its operations by forming teams that will be responsible for performance of all juvenile functions within an area of the city or station/precinct. The areas may be determined by identifying each senior high school and its "feeder" junior high and elementary schools as an area, or areas may be determined based upon the juvenile population in given areas of a city or station/precinct. This approach is logical for departments in relatively large cities with a juvenile division of fifteen to twenty or more personnel.

A generalist approach to juvenile work follows. Personnel assigned to each team should be sufficiently well trained and qualified to perform all functions in a reasonable manner. The traditional organizational structure of having functional details or units no longer pertains.

The team in each area will perform the usual investigative functions of follow-up or full investigation of cases involving juveniles and the disposition and referral functions. In addition, it will interact with the other agencies in the area, including the schools, the probation and parole agencies, the recreation department, other public agencies, and the private agencies in the performance of the crime prevention and control functions.

Coordination and direction of the several teams is accomplished by the division commander and a small staff at the station/precinct or departmental headquarters.

Sheriffs' Departments and State Police Organizations

Because of the rural nature of the areas to be policed by sheriff's departments and state police, close contact between officers and juveniles cannot be maintained; thus, work with juveniles is quite different. The responsibility for investigation of cases involving juveniles becomes somewhat more important than the performance of the other juvenile control functions. The disposition and referral function is more complex. Agencies to which referrals may be made are not so prevalent as in a municipality. Servies to youth in the way of recreation, group work activity and other types of activities are not so plentiful in rural areas. This complicates the police activities. However, the same concepts of organization and administration for juvenile control can be applied to these agencies, though performance of the functions may be somewhat different.

There seems to be two logical approaches to organization and administration of a juvenile control unit in a sheriff's department or a state police agency. In agencies having policing responsibilities in highly congested areas contiguous to a large city the problem is somewhat similar to that of the large city. Decentralization is necessary, but performance of the basic juvenile control and delinquency prevention functions in each area is the same as those of a municipal police department. Planning and direction must come from central headquarters. In the more rural areas the problem seems to be one of planning and directing the activities of the regular field officers. The juvenile control unit can be responsible for coordinating investigation activities of all agency units, developing plans and contacts for referral of juveniles apprehended by the agency, and for performance of the staff-service functions necessary for effective operation.

Personnel assigned to the juvenile control unit may be assigned to the headquarters of the agency if they are only responsible for providing staff-service functions. A small staff of officers may work out of central headquarters to assist field officers in making more complex investigations. Those officers can move from field division to field division as needed. Liaison activities with the other agencies can be developed from headquarters in the several areas policed.

THE JUVENILE SPECIALIST

The role of the juvenile specialist is changing. Recognition that much of police juvenile work is performed by the uniformed field officers and that detectives investigate many cases involving juveniles has considerably changed the nature of the juvenile officer's work. Juvenile officers are becoming much more involved in the total operation of the department, with greater emphasis on teamwork. The specialized features of the job are becoming more limited.

Traditionally, the juvenile officer has been the human relations and community organization specialist for the department. A shifting of emphasis by police agencies to community relations has brought about the advent of community relations specialists and community relations programs, the juvenile concerns becoming only one facet of a much broader community concern. The juvenile officer may or may not become involved in working with community organization, and his work with schools and other youth-serving organizations may be limited to the immediate problems of delinquency and misbehavior. On the other hand, some departments have expanded the role of the juvenile officer to include the broader community relations functions. In any event, the juvenile officer has a paramount concern for dealing with community problems and issues that influence the patterns of behavior of juveniles.

The increasing involvement of field officers and detectives in the investigation of cases involving juveniles has placed the juvenile officer in more of an aiding and assisting role in the conduct of investigations. Thus, the juvenile officer provides an element of expertise for investigations, rather than assuming the principal responsibility. However, the cases in which juveniles are readily identified as being responsible and family relations-type cases are often assigned to the juvenile officer as a primary responsibility. The fact that juveniles often manifest behavior quite different than adults calls for a different approach to the investigative process. This is particularly true with respect to interviewing. Juveniles just do not respond the same as adults. It is the peculiarities of the juvenile and his behavior that require the expertise of a juvenile officer.

It is in the disposition of the juvenile that the juvenile officer fulfills a specialized role. The juvenile officer should monitor and follow up, when necessary, the dispositions made by field officers. This is not to say that the field officer's disposition is not correct. Rather, the concern is with taking appropriate steps to prevent recurrences of the actions of juveniles that indicate a pattern of misbehavior. A requirement here is that the field officer notify the juvenile unit of action taken. The disposition of juveniles when formal action is initiated is a primary responsibility of the juvenile officer. He should be the expert on filing of petitions, making of referrals to the school counselors, clinics, or other youth-serving agencies, and in dealing with family situations.

In addition, the juvenile officer can provide invaluable service in identifying and working toward alleviation of community situations that contribute directly to delinquency. This requires a certain amount of field patrol activity, which should not replace regular patrol by uniformed personnel but rather supplement it.

Coupled with information on the role and functions of a juvenile unit the preceding provides specifications for the job of juvenile officer. These specifications call for skills and attitudes that are different than those required for dealing with adults. Basically, an understanding of juvenile behavior, values, and psychological makeup is fundamental. An ability to work closely with a variety of people and community agencies is also necessary. But, just as important is the ability to work as a team member with other police personnel in dealing with juveniles and their problems.

SELECTION

The general upgrading of police personnel in the United States through adoption of minimum standards for recruitment and selection with an increasing emphasis on academic education is raising the general level of qualifications for all police personnel. This is negating the emphasis that has previously prevailed for selecting the "elite" officers of a department for juvenile work. Focus is turning more toward the officer who by temperament, personal appearance and mannerisms, interest in juvenile work, and academic preparation in fields such as education, psychology, and social welfare has developed the greater expertise in dealing with juveniles and their problems. The base for selecting the juvenile officer, of course, is limited by the number of officers within the department.

If competent officers have been recruited at the entrance level, the problem of selecting a juvenile officer is somewhat simplified. The methods used in any department will of course depend upon departmental organization and policies. Although few departments have established any formal criteria for selection of their juvenile officers, a few departments have adopted what might be termed *formal selection procedures*.

The most common procedure is to allow the head of the juvenile control unit to select the officers, within reason, of course. This procedure normally involves an interview with those officers who have indicated an interest in juvenile work and officers whom the head of the unit may want transferred because of personal knowledge of the officer's qualifications. At the interview the director notes personal appearance, personality, mannerisms, and the expressed interest of the applicant. The director may then classify the applicant on the basis of the impression he received concerning the traits previously mentioned. If the impressions are favorable, the director then consults the personnel record of the officer in question and looks for other traits and experience.

Reviewing of the personnel record should cover such things as the officer's entrance and promotional examination scores, his reputation as indicated by the presence or absence of complaints and commendations in the record, and the officer's educational background and field of study, if a college person. In-service training courses taken should be reviewed, as they concern the officer's interest in juvenile work. A few directors have set an arbitrary minimum of police experience. In larger departments the minimum may vary from two to five years. Use of psychiatric or psychological testing should be considered. Juvenile work requires exposure of the officer to psychotherapeutic skills used by social workers and probation officers and to some extent use of such skills himself.

Following completion of the steps indicated, the director should evaluate each officer and place him on a "list," the list to contain the names of the officers interviewed and ranked in order of the evaluation. Transfers can then be made to the juvenile control unit from the list.

Occasionally, a department has decided that none of its officers are qualified to assume responsibility as a juvenile officer. In these instances, the department has looked outside for a qualified person. The problem of orienting the officer to the job and his gaining acceptance by other members of the force makes the procedure not too advisable. However, if it is necessary to bring an officer in from the outside, the following selection procedure appears worthwhile.

Basic qualifications to be established should follow closely those established for selection of an officer within a department. Education, intelligence, character, appearance, and social adaptability requirements should be high. If it is at all possible the experience requirement should include at least five years experience in the law enforcement field or in an allied agency, such as a probation department or a parole agency, where the officer has gained knowledge of working with law enforcement personnel. At least two years of the experience should be in working with juveniles.

In recruiting juvenile officers outside of the department clear specifications must be established as to requirements and a statement of what the job entails. In bringing officers in at a rank higher than patrol officer with a higher salary schedule the education and experience requirements can be adjusted upward in order to get a properly qualified applicant.

Under the team policing model of organization, each operational team would be assigned the requisite number of juvenile specialists. Basic requirements would be the same as those previously discussed.

Tobias has provided some useful criteria to be considered in the selection of juvenile officers and has developed some desirable characteristics to be considered. Key criteria for selection follow:

1. Men and women should be considered on the same basis.
2. The person should be an integral member of the police service and trained in police procedures with emphasis on juvenile law.
3. It should be a person who is committed to the idea that young people will enhance their development and correct antisocial behavior and attitudes if given an opportunity to experience a professional relationship that helps them to better understand themselves and their environment.
4. A person who believes the following:
   - Each juvenile is a unique person and has within him the ability to change and do that which is socially acceptable.
   - The police service may, in itself, because of its very nature and what it stands for, create conflict among today's young people and consequently require a special person to interpret its role in society.
   - Today's society, because of its complexity, rapid changes, and pressures, may create frustration and thereby bring about antisociality for some young people.
   - The juvenile officer, as a police officer with professional competencies, behavioral science training and guidance orientation, may provide professional assistance and be a very special friend to young people in trouble.

Some desirable characteristics for juvenile officers follow:

1. Philosophically a juvenile officer should believe that prevention of antisocial behavior is one of the most important functions that he/she can perform. Thus, development of a guidance-oriented approach in dealing with young people and their problems is needed.
2. To accomplish the guidance-oriented approach he/she should possess the following personal attitudes and characteristics:
   - Likes youth work and is totally dedicated and committed to it.

- Is genuinely interested and personally concerned for young people and their healthy socialization into the community and society.
- Is mentally healthy, emotionally mature, and a levelheaded, commonsense type of individual.
- Is sensitive to both himself and young people, understanding of their characteristics and background, and accepting of their behavior, even though he may personally disapprove of same, and capable of feeling with them and their difficulties.
- Strives to be a tolerant, patient, nonjudgmental, and unbiased person.
- In dealing with young people is warm, honest, respectful, truthful, and sincere.
- Is capable of devoting much time and energy to his work and the concerns of youth.
- Must be a well-rounded, humane person.
- Must possess a high level of communicability and be able to establish a trusting relationship with those with whom he deals.
- Must be able to provide a safe, secure, and comfortable atmosphere so that young people will be able to discuss their antisociality.
- Must be a good listener and the type of person that young people feel they can approach and "rap" with at anytime.
- Today's juvenile officer must be the kind of person who is flexible enough to adapt to today's scene.

TRAINING

Police training and education in the United States has greatly improved in the past two decades. Over four hundred universities and colleges now include in their curricula police and criminal justice programs. State-mandated standards and training programs that by subvention offer assistance to local police agencies for training are on the increase, having begun in California in 1959 with the establishment of the California Commission on Peace Officer Standards and Training. The federal government with the passage of the Law Enforcement Assistance Act in 1965 followed by the Omnibus Crime

Control Act in 1968 made considerable federal funds available for both police education and training, the result being the initiation of a number of new programs and expansion of existing programs. The Federal Bureau of Investigation has continued its yeoman service in providing training for local police through its "zone" and departmental programs as well as expanding its National Police Academy Program. And the International Association of Chiefs of Police has encouraged improvement programs, including the holding of workshops and seminars in a number of specialized areas.

The police service is benefitting from these developments. An increasing number of academically educated personnel are entering the service of local police agencies; scholarships are made available to employed personnel for either full-time or part-time academic study by the Law Enforcement Assistance Administration established under the Omnibus Crime Control Bill, swelling the ranks of the "scholar-practitioner." State subvention and local government tuition reimbursement programs are returning an increasing number of officers to universities and colleges for specialized educational programs. Recruit and in-service academy programs are being expanded to include an increasing number of subject-matter areas.

Training and education for police work with juveniles is not being neglected. Both the academic and academy programs are increasing their emphasis on human relations and juvenile control subjects. Appropriately, all officers are being exposed to the subject matter, expanding the capabilities of the police to meet more effectively their juvenile control and prevention requirements. More training and education is also available for the specialist juvenile officer.

The increased emphasis on preparing all officers for work with juveniles is in accord with research findings that the uniformed field officer carries the large share of work with juveniles in routine day-to-day activities. The patrolman has the basic responsibility for police-juvenile relations, since he comes into face-to-face relationships with a far greater number of juveniles than does the juvenile officer. His demeanor in these relationships is of the utmost importance in achieving or maintaining desirable behavior by juveniles.

The philosophy of police-juvenile relations are best based on the following: (1) respect for the individual whether a victim or suspect;

(2) accepted criteria of human relations; (3) therapy and treatment rather than punishment as an end goal; (4) crime prevention and deterrence rather than apprehension, detention, and court procedures; (5) police involvement and active cooperation with local youth-serving agencies and institutions with a view to decreasing delinquency. This philosophy applies equally to all officers and implies that there is no justifiable philosophical basis for a different approach to juveniles by juvenile specialists as contrasted with other officers.

The fact that officers may have taken academic courses in human relations and juvenile work does not negate the need for recruit and in-service training. There is such a wide variation in academic courses that often basic material essential for field operations may not be covered. Furthermore, officers need to be familiar with the laws, statutes, and codes as they pertain to delinquency, the processing of juveniles in local jurisdictions, and policies and procedures of the local departments. In addition, the officers need to become familiar with local conditions, youth-serving agencies, and social welfare agencies serving families and youth.

What then constitutes a curriculum for police training in juvenile matters? Probably the most comprehensive suggested curriculum is that developed by Kobetz of the International Association of Chiefs of Police. The curriculum reflects identified needs of representatives of police departments from almost every section of the United States. Thus, with adaptation to meet local needs the suggested curriculum provides coverage of almost all conceivable subjects. The report suggested curriculum for general training, workshops, in-service and recruit training programs, and supervisory training. The major subject matters covered in the suggested curriculum are as follows:

Orientation and definitions
Police-juvenile attitude relationships
Juvenile court
Laws relating to juvenile offenses
Legal limitations and provisions
Departmental procedures and methods
Juvenile records and statistics
Visual aids and field trips
Functions of the juvenile court

Responsibility of line officers
Treatment of juvenile delinquent problems
Social aspects of delinquency
Special problems such as alcohol and narcotics
Youth gangs
Public relations
Supervision
Administrative checks
Juvenile interrogation techniques
Police-community service relations
Juvenile patrol techniques
Abnormal behavior patterns and delinquency
Causation of delinquency
Child abuse

These subject matters coincide closely with subjects covered in the special delinquency control institutes that have been held at various locations throughout the United States under various sponsorships since 1946 when the model institute program was inaugurated by the Delinquency Control Institute at the University of Southern California.

Since many departments are too small to operate their own academy programs, regional academies or individual department academies open to other agencies' personnel are commonplace. Usually, the subject matter covered in these academies has general application for all departments. What remains is for each department to train its officers in departmental procedures to cover local community problems and situations.

SPECIALIZED TRAINING

A number of training and educational programs for the juvenile officer specialists are provided regularly. These vary in length from three days to ten weeks. Curricula generally covers the subject matter either in whole or in part developed by the International Association of Chiefs of Police (IACP) with a heavy emphasis on the sociopsychological aspects of behavior.

The IACP regularly schedules annual, one-week seminars on juvenile justice administration. The seminars are conducted in strategic locations to serve the maximum number of agencies. The University of Florida's Institute for Law Enforcement is held annually in the summer. Indiana University offers special juvenile justice programs through its Center for Criminal Justice Training, and the University of Minnesota holds an annual Juvenile Officers Institute.

Delinquency Control Institute

The Delinquency Control Institute at the University of Southern California is the premier program, which was conceived in 1944 and which began operations in 1946. It has since conducted some seventy-four classes and has graduated in excess of twenty-five hundred law enforcement officers and juvenile justice workers. The institute provides a specialized academic program of six weeks, designed to aid law enforcement officers and others to work more effectively with youth and community problems.

The participants in the program learn to:

- Understand the existing laws relating to juveniles and keep pace with new legislation.
- Organize and manage a police juvenile program using modern principles of administration.
- Understand delinquent behavior and the multiple factors contributing to it.
- Make effective case dispositions and divert selected youth from the juvenile justice system.
- Plan citizen participation in the development of community-wide crime prevention programs and traffic safety.
- Interpret law enforcement to the public and create a realistic new image of the police.
- Develop more effective coordination throughout the juvenile justice system and the total criminal justice system.
- Deal with special problems associated with delinquency and offenses committed against children, including child abuse and sexual exploitation, substance abuse, crisis intervention and hard-core offenders and juvenile gangs.

The institute offers classroom instruction and seminar discussion in three major categories:

BEHAVIORAL SCIENCE ASPECTS OF JUSTICE ADMINISTRATION. Sociological and psychological theories of crime, delinquency, and offender behavior. Behavioral science contributions to formulation of justice programs and their administration. Emphasizes growth and change in childhood and adolescence.

ADMINISTRATION OF POLICE SERVICES. Police services to the community and relationships to other components of the justice system. Special emphasis is upon administration of police juvenile programs, community relations, and the role of the law enforcement officer in crime prevention.

ADMINISTRATION OF JUSTICE: A SURVEY OF THE SYSTEM. The system of justice administration of justice administration: police services, judiciary, corrections; agency interrelationships, current system work load and the need for change and planning strategies. Focus is on the improvement of juvenile justice.

The threefold attack on the basic problems as presented in the classroom by regular faculty members of the University of Southern California is reinforced by a wide range of interdisciplinary specialists representing major resources of the Los Angeles metropolitan community and the state of California. Classroom instruction is supplemented by research, field work, and field visits to important agencies and institutions engaged in juvenile work.

REFERENCES

1. Kobetz, Richard W.: *Juvenile Justice Administration.* Gaithersburg, Va., International Association of Chiefs of Police, 1973.
2. Tobias, Jerry J.: Today's youth officer as I see him/her. *Police Chief,* Gaithersburg, Va., IACP, June, 1973.

Chapter 11

POLICE OPERATIONS

P OLICE work is essentially a fieldwork operation. Criminal activity, disturbances, and other activities requiring police attention may happen any place within a jurisdiction. Policemen must be
available to the place of action. Staff support for the field operations
should be only that which is absolutely essential to facilitate effective
and efficient operations. Police work is essentially a team operation.
All men should work together, and specialization should be limited.

In a metropolitan area it is incumbent upon all police agencies to
cooperate actively with other law enforcement agencies. This is particularly true of agencies in suburban areas that must rely on the
larger metropolitan police agencies for much information regarding
the general crime picture in the total area, as well as for assistance in
the apprehension of offenders and recovery of property. This is true
for both routine police operations as well as in the handling of
emergency situations, but is especially necessary in the investigation
of criminal cases and in dealing with juvenile problems.

Police duties generally fall into three categories: (1) cases, (2) field
activities, and (3) community coordination.

Cases provide the tangible evidence of police activities. There are
criminal cases, traffic cases, and service cases. Usually all cases will

result in some kind of a written record being made by the police department.

Field activities are essentially for the purpose of prevention and repression of crime, regulation of conduct, and to have personnel available to handle cases when, where, and as they occur. They include inspectional services designed to reduce the opportunities for the commission of crime. Inspections are made of business and industrial establishments and situations and incidents that arise in the course of a police officer's duty.

The other major component of field activities is that of surveillance. As police officers move around on beats or in assigned areas, they are available to take action in situations requiring it, and it is by this means that they create the impresssion of "omnipresence" that has the effect of reducing opportunity, or belief in opportunity, for the commission of crime. In the course of performing inspectional services and in providing surveillances, officers are available to control and regulate the conduct of people.

The role of the police in community coordination is to achieve crime prevention. It is also a means by which the police make available information on crime and other police activities that are of concern to other agencies and to the public at large. The police have a responsibility to work closely with other agencies in developing what may be called a healthy environment, and it is through activities in community coordinating councils and other community organizations that they can be of assistance.

In order to maintain a complete police service, a police department engages in three broad areas of activities: First are those that have to do with the programs concerned with achieving police objectives. Second are the sustaining activities required for the performance of the primary police duties. Third are the administrative activities essential for management of the department.

The primary police activities may be broken into field operations and investigations. The field operations are essentially those that are undertaken for the purpose of patrol and traffic control. Investigations are for the purpose of clearing cases and include the detective, vice, and juvenile operations as well as field operations. Sustaining activities include records, communications, and property and equipment control. Administrative activities include operation of the office of the chief of police, personnel, budget, planning, public relations, and reporting activities.

It has been emphasized that juvenile control is a function of the entire police department. The establishment of a separate functional unit that is responsible for matters relating to juveniles must be based upon a demonstrated need for more effective utilization of departmental manpower and community demands and legal requirements that dictate that juveniles shall be processed by the police department differently than adults.

Specialization for juvenile control results primarily from the need for application of special investigative techniques for the processing of juveniles, disposition requirements, and community coordination needs. Delinquent juveniles behave somewhat differently than adult criminals, often requiring the use of specialists in the interrogation process and in the collation of information relating to a series of offenses. The making of dispositions of juveniles responsible for delinquent acts, or taken into custody for other reasons, requires a specialized knowledge of community resources and court procedures. Delinquency prevention is a community responsibility, and the police specialist is most helpful in relating to other community agencies the problems of delinquency and behavioral patterns of youth to assure development of effective crime prevention programs.

Logical assignment of responsibilities for overall police work must be considered before specialization. Patrol activities are primarily a responsibility of the field division. Any specialized patrol focused on juveniles should be perceived as strictly a supplement to the routine patrol operation. Preliminary investigations of practically all cases should be primarily a responsibility of the field unit. For the most part, a report of an offense in most cases does not carry with it a designation that a juvenile is responsible. Therefore, a juvenile unit or specialist should not come into the investigative process until later.

Follow-up investigations in most cases is the responsibility of the investigation or detective units of the department. Investigations of cases are normally made on the basis of types of cases rather than persons who might be responsible. There are only a few types of cases in which it can be inferred that a juvenile was responsible at the outset of the report of the offense, and, even in the follow-up of most cases, the primary criterion for assignment of responsibility should be the offense, not the responsible individual. This is important in order to assign investigative responsibility.

For example, a home burglary unit of a detective division should have responsibility for follow-up investigations of all home burglaries. Only when it has been determined that a juvenile was involved should assistance from the juvenile unit be sought. Transfer of investigative responsibility should not take place.

Thus, the juvenile unit of a police department performs a supportive activity. The juvenile specialist supports the field and investigative operations for the most part. In only specified types of cases does the juvenile specialist assume responsibility for follow-up investigations.

It can be generally assumed that the juvenile control unit operation evolves primarily around the investigative process. The juvenile specialist is concerned with the processing of juveniles who are responsible for offenses. He assists investigators of other units as required.

Once the investigation of the offense is complete, then it becomes the responsibility of the juvenile specialist to make the departmental disposition of the juvenile, or juveniles, involved. It is in this capacity that he performs most effectively, because of his knowledge about community resources and court procedures and presumably his ability to ascertain what is best for the individual and the community.

The juvenile specialist role in community organization is quite different from that involved in the law enforcement function of the department. One of the important crime prevention activities of any department is community relations and working with community organizations. In effect, the mobilization of community resources by the department is important for achievement of the objective of crime prevention. By the nature of police juvenile work, the juvenile specialist often becomes the departmental specialist in community organization. This is both traditional and practical.

The departmental organization dictates to a great degree the role and functions of the juvenile unit and its juvenile officers. In the traditional organizations the functional role of the juvenile specialist is emphasized. His activities are usually definitively prescribed, and his relationship to other units and officers is rather precisely defined. As a department adopts a more generalist approach to police work, the juvenile specialist's role and functions become more varied and less precise. His relationship to other units and officers is more flexible usually, signified by a greater involvement of other units and officers in the performance of the juvenile functions.

THE JUVENILE UNIT

Functions

Logically, the functions of a juvenile unit seem to be as follows:

1. Discovery of delinquents, potential delinquents, and conditions inducing delinquency.
2. Investigation of delinquency and causes of delinquency.
3. Disposition and diversion of cases.
4. Protection of children and youth.
5. Community organization.

Although these functions are general in nature, they provide the basis for the operation of the juvenile unit. When viewed in terms of the overall departmental purposes for juvenile control as discussed in the previous chapters, they provide the basis for the juvenile control unit's operation. These functions should be clearly understood by all officers of the department and must definitely be understood by officers assigned to the juvenile unit. Fundamental to the success of any program is an understanding of its purposes and functions.

Patrol and Inspection

Patrol and inspection are fundamental responsibilities of the juvenile control division. Activities of patrol officers of this unit do not in any way relieve patrol division beat officers from routine patrol responsibilities; rather, patrol operations of the juvenile control unit supplement those of the regular field patrol. All complaints received should routinely be answered by beat officers, regardless of whether juveniles are involved. Routine inspections by the beat officer should include places where juveniles may congregate or other places that might be detrimental to youth welfare.

Patrol operations of the juvenile control unit are for the purpose of giving special attention to those places or situations throughout the jurisdiction in which youth are or may be exposed to detrimental social elements. Almost every jurisdiction has its share of such places and situations. Places of commercial recreation, bus and railroad depots, bars, recreation centers for youth, drive-ins, and other places where youth may congregate are common examples.

Officers assigned to juvenile patrol should be ever alert for adults who may molest or harm youth. School grounds, playgrounds, and theaters should be closely checked. Constant attention should be focused upon the formation of gangs or new "hangouts."

Mobility throughout the entire city or jurisdiction gives the juvenile officer on patrol advantages that are often denied the regular beat officer in correcting bad juvenile situations. Opportunity to observe movement of youth from one part of the jurisdiction to another, a common feature of youth activity, makes possible correction of many bad situations that may develop.

The juvenile officer devotes his entire time to youth and their problems and is therefore in a position to know most of the individual youth in an area by sight, and probably by name as well. This, of course, makes him a more effective worker. He is in a position to discover those places or situations conducive to delinquency. All too often the beat officer, of necessity, is so engrossed in regular patrol duties that his attention is diverted from needed control over youth activities.

Special laws affecting working juveniles, attendance at school, or use of alcoholic beverages have been passed for their protection. Enforcement of these laws is important to the success of any delinquency prevention work, though, it unfortunately has not been effective by regular patrol officers in most police departments. Juvenile patrol must assume, as part of its responsibility, enforcement of these laws.

Investigation

Investigation of law violations by youth should be as thorough and complete as investigations of offenses committed by adults. Moreover, these should be made as promptly as possible. Police responsibility is as great in one instance as the other. It is just as important that all of the facts relating to a case be available to the juvenile court as must be available when the criminal procedure is followed.

More important, however, in the investigation of juvenile cases is the ascertaining of all offenses for which the juvenile may be responsible and finding out who the youth's associates may be, if any. Failure to uncover one of a series of separate offenses committed by a juvenile may result in failure of the rehabilitation process. Associates of the youth should be ascertained in order to clear up a bad situation that may be developing from improper associations and misdirected activities.

There is a second, equally important phase in a juvenile investigation — that of determining the causes underlying delinquency. Combined with the offense investigation, a determination of the underlying causes for commission of the offense will provide an intelligent basis for referral or disposition of the juvenile.

Intelligent referral of a juvenile responsible for a law violation is made only when basic causes are understood. All tools should be utilized in making an investigation. The departmental records, records of the school, probation department, parole agency, social agencies (both public and private), and every logical and possible source of information should be tapped. Interviews should be held with the juvenile, his parents, relatives, victims, neighbors, associates, and any other persons who might have information concerning the particular case or information relating to the causes.

Some departments consider it necessary to maintain supervision over the youth in order to complete the investigation. Referral to clinics and other facilities in the community may be advisable in order to complete an investigation. The police, however, should not forget the case even though referral may be made to the probation department and detention ordered in the detention home. All phases of the case should be investigated to the full satisfaction of the police department. Officers should probe incessantly for underlying causes even though the immediate aim is to establish substantiation of a specific offense by a certain youngster or youngsters.

Responsiblity for investigation of specific types of cases by the juvenile control unit is based on whether juveniles are involved as perpetrators or victims, and such is usually known at the time a complaint is received by the department or upon completion of the initial investigation. Cases that may normally be assigned to the juvenile unit for investigation are as follows:

1. Bicycle thefts.
2. Offenses concerning the family situation such as desertion,

abandonment, neglect, or abuse of children.

3. Adults responsible for encouraging delinquency of minors; employment of minors in injurious, immoral, or improper vocations or practices; admitting minors to improper places.
4. Child stealing.
5. Possession or sale of obscene pictures or literature, exhibitions, and so forth.
6. Offenses committed upon school property.
7. Sex offenses, except forcible rape.
8. All other cases involving juveniles not regularly assigned to another division, except vice cases.

In assigning investigative responsibility for specific cases to the juvenile control unit, responsibilities for other divisions for investigating other types of cases in which juveniles are involved must be clearly defined. If juveniles are involved in offenses other than those listed, the detail of the detective division or other division responsible for the specific type of offense should be held responsible for the case investigation. Assistance from the juvenile control unit may be solicited, but responsibility should not be transferred.

Upon completion of an investigation of a case involving juveniles by another division, transfer of the case for disposition or referral should be made. Investigation into the causes beyond commission of · the specific offense or the general cause of the juvenile's delinquent behavior should be undertaken by the juvenile control unit to assure proper disposition or referral of the juvenile.

Dispositions

Disposition or referral of the delinquent juvenile is perhaps one of the most important functions performed by the department. It is in this sphere of activity that the juvenile control unit probably is most needed. The juvenile unit is in a position to develop all community resources for use by the department in effecting rehabilitation and treatment for delinquent youth.

Referrals are made to the probation department and the courts in the more serious cases. Social agencies, both public and private, can be utilized effectively for cases of a minor nature and those involving need for assistance either for the child or for the parents. Religious agencies should not be overlooked. Full support by all churches should be solicited and developed.

Community councils can be effective agencies for development of places for referral and for disposition. Recreation and character-building agencies should be utilized to their fullest extent, and an appreciation of the problems of the delinquent child should be instilled in leaders of those agencies in order to effect rehabilitation.

General agreement has been reached among juvenile officers and police administrators that in cases where treatment and adjustment of a more serious nature is necessary, referral to an appropriate agency equipped for that service should be made. The police agency itself should *not* carry on a comprehensive treatment or adjustment program. In communities where facilities are not available it may be necessary to have voluntary police supervision in order that treatment be initiated. The practice is not recommended, however, and if utilized should be terminated as soon as possible by encouraging the community to provide the necessary services. Police departments should not become vulnerable to criticism by participating in activities that some citizens may point out as being out of the realm of police work.

Many dispositions are made directly to parents or guardians of the child. It is in this type of disposition that the police can be very effective. Their explanation of the delinquency to the parent and suggestions for carrying out an adjustment program in the home become of paramount importance.

The schools are another important agency for disposition or referral. Being in constant contact with the youth of the community, their program affects to a great degree the amount of delinquency that goes on and adjustment of those boys and girls who commit law violations.

Upon completion of an investigation, the police officer must determine whether the child should be detained or released to his parent or guardian. In some cases detention is necessary. Generally speaking, detention should be considered only when the youth fall under one of the following categories:

1. *No supervision*—when a juvenile concerned is destitute or obviously in need of supervision or protective custody.
2. *Danger to person*—when release of the juvenile will endanger his person or morals.
3. *Record of runaway*—when a juvenile has a record as a runaway,

and it is reasonable to assume that upon release the juvenile
will leave the jurisdiction of the court.
4. *Danger to public*—when the record of the juvenile and/or the
gravity of the offense is such that release probably would prove
dangerous to the public welfare.
5. *Investigation*—when a juvenile's release would seriously hamper
the officer's completion of the investigation.

Final disposition of all juvenile cases should be handled by the
juvenile control unit. This should not imply that every juvenile will
be referred to the unit. It means that all reports concerning youth
will be processed through the unit for review and possible follow-up
work, if such is deemed necessary. Cases requiring referral to
another agency can be properly processed and all necessary information acquired before referral is made. For youths apprehended or arrested, this procedure assures that all necessary data as to facts of the
offense and possible causative factors will be ascertained and made
available for use by the agency to which the case is referred. Review
by the unit of reports from other divisions in cases involving
juveniles assures follow-up investigations where necessary and referral for treatment if such is warranted.

Centralization of the disposition function assures uniformity of
dispositions for all juvenile cases. Juveniles in need of treatment are
afforded that treatment, and those who can be handled satisfactorily
in other ways are so handled.

Terminology regarding dispositions varies greatly. Evaluating
the effectiveness of a juvenile program in comparison with another
department is almost impossible because of this difference in terminology. Uniform terminology has not been agreed upon, but
there are certain types of dispositions that are made by almost every
department; therefore, these types can be discussed here and suggested for use by departments. They are as follows:

1. *Application for petition.* A petition is filed when the circumstances
of the case are such that only the juvenile court can reasonably
be expected to safeguard the interests and welfare of society
and the juvenile concerned. A petition means that youth is
subject to its jurisdiction and may be brought before the
juvenile court.
2. *Transfer of case.* Juvenile cases are transferred when another
agency has jurisdiction, such as a probation department, state

training school, or other law enforcement agency.

3. *Referral to other agencies.* A referral is made when it is believed that the case in question should be investigated further and some rehabilitative program set in motion for the guidance and adjustment of the juvenile. Referrals will be made to such agencies as the School Guidance and Welfare Bureau, Department of Social Welfare, family and childrens' agencies, or to a diversion program.

4. *Action suspended.* In cases where it appears that the parents and the juvenile, alone and unaided, can effect a satisfactory adjustment, no further action need be taken.

5. *Insufficient evidence.* When there is conflict in evidence or when there is reasonable doubt as to the responsibility of a juvenile and the evidence is of such a nature as to preclude a determination of involvement, the juvenile should be released and no further action taken.

6. *Exoneration.* When the investigation clearly indicates that a juvenile is not responsible for the delinquency charged, he should be released and exonerated, or cleared of all involvement.

7. *Voluntary police supervision.* This form of disposition is employed when it is felt that the parents unaided are incapable of effecting the child's rehabilitation, but that the officer and the parent working cooperatively can assist the child to self-adjustment without the help of the juvenile court or the probation department or other agency. This disposition consists of furnishing guidance and counsel to the juvenile with the consent and full cooperation of the parents. Without such acquiescence it is valueless. (This disposition is controversial.)

8. *Proves to be adult.* When investigation discloses that the true age of the person arrested as a juvenile to be over the juvenile court age limit, the charges shall be suspended and prosecution of the charge or charges handled as with an adult.

9. *Declared unfit.* The juvenile officer may recommend in his application for petition to the juvenile court that the juvenile be declared unfit for further consideration by the juvenile court and be remanded for trial under the general laws in the criminal court. This recommendation would apply when investigation discloses that the juvenile had committed an offense or offenses of a serious nature and that his previous

record and attitude are such that a program of social treatment under the juvenile court would be ineffective.

10. *Detention.* Although at times detention may form a part of the treatment process it is presumed to be protective in nature, never punitive. All detention not under the order of the courts is temporary in nature. A child must be held no longer than is reasonably necessary for' effective placement or for being brought to the attention of the court.

Protection

Protection of minors is a further function of the juvenile unit, and this may be accomplished in the following ways:

1. Through the removal or control of environmental hazards.
2. Through cooperation with civic betterment groups.
3. By giving assistance in initiating constructive legislation.
4. By carrying on juvenile patrol activities.
5. Through apprehension and prosecution of adults involved in offenses against minors.
6. By opposition to publicity that identified delinquents or juvenile victims of adult crimes.

The police have generally not made use of the weapons available to them in combating the influence of illegally operated amusement centers and other business establishments. Nuisance abatement, red light abatement, or revocation of permits may be utilized. The influence of Parent Teachers Associations, community councils, women's clubs, schools, the press, radio, and other resources may be enlisted in the campaign to control community conditions detrimental to youth. Patrol of streets and places of public resort, coupled with the apprehension and prosecution of offenders, will likewise tend to eliminate environmental hazards.

Arrests

Controversy exists even in police circles as to when a juvenile should or should not be, is or is not, arrested. In some jurisdictions only those juveniles who are referred to the juvenile court are considered as having been arrested. In other jurisdictions the record of

TABLE 11-I

Police Disposition of Juvenile Offenders Taken into Custody, 1980

[1980 population]

Population group	Total[1]	Handled within department and released	Referred to juvenile court jurisdiction	Referred to welfare agency	Referred to other police agency	Referred to criminal or adult court
TOTAL ALL AGENCIES: 11,217 agencies: population 187,842,281:						
Number[2]	1,466,411	495,246	852,411	22,849	25,139	70,766
Percent	100.0	33.8	58.1	1.6	1.7	4.8
TOTAL CITIES: 7,946 cities: population 125,180,778:						
Number	1,215,839	419,613	694,902	18,665	21,185	61,474
Percent	100.0	34.5	57.2	1.5	1.7	5.1
GROUP I						
48 cities, 250,000 and over; population 28,096,166:						
Number	240,356	62,566	166,404	2,575	5,805	3,006
Percent	100.0	26.0	69.2	1.1	2.4	1.3
GROUP II						
105 cities, 100,000 to 249,999; population 15,035,295:						
Number	138,565	49,655	79,990	3,542	2,827	2,551
Percent	100.0	35.8	57.7	2.6	2.0	1.8
GROUP III						
275 cities, 50,000 to 99,999; population 18,761,565:						
Number	184,825	66,355	102,434	4,261	2,929	8,846
Percent	100.0	35.9	55.4	2.3	1.6	4.8

GROUP IV						
581 cities, 25,000 to 49,999; population 20,020,031:						
Number	221,264	83,671	120,340	3,131	3,971	10,151
Percent	100.0	37.8	54.4	1.4	1.8	4.6
GROUP V						
1,470 cities, 10,000 to 24,999; population 23,010,868:						
Number	232,026	88,270	122,489	2,870	2,937	15,460
Percent	100.0	38.0	52.8	1.2	1.3	6.7
GROUP VI						
5,467 cities under 10,000; population 20,256,853:						
Number	198,803	69,096	103,245	2,286	2,716	21,460
Percent	100.0	34.8	51.9	1.1	1.4	10.8
SUBURBAN COUNTIES						
894 agencies; population 35,456,591:						
Number	166,773	52,703	105,723	2,240	1,762	4,345
Percent	100.0	31.6	63.4	1.3	1.1	2.6
RURAL COUNTIES						
2,377 agencies; population 27,204,912:						
Number	83,799	22,930	51,786	1,944	2,192	4,947
Percent	100.0	27.4	61.8	2.3	2.6	5.9
SUBURBAN AREA[3]						
5,088 agencies; population 85,188,675:						
Number	650,574	252,407	341,932	8,005	8,808	39,422
Percent	100.0	38.8	52.6	1.2	1.4	6.1

Source: Federal Bureau of Investigation, U.S. Department of Justice, *Crime In The United States*, U.S. Government Printing Office, Washington, D.C., 1981.

[1] Includes all offenses except traffic and neglect cases.

[2] Because of rounding, the percentages may not add to total.

[3] Includes suburban city and county law enforcement agencies within metropolitan areas. Excludes core cities. Suburban cities also included in other city groups.

juvenile arrest includes those referred to the juvenile court and those cases of the more serious law violations by juveniles in which a juvenile is referred to some type of social or community agency for action. In some jurisdictions, although no official referral is made to another agency if the law violation is of a sufficiently serious nature, an arrest record will be made and disposition made by the department only. In some departments if a law violation is of a somewhat serious nature, and it is felt by the officer that the juvenile will engage in further delinquent behavior, the juvenile will be arrested.

In most departments the final decision as to whether an arrest will be made of a juvenile or will not be made rests with the head or officers of the juvenile control unit. This procedure minimizes criticism from the public for any mishandling of juveniles that might occur and makes possible more uniform processing and handling of juveniles contacted by the department.

The problem of adequately defining a juvenile arrest has continued to confront police agencies. Because of great variation in the practices of juvenile processing by the police, the need for some useable operational definition for juvenile arrests persists. The Bureau of Criminal Statistics of the California Department of Justice has developed, in cooperation with local police officials, guidelines for reporting arrest statistics. Although these guidelines are simply guidelines, they do provide a logical basis for determining when an arrest of a juvenile has in fact been consummated.

A juvenile arrest is the taking, seizing, or detaining of the juvenile, either by touching or putting hands on him or by any other act that indicates an intention to take him into custody. It subjects the juvenile arrested to the actual control and will of the person making the arrest. The act must be performed with the intent to effect an arrest, and the person making the arrest must be acting under some legal authority for taking the juvenile into custody.

An application of actual force or physical restraint is not necessary. It is sufficient if the juvenile arrested understands that he is in the power of the one arresting and submits to his custody. But if there is no manual touching, intent becomes very important. The one arresting must intend to arrest, while the juvenile arrested must intend to submit.

Arrest involves four separate elements:

1. There must be intent to take into custody.

2. There must be authority, either actual or pretended.
3. There must be actual or constructive restraint or detention.
4. The juvenile arrested must submit to the authority of the one arresting.

Although there has been no suggestion that the principles enunciated in this definition be changed, the need for a restatement in terms more readily identified with established police terminology, procedures, and practices is believed desirable.

Because of the wider range of police involvement in juvenile control than in the control of adults, a major problem is to specifically define police contacts that for statistical purposes are arrests and those that are not considered arrests. Police contacts in the juvenile control field can be separated into two basic types: (1) contacts that require subsequent action, and (2) contacts that do not require subsequent action.

1. Contacts that require an action subsequent to the initial contact are arrests. Contacts of this type include those that result in the transportation of juveniles to the officer's headquarters and a subsequent arrest report or booking record completed, whether released to parents, placed in a juvenile hall, jail, or other detention facility, or released on their own recognizance. Also included in this group are juveniles released after they have been issued citations, wherein they agree to appear at the probation department for further consideration of the case. It will be noted that each type of action listed requires an action subsequent to the initial contact before the incident can be terminated.

2. Contacts that do not require subsequent action are generally thought of as field contacts or field interrogations. They involve situations where juveniles are stopped, questioned, or identified and, on occasion, reprimanded or requested to disperse or return home. In these situations no further action is taken by the police, and the matter is closed. This type of contact is not considered an arrest for statistical purposes.

Other contacts that are not to be identified as an arrest for statistical purposes are requests made during field contacts for juveniles to call at the officer's headquarters or some other specified location for an interview. These appointments, usually investigative interviews, are considered voluntary actions of the juvenile. If the juvenile refuses to comply with the officer's request and is thereafter ordered to comply, his compliance would then be considered an arrest. However, there are some situations requiring only an initial contact that are classified as arrests. These are contacts with juveniles where the individual's responsibility for an offense is admitted, but the incidents are recorded and closed by the police during the initial interview. These contacts are considered arrests. This type of action may be more clearly defined by citing an example:

A juvenile has stolen property from a neighbor. An officer called to the scene may apprehend the juvenile, reprimand him, secure the return of the property, and conclude the entire case without the necessity of subsequent action.

In the situation, as outlined, there was an offense, the offender was arrested, the investigation was completed, the official action was taken, and the case was terminated while the officer was at the scene.

Some jurisdictions may desire to use some term other than arrest in the handling of juveniles. The Standard Juvenile Court Act refers to apprehension and release of children by stating that "when any child found violating any law or ordinance, or whose surroundings are such as to endanger his/her welfare, is taken into custody, such taking into custody, shall not be termed an arrest. The jurisdiction of the court shall attach from the time of such taking into custody...." An alternative to the term *arrest* may be *investigation* or *taken into custody* to avoid any stigma associated with it. If a juvenile has not been labeled with an arrest, his future may be brighter in obtaining employment, furthering his education, or making his life more socially successful.

Truancy

Police agencies should work very closely with the schools in the handling of juveniles who are truant from school. The juvenile specialist unit, which maintains liaison with the juvenile court, should also maintain liaison for this purpose with the schools. Generally speaking, youngsters found to be truant should be referred to the schools for handling within the school framework. There are usually specialists on the staff of the school district administrator who work with these cases. The policies behind and mechanisms for these referrals should be worked out in a joint cooperative effort by police and school personnel. Truancy referrals to juvenile court should usually be made by school rather than by police personnel.

Incorrigibility and Ungovernability

Incorrigibility and ungovernability are concepts that are much harder to discuss than truancy. These are interchangeable terms establishing catchall categories, much less specific ones, both in inherent meaning and in application. Such situations usually involve older children and reflect a breakdown in the child-parent relationship. Children fall into one of these categories when they are beyond the control of parents but have not yet been involved in violations of law as far as anyone knows. These allegations are frequently made to juvenile courts by the parents themselves.

There does not seem to be any compelling reason for police activity in these cases, unless the parents are mistakenly using these terms to describe a case that does involve violation of law. In such a situation, the police should act just as they would on a similar complaint from any other source. By definition, however, they will have the advantage of the assured cooperation of the parents from the start. If the parents approach the police in a true case of ungovernability not involving violation of law, they should be sent directly to an appropriate social agency or to the juvenile court with their problem.

Use of these general catchall categories frequently results in abuse. Juveniles are taken into custody on the basis of an alleged violation of law when there is insufficient evidence to establish probable cause that they actually committed that violation. In these circumstances, the specific violation charge is dropped and a general allegation of incorrigibility or ungovernability substituted. This allegation is also sometimes used in an effort to minimize publicity when the offense involved is a sex offense. The result in either case is that there is no fair opportunity for the juvenile to challenge the basis for jurisdiction of the juvenile court.

Incorrigibility and ungovernability are all too often regarded as catchalls that can justify court jurisdiction in any case in which a specific basis for jurisdiction cannot be demonstrated. This is an abuse of juvenile court process that can and should be stopped. There are a number of case decisions in appeals from juvenile courts that hold that a pattern of antisocial conduct must be proved to establish one of these vague, general allegations. If this theory were pressed, such an allegation would be more difficult to prove than the more simple one of specific violation of law. Elimination of these categories as a basis of juvenile court jurisdiction is being seriously considered. More lawyers involved in juvenile court actions and more appeals in these kinds of cases would clarify the law of incorrigibility and ungovernability.

Absconders, Escapees, and Runaways

It is a common responsibility of each police agency to work out procedures for the return of juvenile probationers and parolees who have absconded from probation or parole supervision within the state in which the police agency is located. These procedures may be dictated by local law. The procedures to be worked out will not necessarily be the same as those for adult absconders, since juveniles who are on probation or parole as a result of juvenile court action have not been convicted of a crime.

In some states, no satisfactory statutes have been enacted to meet this difficulty. In these situations, it is particularly important for representatives of police agencies to meet with juvenile court, public welfare, and probation and parole authorities to work out satisfactory procedures that can be implemented by administrative action and to then press for legislation that will make it possible to adopt better procedures.

When it is discovered that the juvenile has absconded from probation or parole supervision in another state, the same problems may exist. In such cases, help can usually be obtained from the local probation and parole authorities. In some states, however, this situation is covered by the Interstate Compact on Juveniles. When a police officer encounters a juvenile who has absconded from probation or parole in another state, the procedures of the compact are available. In such a situation, the police officer takes the juvenile into custody and delivers him to the local juvenile court. The court will contact the local state compact administrator, and the juvenile will then be returned to his home state by compact procedures, unless he/she is in additional trouble locally. In that case, the local difficulty will be cleared prior to return. Police administrators in states that have not adopted the compact should work toward its adoption.

Escapees

Much the same situations are encountered with escapees as with absconders. Police administrators have a responsibility to survey the local law and work with the institution officials of the state in establishing procedures under those laws. The compact is again available if the state in which the juvenile is found and the state from which he has fled are both signatories of the compact. In these circumstances, the compact also provides that the police deliver the juvenile to the local juvenile court, which handles the matter from that point on.

With both absconders and escapees, the compact authorizes the issuance of a "detention order" by the local state compact administrator or by the local juvenile court for the apprehension and detention of the juvenile. This order may be served by any officer anywhere in the state. In serving these orders, the same procedure should be followed as in the serving of all other orders for taking into custody. In addition, the compact provides that if a police officer has "reasonable information" to the effect that a certain juvenile is an absconder or escapee, that juvenile may be apprehended and delivered to the local juvenile court without a written order.

Runaways

In dealing with runaways, the police have an additional problem that does not exist with absconders and escapees. The latter categories are already being given help by a state in meeting their problems. Their cases have already come to the attention of the juvenile service agencies. With runaways this is not so. As a result, the police may be responsible for returning the juvenile home to juvenile court; however, some states have made this a status offense, limiting police jurisdiction.

Those who study the mental health problems of juveniles agree that running away from home is quite often indicative of deep-seated problems within the family. This is substantiated by the experience of the police. The police frequently have their first of many contacts with a juvenile in a runaway situation. Runaway cases should be referred to the juvenile specialist unit.

Because a runaway situation usually means that the family has a serious problem, it is good practice for a police agency to get the assistance of a social agency in helping both the juvenile and his parents come to an understanding of their difficulty. The police department taking a runaway juvenile into custody should, at the same time the parents are notified, notify a local social agency, which will give help in such cases, unless the case is referred to the juvenile court.

A social worker can then be working with the juvenile pending the arrival of the parents or the making of other arrangements for the return, attempting to help the juvenile arrive at a satisfactory solution of the problem that led to his/her running away. At the same time, the police department in the juvenile's hometown should notify the parents of the runaway and give the parents skilled help in understanding their child's conduct. In the many communities where such social services are not available, the local department of public welfare may be able to help.

Every report of a runaway juvenile within a jurisdiction should be considered like any other complaint. It should be investigated by the police department or by a local social service or welfare agency to determine whether the juvenile court jurisdiction that probably exists should be invoked. In case of doubt, the case should be referred to juvenile court. Occasionally, there will also be a question as to whether there actually is a runaway. This will be true particularly when the child is taken into custody in his hometown soon after being reported missing. Here the police will have to decide upon the evidence available to them whether an actual intent to run away from home existed.

Special problems are presented when the runaway is from another state. Again, contact with the hometown police agency should be made through police communication channels. These channels should be used to minimize expense. Usually a state police or state highway patrol will be happy to cooperate by contacting its equivalent state law enforcement agency in the other state through police communication channels. The information will then be relayed to the municipal police agency in the other state.

This service is available to courts as well as to police agencies. This does not preclude the use of social agencies as discussed above. When the answer is that the parents or other relatives will come to pick up the juvenile, these cases can be handled just like those of runaways from within the state. Special problems are presented in either case when the family of the juvenile would like to come for him but is not financially able to make the trip. This is frequently a problem where great distances are involved.

Police officials in every state should know whether funds are available through the public welfare agency. If they are not, every effort should be made to persuade the state public welfare director to provide for their availability. When these funds are not available, private charitable funds may be, on a local basis. Travelers aid will advance money in emergency situations where funds for reimbursement will be available at a later time and, in some communities, even when there is no possibility of reimbursement. Travelers aid will also assist when the parents and the police are able to obtain the juvenile's cooperation in returning home by himself. In such a case, the parents may send the money for return transportation, and travelers aid will assist in getting the child from one train, bus, or airplane to another as required on the trip back.

Little difficulty can arise for local police officials when the juvenile consents to return to his home and when his parents come and pick him up. There are possible difficulties if the juvenile is to return alone, however. If the juvenile is injured during the trip or if he runs away again, the local police agency may be subjected to adverse criticism. Difficult problems are also presented when a runaway child must be kept overnight. Where there is any doubt about such cases, they should probably be referred to the local juvenile court. Where the Interstate Compact on Juveniles is available, its provision for voluntary return should be utilized. What this provision does is to make formal the giving of consent by the juvenile so that it will be readily provable at any later date.

In this procedure, the police take the juvenile to the local juvenile court. Under the compact, the court has discretion whether to appoint a guardian ad litem (i.e. a guardian for the purpose of this court proceeding only) for the juvenile. The judge then explains the situation to the juvenile, making sure that the juvenile understands fully what is happening and what his/her rights are. The juvenile then signs a written statement of consent. If a guardian ad litem has been appointed, he then also signs a statement that he believes that the juvenile should be allowed to return as directed by the court and that he consents to such return. The judge then signs a statement that he has explained the situation to the juvenile, and that the consent of the child is voluntary. This is an excellent protection for the local police agency and should be followed where possible in every case when the juvenile is not delivered directly to the parents or their representatives.

Another provision of the compact makes a procedure available for those cases in which the parents of the juveniles are not financially able to provide for his return and funds are not available from any other source. Under this procedure, the custody agency delivers the child directly to the local juvenile court. Here, as in the case of absconders and escapees, the subsequent procedures are the responsibility and concern of the court and not of the police. Under this procedure, the cost of the return is eventually borne by the state from which the juvenile fled.

As with absconders and escapees, the taking into custody may be by virtue of a "detention order" issued by the compact administrator or by the local juvenile court judge, or it may be made by virtue of "reasonable information" available to the police without any written order.

The above discussion has been concerned with the action of the police department in taking into custody runaways. Attention must also be given to the response of the department to reports that juveniles are missing. Many missing person reports are made by some member of the family at police headquarters. When the report is made by telephone, the patrol unit on whose beat the family resides should go to the home and take the report. Factors to be determined for the report are the age and sex of the missing juvenile, personal description, time and date left, whether there is any apparent reason for the disappearance, the circumstances surrounding the disappearance, and whether the child has run away before.

If the information in the report indicates that kidnapping or homicide may be involved, detective specialists should be brought into the case immediately and the usual investigative procedures initiated. Where kidnapping is suspected, this may include notification of the Federal Bureau of Investigation. if the information indicates that a young child has merely wandered off, preplanned procedures for a search of the area should be activated. Arrangements for mass media publicity may also be indicated. If there is reason to believe that an older juvenile has left the area or the state, other police departments should be alerted.

A law has been presented to the United States Congress entitled "Missing Child Act of 1981." This law would set up a national data bank for runaways and missing children. A national system of this type would be extremely valuable to local law enforcement agencies.

There is an innovative and effective system in the state of California. Under a law implemented in 1979 the California Dental Identification System was established. This system is based on the fact that all law enforcement agencies in the state must forward dental information on missing persons who are still missing after forty-five days, and that all medical examiners and coroners must likewise forward dental data on all unidentified bodies. Technicians at the Special Missing Person Unit, California State Department of Justice, Sacramento, California, with the aid of forensic odontologists, compare the data in an effort to establish identifications.

As of August 1981, twenty-five adults and juveniles have been identified through this system, for a successful identification rate of approximately 10 percent. Twenty-two of the victims identified were victims of homicide. Although most of the victims have been reported missing and found in California, at least three victims have been identified in other states, because California is accepting dental data from other states at this time.

This concept is innovative and timely. According to Dr. Norman D. Sperber, D.D.S., a forensic odontologist and one of the originators of this concept, California is the only state with an operational dental identification system. Dr. Sperber, who currently is a consultant to the San Diego Coroner's Office, is attempting to have this dental identification system included in the federal missing persons bill in order to have this methodology carried out on a national scale, which would be of significant aid to law enforcement.

Traffic Safety Activities

Traffic safety activities in police agencies are normally a responsibility of the departmental traffic unit. However, they are an integral component of an agency's efforts to meet the needs of juveniles. Often the program activities are a shared responsibility with the juvenile unit. Presentations by officers in schools often include traffic and bicycle safety, as well as delinquency prevention subjects. Specialized bicycle and junior safety patrol programs involve considerable interaction between the police and a large number of juveniles in the community. The latter provides continuing opportunities for the police to emphasize delinquency prevention as well as traffic safety.

It is just good police work to include traffic safety for juveniles as an integral component of an agency's juvenile program. Whether the program will be placed in the traffic or juvenile unit depends on how a department is organized.

Bicycle Programs

There are a number of departments throughout the United States that have developed programs for the control and operation of bicycles. Programs differ from city to city, but basically the programs provide for yearly inspection, registration, and licensing of all bicycles in the city. Emphasis is placed on enforcement and safety education in many of the programs. Organizationally, these programs may come under the direction and supervision of the traffic division or juvenile control division.

In most states the bicycle safety and control program can be effected under state laws. Many cities, however, design local ordinances to provide special regulations not covered by other laws. The local ordinances usually establish a system for bicycle registration and licensing and regulate the buying and selling of bicycles, both new and used.

Because it is well-known nationally and has been unofficially referred to by the National Safety Council as a model program, the basic program of the Berkeley, California, Police Department will be reviewed here.* The bicycle bureau is a subdivision of the traffic

---

*The program is a classic for administrators interested in programs of management by objectives. Inaugurated in 1939 the program was designed to reduce injury and fatal accidents, which were running 40 to 50 per year, in the city of Berkeley. Since 1940, bicycle injuries and fatal accidents have maintained a level under fifteen accidents per year, even with a great increase in the use of bicycles.

division. It is staffed full time by a regular police officer who bears the title of director of the bicycle bureau.

The Berkeley program performs three main functions: licenses and inspects bicycles; controls bicycle dealers; carries on an educational program and supervises the bicycle traffic court. Under the licensing program yearly renewals are required for all bicycle owners. At the time the licenses are renewed, the bicycles are inspected for mechanical condition and equipment. The director of the bureau exercises an opportunity during the registration period to keep bicycle riders fully acquainted with current laws governing bicycle operation, and it is an excellent means of carrying out a public relations program with juveniles and their parents.

Bicycle dealers within the city of Berkeley are controlled, being required to obtain a permit from the chief of police for establishing and carrying on a business. Before the permit is issued, the applicant is subjected to an investigation to determine that he is the proper person to be dealing with juveniles. The permit may be revoked at any time. The dealer is required to report the sale or purchase of any bicycle, new or used. All dealers are required to maintain complete records of all deals involving bicycle transactions in their office. It is a function of the director to make regular inspections of the books to insure that dealers are conducting their business in a legal and satisfactory manner.

An important duty of the director of the Bicycle Bureau is to carry on an active educational program throughout the year. To do so, it is essential that he work closely with administrators of the school department and with the principal of each school. At least once a semester he appears before the students of each school in the city and either delivers a lecture on bicycle safety or presents a film on the same subject. His responsibility also includes working in close cooperation with individual groups such as the Boy Scouts, PTA, and YMCA.

One of the most important activities of the bicycle bureau is supervision and operation of the bicycle traffic court. Basically, the court operates in a similar fashion to the regular traffic court. The enforcement of the bicycle laws is the responsibility of all patrolmen assigned to street duty. They cite juveniles to the bicycle traffic court. Adult violators are treated in the same manner as for violation of any traffic law, i.e. being cited directly to the municipal court. All violators between the ages of eleven and seventeen years inclusive are required to appear in bicycle court. Those under the age of eleven are handled through a direct contact with their parents by the director of the bureau. Bicycle offenses committed on the school grounds are normally handled by school authorities in the same manner as any other violation of school rules. In exceptional cases referrals may be made to the juvenile court.

The bicycle traffic court is staffed with personnel selected from the junior and senior high schools and parochial schools in the city. Selections are made by the faculty and student body representatives in each of the schools concerned. Four students are selected from each junior high school and three students from the senior high schools and from each parochial school. Selections are based upon scholastic ability and leadership and are made for a period of one semester. It has been customary, however, to retain a few of the judges from one semester to the next, thereby providing a nucleus of experienced personnel about which to build each subsequent court.

For operating purposes four students take part in each session of the court. One serves as chief justice, two as associate justices, and one as bailiff. The director of the bicycle bureau is also present at each session as an adult counselor. Each member of the court sits in on at least four sessions and serves as bailiff, associate justice, and chief justice. The position of chief justice changes each court day.

The bicycle court convenes at 10:30 A.M. every Saturday morning, each week of the year, in a municipal courtroom located in the hall of justice. The program continues throughout the summer months.

The judges are given an oath of office by the local court judge, following which they attend a session of the court to observe the proper operation of a court. Prior to the first session as judges they are given an orientation course whereby they become acquainted with the history and operation of the court.

Juveniles are cited to the traffic court by a special citation form, the stub of which is routed to the director of the Bicycle Bureau. The director prepares the calendar for use by the judges and the traffic court. The juvenile must appear before the court. His parents may or may not be present since it is operated in a very informal manner.

The following "sentences" may be meted out by the court if the child violated a law:

1. Reprimanded or suspended "sentence."
2. Preparation of a composition of 200 to 1000 words on various aspects of safety; for example, quote reasons for safe-riding rules.
3. Required attendance at bicycle traffic school for a period of six consecutive Saturdays, each period lasting one hour, from 9 A.M. to 10 A.M.
4. Impounding the bicycle at the hall of justice for a period of from seven to thirty days.
5. Parents to deprive the offender of use of bicycle for from one to three days.
6. Failure to obtain license during renewal period must pay fifty cents additional to required fee as provided by the ordinance.
7. Copy a specified section of the bicycle ordinance from one to five times.
8. Any combination of two or more of the above dispositions.

Subsequent to issuance of a citation to a juvenile violator and prior to his appearance at bicycle court, a letter is sent to the violator's parents informing them of the violation, the citation, the required appearance in court, and outlining the objectives of the court. Stress is placed upon the fact that it is educational, not criminal. After appearance in court, another letter is sent to the violator's parents, outlining the "sentence" received and requesting their cooperation in seeing that the directions of the court are obeyed.

It is the responsibility of the director of the Bicycle Bureau to insure that all sentences are complied with. If the juvenile fails to comply with the sentence, he may be called to the office of the director for an interview. If the violator still fails to obey instructions after the interview, his or her parents are interviewed. If this interview fails to obtain necessary results, the violator's bicycle is impounded or the case is referred to the juvenile court.

School Safety Patrols

Providing necessary traffic control at busy school crossings is an essential police responsibility performed by police officers or crossing guards in almost every community, be it rural or urban. The responsibility is becoming progressively greater because of the increasing traffic problem, and the number of crossings that must be controlled is ever increasing.

Many cities assign a considerable number of officer man-hours to the manual control and supervision of school crossings. Some communities employ crossing guards, either women or older men. Another method has been initiated for school crossings control and supervision: the school safety patrol or, as it is sometimes called, "junior traffic patrol."

The school safety patrol program utilizes school boys and girls for full traffic control at most intersections near schools. They control both vehicular and student traffic without immediate adult supervision, either on the part of school authorities or the police department. Training and general supervision for the boys and girls is afforded by the police agency with assistance from school officials.

That such a program is practiced has been known and utilized by many police agencies. Officially, the program was recognized in California by the State Department of Education in 1948 when the school code was amended to provide for establishment of such patrols. Not only was their use approved, but detailed specifications with respect to equipment and method of operation was developed and incorporated into the rules and regulations of the State Department of Education.

Departmental responsibility for administration of the junior safety patrol program is normally placed either in the traffic division or juvenile control division. In the average city no more than the services of one officer is required to head the program.

The school safety patrol program has been utilized by many departments. However, there are some areas where the legality of the program is questioned and the program has not been effected. It remains, however, that a conservation of police man-hours is achieved, especially valuable in days of emergency and curtailed budgets.

Traffic Education

Traffic education has been accepted as a major function of traffic divisions in law enforcement agencies. Effective traffic education, however, is predicated upon full support of interested community agencies and, in many jurisdictions, relies considerably upon the court or the local chapter of the National Safety Council, local automobile clubs, and the school system. In the case of juveniles the need for traffic education has been emphasized; consequently, juvenile traffic schools have been established in a number of jurisdictions.

Police officers participate in other types of traffic safety education programs. In many states it is either required or possible that safety education be taught in the school curriculum. Oftentimes, instructors are from the local police department or highway patrol or state police. The police are in a position through these programs to influence the driving habits of youth throughout the country. If such a program is not in existence in a community, the police can be the promoters. The value of the programs cannot be overestimated because they reach the juvenile in many instances before he ever sits behind the wheel of an automobile. Since the police are more concerned with preventing accidents by encouraging observance of traffic laws than in punishing offenders after the accident occurs, this medium seems particularly effective. It has been found that in a majority of traffic accidents at least one traffic regulation was violated.

Chapter 12

INTERVIEWING

I NTERVIEWING is one of the most important parts of every law enforcement officer's job. It has been estimated that over 80 percent of an officer's investigative work consists of obtaining information through interview. He is constantly interviewing juveniles, parents, witnesses, victims, correctional workers, citizens, community leaders, and others. The reputation of the individual officers and that of his department will depend a great deal upon how efficiently and considerately the officer carries on his interviews as the core of his investigation responsibilities.

Interviewing is a skill and not an inborn trait. Each officer should continually strive to improve his knowledge of interview and communication skills. The challenge is one that will add interest to those years in which the investigator works towards increasing his proficiency in this art.

PURPOSES OF INTERVIEWS

There are various purposes or objectives for the interviews. They include the following:

1. To obtain the element of the alleged offense.

2. To determine whether a particular juvenile or juveniles were involved in the offense.
3. To learn all significant facts about the juvenile and his overall situation.
4. To obtain information about a complaint regarding harmful home conditions or dangerous conditions.
5. To determine information about a juvenile found under questionable circumstances, e.g. officers find a juvenile on the street very early in the morning.

The above purposes might be called the *immediate purposes* or *objectives*. The long-term purpose of the interview would be to obtain information to file a petition or plan a constructive treatment program for the juvenile and his family using diversion and community-based services.

PREPARING FOR THE INTERVIEW

Thorough preparation for interviews with juveniles will lead to the most effective results. These preparations include the following:

1. Obtaining the basic facts about the case from police reports and any other possible sources.
2. Learning about the juvenile's past record and personality traits through search of departmental files, which might also provide valuable information about the family situation. Consultation with other officers acquainted with the juvenile could also prove helpful. Clearance with a central juvenile index, if one exists, is essential.
3. Choosing the best setting for the interview. The three basic alternatives are the law enforcement office, the juvenile's home, and a neutral location such as a school office. Although most officers prefer the departmental office as the exclusive choice, consideration should be given to the juvenile's home. In the family setting the officer can observe the living conditions and the more natural interaction between juvenile and parent during the interview. These items can be valuable in making the final disposition.
4. Scheduling the interview as soon as feasible after the original police contact, usually by a patrolman. An early interview will

Giving of Rights

Of paramount concern in every arrest and investigation is the proper giving of rights to juveniles immediately upon arrest, usually by a patrolman. It is also essential that a juvenile fully understands these rights and the meaning of his waiver of his rights.

The *Illinois Youth Officer Manual* provides a sound set of guidelines on the questioning of juveniles and the giving of rights, as follows.

Questioning Juveniles

These rules are suggested for consideration and in themselves are not binding either on patrolmen or the juvenile officer. They may be useful in helping determine departmental procedures for questioning juveniles.

1. Before questioning, the officer should identify himself. If in plain clothes, he should show his identification card and badge.
2. His attitude should be friendly and helpful, not formal, overbearing, and officious. For the victim of a crime, be sympathetic even if you don't feel that his condition is serious.
3. Consider the normal emotional state of the youngster being questioned, particularly where crimes of violence have been committed. Excitement and tension may obscure their perceptions of what occurred. Try to obtain accurate information on what the circumstances were immediately before, during, and after the incident.
4. Persons being questioned as witnesses or victims of a crime should be allowed to give an uninterrupted account while the officer makes mental notes of any omissions, inconsistencies, and discrepancies that may require clarification at a later time. Phrase all questions to keep the individual on the subject and to the point. Avoid taking narrative statements from juveniles by using the question-and-answer approach whenever possible.
5. When the juvenile being questioned is a suspect, ask him to identify himself and explain his activity. You have no power to compel an answer and you should not attempt to do so by insinuating consequences of fear or favor.

6. Refusal to answer your questions should not be the entire basis for taking the child into custody. You need probable cause to take into custody. If the youth runs, don't jump to conclusions; fear and fright can cause the most innocent to panic.

7. Once you take a juvenile into custody for any offense where he is alleged to be a delinquent, read him the Miranda warnings and make sure he understands them. These warnings are necessary to ensure that the youth being questioned or interrogated knows that he has a right not to speak or incriminate himself, then when he speaks it is voluntarily and not because of police pressure.

8. The Miranda rules apply to all "interrogations" of a person "in custody" or arrested. A youth is in custody when he has been deprived of his freedom of action in any significant way. As a matter of practice, the Miranda warnings should be given when the officer's questions are intended to elicit incriminating or exculpatory admissions or a confession from the juvenile.

9. If a youth waives his right to have a lawyer present and proceeds to answer questions, there is a heavy burden on the police to demonstrate that the accused did in fact knowingly and intelligently waive his right to counsel. Get it in writing by having a prepared statement, approved by the state's attorney and the judge of the juvenile court, which clearly indicates the voluntary waiving of the Miranda protection. No threats, inferences, or any statements that contain a coercive implication should be engaged in by the officer.

10. Simple street questioning of a juvenile concerning his identity and activities does not necessarily constitute an "interrogation" or unnecessary limitation on freedom of action. If your questions are only a few direct, preliminary questions such as "Who are you?" and "What are you doing here?" you do not have to give the Miranda warnings. (If the juvenile you have stopped is being approached under the "stop-and-frisk" law, you do not have to give him the Miranda warnings.)

11. At any point where your questioning becomes more extensive than a few informational questions about name, age, place of residence, and destination, then the safest rule to follow is to

give the Miranda warnings.

12. Interrogation designed to break a youth's story or to get a confession should never be conducted on the street. This is not the job of the patrolman. If there is a reasonable cause to take a youth into custody, you should do so and immediately take him to the juvenile police officer. If not, take notes on his identity and answers to your general questions, then allow him to leave.

13. Any time you take a youth, on what will constitute a delinquency charge, to the police station always give the Miranda warnings.

14. If a juvenile, at any time and in any manner, prior to or during questioning, indicates that he wants to remain silent, all questioning must cease. If he states he wants a lawyer, all questioning must cease until a lawyer is present.

15. Neither physical force nor psychological pressure should ever be used to compel a child to confess or answer questions.

16. The "consent" given by a youngster may not be enough to legalize the information received if the child is too young to realize the consequences of his statements without the presence of his parents or lawyer to counsel him.

17. Patrolmen should not enter into extended or systematic interrogation of juveniles or attempt to get a written statement. This is the job of the juvenile officer, who, it is hoped, will likewise bind himself to the aforementioned rules.

18. CUSTODIAL INTERROGATION (MIRANDA) WARNING

After each part of the following warning, the officer must determine whether the suspect understands what he is being told:

You have a right to remain silent. You do not have to talk to me unless you want to do so.

If you do want to talk to me, I must advise you that whatever you say can and will be used as evidence against you in court.

You have a right to consult with a lawyer and to have a lawyer present with you while you are being questioned.

If you want a lawyer, but are unable to pay for one, a lawyer will be appointed to represent you free of any cost to you.

After advising the warning, you may follow up with:

Knowing these rights, do you want to talk to me without having a lawyer present? You may stop talking to me at any time, and you may also demand a lawyer at any time.

QUALIFICATIONS OF THE INTERVIEWER

Authorities agree that the following qualities are required for the successful interviewer:

1. A basic knowledge of psychology
2. Salesmanship
3. Ability to act or role play
4. Discretion
5. Perseverance
6. Insight
7. Intelligence
8. Persuasiveness
9. Good speech habits
10. Verbal communication skills
11. Nonverbal communication skills
12. Well-groomed, clean and neat appearance
13. Experienced in investigations
14. Basic knowledge in a variety of areas
15. Constantly strives for proficiency
16. Interest in people
17. Frankness
18. Understanding
19. Alertness
20. Self-assurance
21. Professional attitude
22. Good self-image
23. Integrity
24. Ability to command respect
25. Logical mind

Although these demands are great, officers should constantly strive to improve their individual skill in the art of interviewing.

RAPPORT

Rapport is a basic ingredient to be developed between the subject and the interviewer. It will usually determine the final outcome of the interview. Rapport embodies an understanding between two individuals and conveys a sense of identification on the part of both parties, plus the ability to communicate. If the relationship is strained or marked by mistrust or a feeling of strangeness, the subject may be reluctant to furnish the desired information. The interviewer must endeavor to win the confidence of the subject, since a completely voluntary offer of information is the ideal result of a successful interview.

Rapport may be gained through good personality traits. The interviewer should show a forcefulness of personality and induce confidence by strength of character so as to induce trust. There should not be an air of superiority, but rather feelings of sympathy and understanding.

Rapport may be established by starting the conversation on neutral subjects of mutual interest such as sports, hobbies, school, friends, automobiles, or racing.

HOW TO INTERVIEW

Various successful interviewing techniques have been developed by experienced police officers. It would be impossible to standardize interviewing, because each officer will naturally have his own particular method that makes him feel comfortable. We can, however, list some basic techniques which have been successful and which can be adopted by officers who are interested in developing greater skill in this important responsibilty. Many of these techniques are applicable for interviewing both juveniles and adults.

Original interviews with most juveniles will be made by uniformed patrolmen who particularly need to use a constructive approach that will not antagonize or completely alienate youth. The following suggestions focus on the follow-up investigation, which should be conducted by juvenile officers or detectives with a sound juvenile orientation. Perhaps the best general guideline for officers would be to interview juveniles in the same considerate manner as they would want their own children interviewed.

Police investigation of juvenile delinquency complaints involving alleged violations of law should be made with the following three questions in mind:

tion in the offense. Pointing out discrepancies also helps.

5. Explain why the truth is necessary. Make it clear that your constructive purpose is to settle the complaint and arrive at a disposition that is best for him and the community.

6. Be patient if resistance develops. Sometimes the use of humor can reduce negative feelings. Be understanding of anti-authority feelings of most adolescents.

7. If tape recordings are to be used, they should be with the knowledge and consent of the juvenile.

8. Encourage him to clear up any other offenses committed so he can continue with a clean slate.

9. Written confessions are desirable but must be consistent with legal controls.

10. Accomplices should first be interviewed alone and then, if necessary, in a group to clarify any discrepancies.

11. Express appreciation for his cooperation, and indicate your long-term interest in his welfare. Ask how he sees himself behaving in the future in order to evaluate his motivations toward constructive conduct.

Don't Do This

1. *Don't resort to vulgarity, profanity, or obscenity.* The use of such language by a police officer is especially reprehensible and should not be tolerated under any circumstances.

2. *Don't "brand" the juvenile.* Epithets such as "thief," "liar," "burglar," "forger," and so on should never be used toward juveniles whether in custody or not; nor should such terms be used in reference to juveniles in their presence or in the presence of their parents or relatives, or of any other person not a member of the police department—nothing is to be gained by it, and there is definite indication that it is very injurious to the child. Such epithets give rise to justified complaints. They are rightfully resented by the parents of nondelinquent children and, in the case of delinquent children, by the state. The use of such epithets towards juveniles is a reflection upon the character and intelligence of the officer using them.

3. *Don't lose your temper.* To do so is an admission of inferiority to

the person being interviewed.

4. *Don't lie to gain a point.* Sooner or later the lie may be discovered, and you will have lost the respect you are trying so hard to gain.

5. *Don't use physical force.* Rough treatment does not gain respect but tends to develop greater hostility. If you can't settle the case through accepted methods, be content to solve the case at some later date or to get the necessary facts on some future offense.

6. *Don't take notes immediately.* Wait until the person feels comfortable with you. Otherwise he may "freeze up" if he sees you writing too soon.

Interviewing in Presence of Parents

Whenever possible, and especially in the case of younger children, police interviews with juveniles should be conducted in such a manner as to protect the rights and best interests of the minor. The interview should take place in the presence of the parents or guardian of the minor, except when the parents, or their presence, would interfere with the officer's duty to obtain the facts surrounding the alleged offense, or where the parents or guardian have themselves participated in, or contributed to, the conduct of the minor being investigated. It is the police officer's duty to protect the guaranteed rights and best interests of the minor, but it is also his duty to learn the truth. There may well be instances in which the presence of the parents will tend to "block" or impede the investigation; in such a case the officer may refuse such parents the right to be present at the interview. The officer, however, must always remember that he may be charged with having obtained a statement from a minor by means of duress or by the infringement of the minor's guaranteed rights.

Learn Through Close Observation

Much of value can be learned for making the proper disposition if the officer observes the juvenile carefully from the moment of first contact until the interview is completed.

POSTURE. How a boy carries himself may be an indication of his feeling toward himself and others. A slouched, dejected posture may indicate lack of self-confidence. It may indicate fear of persons in authority or a giving in to extreme pressures from his social environment.

PROPORTION. Any undue disproportion such as an overly large head, hands, feet, ears, or nose may affect the boy psychologically and cause others to joke about him. His delinquency may represent a fighting back against society for these slights.

WEIGHT. Extremes in weight are often significant to note. An overweight child may be unconsciously trying to gain satisfactions through excess eating if he can't get affection normally from the parents. An excessively thin child may reveal inadequate dietary knowledge on the part of the parents. Glandular disturbances may be the main cause of the weight extremes.

DEFORMITIES. Physical handicaps such as club foot, deformed arm or leg, or unusual body growths may be the basis for some delinquencies. They may cause the child to try to overcompensate for his lacks through antisocial conduct.

FACIAL APPEARANCE. Birthmarks, acne, harelip, and so forth may be very disturbing to a youngster and condition his attitude toward the world. Adolescents are usually very sensitive about their facial appearance.

GLANDULAR DEFECTS. Bulging eyes, excessive perspiration, hyperactivity, sluggish reactions, and so forth may be indicative of some glandular disturbance that needs treatment.

TICS. Intermittent and spasmodic jerky movements are easily observed and may be indicative of deeper lying emotional problems calling for specialized treatment by other agencies.

SPEECH DEFECTS. Stuttering, inarticulate speech, or hesitating speech may be symptomatic of deeper emotional problems or results of physical defects that can be remedied.

NAIL BITING. Nervous biting of the nails may be a clue to inner feelings of inadequacy and insecurity.

SWEATING HANDS. May show excessive fear and insecurity.

HYPERACTIVITY. Some children are constantly on the go, moving their hands or feet or twisting around in their chairs. They just can't seem to sit still in a normal manner. Their excess energy may be an important factor in their getting involved in antisocial behavior and may indicate a need for medical care.

INTERVIEWING PARENTS

In order to make an effective disposition of each case the parent(s) or guardian should be interviewed with certain objectives in mind. Every effort should be made to interview both father and mother, whenever possible, in order to obtain a more complete understanding of family circumstances. Too often the father is never interviewed because he is at work during the normal day shift. Officers, therefore, need to make special arrangements to involve the father as the authority figure in the total investigation process.

It is recognized that officers do not have a great deal of time to gather detailed information on the family, nor is it the province of police departments to make social investigations. The focus of interviews with parents must therefore relate to the juvenile's behavior that brought him to the attention of the department. Within this context officers need to obtain certain basic information so they can make intelligent decisions.

Following are some of the key objectives to be attained:

1. Officers should introduce themselves as representatives of a law enforcement department that is interested both in the welfare of the juvenile and in the protection of the community. It is advisable to hand the parents a business card containing the officer's name and telephone number for possible use.

2. The legal rights of the juvenile suspect should also be explained to the parents so they have a clear understanding of what these mean.

3. Parental attitudes toward the juvenile's involvement in the offense are important to explore. If the juvenile has been interviewed alone and has admitted his misbehavior, it is advantageous to have him repeat the story in the presence of the parents. Are they objective, overprotective, or rejecting of the facts? What is the parental value system toward personal and property rights? What moral values have they tried to teach their children?

4. It is also essential to learn about the quality of parent-child relationships. To what degree do the parents provide love, security, recognition, guidance, and control? Is their discipline fair and firm, consistent or inconsistent, too lenient or too harsh? What is the quality of supervision, especially during

nonschool hours?

5. The interview should reveal how the parents feel about their ability to cope with the juvenile's problems in the future. Do they think they can handle the situation within the family, or do they recognize the need for help from some social agency or other resource?

6. Finally, the officer should obtain sufficient information about family stability so he can make a more effective disposition. How stable are the parent-parent relationships? What is the employment situation? Are the parents receiving assistance from social or other agencies?

NONVERBAL COMMUNICATIONS

The communication process consists of more than the spoken or written language. We also communicate through a variety of nonverbal communications.

A person's nonverbal communication, or body language, is usually involuntary, and the nonverbal signals that one transmits often are a more valid source of gleaning information than are the signals that are expressed verbally.[3]

When a person's verbal and nonverbal communications are congruent we tend to relax, trust and believe that person. If incongruent, we tend to distrust, doubt and suspect.

Although we can manipulate and disguise our verbal messages at will, our bodies are predisposed to convey only the true meaning of our expressions in an involuntary manner.

When verbal and nonverbal messages conflict, the listener invariably relies on the nonverbal, i.e. we trust actions more than words.

The transmission of mixed or contradictory messages lends an overall negative feeling toward communication.

Types of Nonverbal Communications

1. Gestures
2. Postures
3. Facial expressions
4. Eye contact

5. Body movement
6. Timing and silence between verbal exchanges
7. Touching
8. Sounds
9. Interpersonal space
10. Clothes
11. Signs

Importance of Nonverbal Communications

1. Increase congruency of verbal and nonverbal communications
2. The feedback function: Are you getting your message across?
3. Increase listening effectiveness
4. Increase cooperation/reduce defensiveness
5. Recognize patterns of increasing conflict/cooperation
6. Recognize real and/or hidden differences and needs
7. Strengthen empathy and understanding

Guidelines

1. Check for clusters of nonverbal signs to increase accuracy. Also, look for patterns in another person over a period of time.
2. Be careful not to read too much, but most of us are at a low level of awareness.
3. Some people display nonverbal behaviors that are unalterable or are due to physical factors.

Nonverbal Clusters

Openness: Open hands
Unbuttoned coat
Coat removed

Defensiveness: Arms crossed on chest
Legs over chair arm while seated
Crossed legs
Fistlike gestures
Pointing index finger

Karate Chops
Straddling a chair

Evaluation: Hand to cheek
Hand to chin/index finger along cheek
Head tilted
Stroking chin
Peering over glasses
Taking glasses off — cleaning
Glass earpiece in mouth
Pacing
Pinching bridge of nose

Suspicion: Not looking at you
Arms crossed on chest
Movement away from you
Sideways position
Sideways glance
Feet/body pointed towards exit
Touching/rubbing nose
Rubbing eyes

Readiness: Hands on hips
Hands on mid-thigh when seated
Sitting on edge of chair
Arms spread gripping edge of table/desk
Moving in and speaking confidentially

Reassurance: Clenched hands
Pinching fleshy part of hand
Chewing pencil
Fondling paperclip
Holding cup of coffee

Cooperation: Sprinter's Position
Sitting on edge of chair
Hand-to-face gestures
Unbuttoning of coat
Tilted head

Frustration: Running hand through hair
Rubbing back of neck
Breathing patterns
Tightly clenched hands
Wringing hands

Confidence: Steepling
Hands joined together at the back
Hands on lapels of coat
Feet on desk/chair
Placing object on a desired space
Elevating oneself

Nervousness: Clearing throat
Fidgeting in chair
Hands covering mouth while speaking
Not looking at other person
Tugging at pants while seated
Tugging at ear

Self-Control: Holding arm behind one's back
Locked ankles and clenched hands
Restraining an arm or gripping the wrist

Boredom: Drumming on table/tapping with feet
Head in palm of hands
Blank stare
Head erect/back straight

Acceptance   Hand to chest
Touching gestures
Moving closer to another person

Authorities have estimated that about 8 percent of our attitudes and feelings are expressed by words, 37 percent by vocal intonation and *55 percent* by body language. Interviewing officers must be aware of this phenomenon and utilize it as a productive tool.

Emotional conditioning of the body is frequently incited by past activities that have developed through repeated emotional reaction to certain situations. This is called a "conditioned reflex" and exists in almost all persons with respect to lying. Most people exhibit some emotion whenever they tell a lie.

PHYSICAL SYMPTOMS OF EMOTION

1. Dryness of mouth, frequent requests for water, dry cough.
2. Restlessness, frequent change in position, tapping of foot, fidgeting, gripping arms of chair, elbows held tight to body, running hands through hair, chewing fingernails, pencils, or other objects.
3. Excessive sweating, particularly of hands, armpits, and temples.
4. Unusually pallid or ruddy complexion, changes in complexion.
5. Pulsation of the carotid or temporal arteries.
6. Excessive swallowing, indicated by the unusual activity of the Adam's apple, dry cough.
7. Avoiding direct gaze of the interrogator's eyes, sidewards glance.
8. Excessive assertions of truthfulness, such as "I hope to die if I am lying," or "I'll swear it's the truth standing on my mother's grave," or "My right arm to God."
9. Evasive or vague answers, such as "I am not sure what happened;" "I can't remember;" "I have forgotten;" "I don't think it could have been that much."
10. A disturbing feeling of tenseness and turbulence in the pit of the stomach.

An experienced interrogator will constantly "body scan" the subject for any of these telltale signs that may aid him.

PROXEMICS AND THE INTERVIEW

The following ideas on proxemics and interviewing are to be viewed as suggestions, though some methods may well be integrated into an interviewing technique.

Behaviorists have shown that lower animals establish territories within which they hunt, raise their families and fight. There is a similar phenomenon in man. The lower mammals learn territoriality while man learns appropriate social distances as a result of interaction with his culture. This may vary from person to person depending on cultural differences and gender.

The social distances one assumes when sitting, standing, or talking are all culturally dictated. The culturally dictated body space maintained in a foreign country may vary from the traditional United States standards. The United States State Department attempts to prepare diplomats for this cultural phenomenon, which is a part of the "culture shock" an American can suffer when in foreign countries.

Dr. Edward T. Hall, an anthropologist from Northwestern University, has conducted an exhaustive cross-cultural study of body space and has reported the findings in his book, *The Hidden Dimension*.[4] He has observed different "social distances" in many nations and recorded them in what he calls a study of "proxemics." Dr. Hall has subdivided his "body space" categories into several substructures: public distance, formal social distance, personal or informal distance, and intimate distance.

Public Distance

Public body space is generally reserved for meetings, lectures, church services, and public meetings. This distance usually runs from twelve to twenty-five feet.

Formal Social Distance

People in formal social settings, such as in normal business transactions or at cocktail parties, usually maintain a distance from four to seven feet. The degree of closeness can be a part of effective communication. It may reflect trust, friendship, or that one is comfortable in another's presence or wants to communicate more effectively. Unilateral closeness, however, can raise anxiety in one of the parties if the warm feelings are not reciprocal.

Personal or Informal Distance

Personal distance can vary from one-and-one-half to about three feet. When communicating at this distance one is very aware of the other's presence, the lines in his face, stains on his teeth, as well as other factors that make this individual unique. However, when a third party joins the conversation, a minor adjustment is usually made to accommodate the new arrival. The distance between two persons in a conversation can be used to gauge the closeness or relationship between them. Many psychological counsellors use personal distance as one key in evaluating the health of a marriage, for instance.

Intimate Distance

Intimate distance is from zero to one-and-one-half feet. Here the presence of the other person is overwhelming. Every movement of the person is apparent. This degree of closeness can be very anxiety provoking if the other party does not have permission to transgress this intimate frontier.

Proxemics and Law Enforcement

The use of creative anxiety in the law enforcement interview has been recognized by various authorities. The knowledge and subtle use of body space theory can be of value to the interviewer in creating an atmosphere conducive to learning the truth. This tactic of moving closer to the subject is a very effective device in raising anxiety. The same is true in the police interview. Proxemics can be a two-edged sword. The police officer who is unable to use proxemics while interviewing should be aware of these techniques lest they be used against him by a subject. A high level of anxiety makes lying increasingly difficult for the normal person. The psychological energy required to maintain a lie is diverted and consumed as the interviewer subtly closes the distance between himself and the person being interviewed.

To generate anxiety, begin the interview at a comfortable distance with general-information questions, then subtly begin to ask more pertinent questions, while at the same time slowly closing the distance between the interviewer and the subject. Pinpoint any inconsistencies. This procedure may continue as the interview progresses. The subject will become so preoccupied with the interviewer's presence that truth will become the most anxiety-relieving course of action. Prior to telling the truth, the subject may cross legs, fold arms across chest, or lean back in the chair. These body-language clues are psychologically defensive and protective in nature and signal the alert interviewer that anxiety is being produced. Investigators using this technique of slowly varying the body space between themselves and the subject have reported high levels of success. However, use of this technique requires a great deal of preparation and self-awareness. If the interviewer is the one who becomes anxious rather than the subject, the process becomes self-defeating.

The subject may also be rewarded for being cooperative and telling the truth by the officer moving away from the subject, giving him more body space or "room to breathe." The interviewer must be aware of and carefully plan his body movements for a successful interview.

Certainly these techniques are not designed as a panacea for a successful interview. Each officer will develop his very own style of interviewing. A knowledge of these techniques will aid the officer to build upon and improve his interview technique.

The consideration and planned use of these techniques, integrated with individual style and personality, may be the key to increased effectiveness during the interview process.

SUMMARY CHECKLIST

Consider the following checklist to evaluate your interviewing skills:

1. *Fundamentals*

- Admit your weakness (to strengths).
- Customize your approach (to situation).
- Be aware (concentrate, alertness).
- Be patient (people think and analyze at different speeds).
- Be considerate (comfortable).
- Do not be vague (no confusion, misinterpretations).
- Choose your words to suit your listeners (level).
- Express your thanks when appropriate (stroke).
- Do not be afraid to pay a compliment (awareness).
- Control your temper (emotion vs. reason).

- Keep your cool (self-control).
- Get off to a good start (strong, warm, rapport).
- Say what is on your mind (do not beat around the bush).
- Always use positive approach (no negative questions).
- Use persuasion (persuasive, reasonable, rational).
- Think twice when you have an impulse to speak.
- Do not be supersensitive (by generalities).
- Be aware of your facts (or qualify).
- Know your subject (authority, credibility).
- Be responsive to question (direct an answer).
- Relate (enthusiastically, naturally).

2. *Philosophies*

- Do not exaggerate (lose your credibility).
- Do not start until you have all details straight.
- Do not stereotype by working broad generalizations (criticisms of group alienates individual).
- Be alert to others' reactions (study reaction, body languages).
- People hear what they want to hear (misinterprets).
- Think before you speak (foot in mouth!).
- Do not kill people's enthusiasm (be positive).
- Do not press too hard (give them space).
- Do not dispense criticism needlessly.
- Do not show indifference (be an "equal").
- Be sensitive (to feelings of others).
- Give people the benefit of the doubt (their side).
- Get a positive tone (defer until appropriate).
- Maintain flexibility (be prepared to divert).

3. *Mannerisms*

- Do not make noise (interruptions).
- Give speaker your undivided attention (eye contact).
- Keep your feet off the desk.
- Speak up (loud, authoritative voice).
- Consider people's temperament (do not offend).
- Remember, there are many ways to interrupt (besides verbal).
- Do not be a fiddler (turns people off).

- Do not doodle (shows lack of awareness).
- Settle down (relax, calm, cool, collected).

4. Techniques

- Avoid overuse of favorite words ("super").
- Do not anticipate (listen it out).
- Avoid ambiguities (words with other meaning).
- Know when to stop (end conversation).
- End on a strong note (loud, positive, strong).
- Avoid platitudes ("to be truthful," "now?").
- Practice what you preach (credibility).
- Ask your question, then listen (listen carefully to the entire answer).
- Give people the time they need to respond.
- Use words everyone can understand (lay terms).
- Set the stage (who and what you want).
- Silence can be refreshing (restful "um-hum").
- First things first (open pleasant — get to objectives).

5. The Telephone Interview

- Identify yourself (who you are and the purpose of the call).
- Speak into the mouthpiece.
- Do not eat while on telephone.
- Listen to yourself (check your style — you have no eye contact or body language to guide you).
- Be quiet (no off-stage noises, papers, etc.).
- As always, be considerate.
- Remember the golden rule: Do not interrupt (listen to his entire story, answer, etc.).
- Avoid extended silences (when they pause, make appropriate, courteous comments; let him know you are still with him and listening).
- Do not let others interrupt your conversation.
- Concentrate (success in communications depends heavily on being a good listener).
- Do not be a daydreamer (do not drift away).
- State your case (get to objectives).

- Your tone of voice sets the stage (appropriate).
- Do not shout (self-control, normal voice).

6. Courtesies

- Do not disagree needlessly (offensive).
- Be fair (use the golden rule).
- Do not be doom and gloom (some people take perverse pleasure in predicting what can go wrong; they keep others from relaxing and enjoying themselves).
- Avoid humor at other people's expense.
- Be yourself (do not put on an act or airs).
- Hide your prejudices (any chance of communicating is lost if your biases are obvious and influencing what you say).

7. Conclusion

- The last word is *listen*. If you do not, you will probably miss the last word.

USE OF THE POLYGRAPH TECHNIQUE

Although the results of a polygraph interview may not be admissible as evidence in court, this technique may be invaluable in a wide variety of juvenile cases that may not necessarily end in judicial process.

The polygraph should not be used as a "crutch" for inadequate investigative efforts, and any information developed should be thoroughly investigated and corroborated.

Responsibilities of the Investigator

1. Study and become thoroughly familiar with organizational directives and policies concerning polygraph utilization.
2. When polygraph examination is contemplated ascertain if the person involved is willing to voluntarily submit to the examination. If a voluntary waiver is obtained, discuss the case with a supervisor.
3. Discuss the examination with the polygraph examiner, and be

prepared to justify your request logically.

4. Be prepared to provide polygraph examiner with all information available to you. This would include key items that only the perpetrator could know if they are available.

5. Be present at the time of the examination to monitor and observe the examination, if approved by polygraph examiner.

6. Following the examination be prepared to obtain tape-recorded confessions or written statements as applicable.

Dos and Donts for Investigators

1. Do interview and, if possible, obtain an audiotape or written statement from the prospective examinee before requesting the examination.

2. Do advise of the effectiveness of the polygraph technique. Don't describe it as infallible.

3. Do withhold key information from the examinee. The Peak Of Tension Test (POT) is generally accepted as one of the most effective examinations. However, its use depends on key information known only to a guilty party. The disclosure of pertinent details such as color of car, amount of money, quantity of weapons, type of rings, number of shots fired, and kind of weapon used can make this test ineffective. Don't tell the prospective examinee the key questions.

4. Do tell the prospective examinee how experienced and highly qualified your examiner is. Don't attempt to explain the examination to him, as this is the responsibility of the examiner.

5. Do tell the prospective examinee of your personal confidence in the polygraph technique. Don't act as a polygraph expert. Don't volunteer the information that polygraph results are inadmissible in court.

6. Do recognize the value of a polygraph test as it might affect your case. Be prepared to reinterview if the examiner tells you the results were deceptive.

7. Do tell the nondeceptive (truthful) examinee that he will be informed of the results when the examiner has completed his analysis of the charts.

8. Do attempt to obtain a written or taped statement from the untruthful examinee immediately after the examination. Don't

delay or postpone reinterview of an untruthful examinee, and don't assume that a statement given to the examiner is enough.

9. Do advise a prospective examinee to get a good night's sleep and to try to refrain from using drugs or overindulging in alcohol during the night before the examination. Don't tell him that he can't be tested without a good night's sleep, or that the use of drugs or alcohol could confuse the test.

10. Do ask the examiner any questions that may be bothering you. Don't assume that he does not want to discuss your polygraph test or the case in general.

11. Do cooperate and work with your examiner as a team member. Don't assume that he prefers to be independent.

12. Do concentrate on primary issues, and advise the examiner of the basic issue you want resolved. Don't present the examiner with a list of questions that you'd like to have answered. A polygraph examination must be confined to a few key issues or questions and only the examiner can determine what they should be for best results.

13. Do confine your request to specific key issues that must be resolved.

14. Do respect the examiner's opinion as an aid to your investigation. Don't expect the examiner to give you all the answers. The best he can do is tell you whether or not the examinee actually believes what he is saying. For example, a rape victim, who identifies a suspect as her assailant because she actually believes that he was the offender, will run truthful on the polygraph even if she has identified a totally innocent person.

15. Do confine your examination to one specific offense. Don't attempt to clear several crimes with one examination. To work properly, each specific examination must pertain to only one incident. Incorporating more than one incident contaminates the procedure and nullifies results.

16. Do tell the examiner all you know about your examinee. Don't hold back information regarding past record, mental condition, or use of drugs, as this can only confuse issues and adversely affect results.

17. Do level with your examiners. Don't conceal certain investigative techniques or other means you've utilized in

developing information.

18. Do accept the polygraph technique for what it is — an invaluable aid to your investigation when its use is indicated. Don't assume it can answer all questions or resolve all issues. It cannot do your work for you, but it can help you if properly utilized.

19. Do utilize polygraph examination as soon as deemed advisable and all logical investigation has been completed. Don't put it off to an inappropriate time.

20. Know your polygraph examiner.

REFERENCES

1. National Advisory Commission on Criminal Justice Standards and Goals: *Corrections*. U.S. Government Printing Office, Washington, D.C., 1973, p. 264.
2. Manella, Frank L., Nedrud, Duane R., and Taylor, Charles R.: *The Illinois Youth Officer Manual*. Police Training Institute, Division of University Extension, University of Illinois, Champaign, 1972, pp. 24-28.
3. Nierenberg, Gerard I., Calero, Henry H.: *How to Read a Person Like a Book*. New York, Hawthorne Books, Inc., 1971, p. 1.
4. Hall, Edward T., *The Hidden Dimension*. Garden City, New York, Doubleday and Co., Inc., 1966, p. 5.

Chapter 13

FORENSIC HYPNOSIS: ITS USES IN
LAW ENFORCEMENT INTERVIEWS

HYPNOSIS is almost as ancient as civilization itself. Although it is shrouded in mystery and greatly misunderstood, the phenomenon has substantial contributions to make to law enforcement now and in the years ahead.

One of the more striking aspects of the phenomenon is its unique capability to elicit a myriad of repressed and forgotten memories from witnesses and victims of crisis, often with a high degree of accuracy. Unfortunately, this type of data is seldom available to the investigator at the nonhypnotic level. The reasons are comparatively simple. Amnesia, trauma, or even simple nervousness frequently accompany the initial shock of witnessing or being victimized by a criminal act. Vital facts seemingly vanish from the memory to become deeply buried in the subconscious at the very moment when their disclosure could spell the difference between success or failure.

Hypnosis cuts through inhibitory fears, enabling the subject to experience a relaxed, concentrated state of awareness in which all of the five senses are heightened to a marked degree. He thinks and remembers better because the conscious mind swings aside permitting direct access to the vast repository of the subconscious. Scien-

256

tific research has established that by the age of fifty the human brain contains some seventy trillion bits and pieces of data as part of the total experiential background. Thus, there is a broad field in which to operate when hypnosis is utilized to stimulate the brain's storage capacities.[1]

HISTORY

Assyro-Babylonian priests employed hypnotic incantations fifty centuries ago to heal the afflicted. Early Greeks and Romans were acquainted with its curative powers. The Ebers papyrus over 3,000 years old provides one of the richest sources of documentation that hypnosis or a similar induced state of consciousness was a regular form of treatment in Egyptian "sleep temples" along the river Nile. It was known to witch doctors and medicine men of Africa and pre-Columbian America as an expression of some supernatural power.

In the Middle Ages, sufferers by the millions turned to faith healing, a form of hypnosis. Kings healed by the "royal touch." Sorcerers, magicians, and wizards kept the phenomenon alive under a cloak of black magic. It evolved to become known more as an evil power than a natural beneficial state. Hypnotists were considered as agents of the devil, victimizing helpless subjects under their strange spells.

In 1843, James Braid, a Scottish physician, became interested in mesmerism and later explained the effects as due to expectation and suggestion rather than mysterious fluids and magic. He coined the term *hypnosis*, which means sleeplike, but later realized that hypnosis was not the same as sleep. However, the word caught on and has remained the most popular term.

The phenomenon spread from Europe to the United States. Aside from some clinical experimentation, it was neglected in the twentieth century to become a pathetic stepchild put on display by stage hypnotists. Finally, in World War II, psychosomatic illnesses were treated successfully by hypnosis, and the stage was set for even greater acceptance by the scientific community. This was to come in 1958 when the American Medical Association formally recognized hypnosis as a legitimate medical tool.

The Los Angeles, California, Police Department instituted a hypnosis interview program during 1970 and was soon to be followed by others, including the Federal Bureau of Investigation in 1976.

Guidelines usually limit use of the technique to consenting witnesses and victims for the purpose of enhancing their recall of past events. Suspects are not considered candidates for hypnosis on ethical and legal grounds.

Justifications for requests are usually screened by experienced investigative supervisors.[2]

COMMON MYTHS

The myth of hypnosis as a form of mind control has been perpetuated by the media in many variations of the Svengali-Trilby story of du Maurier. Actually, most hypnosis is self-hypnosis and requires the cooperation of the subject. Although the word *hypnosis* originally meant sleeplike, the state does not involve unconsciousness or sleep. Rather it is an altered state of consciousness in which increased physical relaxation is combined with varying states of mental concentration and quiet. Most subjects in light-to-medium hypnosis are fully aware of their surroundings and of what is transpiring.

Another myth is that weak-minded people are more susceptible to hypnosis. Actually, it is the reverse. Intelligent individuals with the ability to relate interpersonally and to use imagery tend to be better subjects.

The fear that there will be difficulty in coming out of hypnosis is unfounded. Individuals who are reluctant to leave the pleasantness of the hypnotic state usually desire to extend the period of rest and relaxation. In other instances, some interpersonal resistance may be involved, which can be easily handled by an experienced operator.

The myth that hypnosis is dangerous is misplaced. Like driving a car, it really depends on the person using it rather than on the vehicle itself. There is nothing innately dangerous about the state of hypnosis; however, as with any other tool, it can be misused by unethical or untrained people.

About 90 percent of the general population can be hypnotized to some degree. Children between the ages of seven and fourteen years of age tend to be the best possible candidates, perhaps because they still retain their imaginative ability and sense of trust. Hypnotizability drops off somewhat with age, generally being more difficult in the elderly. However, there are always exceptions, since hypnotic ability varies with each individual.

Most of us have experienced hypnoid or hypnotic states without consciously being aware of it. The drowsiness that occurs while driving on a straight road has been labeled *highway hypnosis*. The fascination with and responsiveness to T.V. commercials is a form of waking hypnosis, and our reactions to religious rituals and spellbinding orators are common "hypnosis" experiences.

RESULTS

Examples of relevant information available at the hypnotic level include memories of crime scenes, makes and models of automobiles, license numbers, and detailed physical descriptions of suspects. Vivid likenesses of some suspects have been sketched by composite artists.

Solution of the 1976 kidnapping of twenty-six frightened school children and their bus driver who were entombed in a Chowchilla, California rock quarry was expedited through the use of hypnosis. The identity of a habitual sex offender who kidnapped two little San Francisco-area girls and took them into Mexico would not have been solved without hypnosis. An organized crime case involving professional hit men was materially aided through the technique.

Authorities in departments around the country reported that in approximately 85 percent of those interviews conducted under hypnosis additional information of value will be obtained. In about 10 percent of the cases the information obtained under hypnosis was credited with leading to the final solution of the case. This is indeed a cost-effective law enforcement tool.

Of course, all information obtained under hypnosis must be substantiated and corroborated by diligent investigation.[3]

METHOD

Surprisingly enough, medical science today is unable to provide an acceptable theory or explanation of what occurs in the human organism during hypnosis. What cannot be explained may be defined. Thus, *hypnosis* is a relaxed, yet heightened, state of awareness and concentration, which is induced through suggestion and misdirection of attention in any highly motivated individual. *Suggestion* has been defined as the uncritical acceptance of an idea. It follows that suggestibility is an inherent behavioral characteristic of all human beings.

The skilled hypnotist takes full advantage of all these factors. First, he asks his subject to stare at an object. This narrows concentration and promotes strain on the small eye muscles. Soothing suggestions for relaxation and heaviness of the eyelids are given. At this point, misdirection of attention comes into play. As the subject concentrates on the fixation-object, additional suggestions for heaviness of the eyelids are timed to coincide with the natural fatigue and strain that occurs. One suggestion follows another.

These verbal suggestions in combination with eyestrain act as a cue for the highly motivated subject to begin drifting into a relaxed state of heightened perception. It is here that direct communication is established with the subconscious.

A variety of phenomena interact to bring recollections to the surface of conscious awareness. Hyperamnesia, age regression, and revivification, among others, help susceptible subjects to return to that point in time of the scene of their experiences and report them in vivid detail. Other factors are essential to a successful hypnotic experience. Rapport with the hypnotist, good preinduction education, and expectation combine with the imagination to produce the desired effect.[4]

HYPNOSIS AND THE LAW

There are no published cases in California addressing the issue on the admissibility of testimony that has been refreshed through hypnosis, although there are some pending. However, looking to an unpublished California case and to several other state decisions, it would appear that it is proper to use hypnosis to refresh a witness' memory where the fact of hypnosis is disclosed to opposing counsel and to the jury; the witness is subject to cross-examination, and the jury is instructed to consider the hypnosis process in weighing the evidence. Additionally, the court should make sure that the safeguards traditionally exercised when a witness' memory is refreshed by a memorandum are also followed when hypnosis is used as the means of refreshed memory.

Of course, all current local department rules, regulations, and policies, as well as those of the prosecuting attorney, state and federal laws, and court decisions must be closely followed.

TEAM VS. INDIVIDUAL APPROACH

The field is divided on the best approach to forensic hypnosis by law enforcement organizations. Some agencies use a team approach. In this model the agency uses a trained investigator–hypnotist to conduct the interview after a licensed consultant from the health-service field actually does the hypnotic induction. This approach has an added expense but has the advantage of a health-service person in attendance. Many local doctors, psychiatrists, dentists, psychologists, and others are trained in hypnosis and are willing to assist local law enforcement agencies.

The other approach is to utilize a mature experienced investigator who is specially trained in forensic hypnosis. This model is cost effective and assures that the trained investigator will not be hampered in his interview by another party. In either case, the entire hypnosis interview session must be recorded on videotape or audiotape and preserved the same as any other evidence for possible use in later prosecutions.

Further information may be obtained from The International Society for Investigative and Forensic Hypnosis, Post Office Box 1208, Los Angeles, California 90053 and The International Professional Association of Hypnosis-trained law enforcement investigators.

ARTIST COMPOSITE

While under hypnosis the cooperative witness or victim may have vivid recall of the physical characteristics of the suspect or subject. All efforts should be made to obtain a thorough and complete detailed physical description. Some agencies utilize the plastic overlay descriptive-type kits to obtain a facial image of the suspect. Although very useful, these kits are somewhat difficult to use during a hypnosis interview due to the victim's relaxed state.

Excellent results have been obtained by the use of the police composite artist. The hypnotized victim is directed to work with the composite artist in an effort to complete a composite drawing of the suspect. Numerous investigations have been successfully concluded based on the circulation of an artist's composite drawing. When considering the investigative man-hours that may be saved by a rapid solution of the case, the artist composite is extremely cost effective in the more important cases.

Agencies that do not have a composite artist may obtain one from nearby departments or perhaps county, state, or federal sources or develop a local portrait artist on a volunteer or consultant basis.

THE FUTURE

Advances by some law enforcement professionals tend to assure hypnosis of a future. Progressive departments must be congratulated for their impressive accomplishments. Some opponents of hypnosis argue that such a suggestive technique in the hands of law enforcement poses serious threats to the rights of offenders and victims alike. Others legitimately contend that improper questioning under hypnosis could cause a subject to distort his memory. To say that we must always adopt an alert position when utilizing this technique would be an understatement. It is axiomatic that hypnotized subjects can misremember, fantasize, or even lie if it suits their purposes. Seasoned investigators need no one to remind them that hypnotically related evidence requires independent corroboration.

Many Americans today regard crime as a very narrow range of human behavior. We know otherwise. In a sense, every citizen is victimized. If society proposed to reduce its insidious effects, law enforcement must be equipped with every tool available.

All efforts are being made by professionally trained hypnotist-investigators to retain this valuable tool in the hands of law enforcement.

REFERENCES

1. Douce, Richard G.: Consulting Forensic Hypnotist, Retired Special Agent Federal Bureau of Investigation. Lectures at Delinquency Control Institute, University of Southern California, 1980.
2. Nielsen, Michael: Captain, Investigative Hypnosis Program, Bunco-Forgery Unit, Los Angeles Police Department, Los Angeles, California. Lectures at

Delinquency Control Institute, University of Southern California, 1981.

3. Law Enforcement Hypnosis Institute: Attendance Basic Course, April 6-9, 1978; Advanced Course, June 23-25, 1978. Los Angeles, California.

4. Reiser, Martin: *Handbook of Forensic Hypnosis.* Los Angeles, LEHI Publishing Company Inc., 1980.

Chapter 14

JUVENILE COURT AND PROBATION SERVICES

T HE juvenile court continues on its inexorable path toward becoming a criminal court for young offenders. Lacking only the
right to bail and a jury trial, the procedural differences are
diminishing as today's sophisticated juvenile offender torments the
conscience of the court while frustrating law enforcement, probation, corrections, and the public. The hopes of liberals have been
dashed as favorable court decisions extending due process rights
through *Gault* have plunged society into a plague of fear while
juvenile offenders, represented by newly minted "jailhouse lawyers,"
exercise their constitutional rights. *Parens patriae*, if ever valid, has
withered and receded. Motions practice is brisk; the law is now
relatively rich in juvenile cases, and today's youthful ward of the
state sounds like a young John Dillinger in describing his lawyer's in-
competence, the "trumped up" charge on which his commitment was
based, the inhuman treatment that he is receiving, and anything else
one will listen to. The fact remains that today's urban, juvenile court
is dealing with sophisticated juvenile offenders whose prior offenses
are substantial and whose propensity for violence has been on the

upswing. Whatever influence the court may have had earlier in deterring the first- or second-time offender seems now to have yielded to consuming involvement in delinquent acts, felonious in nature, protected by a full panoply of constitutional rights. Only the status offender has been, for the most part, excluded from the arena.

The juvenile court has become a repository for demented juveniles, sophisticated youthful offenders, youth gangs, and, on occasion, a runaway, incorrigible, or habitual truant. Thus, a metamorphosis has occurred over time in the juvenile court. The casual petty thief has been replaced in court by the streetwise sophisticate who "knows his rights." This enormous dumping of youth on a branch of government, often still playing by the rules of earlier times, seems at times incongruous, inefficient, costly, and frustrating. Judges are frustrated by the paucity of dispositional alternatives. In what may become a classic comment, a New York Judge lamented, ". . . While incarceration is merited, (homosexual) rape, torture and brutality are not. We take judicial notice of a defendant's slight build, his mannerisms, dress, color, and ethnic background and are cognizant of the unfortunate realities that he would not have lasted for ten minutes at Riker's Island." The defendant was not incarcerated, but given community-service tasks, a fine, instructed to make an apology, and compose a 5,000-word essay.

While the judges express frustration at dealing with errant youth, law enforcement and prosecutors stand tight-lipped in courtrooms as motions to suppress are granted. Law enforcement views judicial protections as technical in nature and preventive of "just desserts." The technicalities of acquittal seem prejudicial against victims and apologetic toward defendants. While the guilty seem constitutionally protected, the victims and society seem fearful of walking the streets without a trained canine escort, a hand-operated radio, and a can of mace held at the ready. Some citizens view the institutionalized juvenile as living in splendor at a cost exceeding the tuition at Harvard University, totally devoid of responsibility, and just waiting for the opportunity to return to the streets and seek vengeance for his "inhumane treatment." A free society may well ask itself why it is that juveniles roam the streets terrorizing the elderly and innocent passersby while the courts return the violators immediately, or soon thereafter following a brief incarceration, only seemingly to have launched the juvenile on a serious criminal career.

One may well ask what has gone wrong with the system, particularly the juvenile court and the probation system. No institution can perform its task successfully if it continues to incur the wrath of society, the media, and, in particular, law enforcement and the public prosecutor. In addition, despite abundant cases to the contrary, the nation's public defenders often complain that few juveniles, or adults for that matter, go free due to the exclusionary rule: that is, *on the average*, or in considering the totality of cases. Thus, the various state supreme courts interpreting state constitutions or interpreting the United States Constitution as directed by the United States Supreme Court through the "equal protection clause" of the Fourteenth Amendment seem to be on a collision course with those having responsibility for implementing statutory and decisional law.

There can be little doubt that the situation will not be relieved by population decline. A baby boom exists as we move from the 1970s to the 1980s. Within 10–15 years large numbers of youths will be poised to make their mark on society. What evidence suggests that the courts will be ready for such an onslaught?

The juvenile court depends substantially for its day-to-day, dispositional support on its probation services. Probation provides initial intake information, screens offenders for possible diversion from formal court processing, involves the family when possible, explores the psychodynamics of the youth and family, postulates dispositional alternatives to the court, and often aids the court in expediting the court process. Probation mobilizes existing system information regarding the youth from among law enforcement, school, social services, family and friends. Furthermore, it casts itself in a dual role of recommending a particular disposition to the court while at the same time providing probation supervision if the court so orders. To avert what might be construed as a conflict of roles, probation often organizes itself so that the intake decision is made by one unit of probation and the supervision function by another unit. In the event that the youth is already under court supervision, the youth's probation officer is faced with the dilemma of retaining court supervision or recommending transfer to the state correctional agency.

Probation officers typically view themselves as not appreciated by other components of the juvenile justice system. Dispositional recommendation is clouded by having worked with the youth. The offender and family may be hostile. Should placement arrangements be inchoate, the court may hold probation responsible. In many jurisdictions probation services are administratively responsible to the court rather than the executive branch. In these instances, even courtroom demeanor may be evaluated. Seen as "do-gooders" by law enforcement, seen as suspect by the offender and family, seen as biased by the prosecution or defense, and viewed as a support arm of the court, the probation officer views his position as rather powerless. In fact, the probation officer influences the court outcome substantially. By obtaining and presenting case information in a particular way, the court may be persuaded by the social "context" of the youth and family. By arranging a "suitable" placement the court may be relieved of uncertainty as well as narrowing its alternatives.

Evidence suggests that the court frequently, if not usually, follows the recommendation of the probation officer. Dispute exists, however, as to whether or not the probation officer simply recommends what the judge wants to hear. The experienced probation officer will know the dispositional limits of each judge. It is probable that, just as a particular judge rules on motions in a particular way, the judge will be predictable with respect to dispositional preferences.

Despite probation's low esteem of itself, one should recognize the important contribution that it makes. Naturally, one can differ philosophically with probation though, just as within each component of the juvenile justice system individual officers vary widely in view. It is precisely the function that probation performs that fuels its perspective. It is asked to explain the entire juvenile justice system to the youth and families. It is asked to act as a "buffer" between the system and the street. It is asked to involve itself in the families of offenders while manipulating case loads, sometimes in excess of 100. It is asked to expedite and facilitate the court process while fending off antagonisms from other components in the system. It may even be asked to supervise youth for whom the probation recommendation was "confinement in a structured setting." One need not feel apologetic nor even sympathetic to the probation officer. What should be recognized is the *human* element that probation provides in an otherwise dehumanizing process. This phenomenon perhaps sets juvenile probation aside from its adult counterpart. Today's juvenile probation officer still believes that a youthful offender may be detoured from a life of crime. That the youthful offenders of today may have transcended any viable probation approaches causes probation as much consternation as other components of the system.

JURISDICTIONAL TRENDS

Reformers aver that today's juvenile court cannot succeed as presently constituted. The presence of youthful, hardened criminals in juvenile court invites scorn of those wishing to prosecute them as adults. Increased transfers of juveniles to adult court are urged. Lowering of juvenile court age jurisdiction is attempted. Direct filing in adult court for heinous crimes, often adding felonious matters in general or crimes against persons in particular, is attempted. Knowledge that a juvenile's first prosecution in adult court may result in probation does not deter.

Other reformers seek to preclude jurisdiction over the status offender. It is argued that the child in need of supervision is an anachronism in a youthful criminal court. The status offender simply becomes quickly educated in pre-delinquent or pre-criminal activity. Perhaps the time has come for two courts: one for the early offender and one for the youthful "veteran." In fact, certain jurisdictions, if not most, have acted by virtually excluding the status offender from juvenile court while concentrating increased penalties on the delinquent offender. To some extent, the juvenile court attempts to sort out its intake of youths, casting out the status offender, advancing the serious, delinquent offender to criminal court, and attempting to deal with the remaining melange of "intermediate" offenders whose history of property crimes now exhibit definite trends toward injury toward persons.

For the most part, courts have not known what to do with the juvenile traffic offender. Some courts have reposed this function in the courts of limited jurisdiction in the hopes that more significant matters would be taken up in juvenile court. In the event that the traffic charge did not involve joyriding or auto theft, this bifurcation seemed viable. If the traffic violations involved criminal activity, the court of limited jurisdiction sought relief in the juvenile court by transferring the remaining allegations to juvenile court. The latter court often seemed somewhat inhospitable to such a practice. In other jurisdictions, juvenile traffic matters fall within the juvenile court jurisdiction, thus avoiding the bifurcation problem while adding substantially to the work of juvenile court. The press of delinquent matters in today's juvenile court seems likely to force juvenile traffic matters away from the normal flow of juvenile court, as it seeks to cope with the avalanche of property and person-to-person crimes and exclude the relatively minor or first-time offender.

During the seventies, substantial interest developed around the concept of the family court. This court, it was argued, would enjoy full jurisdiction over the entire family and include not only the typical juvenile jurisdiction but divorce and paternity as well. Thus, in concert with its dependency jurisdiction, the family court could acquire jurisdiction over an entire family in the event that one of the members fell within its jurisdiction. Child custody could be arranged or rearranged without fear of contravening a court order issued by the divorce court, now a separate court in most jurisdictions. Similarly, in a delinquency matter, parents could be ordered into psychological, drug, or alcohol counseling as part of the disposition against a child whose behavior had been strongly linked, for example, in rebellion against the parents. In this way, it was hoped that the court could intervene jurisdictionally, as necessary, in order to interrupt the process of delinquency-producing parents whose offspring seemed known throughout probation- and protective-service agencies; in some cases, for generations.

Whatever the hopes may have been for the family court, the progress has been modest. Few jurisdictions have made major inroads against the "problem families." The increase of gang activity as well as juvenile crime, in general, seems to have overwhelmed most juvenile courts to the point of complete frustration. The family court seems best designed for a parallel coordination of court services, which requires cooperation among the criminal justice and social-serving agencies. This cooperation has been difficult to obtain. In light of increasing case loads, strained governmental budgets and employee dissatisfaction, the promise of family court seems a matter to be postponed.

Chapter 15

STATE PROGRAMMING

T HE commencement of the 1980s saw a decade of national influence over state juvenile justice programming come to a halt.
In the later seventies, national funding decelerated. With the loss of
funding to the Law Enforcement Assistance Administration and the
Office of Juvenile Justice Delinquency and Prevention, a massive
experiment in federal noblesse oblige withered and died. The
millions of dollars spent had provided national bureaucrats with
leverage over a myriad of antidotes to crime and, with it, anguished
compliance from state and local officials. Attempts to impose national reform were sustained by funneling funds to state and local
government under conditions generated from above. Local officials
accepted this financial assistance in the hopes that crime might be
combatted with newfound resources. That conditions required
separating juveniles from adults or delinquents from status offenders
seemed improbable but worth attempting. In fact, national programming brought about its own demise, and with it, whatever
merit attached to national standards sputtered out of existence.

State and local officials always seemed to treat the national
"greening" of delinquency programs as "bonus" programs ancillary to
the basic business of juvenile crime. Diversion, prevention, and

alternatives to institutionalization seemed desirable as long as *serious* offenders were apprehended, processed, and assigned to closed facilities. There was long a suspicion that federal programs were best implemented with the first-time offender as well as the status offender. That juvenile crime continued and closed the seventies with an upsurge in violent crime seemed to preoccupy not only local officials but the public as well. Few agonized over the inability to ac- comodate the early offender when burgeoning case loads of youthful criminals awaited court processing and crowded institutions. So- ciety's view of the youthful offender, as the eighties commenced, was that of a vicious gang member hell-bent on violent crime. Only in one's most reflective moments would the enigma of how to interrupt the flow of the early offender into the violent ranks cause serious debate. Most seemed resigned to the passing of the "experiments" of the seventies, noting, in passing, that maybe the best that could be said was that everything might be far worse were it not for the federal initiatives. In fact, America must concern itself with why one juvenile seeks crime and another turns away. The baby boom of the late seventies and early eighties will be poised in ten to fifteen years to remind us of its presence. If national dictates are not the answer, then the states and local governments need to assess their options.

STATE INCARCERATION

There is little to suggest that incarceration in state institutions does more than incapacitate the offender. The recidivism rate for youthful offenders seems destined to hover around 50 percent in state institutions, regardless of programs in the institutions *as they now exist.* Worse, certain offenders, embittered by their incarcera- tion, return to society without intent, motivation, or skill to change their ways. Society finds, to its horror, that these individuals seem intent only on repaying innocent victims for whatever dehumaniza- tion occurred while incarcerated. That some do not may reflect more upon their inner impulse control than on any "learning" experience in the institution. Liberals would close the institutions and place of- fenders in the community. Conservatives would build additional in- stitutions. The answer may lie in radically different institutions than those presently designed.

EXECUTIVE BRANCH ROLE

In the absence of federal largesse, the state, through its executive branch, provides the main institutional component of the state criminal justice system. Local government naturally supplements these efforts.

Despite the periodic concern of elected officials, a state's criminal justice expenditures, quality of staff, and general climate of institutional care is dependent upon the expertise, commitment, and motivation of the criminal justice professionals. During the 1970s substantial numbers of professionals were attracted to criminal justice programming. In addition to institutional care, several states embarked upon diversion programs, acquired local detention centers, and, through criminal justice planning, attempted to launch major inroads into the cycle of crime and recidivism. With the passing of federal funding, the states tended to return to primary emphasis on institutional care.

State institutions for juvenile offenders vary from virtual nonexistence in Massachusetts, which opted for local alternatives, to a varied network of institutions such as in California, where they are attempting to group *like* offenders in *like* institutions. Despite years of professional experimentation with various programs, the only consistent feature of most juvenile institutions, as now designed seems to lie in their ability to incapacitate the juvenile from further street crime while serving time in locked facilities. Recidivism continues, few juveniles appear to be equipped for maintaining a nondelinquent parole period (and those that do seem enigmatic to parole), and aftercare professionals' attempts at assistance seem misplaced, misguided, and racist to many juveniles. In short, there is little about which to be enthusiastic in reviewing the state's efforts to modify juvenile delinquent behavior.

The state's efforts to act as the "jailer" for masses of urban delinquents seem least of all appreciated by other members of the criminal justice system, the media, politicians, and the public at large. Often filled to capacity, manned by staff whose financial status seems exploitive (to them), and unable to control its own admissions, the state institutional system seems to survive rather than progress. Attempts at humanizing the delinquent's stay may appear as "coddling" the juvenile, and an early release may result in some heinous crime (incomprehensible to the general public). Perhaps worse than the public's reaction is that of other criminal justice professionals. As now designed and administered, those who feed the institutional system lack confidence in the likely result. For whatever reason, those responsible for administering the institutional system have been unable, for the most part, to enlist the support of other professionals. Liberals view institutions as anomalies, while conservatives view them as costly "country clubs." Every governmental institution needs at least a modest base of professional or political support. In the absence of federal attention, state institutions seem particularly vulnerable to political second-guessing and eroding public support.

Not without obvious influence is the fact that most juvenile commitments to state institutions do not occur until a pattern of delinquent behavior has become well-established. Those feeding the institutions see this commitment as the last step after probation, as local residential and other local programming has been found to be inadequate. Few professionals contemplate committing a youth to a state institution after sustaining a petition for the first offense. Not only are the facilities presumably unable to admit large numbers of first offenders, but it has been assumed that all other alternatives should be exhausted before state commitment. Consequently, the population in most state institutions consists of recidivists who have graduated to the "big time." That such offenders are difficult to rehabilitate seems unavoidable. This whole process seems to be stuck on dead center and continues to plague all criminal justice professionals. In frustration, we turn toward prevention programs in junior and senior high schools. Yet, the flood continues.

JUDICIAL BRANCH ROLE

Unlike the executive branch, the judicial branch affects juvenile justice programming in a slightly less direct manner. Naturally, there are states such as Colorado that administer probation programs and other direct service. However, these services more typically fall within the executive branch. Nationwide, however, the judicial branch affects the *behavior* of system participants as well as the initial fate of juvenile defendants.

The state, through its judicial branch, equalizes interpretation of federal and state constitutions and federal and state statutes. States are known to differ among *themselves*, and though motions practice and court procedure *within* the same state may vary, it does not deny that general practice (e.g. admissibility of evidence, search and seizure, and a host of other substantive rights) gains definition through judicial interpretation. These effects are far-reaching. Judicial interpretation provides the foundation for law enforcement and district attorney manuals of procedure and practice. It sets the framework for plea bargaining, and it influences police discretion in exercising arrest powers. Through its sentencing powers the judiciary signals law enforcement officials, defense counsel, and the public as to who will be punished, for what crime, and for how long. It directly affects the flow and volume into the state's institutions, as well as local and state probation and parole.

Naturally, there are judges whose records comport more closely to those who favor sustained petitions and maximum sentences, just as judges exist in the same states of other persuasions. Despite potentially biased arguments by inmates that sentencing lacks standardization, disparities do exist. In states having determinate sentencing, juveniles will tend to be sentenced for similar terms but may encounter varying release dates, depending upon their behavior in an institution. It is acknowledged that juveniles from rural areas may be committed much earlier in their pre-delinquent lives than the sophisticated urban youth. Despite these differences, only two proposals have gained much credence toward standardizing sentencing. The first utilizes a matrix or table that weights such factors as prior record, severity of instant offense, age, sex, and others, assigns points for each factor, and compiles a total score, which may then be related to a standard sentence. Judges sentencing more harshly or more leniently would need to explicate their reasons. The second proposal is to utilize a sentencing panel, most likely of three judges, to either review sentences or set them in the first place. The former proposal seems to have gained more ascendancy than the latter.

Naturally, there are many other proposals affecting the judicial branch, most of which would limit its discretion or increase its accountability. It is believed that such proposals will further prescribe desired outcomes and proscribe undesirable decisions. These proposals do not seem to deter the judiciary from defending its need for independent judgment though it is apparent that the American system of trying a case on the record frustrates the prosecution. It is often argued that this practice, coupled with the "exclusionary rule" and voluminous appeals, generates the appearance of bias toward the defendant rather than the victim. As police officers strive to follow the dictates of the law, they will encounter frustration, particularly in those states that vacillate or break new ground with each new appellate decision.

LEGISLATIVE BRANCH ROLE

State legislatures influence the juvenile justice system in two primary ways: substantive legislation and appropriations. The legislature reflects the general mood of its constituents and often attempts to legislate change by setting jurisdictional limits, separating juveniles from adults in local and state institutions, maintaining jail standards, and many others. Through its power of the purse it can affect efficiency as well as effectiveness in state institutions, as well as locally in those instances involving money transfers or "bailout funds." In addition, it can inaugurate new juvenile programs, terminate others, and maintain others at substantial levels or at minimal levels. In certain situations, a legislative act may directly affect local expenditures, as in requiring the existence of a separate detention center, i.e. separate and apart from any adult jail or lockup. Despite this requirement, local government varies in its willingness or authority to supplement the county's coffers to follow state dictates. Of course, the judicial branch can similarly impose its will on local government by ordering a juvenile placed in a particular institution that may require local governmental funding. In fact, the uneasy alliance of the executive, judicial, and legislative branches is often in conflict over "the right" of one branch to affect the mission of the other by providing or withholding funds. The judiciary, for example, is well aware that the legislature can, if it wishes, be less than enthusiastic about granting judicial salary increases were it to conclude that the judges were not deserving. These checks and balances presumably balance the power among the three and maintain their independence. Nevertheless, the custom of legislating desired outcomes may gain its legitimacy through the enthusiasm of administrators and the availability of funding. In precluding certain activity as criminal in nature or in "enhancing" certain criminal acts by doubling time to be served, the added responsibility for providing for appropriate correctional facilities to deal with these offenders typically lies with the executive branch.

Legislatures are not in agreement as to the appropriate age of juvenile versus adult jurisdiction. In making this determination it is clear that a sixteen- or seventeen-year-old may be treated as an adult in one state, e.g. New York, Connecticut, and North Carolina, whereas in others a juvenile is statutorily defined as less than eighteen years of age. The effect of this, one would argue, is to reflect the sophisticated, criminal behavior of sixteen- and seventeen-year-olds in New York and Connecticut. The practical effect is to raise the volume of court and correctional cases in the adult system, while possibly creating a cadre of young offenders who cannot be placed in most adult institutions and who may need to be separated from other juvenile offenders. This is not to say that the theory behind the legislation is wrong. It suggests that the impact of criminal justice legislation may be left somewhat to chance rather than plan or design.

One legislative activity that exemplifies the states acting in concert with national strategy has to do with commingling juveniles and adults either prior to or following adjudication. The Juvenile Justice and Delinquency Prevention Act of 1974 established a goal of not detaining or confining a juvenile ". . . in any institution in which they have regular contact with adult persons incarcerated because they have been convicted of a crime or are awaiting trial on criminal charges." Interpretation of this language has defined *no regular contact* as being separated by *sight and sound*. In order to qualify for financial assistance from the Office of Juvenile Justice and Delinquency Prevention (an office within the Law Enforcement Assistance Administration), the states moved statutorily to comport with the *sight and sound* doctrine. Thus, in this instance, state legislatures acted statutorily to increase the flow of federal funding to states that, in turn, had substantial impact, not only on state institutions, but on local government and their responsibility for jails, detention centers (when a local responsibility), and other correctional programming. Thus, the juvenile justice system embodies not only constitutional, statutory and interpretative checks and balances, but there further exists an intergovernmental leverage particularly from the federal level downward. With the demise of LEAA, implementation of tight budgets, and public interest in retribution, the influence of inter-governmental leverage would seem to be attenuated.

Chapter 16

REPORTS AND RECORDS
PERTAINING TO JUVENILES

REPORTS and records are required of all juvenile justice agencies involved in the processing of juveniles who come under the purview of the juvenile court. They reflect both official and unofficial actions taken and provide the means by which accountability for the actions taken are assured. As recordkeeping methods have become increasingly sophisticated, there has been a growing concern over the stigmatization caused by the maintenance of a person's childhood mistakes for decades after the person has reached adulthood, as well as over the accuracy, use, and misuse of data concerning juveniles and their families by both private and public agencies. Except for records maintained by schools there is a wide variation in legal requirements covering the collection, processing, and retention of information collected about juveniles, and few agencies or jurisdictions have developed comprehensive systems for the management of juvenile records.

It will be the purpose of this chapter to present some definitive guidelines pertaining to juvenile reports and records in general and some specific guidelines for the administration and management of police, juvenile court, and probation records in particular. Emphasis will be on those official reports and records essential for the processing of juveniles through the juvenile court.

The National Advisory Committee for Juvenile Justice and Delinquency Prevention provides us with general standards for reports and records pertaining to juveniles. The committee in the preparation of its standards sets forth guidelines, which in effect are statements of public concern for the protection of juveniles and society by prescribing or circumscribing practices and procedures to be followed by all agencies. Basically, the standards viewed collectively provide a philosophy for reporting and recording official information about juveniles involved in the juvenile justice system.

First, let us direct our attention to the more general standards that deal with security and privacy; retention and destruction; confidentiality; completeness and accuracy; and access for the purpose of conducting research, evaluative, or statistical studies. These standards should be carefully reviewed and followed by all agencies. They provide key guidelines for the establishment and management of an agency's juvenile records system.

The past decade has brought the development of a public policy designed to assure a person's right to privacy; thus public and private agency records must be maintained in a secure manner to preclude their unauthorized use. The fact that some states have not officially proclaimed the policy has prompted the committee to urge that they do so posthaste. The standard sets forth a positive approach for achieving security and privacy of juvenile records.

> Each state and the federal government should enact statutes governing the collection, retention, disclosure, sealing, and destruction of records pertaining to juveniles to assure the accuracy and security of such records and to protect against the misuse, misinterpretation, and improper dissemination of the information contained therein.
>
> Recordkeeping practices should be reviewed periodically to determine whether the information collected is necessary and whether it is being gathered, retained, utilized, and disseminated properly. Privacy councils should be established at the state and federal levels to assist in this review and in the enforcement of the statutes and regulations governing records pertaining to juveniles.

The standard relating to the collection and retention of records makes it quite clear that only *essential* information and data should be collected and retained. The long-standing practice of many agencies to collect and retain extraneous information and data that "may" be valuable for the processing of a juvenile or controlling juvenile delinquency is deemed improper and undesirable. The standard reads as follows:

Information identifiable to a juvenile or family should not be collected by law enforcement agencies, prosecutors' offices, courts, public agencies legally responsible for providing services to juveniles and to their families, or private organizations or programs under contract to such agencies or licensed to provide those services, unless essential:

a. To provide necessary services;

b. To make decisions regarding the juvenile or family in conjunction with the initiation, investigation, processing, adjudication, and disposition of a complaint or petition submitted pursuant to the jurisdiction of the family court over delinquency, noncriminal misbehavior, or neglect and abuse;

c. To make decisions regarding the juvenile or family in conjunction with the appeal of the adjudication or an order in a delinquency, noncriminal misbehavior, or neglect and abuse proceeding;

d. To provide services pursuant to a referral from an intake unit or the dispositional order of the family court;

e. To administer the court, agency, organization or program effectively and efficiently;

f. To monitor and evaluate the court, agency, organization or program; or

g. To conduct authorized research, evaluative, or statistical studies.

Such identifiable information should be retained in retrievable form only if it is accurate; protected from unauthorized access, disclosure, and dissemination; physically secure; and essential to accomplish one of the purposes specified in paragraphs (a) through (g). The subjects of such information should be notified that the information has been retained, and that they have the right to inspect the records and to challenge their accuracy and retention.

Supplementing the standard on collection and retention of records are the standards relating to confidentiality, accuracy, and completeness of records. With respect to confidentiality the committee states that, "Identifiable information retained...should not constitute a public record. Access to such information should be strictly controlled." Completeness should be assured. "Procedures should be developed to assure completeness of records maintained." Included in those procedures should be provisions requiring:

a. That written notice of the disposition or dismissal of a delinquency, noncriminal misbehavior, or neglect and abuse complaint or petition be sent within thirty days to law enforcement, protective services, supervision, and other public agencies or programs involved in the investigation of the report complaint or petition, in the taking into custody, detention or custody of the juvenile, or in the supervision of the juvenile and/or family, and

b. That the information contained in the notice be entered within fifteen days of its receipt on any identifiable records pertaining to the juvenile which are maintained by such agencies.

In addition, "Procedures should be developed to assure the accuracy of records maintained. Included in those procedures should be provisions which permit the subject of an identifiable record to challenge its accuracy or completeness and which provide for administrative and judicial review of a refusal by the maintaining agency to correct or destroy challenged information."

Pursuant to the need to reduce or limit the stigmatization associated with a juvenile's wrongdoing a positive plan for the destruction of juvenile records is proposed by the committee. The chief executive of a juvenile agency should ascertain from the jurisdiction's attorney or the state archivist, who is the final authority, the legal requirements associated with records destruction. The committee's proposed standard is as follows:

> The destruction of a record should be mandatory and should not be contingent upon receipt of a request by the subject of that record.
>
> Records retained under Standard 1.52, which result from the investigation, initiation, processing, and disposition of a delinquency complaint or petition, should be destroyed no more than five years after the date on which they were created unless:
>
> a. The allegations in the petition are proven beyond a reasonable doubt, in which case the records should be destroyed no more than five years after termination of the disposition imposed; or
>
> b. An adjudication is held at which the state fails to prove the allegations in the petition beyond a reasonable doubt, in which case the records should be destroyed immediately.
>
> Records retained, . . .which result from the investigation, initiation, processing, or disposition of a noncriminal misbehavior complaint or petition, should be destroyed no more than five years after the date on which they were created or at the time the juvenile named in those records attains the statutory age of majority, whichever occurs first, unless an adjudication hearing is held at which the state fails to prove the allegations in the petition beyond a reasonable doubt, in which case the records should be destroyed immediately.
>
> Prior to destroying a record, the maintaining agency should advise the

subject of the record that the record is being destroyed and that the subject and his/her family may inform any person or organization that, with regard to the proceedings from which the record resulted, they were not arrested, held in custody, named in a complaint or petition adjudicated, or subject to a dispositional order of the family court.

Notice of destruction of a record should also be sent to all persons, courts, agencies, and programs which may have copies of or notations regarding such records. Persons, courts, agencies and programs receiving such a notice should promptly destroy all copies of the record or portion or notations thereof contained in their files, unless the information was obtained for research, evaluative, or statistical purposes. . . .

Research, evaluative, and statistical studies are essential for the advancement of our understanding of juvenile delinquency and the administration of juvenile justice and to assist in the management and assessment of juvenile service system agencies and programs and in the monitoring of recordkeeping practices. The committee has addressed these needs in the following standard:

Access to records maintained under (the standard for the collection and retention of records) should not be granted to individuals or agencies for the purpose of conducting a research, evaluative, or statistical study unless an application is filed with the court or agency maintaining the record, which describes:

a. The purpose of the study;
b. The qualifications of the individuals conducting the study;
c. The identifiable information sought and the reasons why the purpose of the study cannot be achieved without using information in identifiable form;
d. The methods to be used to assure that the anonymity of the subject of the records is preserved; and
e. The methods to be used to assure that the information will be physically secure.

Decisions approving or disapproving applications for access should be in writing and should be subject to review.

Identifiable information collected for research, evaluative, or statistical studies should be immune from legal process and should not be used for any purpose in any judicial, legislative, or administrative proceeding without the informed written consent of the person to whom the information pertains.

POLICE REPORTS AND RECORDS

Police records provide the hub for police operations. An adequate system for recording complaints, police contacts, arrests, investigations, and dispositions must be maintained. Records provide the basis for decision making in all steps of the investigation process, for administrative control and policy making, as the basis for the development of crime prevention programs, and for use by the courts and other agencies involved in the administration of criminal justice.

The extent to which records serve the operation is directly proportional to the needs of the department and to the quality of records themselves. The dimensions of the crime and delinquency problem confronting a community must be known before effective plans can be made.

Factual information on the amount and extent of delinquency in a community provides the basis for planning. The police department is concerned with effective utilization of its personnel in keeping the peace in the community. The community is desirous that order, security, and stability are maintained and that a healthy environment prevails for the growth and development of its youth. Police records provide the primary source of information for both the operations of the police department and actions of the community in coping with problems of delinquency.

Much controversy exists over the problem of keeping juvenile case records. Major emphasis is on the protection of the individual juvenile. The primary concern is that the delinquent acts of youth will not handicap them as an adult. The other argument is that without adequate facts and information effective delinquency programs for the community cannot be developed. It would seem, however, that these two arguments are not incompatible. In a democratic society both the individual and the community are important.

There is a special problem in the management of police records regarding cases of individual juveniles. Previous theory and practice in governmental reaction to juvenile delinquency was based on rehabilitation and reeducation of juveniles in an attempt to help them become acceptable members of the community. Recently, legislation has been passed in several states which specifies that juveniles as young as thirteen when they commit certain offenses will be processed the same as adults. This means that the police are confronted with two sets of rules relating to the preparation of reports and the maintenance of records on juveniles.

A variety of records must be kept on police work with juveniles.

To serve its function of preservation of life and property, the police department must have a system for the collection of information that will make it possible to anticipate some antisocial action by juveniles as well as by adults. These records are essential for preventive action as well as for effective investigation when such conduct does occur. Records must also be kept of complaints about unlawful activity, and information about the investigative process which follows complaints must be recorded. The same is true of the actual processing of juveniles who have been referred to juvenile court. This means that information as to citation, taking into custody, and court disposition of a case should be available.

Each of the different files of police records concerning juvenile cases should be purged at regular intervals. This means that the records of defined categories of juveniles should be taken from the files and destroyed. This is necessary first of all for efficient use of the files.

Purging the files is also necessary to implement the philosophy of allowing young persons to begin their adult lives with a clean slate. Although accurate statistics are nonexistent, experience indicates that despite the fact that many adult criminals were juvenile delinquents, only a very small percentage of juveniles who have contact with police while growing up actually become criminals. Those who do achieve satisfactory social adjustments as adults should not have the shadow of a police record jeopardizing their futures.

There are actually several facets to the general problem of confidentiality of police records in juvenile cases. Three of these are the separation of juvenile records from adult records, the guarding of the separated records against unauthorized access, and the deliberate releasing of information to mass communication media.

There are a number of justifications for separating juvenile records from adult records. The first is the philosophical one that records of adult antisocial conduct investigated by police agencies are records of criminal conduct while those on juvenile antisocial conduct are not criminal records. And there is the added fact that control over police records has been lax in many departments, with unauthorized persons sometimes allowed access to them. Because this can be particularly harmful in the case of juveniles, it has sometimes been easier to provide safeguards for a separate system of juvenile records than to revise the entire record system of the department. With increasingly effective police record management, this argument has been considerably weakened. Separation does make it easier, however, to carry out special record management programs with juvenile records, such as the periodic purging program. Again, the separation can be accomplished by a separate section of the general file of the same type in a well-managed record system as well as by a completely separate set of files in the juvenile division.

Control over access to police records has long been a serious problem. Information that should have been kept confidential has been made available to the mass communication media, to the personnel offices of business and industry, to private investigators working on a variety of types of cases, to lawyers, to insurance agents, and to just plain curious private citizens. The Federal Bureau of Investigation and other federal investigative agencies were among the first to demonstrate that controlled access could be made a reality. This aspect of record management has also been developed to a fine art by the agencies responsible for our national defense, particularly by the civil and military intelligence agencies, and by many progressive state and local police agencies. One of the factors that has held back police progress in control over record access is that security systems cost money. Concerted effort can convince budget agencies of their necessity, however. Any community that wants a secure police record system can have it.

Many state juvenile court acts have provisions protecting the privacy of court matters, and an appreciable number have extended the provisions to police records in juvenile cases as well. By implication there is authority in juvenile court acts which is considered binding on police agencies regarding the privacy of police juvenile records. This is deemed necessary in order to make the provisions regarding the privacy of court records in juvenile cases an effective one. A number of national associations including the National Council on Crime and Delinquency support the privacy thesis.

Privacy of juvenile records is a matter on which there must be community agreement. Because the information may be available from several agencies, the policy of one may be negated by the others. This calls for cooperative action on the part of the juvenile court, the police, the community press, and related agencies.

According to O'Connor and Watson, factors to be considered in the evaluation and development of policies for control of police juvenile records are as follows:

1. The functional value of individual criminal histories in police investigations.
2. The research potential of the data contained in the records, bearing in mind that longitudinal studies of behavior may require information dating back many years.
3. The significance of the events recorded.
4. The fact that the skeleton notation appearing on a fingerprint record made in serious cases and forwarded to state and national repositories lacks explanatory and mitigating circumstances. Such a data skeleton record may survive the destruction of the more complete data with consequent loss of explanatory material.
5. The feasibility of extracting useful statistical data and discarding the rest.
6. The fact that the record may ultimately prove to be a liability to the community in that it adversely affects the career of one who is truly no longer a behavioral risk but a potentially productive citizen.

From the above factors four significant policy guidelines are suggested by Kobetz.

1. Police are, as a matter of policy, opposed to any blanket rule requiring the automatic and unconditional destruction of documents recording the police history of persons based on a criterion of age alone—either at the time they pass the statutory juvenile age or at age twenty-one.
2. Police should exercise discretion and judgment following the evaluation factors set out above and
   a. Refrain from making permanent records of trivia.
   b. Periodically purge their files of records having no lasting value.
   c. Take steps through training and administrative regulations to insure that all records will be complete and clear.
   d. Establish tight administrative controls so that records will not be available to unauthorized persons.
   e. Provide explanations and interpretations as necessary when records are reviewed for official purposes.
3. Police should actively participate in deliberations, official and

nonofficial, in which matters affecting police recordkeeping policies are discussed.

4. Requests for information on juvenile records that come from other than governmental agencies should be referred to the juvenile court for reply. This practice will eliminate the problem of the police providing data lacking in final case dispositions.

In a number of states statutes provide for the sealing and/or the destruction of juvenile records upon application to a court by an individual. Proof of rehabilitation is required, but when the court orders the sealing or destruction all concerned criminal justice agencies are affected. The sealing and destruction statutes also apply in many adult criminal cases.

Some states have statutes that forbid the destruction of public records, including police records. These statutes are often interpreted to mean that *all* records developed may not be destroyed. However, careful analysis of statutes suggests that only records related to authoritative actions taken must be retained. A check with the city or county attorney will usually resolve any questions regarding the retention of records; however, the most authoritative source is the state archivist who has the unenviable job of determining what are or are not "official" records.

Reports

Myren and Swanson in their premier study of police services to juveniles set forth sound principles and procedures governing the preparation of police reports of actions taken with juveniles.

General Information Reports

One kind of police reporting seeks to establish files of general information that will allow the anticipating of trouble before it actually occurs. It also stockpiles information that may be useful in the solution of offenses through the systematic analysis of fragmentary bits of information that may tell a story when properly assembled. For example, bicycle registration programs facilitate the recovery and return of stolen bicycles to their owners. Development of files on cars owned and operated by juveniles suspected of illegal activity, on the membership and characteristics of gangs with a history of trouble-making, on nicknames and associates of juveniles suspected of law violations, and on places where troublesome juveniles are known to hang out can be extremely useful during both preventive and investigative procedures.

Information can also be developed on the location of individuals and property particularly subject to attack by juveniles. Any one of such files may provide the one additional clue that, although not too significant when considered alone, may fall into place with other available evidence to identify some juvenile as dangerous to himself and to society.

These files must necessarily be limited to confidential use by police agencies only. They will contain many facts that are innocent standing alone, but proof of antisocial conduct frequently consists of a chain of related facts, each of which might have a possible innocent explanation, but which, when taken together, make it clear that the possible innocent explanation is not the actual explanation. Investigation is merited long before authoritative action can be justified. Files of this type require close management control, however.

The dangers are twofold: general information that justifies only suspicion may be acted on by some officer as though it constituted probable cause, or some inquiring agency, such as the military or some potential employer, may be told of the contents of the file although it does not constitute proof of antisocial conduct by the juvenile. But these are abuses of general information files that do have a legitimate use. This logically calls for tight administrative control of the information once collected rather than a decision not to collect it.

General information files are peculiarly police files. They should certainly be kept private — for the use of police officials only on a need-to-know basis. They do not contain the kinds of information that should be spread upon the public record for the protection of the public. Police records that should be public records are those that are necessary for a proper accounting for expenditure of funds and use of facilities and equipment and those that record authoritative action by the police with regard to particular citizens. These elements are not involved in the keeping of police general information files. On the contrary, the protection of both society and of individuals whose names might fortuitously appear in such files requires that access be strictly limited.

Complaint Reports

Complaints in cases involving juveniles come from a variety of sources in a community. Recording these complaints in a consistent and uniform manner is necessary if the community is to achieve any measure of insight into its problems with children and youth. Complaint reports should contain as much of the following information as is available:

1. Source of the complaint, with the name, address and telephone number of the complainant.
2. Date and time of the complaint.
3. Name, address, telephone number, birth date, and sex of the juvenile involved.
4. Name of school attended or of employer.
5. Name, address, and telephone numbers of parents or guardians or of the spouse, if married.
6. Reason for complaint (conduct that would be a violation of law if committed by an adult; conduct that would not be a violation of law if committed by an adult; traffic law violations, and cases requiring protection or care but not involving violation of law by the juvenile).
7. Previous police contacts with the juvenile.
8. Police disposition of the complaint.

Complaint reports should probably be kept in a separate juvenile section of the central complaint file. Further processing of the information obtained will vary from department to department. In one system after verification of the complaint, the information is transferred to index cards in triplicate, which are then filed under name of complainant, name of the juvenile, and location of the action which is the basis of the complaint. The complainant file will result in the rapid identification of chronic complainants whose reports must be taken with a grain of salt. The location file will pinpoint high-risk areas for community preventive action. The juvenile name file will turn up previous police contacts and serve as a master index to all files on that individual.

It will readily be recognized that the complainant and location files are essentially general information files. Only the complaint file itself and juvenile name index files are used in investigation to determine whether the juveniles mentioned should be referred to court. As with all police juvenile files, tight administrative controls must be maintained to assure that these are kept completely private.

Investigative Reports

Investigative reports record the heart of the work of the police department with juveniles on individual cases. The basic purpose of the report is to record the facts relied on in making the three decisions for which police are responsible in every case that they send to the juvenile court. These decisions are whether a situation presents a basis for juvenile court jurisdiction, whether that jurisdiction should be invoked, and whether invoking jurisdiction requires that the child be taken into custody.

Investigative reports are made for cases involving criminal offenses, delinquent acts which are not considered criminal in nature and for cases requiring protection of juveniles or related to a juvenile's welfare. Such reports should reflect as complete and comprehensive an investigation as for adult cases.

Investigative reports need not be filed on all police actions with juveniles. Officers often counsel juveniles against playing ball in the streets or receive complaints of thefts or vandalism by juveniles which are unfounded. Information reports for such are all that are needed, with information, if deemed valuable, transferred to a general report file.

When investigations prove negative, only sufficient information should be retained temporarily to allow supervisory evaluation. Data which are positive in nature may be retained as required for any information report.

The processing of investigative reports are usually dictated by the procedures of the department and the requirements of the juvenile court and probation department. Normally the department will maintain one copy of the report in its files and pass along one copy to the appropriate agency.

There is little reason why the format of the investigative report used in juvenile cases should be much different from that used in adult cases in the department. Using one format will be desirable in most cases because of its tendency to reduce confusion. Departmental policy may specify that specific procedures be positively recorded as having been followed in juvenile cases, such as notification to the parents of the police contact with their child with an accompanying explanation of the significance of that contact, and other similar recommended procedures for juvenile cases. If fingerprints were taken during an investigation, the single set taken should be handled as indicated in the section on fingerprint and photograph files.

There has been much controversy about the extent to which the investigative report should carry social information. The answer seems apparent. It should carry the amount of social information that is necessary in making the three basic police decisions that have been referred to so frequently in this publication. It is beyond the scope of the police investigation to go further in the gathering of social data.

As with all records relating to police contact with juveniles, access to investigative reports should be carefully guarded. They should be available to police personnel only on a need-to-know basis. Investigative reports will be prepared just as in other cases.

Taking into Custody Reports

Because the act of taking a child into physical custody is of such strategic importance, its emergency nature should be stressed by requiring the filing of a report in every instance in which a juvenile is not left with the family. This report should contain a brief summary of the facts which are recorded in more detail in the investigative report. It should also contain a statement of the interpretation of the officer of those facts which justified the taking into physical custody. Close administrative supervision over access to these reports would obviously be required.

In those cases in which, under policy determined by the chief administrator of the department, the juvenile is taken directly to the juvenile court, there will not be a booking at the station in the same sense that there is in criminal cases. The officer can notify his department by telephone or radio immediately after the taking into custody. This is necessary so that information will be available at headquarters if parents or other persons with a legitimate interest make inquiry.

The officer will make out whatever records are required by the court at the detention facility. The record of the police department will be the taking into custody report filed at the time of the action and the investigative report filed later. Since follow-up on these cases is crucial for evaluation of police judgment on taking into custody, arrangements with the court for sending information to the police department about the eventual disposition of juveniles taken in custody should be made. Under these procedures, the question of "secret arrest" which has arisen in the past is eliminated, since custody and control are in the court rather than in the police.

Fingerprint and Photograph Files

Myren and Swanson address the controversial question of fingerprinting and photographing juveniles as aids in investigation of anti-social conduct of juveniles. There are three basic uses for fingerprints in police work:

1. Positive identification of latent fingerprints found at the scene of an offense as those of a particular person from a limited group of persons known to have had opportunity to leave the latent prints. This does not require the maintenance of fingerprint files. All that is required is fingerprinting of the known group and comparison of those cards with the latents.
2. Positive identification of a person printed on a given occasion as the same person who was printed on a previous occasion. The purpose of this procedure is to establish the presence or absence of a record of previous offenses. This information is of more importance to court and institutional personnel than it is to police officials. It requires a file of fingerprints against which to make comparisons.
3. Positive identification of latent prints found at the scene of an offense as those of a person previously fingerprinted, thus establishing that the previously printed person was at the scene of this offense. This technique has resulted in the solution of many serious cases. It requires a file of fingerprints against which to make comparison. These may be files maintained by the individual police department or in a consolidated fingerprint file maintained on a regional or state basis. For the more serious offenses reference may be made to the FBI maintained

central repository of fingerprints.

The argument for maintaining fingerprints of juveniles is simple: they result in the positive identification of the juvenile. Arguments against maintenance of fingerprint files on juveniles are as follows:

1. The simple act of fingerprinting in and of itself is possibly harmful to a sensitive juvenile.

> When the act of fingerprinting is viewed in context, this statement is difficult to accept. In situations 2 and 3, the police have already decided that a basis for juvenile court jurisdiction does exist. These are cases in which fingerprints of persons currently in trouble are being taken for future use.
>
> Assuming that this is true, the isolated act of fingerprinting in the context of developmental and environmental background leading to the violation of law, to reaction to that violation, and to police investigation, including in all probability both questioning and taking into physical custody by the police, is not significant. With all of this already having happened, the additional simple act of fingerprinting does not seem to be sufficiently harmful to outweigh the protection of society that will accrue from a limited fingerprinting program.

2. Even if the simple act of fingerprinting is not in itself harmful, the act shows a lack of faith in the juvenile on the part of society that may block his rehabilitation and reintegration into society. This stems from the fact that putting the juvenile's prints into a file is justified only by the assumption that he is going to commit another violation of law in the future that may require positive knowledge of the current violation to enable society to react properly to that future violation.

> This is a plausible hypothesis, but it can neither be proved nor disproved. Regarding the occurrence of fingerprinting in context once again and assuming that it may be a factor in the success of "rehabilitation," it is not a significant factor in the light of all others. This possible-negative impact can be minimized by proper interpretive comment by the officer doing the fingerprinting, during the process. The special aptitude, training, and experience of the juvenile officer is especially helpful here. The possible significance in rehabilitation does not outweigh the social protection that is being forfeited by failure to utilize limited fingerprint files as an investigative tool.

3. Even assuming that fingerprinting is not of itself harmful and that it can be so interpreted to the juvenile that it will not adversely affect rehabilitation, it creates a tangible police record that can present an obstacle to reintegration of the juvenile into the community.

This is particularly true if the record gets into the hands of a military service into which the juvenile is attempting to enlist or of an employer with whom he is seeking employment.

> It is true that this kind of nonpolice use of the fingerprint files is detrimental to the juvenile. But this is also true of all other police and court records in a particular case. Limiting the use of this file to police officials on a need-to-know basis will prevent this abuse while still allowing legitimate use.

4. If the police are allowed to keep fingerprint files on juveniles, some juveniles will seek fingerprinting as a status symbol with their peer group. This may result in more delinquency.

> Although there is anecdotal evidence that this does happen on occasion, there have been no systematic studies to indicate its frequency. There are certainly many cases in which this is not true. It again seems pertinent to look at the act of fingerprinting in context. Within the framework of violation, apprehension and, frequently, referral to court, the act of fingerprinting does not give much additional "status." This again is not a sufficiently important factor to outweigh the added protection for society which will result from a limited police fingerprint file on juveniles.

These arguments and their analysis make it evident that this matter is not clear-cut. This means that there must be a careful weighing of advantages and disadvantages, of the possible negative effect of keeping limited fingerprint files against the positive additional social protection which would result. With this in mind, a system of juvenile fingerprint files that will achieve the lion's share of the possible social protection and, at the same time, minimize the possible negative effect has been worked out.

If the juveniles are to be fingerprinted the following considerations are suggested and should be implemented only under a definitive policy developed in cooperation with the juvenile court judge:

• Police agencies should be allowed to keep a limited file of fingerprints of juveniles on a local basis only. Copies of the fingerprint cards should not be sent to central state or federal depositories, except in national security cases. These would be extremely rare.

• Cards could be added to the fingerprint file only when the offense is one in which police experience shows that prints are useful in solving future cases. Any person, *regardless of age*, arrested in connection with a crime in which fingerprints have been found or in which fingerprints may be expected to be found on yet undiscovered evidence should be fingerprinted for the purpose of verifying or disproving their personal contact with objects pertinent to the offense.

In addition to those fingerprints that will go into the file, prints of juveniles may be taken as an investigative aid in a current case. If latent prints are found at the scene and there is reason to believe that a particular juvenile participated in the offense, he may be printed for purposes of immediate comparison, even if his prints could not be filed under the above criteria — if, for example, the juvenile was under fourteen years of age or the offense involved would not qualify under item 2 above. If the result is negative, the fingerprint card should be immediately destroyed. If it is positive, it should be made a part of the investigative report forwarded to the court. If the case is not sent to court despite a positive comparison, the prints should be destroyed or, with the special permission of the juvenile court judge, filed with the police copy of the investigative report. It should not go into the juvenile fingerprint file.

- No fingerprints of children under fourteen should be placed in the file.
- The files should be kept by the police separate from the adult criminal fingerprint files and under special security procedures limiting access to police personnel on a *need-to-know* basis. They would not be available to representatives of the military services (except in background investigations for placing men and women already in military or civilian governmental service or in the employ of defense contractors in a particularly sensitive position), of prospective employers, or the schools, or of any other nonpolice agencies except the juvenile court.
- Cards should be pulled from the file and destroyed.
  a. If the decision after investigation of the case is that no basis for juvenile court jurisdiction exists.
  b. When the juvenile reaches his twenty-first birthday, if there has been no record of violation of law after reaching his sixteenth birthday. If there is a record of violation during the juvenile's sixteenth and seventeenth years, the police would exercise discretion as to whether to destroy the fingerprint card or to transfer it to the adult criminal file.
- When the decision after investigation of the case is that a basis for juvenile court jurisdiction does exist but that the case should not be referred to court despite this fact, the card should be destroyed or,

with the special permission of the juvenile court judge, placed in the juvenile file.

• The contention that the process of fingerprinting is degrading or traumatic is often without merit and the decision to take or not to take fingerprints should not be based solely on the age of the subject.

• Where the police have reasonable cause to believe that the individual they hold is likely to repeat his offensive behavior in the future and that such behavior is likely to result in criminal offenses which generally have fingerprint evidence, the individual should be fingerprinted.

• In cases involving habitual runaways, police should fingerprint the subject for the purpose of providing a firm identification record for future comparisons.

• The fingerprints of juveniles arrested for technical delinquencies rather than for traditional adult criminal conduct should be filed in "civilian" rather than "criminal" files since the purpose of such printing is solely to provide a reference for verifying identity as opposed to cases in which evidentiary comparisons are likely.

• Fingerprint files have their greatest value in cases of persons who are recidivists. Frequently the ability to positively identify a recidivist depends entirely on fingerprint records. Those persons whose backgrounds, environment, and attitudes suggest a high likelihood of repetitive criminal behavior should be fingerprinted.

• The desirability of establishing standards and procedures for making certain identification records inactive or inaccessible deserves further deep study. Such study must be made by persons fully aware of all the factors. Thus, representatives of law enforcement, the courts, youth-serving agencies and others must be convened for this purpose. Neither the police nor the legislative bodies can act without full and complete understanding of all viewpoints.

This system is believed to make fingerprinting available to police in the great majority of cases involving juveniles in which it would be of practical assistance. At the same time, it prevents indiscriminate, unnecessary fingerprinting and abuse of the prints, once obtained. Consultation with the juvenile unit would be good practice in cases where juveniles are to be fingerprinted.

Photographing juveniles presents somewhat different problems than does fingerprinting. Police officials find photographs particularly helpful in two kinds of situations involving juveniles. With chronic runaways, the photograph can be reproduced and distributed to other law enforcement agencies and to television and newspaper outlets as an aid in finding the juvenile. The other use is for "rogue's gallery" purposes. If all juveniles arrested for a specific serious crime are photographed, these photographs can then be shown to future victims of the same kind of crimes who may have gotten a look at the assailant.

These arguments are not persuasive. Identification by photograph is not very reliable. This is particularly true with juveniles who are changing appearance very rapidly. Eyewitness testimony is notoriously inaccurate. In runaway cases, recent photographs can almost always be obtained from the families of the juveniles involved. Situations in which juveniles should be photographed might possibly arise, but they would be rare enough to make special permission of the juvenile court judge not an onerous provision.

The National Advisory Commission on Criminal Justice Standards and Goals in its report on *Corrections* recommends unequivocally against the fingerprinting and photographing of juveniles: "Juveniles should not be fingerprinted or photographed or otherwise routed through the usual adult booking process."

An Area or Central Juvenile Index

Numerous areas of the country have broadened their ability to deal with juveniles through the establishment of a county or areawide juvenile index. The system centralizes the records of contacts and dispositions which the contributing departments and agencies have had with the individual youth who has come to their attention.

The purpose of this index is to provide more information about a juvenile upon which to base a decision as to appropriate action. The police officer or the representative of a nonpolice contributing agency obtains from the index information concerning previous delinquent and antisocial behavior of a juvenile being processed. The information may establish a behavioral pattern which requires quite different action than that which would have been taken, based on the immediate set of facts bringing the youth to the attention of the official.

Tight control must be maintained over the use of index files. Access should usually be limited to contributing agencies. The files, however, can be most helpful in research, providing their integrity for official use only is maintained.

The IACP policy recommendation follows:

Police departments as well as other agencies that deal with delinquent youths should pool their information so that each may take action in individual cases upon the basis of a complete inventory of the youth's involvement with the law. Such central county or area indices may be established in any facility provided there is twenty-four hours access for officers on the street. Such access through agency communication centers must be accompanied by swift and reliable interpretation of data by those operating the files.

ACCESS TO POLICE RECORDS

The National Advisory Committee for Juvenile Justice and Delinquency Prevention has proposed a standard that if adopted effectively deals with the access to police records. The standard reads as follows:

> Access to records and files maintained by law enforcement agencies should be restricted to:
> a. The juvenile who is the subject of a record and his/her counsel;
> b. The parents, guardian, or primary caretaker of a juvenile named in the record and their counsel;
> c. Law enforcement officers when essential to achieve a law enforcement purpose;
> d. Judges, prosecutors, intake officers, individuals conducting a predisposition investigation, and individuals responsible for supervising or providing care and custody for juveniles pursuant to the dispositional order of the family court, when essential to performing their responsibilities;
> e. Individuals and agencies for the express purpose of conducting research, evaluative, or statistical studies; and
> f. Members of the administrative staff of the maintaining agency when essential for authorized internal administrative purposes.
>
> Access under paragraph (c) should only be granted to law enforcement officers in another jurisdiction when the juvenile has been adjudicated or when there is an outstanding order to take the juvenile into custody.
>
> Access under paragraph (e) should be subject to the conditions set forth in standard (on access for the conducting research, evaluative or statistical studies).
>
> Intelligence information—identifiable information compiled in an effort to anticipate, prevent, or monitor specific acts of delinquency—and

investigative information — identifiable information compiled in the course of the investigation of specific acts of delinquency — should be maintained separately. Access should be limited to law enforcement officers within the agency when essential to achieve a law enforcement purpose, and to officers in other agencies to confirm information in the files of the other agencies or to assist in an ongoing investigation.

JUVENILE/FAMILY COURT AND PROBATION REPORTS AND RECORDS

The probation department is responsible for the processing of juveniles referred to the juvenile court. Policing agencies refer the bulk of juveniles charged with criminal law violations. Welfare agencies, the schools, and a number of other agencies providing juvenile service refer some clients for which juvenile court adjudication is required by law. The dependency of the probation department on the receipt of complete and accurate reports and records from the referring agencies suggests that a discussion of the key documents prepared by the probation department is in order to demonstrate the process by which juveniles are brought before the court and/cases adjudicated.

All cases are initially referred to the intake unit of the probation department. If a juvenile has been taken into custody and placed in juvenile hall or jail, the intake officer is responsible for arranging a detention hearing before the court to determine whether the juvenile is to remain in custody or released. The reports provided by the referral agency and information available in the probation department, if any, are collated and presented at the hearing.

The first major action taken by the probation department, whether a juvenile is detained or not, is the intake investigation made by an intake officer. The National Committee for Juvenile Justice and Delinquency Prevention has proposed standards for the investigative process and the report that is to follow. These standards read as follows:

Intake Investigation

The intake officer should be authorized to conduct a preliminary investigation in order to obtain information essential to the making of a decision regarding the complaint. In the course of the investigation, the intake officer should be authorized to:

a. Interview or otherwise seek information from the complainant, the victim, and any witnesses to the alleged conduct;

b. Examine court records and the records of law enforcement and other public agencies; and

c. Conduct interviews with the subject of the complaint and his/her family, guardian, or primary caretaker.

Additional inquiries should not be undertaken unless the subject of the complaint and, if that person is a juvenile, his/her parent, guardian, or primary caretaker, provides informed consent.

The subject of a complaint and his/her family, guardian, or primary caretaker should have the right to refuse to participate in an intake interview, and the intake officer should have no authority to compel their attendance. In requesting an interview with the subject of a complaint and at the inception of that interview, the intake officer should explain that attendance is voluntary, and that the subject of the complaint is entitled to be represented by an attorney and has the right to remain silent. At the inception of the interview the intake officer should also explain the nature of the complaint, the allegations that have been made, the function of the intake process, the procedures to be used, and the alternatives available for disposing of the complaint. The family, guardian, or primary caretaker of the subject of the complaint should be similarly advised of the rights to which they are entitled, the nature of the complaint and the allegations therein, and the purpose, procedures, and possible consequences of the intake process.

Notice of Decision

Upon determining that the allegations contained in a delinquency, noncriminal misbehavior, or abuse or neglect complaint should be submitted to the family court, the intake officer should send a written report to the family court section of the prosecutor's office explaining the reasons for the decision and recommending that a petition be filed. A copy of the report should be sent to the subject of the complaint and to his/her attorney. If the subject of the complaint is a juvenile, notice should also be sent to his/her parents, primary caretaker, or legal guardian.

Upon determining that a complaint should be dismissed, the intake officer should send a written report to the complainant explaining the decision and the reasons therefore and stating that the complainant may resubmit the complaint to the family court section of the prosecutor's office. The intake officer should send a copy of the report to the subject of the complaint and his/her attorney and, if the complaint is based on the jurisdiction of the family court over delinquency, to the family court section of the prosecutor's office.

Upon determining that the intake decision should be delayed and the subject of the complaint referred to services, the intake officer should send a written report advising the complainant of the determination, the reasons therefore, and the date by which final decision will be made.

Following completion of the intake investigation the intake officer determines whether a petition will be filed to bring the juvenile before the juvenile court. If he so determines that a petition should be filed, his report and all supporting documentation is either presented directly to the court or the prosecuting attorney, if the law so requires, who makes the final determination of whether a petition will be filed. If the court accepts the petition, then a date is set for the formal hearing. The proposed committee standard related to the decision to file a petition states:

> All petitions should be prepared and filed by the family court section of the prosecutor's office and signed by the attorney in charge of that section.
>
> A petition should not be filed unless it is determined that the allegations contained in the complaint are legally sufficient. If the allegations are not legally sufficient, the complaint should be dismissed.
>
> When a complainant resubmits a complaint dismissed by the intake officer, an attorney from the family court section of the prosecutor's office should consider the facts presented by the complainant, consult with the intake officer who made the initial decision, and then make the final determination as to whether a petition should be filed. This determination should be made as expeditiously as possible and in no event more than thirty calendar days after the complaint has been resubmitted.

If the court sustains the petition at the hearing, the probation department will be directed to prepare a predisposition report that will assist the court in making its final disposition. The proposed committee standard for this report follows:

> Predisposition reports in delinquency, noncriminal misbehavior, and neglect and abuse matters should contain only information that is essential to making dispositional decisions. Written rules and guidelines should be established to govern their preparation and dissemination.
>
> The predisposition report should be divided into three sections. In delinquency proceedings, the first section should contain information concerning the nature and circumstances of the offense upon which the adjudication is based, the juvenile's role in that offense, the period, if any, for which the juvenile was detained pending adjudication and disposition, the juvenile's age, and the juvenile's record of prior contacts with the intake unit and the family court.
>
> In noncriminal misbehavior and neglect and abuse proceedings, the first section of the predisposition report should contain information concerning the nature and circumstances of the conduct, neglect, or abuse upon which the adjudication was based, the prior contacts with the family

court or intake unit which the person adjudicated and his/her family, guardian, or primary caretaker have had, the results of those contacts, and the age of the juvenile with regard to whom the petition was filed.

Section two of predisposition reports should contain only that information essential for selecting a particular dispositional program. Such information may include:

a. A summary of the home environment, family relationships, and background;

b. A summary of the juvenile's educational and employment status;

c. A summary of the interests and activities of the juvenile with regard to whom the petition was filed;

d. A summary of the interests of the juvenile's parents, guardian, or primary caretaker; and

e. A summary of the results and recommendations of any significant physical or mental health examinations.

Section three should contain an evaluation of the foregoing information, a summary of the dispositional alternatives available, and a recommendation as to disposition.

Predisposition reports should be written, concise, factual, and objective. The sources of the information, the number of contacts made with such sources, and the total time expended on investigation and preparation should be clearly indicated.

The predisposition report and any diagnostic or mental health report should not constitute a public record. However, these reports should be made available to counsel for the state, for the juvenile, and for the parent, guardian, or primary caretaker sufficiently prior to any dispositional proceeding to allow for independent investigation, verification, and the development of rebuttal information. No dispositional decision should be made on the basis of a fact or opinion that has not been disclosed. Predisposition and diagnostic reports should also be made available to the public agency directed to take custody of or provide services to the juvenile.

If the court disposition is to place a juvenile on probation, the probation department is required to develop a plan and to provide supervision. Basically, the plan calls for classifying the juvenile's need for level of supervision. The level of supervision required is the basis for case assignment, which ranges between relatively large case loads for those cases requiring minor verification and follow through to small case loads for those cases needing a high level of supervision, support, or verification. Reporting requirements will vary depending upon the level of supervision required.

Probation supervision is the process by which the court monitors the juvenile's compliance with the terms and conditions of the contract (grant of probation). It verifies to the court the nature and degree of such compliance. It provides a means for appropriately and promptly enforcing the conditions of probation, prevents a failure of compliance, and maintains the credibility and integrity of the court order and the probation supervision process. Counseling, guidance, education or other assistance is provided as is available and may be appropriate to aid the juvenile in fulfilling the conditions of the probation grant.

The probation officer is responsible for maintaining the juvenile's compliance with the court, for acting promptly and appropriately in instances of noncompliance, and for maintaining and providing the court with accurate and timely information on the juvenile's behavior and such recommendations as are lawful and appropriate.

In some states probation departments are permitted to place juveniles on voluntary probation for periods of up to six months without the benefit of court action. The supervision is provided in cases requiring only limited adjustment for the juvenile and with the juvenile's and his/her parents' permission. Complete and accurate reports and records must be maintained the same as for juveniles on official probation.

ACCESS TO JUVENILE COURT AND PROBATION DEPARTMENT RECORDS

As is the case for all juvenile records, access to juvenile court and probation department records should be limited. The standards relating to the collection and retention of records and access for the conducting of research, evaluative, and statistical studies proposed by the National Advisory Committee for Juvenile Justice and Delinquency Prevention should govern juvenile court and probation department records. In addition, the committee has proposed specific standards relating to access to intake, detention, emergency custody, and dispositional records; to court records; and to child abuse records. These standards read as follows:

1. Access to case records and files maintained by court...should be restricted to:
    a. The juvenile who is the subject of the record and his/her counsel;
    b. The parents, guardian, or primary caretaker of the juvenile named in the record and their counsel;
    c. Other parties to the proceedings and their counsel;
    d. Intake officers, judges, prosecutors, and individuals conducting

predispositional or presentence investigations, when essential to
performing their responsibilities;

e. Individuals and agencies for the express purpose of conducting
    research, evaluative, or statistical studies; and

f. Members of the clerical or administrative staff of the family court
    if essential for authorized internal administrative purposes.

In addition, objective information such as the nature of the complaint
or petition and its disposition should be available to an individual or public
agency directed by a dispositional order to take custody of a juvenile or to
provide services to or supervise a juvenile and/or his/her family; to a law
enforcement agency when such information is essential to executing an arrest warrant or other compulsory process or to conducting an ongoing
investigation; to the state motor vehicle department for licensing purposes
when the juvenile has been found to have committed a traffic offense; or to
an agency or individual when essential to secure services or a benefit for
the juvenile. Notice of such disclosures should be sent to the juvenile and
his/her parents, guardian, or primary caretaker.

2. Access to records regarding intake, detention, emergency custody, and
    dispositional decisions and proceedings maintained by courts...and
    public agencies responsible for intake, detention, and emergency
    custody decisions; public agencies responsible for supervision of
    juveniles and/or families prior to disposition or pursuant to a disposi-
    tional order to the family court; public agencies responsible for
    preparation of presentence reports; public agencies responsible for the
    care and custody of juveniles prior to disposition or pursuant to a
    dispositional order of the family court; or private programs under con-
    tract to or licensed by such agencies to provide for the care and custody
    of juveniles subject to the jurisdiction of the family court, should be
    limited to:

    a. The juvenile who is the subject of the record and his/her counsel;

    b. The parents, guardian, or primary caretaker of the juvenile
        named in the record and their counsel;

    c. Intake officers, judges, prosecutors, and individuals responsible
        for conducting predispositional or presentence investigations or
        for supervising juveniles or families prior to disposition or subject
        to the dispositional order of the family court, when essential to
        performing their responsibilities;

    d. A public agency directed to take custody of or provide services to
        the juvenile who is the subject of the record;

    e. Individuals and agencies for the express purpose of conducting
        research, evaluative, or statistical studies; and

    f. Members of the clerical or administrative staff of the maintaining
        agency when essential for authorized internal administrative pur-
        poses.

The maintaining agency should also be authorized to disclose portions
of such records to an agency or individual on a need-to-know basis when

disclosure is essential to secure services or benefits for the juvenile and/or family. Written notice of such a disclosure should be sent to the juvenile and his/her parents, guardian, or primary caretaker.

When the subject of a record or his/her parent, guardian, or primary caretaker request access to records which contain information that is likely to cause severe psychological or physical harm to the juvenile or to his/her parents, guardian, or primary caretaker, that information should ordinarily be disclosed to the requesting person's attorney or other independent representative, or through a counseling or mental health professional. In cases in which there is an exceptional risk of severe harm and disclosure through an intermediary is not feasible, the maintaining agency should apply to the family court for authorization to withhold the harmful information or to delete it from the records, such applications should be heard *ex parte*, but the requesting party should be notified of a decision to grant an application to withhold information and of the reasons therefore.

Access to medical and mental health records should be governed by the laws defining the scope of the doctor-patient privilege, the therapist-patient privilege and other applicable privileges, except that records containing information obtained in connection with the provision of counseling, mental health, or medical services to a juvenile which the juvenile has a legal right to receive without the consent of his/her parents or guardian, should not be disclosed under paragraph (b) and should not be granted without the juvenile's informed written consent.

3. Access to records... which pertain to the reporting or investigation of alleged incidents of child abuse as defined in Standard 3.113(b), or to the initiation of a neglect or abuse complaint should be limited to:

   a. The juvenile named in the report or complaint and his/her attorney;

   b. The parents, guardian, or primary caretaker of that juvenile and their attorney;

   c. Individuals or public agencies conducting an investigation of a report of child abuse, or providing service to a juvenile or family on a voluntary basis following such a report, when access is essential to performing their responsibilities.

   d. Intake officers, judges, prosecutors, and individuals responsible for conducting predispositional investigations or supervising families subject to the dispositional order of the family court, when access is essential to performing their responsibilities;

   e. A public agency directed to take custody of the juvenile who is the subject of the record, or to provide services to the juvenile or his/her parents, guardian, or primary caretaker;

   f. Individuals for the express purpose of conducting research, evaluative or statistical studies; and

   g. Members of the clerical or administrative staff of the maintaining agency when essential for authorized internal administrative purposes.

The maintaining agency should also be authorized to disclose portions of such records to an agency or individual on a need-to-know basis when disclosure is essential to diagnosis or treatment of the juvenile's conditions or to secure services or benefits for the juvenile and/or family. The agency should also be authorized to disclose to a person required by law to report instances of possible child abuse coming to his/her attention, a summary of the actions taken following such a report. Written notice of all disclosures should be sent to his/her parents, guardian, or primary caretaker.

REFERENCES

1. National Advisory Committee for Juvenile Justice and Delinquency Prevention: *Standards for the Administration of Juvenile Justice.* Washington, D.C., U.S. Government Printing Office, 1980.
2. Chief Probation Officers of California: *Probation Standards.* San Bernardino, California, Chief Probation Officers of California, 1980.
3. Kobetz, Richard W.: *Juvenile Justice Administration.* Gaithersburg, Va., International Association of Chiefs of Police, 1973.
4. National Advisory Commission on Criminal Justice Standards: *Corrections.* Washington, D.C., U.S. Government Printing Office, 1973.
5. Myren, Richard A. and Swanson, Lynn D.: *Police Work with Children: Perspectives and Principles.* Washington, D.C., U.S. Department of Health, Education and Welfare, Children's Bureau, 1962.
6. O'Connor, George W. and Watson, Nelson A.: *Juvenile Delinquency and Youth Crime: The Police Role.* Washington, D.C., International Association of Chiefs of Police, 1964.

Chapter 17

CHILD ABUSE AND NEGLECT

C HILD abuse and neglect have become serious societal problems and cause particular difficulties for law enforcement. Abuse may take the form of a criminal act; may be grounds for terminating parental rights; may serve as the basis for removing a child from the home; and may result in conduct which challenges the limits of acceptable behavior when viewed by an outsider, for example, the law enforcement officer. The rights of the child versus a parent or parents may be called into question. A division in the family may either cause abuse or result thereafter. A husband or wife may need to testify against a spouse. A child may be psychologically and perhaps physically scarred for life. An abused child, particularly an infant, may cause the observer to act with great emotion toward the perpetrator. A danger exists that adults may be falsely accused with apparent abuse that did not happen. Despite the mix of these factors, which involves the law, parenting, discipline, medicine, psychiatry, and social work, it is to the law enforcement officer that society regularly turns when abuse occurs.

LAW ENFORCEMENT'S ROLE

Law enforcement is one of the few agencies on duty on a twenty-four-hour basis. In recent years, those professionals most likely to observe abuse (i.e. medical, school, and mental health personnel) have been required to notify law enforcement in cases of suspected abuse. Law enforcement has gradually increased its training in detection of abuse. Today's police officer may observe classic symptoms of child abuse while responding to a domestic disturbance call. It is unlawful to abuse one's child, and law enforcement is gradually finding statutory and case law support for intervening promptly in abuse situations. Faced with substantial discretion typically exercised with flexible guidelines the law enforcement officer finds himself exercising a control function unlike that in most other areas of the law. The fact that child abuse and neglect needs the attention of law enforcement and numerous other professionals is the subject of this chapter.

INCIDENCE OF CHILD ABUSE

Estimates of child abuse vary. Since reports of *actual* abuse tend to underrepresent reality, *estimated* figures may overcompensate by inflating the incidence. There can be no doubt, however, that abuse is substantial. Gil's 1965 data estimated 2.5–4.1 million cases of "abuse that resulted in some degree of injury."[1] Gelles' 1975 data estimated 1.4–1.9 million cases of "parent to child violence." Estimates of neglect vary from a 3:1 to 9:1 neglect to abuse ratio. Most researchers agree that physical abuse, when it occurs, is most prevalent among children 0–4 years of age. The first year of life may well be the most critical.

While national estimates tend to be merely representative of reality, a distressing pattern develops when studying the individual abuser. Here the data strongly suggests the danger of an abuse cycle. While not every abused child becomes an abusing parent, a very high probability exists that an abusing adult has experienced abuse as a child. Further, delinquent children have often experienced abuse at an earlier age. Studies in Philadelphia and Denver reported that 82 percent and 84 percent, respectively, of the juveniles studied had experienced abuse prior to school age.[1] A Long Beach, California study reported among mothers guilty of child abuse that 90 percent had been sexually abused as children.[2] It is clear that the abused child may suffer substantial physical and psychological harm, some or all of which may retard intellectual development, impair psychological adjustment, and reduce employment potential as well as pose a threat to one's self and to society.

DESCRIPTION OF THE PROBLEM

Physical abuse involves nonaccidental injury inflicted upon a child that may result in bruises, welts, burns, abrasions, or fractures. Physical abuse perhaps presents the most tangible evidence, since signs of injury may typically be documented by photographs, X-rays, and the recovery of household objects and implements used in performing the injuries. Of course, an adult's hand is capable of inflicting substantial injury and even death. Fingerprints are occasionally available. Teethmarks may well be identified through the use of forensic dentistry. Naturally, a sexual assault on a child involving physical injury may produce saliva, semen, and threads of clothing.

Often, the critical issue in physical abuse is drawing a line between discipline and physical abuse. Certain adults and perhaps certain cultures practice disciplinary measures that, in the eyes of others, might be labeled abuse. While reasonable persons may differ regarding this demarcation, the evidence that suggests severe beating of a child can hardly be labeled anything but an assault, or a crime if committed against an adult. Bruises, however, fade rather quickly, and the passage of time may well blunt the effect of physical abuse. Over a period of time, the signs of abuse may recur. In such instances, practitioners and professionals now accept the landmark finding by Dr. Henry Kempe that a pattern of abuse leads to his label: the battering child syndrome. This syndrome focuses upon repeated injuries, particularly those that can only be caused by a shaking or twisting motion, leading to fractures, subdural hematomas, and burns which require holding a child in place during the incident can reduce the probability of *accidental* causes to less than chance. By substantially eliminating the medical probability that a child may have accidentally injured himself and illustrating the type of injury resulting from inflicted pain, it has now become possible to convince the court of physical abuse. Naturally, testimony may also support the finding, but a child will frequently be unwilling and, in effect, unable to testify against his parents. The anguishing feature of abuse is that a young child is unable to protect itself physically and is psychologically dependent upon the parents. Despite serious abuse, a child will still cling to and seek the love of an abusing parent. The state intervenes to protect the child from further injury and possible death. Though the psychological bond between parent and child may be impaired by state intervention, the separation of child and parent may yield positive results. An abusive parent, just as the child, can often not function effectively without professional assistance. The state seeks to redress the parent-child relationship through sanctions, separation, and treatment.

Emotional, Psychological, or Mental Abuse

Emotional, psychological, and mental abuse injure the psyche of the child. Just as a child is unable to protect himself physically, he cannot always draw upon well-developed defense mechanisms if assaulted by a parent. The dependency created in a parent-child relationship drives the psychological harm beneath the surface and perhaps into the subconscious. The normal reaction of an adult when verbally assaulted would be to respond to meet the assault. A child may feel guilt for causing the assaultive behavior of the adult. This type of abuse includes such behavior as noncaring, absence of love, anger, ridicule, and excessive discipline. Such behavior may be labeled *neglect* when virtually no emotion is showed toward the child. Similarly, a complete lack of parental guidance may also be considered neglect. Parents may well expect behavior of a child that is inappropriate for the particular age. Naturally, a parent may project his or her inadequacies upon a child. Further, a parent may transfer hostility toward a spouse directly upon a child.

Christina Crawford, Joan Crawford's daughter, has written a book entitled, *Mommy Dearest*, now a major motion picture, which is based on her life story and the psychological abuse that she received as a child and which eventually destroyed her love, trust, confidence, and self-respect.[3] The destruction of an ego is agonizing. Only professional assistance and time serves to restore one's ego. While some psychological abuse occurs in physical and sexual abuse, we are able to see from Crawford's book the incredible actions of an adult which might be postulated as a guide for discipline. Even the staunchest believer in discipline would recognize Joan

Crawford's behavior as irrational. Significantly, this type of abuse did not occur in a home denied of material possessions. Economics was not a factor. Professionals accustomed to physical abuse are aware of the incidence cutting across socioeconomic strata. Not surprisingly, this is particularly true of psychological abuse.

An infant requires psychological attention; perhaps more accurately it needs emotional caring. If denied emotional support, an infant may be susceptible to the label of failure to thrive. Essentially, an infant cannot develop physically without food and without emotional support. An infant whose physical development is drastically below its age group for its length (height) makes likely the diagnosis of failure to thrive. Such cases can now be documented in court, particularly when a hospital stay results in dramatic improvement in motor progress and weight gain. Naturally, one would hope for some emotional development depending upon the length of the hospital stay and the medical attention provided, particularly that of the attending nurses.

Sexual Abuse

Sexual abuse involves a sexual act committed upon a child, generally by manipulation and occasionally by force. In an estimated 90 percent of the cases, the perpetrator is known to the child. If the abuse involves incest, the victim is predominantly a female and the perpetrator is the natural father. Other perpetrators may include other family members, boyfriends (of the mother), and other parent surrogates. The incestual act is perhaps one of the most psychologically scarring acts that can occur. The mother may be cognizant of the relationship yet avoid a confrontation with the perpetrator. The perpetrator may be seeking love and affection denied by his spouse. The victim may assume that such behavior is normal.

Upon learning that a sexual act with a family member is not normal, the guilt, anxiety, and anger may cause severe emotional trauma. The interactive effect on the family may destroy trust, love, and dependency. Other family members, particularly brothers and sisters, may not escape their own psychological trauma. Role models may cease to exist, at least within the family. The victim may well become a runaway with a dangerous predilection for drugs, alcohol, and prostitution.

LEGAL CONSIDERATIONS

The critical issue in reporting child abuse centers upon who is to be notified. In forty-two states, reports are sent to the county or state departments of social services or public welfare; in ten states they are sent to the juvenile or family courts; in two states they are sent to court-designated agencies and, in thirty-five states, to law enforcement officials — prosecutors, police, sheriffs, or state police. Only nineteen jurisdictions, including the District of Columbia, limit reporting to one source. Essentially, the majority report *both* to law enforcement and to the governmental social service agency.

Some advocates argue that inclusion of reports to law enforcement essentially precludes the likelihood of reports from private physicians. It is argued that only public medical personnel, usually those in the city or county's general hospital, will feel compelled to report. Naturally, most states having a mandatory reporting law (which includes all 50 states and the District of Columbia) would make no distinction between the private and public medical person. The fact remains that a preponderance of abuse reports emanate from public personnel. It is clear, however, to most professionals involved in child abuse that law enforcement is involved with or without reports. The removal of a child from the home, more often than not, becomes the responsibility of law enforcement. Often, law enforcement is the first public agency called to the scene. It is essential that its information base match that of social services. Dual reporting permits a choice by the person reporting. The system, however, cannot work effectively by only notifying law enforcement when all other efforts fail. States such as Colorado have shown the efficacy of joint sharing of knowledge and joint training and joint strategies toward treatment on behalf of law enforcement and social services. This relationship is strengthened by joint reporting.

CENTRAL REGISTRY

Professionals have long argued for a central child abuse registry at the state level. The purpose of such a registry is to document the behavior of an abusing adult and reduce the likelihood of such a person moving from one area to another without further detection. It is argued that such movements might result in multiple incidents of abuse, which can only be accumulated if reported to a central bureau. Naturally, such reports appear in registries without a formal hearing, raising the question of invasion of privacy and lack of due process. Such a finding was made by a three-judge federal court in Texas and was raised before the United States Supreme Court in *Moore* v. *Sims*.[4] Moreover, once identified as an abuser before the state registry, such a label may have a degree of permanency that is not easily removed. It is likely that the private physician's reluctance to report child abuse stems, in part, from the confidentiality of the doctor-patient relationship. Though absolved of liability by statute, certain physicians find difficult the dual role of therapist and reporter.

CRIMINAL RESPONSE VERSUS CIVIL RESPONSE

Perhaps the most crucial legal decision to be made in child abuse is whether or not to prosecute criminally, or to seek protection for the child temporarily or even permanently. This question involves philosophy, policy, consideration for the child as well as the adults, legal questions of due process, and admissability of evidence.

Philosophy

Certain advocates regard child abuse as an assault on a child and, therefore, punishable as a crime. It is argued that sanctions must be invoked (a) to protect an innocent and often defenseless child and (b) to correct the behavior of the adult before permanent damage or death occurs to a child. Others argue that criminal punishment of a parent causes destruction of the family unit, and that society, in the long run, must find ways to strengthen the family unit. It is argued that the state cannot effectively act as a surrogate parent for all abused children, except those for whom parental rights must be terminated. Naturally, the question ultimately rests upon the dilemma: at what point should the states apply criminal sanctions versus attempt a rehabilitative program within the family? The incest program in Santa Clara County, California, for example, is based upon the assumption that placing the perpetrator on probation *and* placing the entire family in a rehabilitation program is the best solution.

POLICY

Policy questions with regard to proceeding criminally are determined by case law, attorney general opinions, statutes, district attorney's policy, police policy, and particularly the presence or absence of a police child abuse unit. In those jurisdictions having a police child abuse unit one typically finds close cooperation with emergency room medical personnel and, in sexual abuse cases, with special medical teams trained to identify symptoms of sexual abuse. A critical factor in child abuse cases surrounds the age of the child and its ability to talk or, later, to testify. A great deal of evidence in child abuse cases is circumstantial. For this reason, specially trained child abuse teams offer the most promise for accurate investigations and diagnoses and protection of the rights of the parties. These combinations of expertise and the willingness of the courts to admit evidence (for example, color photographs of a badly abused child) set the tone for criminal prosecution.

Parental rights are often weighed against the best interests of the child. The state intervenes cautiously in removing a child from its parents, particularly its natural parents. Termination of parental rights occurs only in convincing cases involving a pattern of abuse and/or neglect. Questions of negligence in child abuse, as well as criminality, are resolved through the adversary process. This process forces perpetrators of abuse and neglect to defend themselves against the accusations of the state. Guilt may well be shielded by the inherent desire to avoid criminal sanctions or the stigma of termination of parental rights. In the process, the rights of the child may be misplaced. The court, by rule, by statute, or by its own motion may appoint counsel, a guardian ad litem, for the child, particularly an infant. It does so in order to create an advocate for what becomes the third corner of a triangle: the child. It is argued that the adjudication between the state and the parent requires additional representation for the child. The court may find, for example, that neither the parents nor the state should take custody of the child, but rather a third party. It is argued that the guardian ad litem will, with greater purpose, argue for the best interests of the child.

Unlike other criminal and civil actions, child abuse has relaxed the barriers for penetrating the privacy of one's home. A law enforcement officer, if he believes child abuse to be imminent, may enter the home without a warrant to protect the child. Evidence seized in the course of such an entry will be admissable. In fact, the officer applies the test for seeking a warrant and enters in the belief that harm may occur or is in the process of occurring. Upon determining that probable abuse has occurred, the officer may temporarily remove the child from the home and, with sufficient cause, may place the adult(s) under arrest. Naturally most evidence considered by the officer will be circumstantial. Longer term removal of the child will be determined by a hearing on the merits in court.

Law enforcement has largely been protected by the courts from false arrest and from improper removal of a child, since the safety of the child has generally been regarded as paramount. Law enforcement, while generally protected, must consider carefully the possibility of sudden infant death syndrome (SIDS) fatality which might appear as a possible homicide. Autopsy will generally rule out the homicide when none has occurred. The SIDS death itself continues to perplex medical personnel, frequently leading to death by causes that are difficult to explain. Children dying from SIDS appear to die of a respiratory disease, though most basically healthy children survive the typical repiratory problems and do not, as does the SIDS child, suddenly stop breathing. The preponderance of children have an innate propensity for breathing, even when sleeping in awkward positions or otherwise impeded by bed clothing.

Unlike criminal matters between two adults, a spouse may testify against a spouse in child abuse. Communications between two spouses are not privileged in child abuse. Since one adult may acquiesce in the presence of abuse, that spouse may later find that he or she is criminally culpable. In fact, the law treats such a passive observer as an accomplice.

Perhaps the most critical evidence will be the testimony of the child when the child is the victim, or a brother or sister is an observer. Knowing right from wrong, separating fact from fantasy, and feeling stress toward recanting the story become problems for the testifying child with few exceptions. In the opinion of most professionals, children do not make up stories regarding their own abuse. The pattern of children who have been seriously injured still professing love for their parents bears witness to the desire of most children to be loved by their parents. Too frequently an abused child believes that it has caused the abusive behavior. Accordingly, in abuse cases involving young children and, of course, infants, the evidence is largely circumstantial. For this reason the "battered child syndrome," and now the "shaking infant death syndrome," have largely been accepted in court as admissable in the absence of direct testimony.

Incidence of Abuse

While the highest percentage of victims of child abuse and neglect occurs before a child reaches its second birthday, substantial abuse occurs until the age of seventeen. Abuse is distributed somewhat equally between males and females until the age of sixteen, at which point girls account for 63 percent (1977) of incidences reported. Of substantiated reports of sexual abuse, 71 percent involved 9–17-year-olds, 29 percent occurred among children aged 0–8. Of all validated reports of maltreated adolescents in 1977, 70 percent involved neglect rather than physical or sexual abuse. A number of researchers have documented the propensity for abuse among premature children.[5] Closely correlated with premature birth is the higher incidence of abuse among children small for their age or possessing deviant congenital characteristics and mental retardation. Naturally, the latter three conditions may have been related to premature birth.

Probability of Abused Child Becoming Delinquent

Various researchers have examined the probability of an abused child coming into contact with the juvenile court, while studies have often been designed without control groups the incidence of abused children again having contact with the juvenile court has varied from 8–17 percent. While certainly not insignificant, it is not known to what extent a control group might yield similar results. It has been observed by some that many assassins, occasionally gaining national notoriety, for example, Sirhan Sirhan and Charles Manson, had been earlier abused. These observations, of course, have been made retrospectively. Very much like the marijuana smoker who does not proceed to hard drugs, the abused child need not assume a future of delinquency. Even the casual observer, however, would not share concern for the abused child whose childhood experiences suggest even an 8–17 percent probability of delinquency. Data for 1976 of the general population, by contrast, show a total of arrest reports for slightly more than 2 million young persons between the ages of 11 and 17, amounting for an arrest rate of 7 percent of the 28.8 million youth in that age cohort (i.e. the status of children, youth, and families in 1979). Naturally, some youths were arrested more than once, therefore partially inflating the figure. Though a tentative linkage may well exist between abuse and delinquency, there is scant evidence to support the view that sexually abused children constitute the bulk of runaway children. Whatever the link, however, it remains a fact that in 1978 the runaway tended to be female (59.4%), aged 16 (25%), and white (74%).

VIOLENCE IN THE FAMILY

Researchers have identified the use of violence in the home as widespread. The demarcation between discipline and violence remains elusive. Nevertheless, abusing families tend toward violence toward children, violence between spouses, periods of desertion, and excessive use of alcohol. Not only do abusing families tend toward violence to children and between spouses, but children may exhibit the same behavior toward siblings, outsiders, and even toward their parents. In addition, violence in the family may lead to self-destructive behaviors on the part of the children. This pattern of behavior forms the basis for a cycle or behavior that may continue until the child reaches child-bearing years. Interrupting this cycle becomes a formidable task.

Psychological Characteristics

Persons abusing children tend toward similar symptoms. Parents of abused children tend toward immature and compulsive behavior, triggered by frustration and anger. Interactive or interpersonal skills of such parents seem limited; flexibility and compassion seem lacking. Abusing parents typically expect behavior of a child that is inappropriate for the age level. Failure to perform at expected levels causes frustration and anger. Should the child be physically or mentally deficient these symptoms would be exacerbated. The tolerance, patience, and understanding of an abusing parent seems constantly to be tested.

SEPARATION

The abused child may be removed from the home temporarily, may be removed for relatively long periods of time, and may, in a termination of parental rights action, be removed permanently. Children may be placed with foster parents, may be placed in residential settings, and, following termination proceedings, may be placed for adoption. These actions simply remove the child from the abusing conditions and rely upon the possibility that the child will enter into a bonding process with other adults, which will create a surrogate or psychological parent. There is an assumption that these adults who are not the biological parents offer greater probability of a nonabusing adolescence than would a return to the natural parents.

TREATMENT FOR THE PARENTS

Though the children might be temporarily removed from the home and might even enter family therapy programs, the target of therapeutic assistance may be for the parents. These programs seek to stabilize the parents, train them to deal with frustration and anger, and share their feelings with other abusing parents. It is assumed that abusing parents need to learn of the existence of other abusers and to confront each other in attempting to modify behavior. Such programs may be voluntary or court-ordered. Obviously, the success of such programs depends upon credibility and expertise of the programmatic personnel.

Cumulative Effect

Very little is known about the cumulative effect of child abuse, detection, adjudication, and disposition upon the child. It might be argued that the trauma created by abuse, separation, adversary proceedings, and treatment success or failure could lead to bitter feelings of rejection, isolation, flattering of emotions, self-destructive behavior, and further violence. The state has generally taken the position that strengthening the family is the most prudent alternative. Where disagreement occurs is in identifying those families in which further presence of the child is counterbalanced by the need to protect the child. Most courts have numerous cases of fatal incidents among children that occurred in homes in which custody of the children had been temporarily removed from the parents and supervision placed with the social services agency. When fatalities occur to children who have been under the court's jurisdiction the bench of that particular court tends toward more prompt and lasting action to protect the child. These tragic events remind professionals of the frail dimension of family life and the caution that should surround returning the child. The rights of natural parents, so often espoused in case decisions, blur the decision-making process following the death of a child or infant.

POLICE PROCEDURES

In no other area of police work do procedures vary so greatly from jurisdiction to jurisdiction as they do in cases involving abuse and neglect of children. This wide variation stems largely from differing community concepts of how abused and neglected children can best be helped and from the differing amount and quality of social services available for implementation of these concepts. In view of these variations, it is important to review briefly the two distinctly different kinds of court action that may result from these cases.

1. *An action on behalf of the child.* This type of action, which is non-criminal, seeks to determine whether the child is in danger and, if so, what action is needed for protection. The parents may be deprived of the custody of the child, required to pay for support, or ordered to make adjustments in the care, custody, and control. This type of action does not permit any punitive sanction against the parents, however.

2. *An action against the parents.* This is a criminal prosecution of the parents on charges that they have committed a harmful act against the child or failed to discharge their responsibility, thus placing the child in acute danger. This action does not involve the status of the child. It is essentially negative rather than positive in nature.

A community program for the protection of children against abuse and neglect involves many agencies providing a variety of services. These include public welfare departments, private social agencies, specialized school services, mental health clinics, hospitals, courts, and the police. In addition, public welfare departments and private social agencies in a number of communities have set up special services specifically designed to focus on neglect situations. This special service has been termed *protective service* by some. It is essentially a casework service staffed by trained social workers. As such, it is appropriate to the function of a social agency rather than to that of a police department. This is a basic service that should be available in every community to prevent neglect and family breakdown.

Every community should have a well-defined and well-known program operating to afford protection to children against abuse and neglect. The focus of this program should be on the welfare of the child and not on the prosecution of the parents. It is important to consider the role of the police in this program. The police are charged with the overall protection of the community. Because of this responsibility, they must be ready to accept complaints of cases of aggravated abuse and neglect requiring emergency action. In such cases the police department, often the first public agency involved, plays a role similar in many respects to its role in a delinquency situation. For the purpose of this discussion, the police processing of neglect complaints is discussed under the heading of receipt and investigation, and evaluation and disposition. A short section is also devoted to the handling of the adults involved.

Receipt and Investigation

Situations involving neglect of children are generally brought to the attention of the police and other community agencies by someone other than the parents. Police themselves often observe instances of neglect when responding to other types of complaints, such as domestic disturbances, or when on routine patrol assignments. Because neglect is not confined to an eight-hour day, a police department, as the only agency with investigative responsibility open twenty-four hours a day throughout the year, receives the initial call in many cases of neglect and abuse. It should not be expected to deal with all such cases, however. The police department is probably in the best position to respond to emergency complaints of neglect where children are in immediate danger, because it does provide continuous service and is able to move without delay.

On the other hand, complaints that appear to be chronic or non-emergency in nature should be referred directly to the community social agency providing service in neglect cases.

Unfortunately, such services are still unavailable in many communities. Where this is true, the police department should take vigorous action to draw this gap in services to the attention of the community agency planning services for children and youth. Meanwhile, the police department should continue to accept all complaints until the proper service can be established. Where such services do exist, neglect complaints of a nonemergency or chronic type that do come to the police should be referred by them directly to the service.

Such a working relationship calls for very close cooperation between the police and the casework agency. Procedures for initial response to or referral of complaints by both agencies should be developed jointly. In cases in which complaints are referred from one agency to another, the referring agency should have assurance that the referral will receive prompt attention. This is necessary because initial acceptance of the complaint carries with it responsibility to see that an investigation is made. The police juvenile specialist unit should carry responsibility for working with the agency in developing these procedures.

Police investigation of a neglect complaint is aimed at protection of the lives of the persons involved and, when necessary, at bringing the situation to the attention of the appropriate community agency without delay. Police investigation should be an impartial, objective, and scientific procedure. Facts must be collected, authenticated, and evaluated.

Two initial questions confront the police officer when verifying reported complaints of abuse or neglect of a child: Does neglect or abuse exist? Is there sufficient evidence to support a referral to court? The answers to both of these questions can be established by a proficient police investigation based upon knowledge of the law of neglect and of the rules of evidence and on previous police experience in handling similar complaints. Wherever possible, investigation of neglect complaints should begin with the complainant. Since the complainant's testimony would probably be needed to support any possible court case, availability and willingness to testify should be determined in advance. The interview may indicate that the basis for the complaint is not sufficient to warrant governmental interference. It may also indicate that the complaint is a spite action growing out of neighborhood animosity.

Whatever the outcome, it is important to tell the complainant that an investigation is underway. The officer must be well informed as to what constitutes neglect under the law. Methods of gathering evidence useful in this kind of case include taking statements of witnesses and the complainant, interviewing parents and children, and making general observations on family life. Poor or dirty physical conditions, in themselves, do not constitute neglect. They may, however, be symptoms of neglect. Obvious cases of abuse or neglect can be verified immediately by observation. Others require the use of additional investigative techniques to obtain more facts. The special aptitude, training, and experience of the juvenile officer is particularly important in such cases.

Evaluation and Disposition

After observing home conditions and discussing the case with the family, complainant, and witnesses, an evaluation of the situation is made by the police officer. The physical condition of the child, the attitudes of parents and child toward each other and toward the situation, and the general conditions of the home are the most significant factors, both legally and socially, in the kinds of cases that require immediate police action. Often the police officer is the first person in an official capacity to enter the home. What he hears and observes can be of considerable help in determining what actions he should take. This evaluation is not the taking of a social history, since the process differs in purpose, scope, and degree but is simply a procedure for arriving at a police disposition.

A patrol officer often finds it difficult to make disposition of neglect cases. One reason for this difficulty is the complexity of factors involved. Special aptitude, training, and experience are necessary to cope with these. In addition, the investigation is generally limited by scope of assignment, tour of duty, and confinement to a specific patrol area. Many neglect cases require facts and social information not immediately available before a sound police disposition can be made. In such a case, the officer should call on the police unit specializing in children's cases.

One of the primary functions of this unit is to provide consultation or conduct follow-up investigations in these cases after the line officer's initial investigation. Follow-up may be required because the case would take the patrol officer too far afield from his assigned patrol, because the use of plain clothes and unmarked cars is desirable, or because the patrol officer is uncertain as to the best disposition for the case.

Juvenile units acquire a specialized competence to deal with cases of neglect and abuse and to make referrals of the families involved to the appropriate community resources. Police departments in rural and semi-rural areas oftentimes do not have a departmental unit or even a single officer specializing in children's cases. In such situations, police officers should seek advice from whatever local resources are available, such as public welfare and probation departments, private social agencies, or visiting school teachers. The chief should also designate one of his men to specialize in these cases in addition to his regular duties.

But, regardless of who within the police department has final responsibility for the case, a final police disposition must be made. Cases in which the complaint is not substantiated should be closed. Cases in which neglect is found are more difficult. The alternatives are discussed below.

As pointed out earlier, the police may refer what appears to be nonemergency neglect complaints to social agencies in the community for investigation and disposition. Even where the police investigation shows the complaint to be unsubstantiated, the police may find that the family needs and wants help, either in the nature of counseling or public assistance. Such a case should be referred to the appropriate social agency.

Once the police officer has decided that a basis for court action exists and that such action is necessary, the case as in a delinquency case, should be referred to the court. The officer should be prepared to file a petition or complaint and present the necessary evidence at the hearing if, in the opinion of the court, further action is necessary, or the court may refer the case for social study to a community agency or to its own staff. Because of its greater resources for obtaining and evaluating social information, the court may decide, at the point of intake, not to use its authority but to refer the case to a casework agency just as the police might have done earlier.

When it has been decided that court action is necessary, the officer must decide whether the child needs to be taken into custody immediately and placed in shelter care. Police have this authority in all communities. In some communities it may also be given to child protection agencies. Whenever a child is taken into custody, whether by a police officer or an agency worker, a referral to court should follow. Exceptions to this would be children temporarily lost or children placed at the request of the parent because of a temporary emergency.

Police Handling of Adults Involved in Abuse and Neglect Situations

The mere fact that a petition alleging children to be neglected has been filed in juvenile court should not, either by law or policy, require that the parents be charged with criminal neglect. Police officers should be permitted to exercise discretion with respect to referring parents for prosecution in such cases. Often a situation that at first appears to involve willful neglect may not be so judged after all the facts become available and are evaluated.

It has been the experience of workers in the field that most parents want to do what is best for their children. The neglect is oftentimes the result of the parents' inability to cope with the tensions and problems of modern living. Before parents are charged with criminal neglect, the case should be discussed with the court and the appropriate community agencies. Whether such action is necessary to gain control over the parents and its probable effect upon the continuing relationship between the parent and child and between the family and the agency providing care and service are two of the factors that should be considered in making the decision.

REFERENCES

1. U.S. Department of Health, Education and Welfare, National Center on Child Abuse and Neglect: *1977 Analysis of Child Abuse and Neglect Research*. Washington, D.C., U.S. Government Printing Office, 1978.

2. Ray E. Helfer and Henry C. Kempe, (Eds.): *Child Abuse and Neglect.* Cambridge, Massachusetts, Ballinger Publications, 1976.

3. Christina Crawford: *Mommy Dearest.* New York, William Morrow and Co., Inc., 1978.

4. U.S. Department of Health and Human Services, Office of Human Development Services, Administration for Children, Youth and Family Research, Demonstration and Evaluation Division: *The Status of Children, Youth and Families in 1979*, Washington, D.C., U.S. Government Printing Office, 1980.

Chapter 18

SEXUAL EXPLOITATION OF CHILDREN

T HE exploitation and abuse of children by anyone is a serious crime, one that should receive the fullest measure of attention from law enforcement personnel. Available information indicates an increase in the scope of sexual exploitation and abuse of children. This type of crime can occur anywhere, and suspects may be rich or poor, ignorant or well-educated, married or single. They can come from any sector of society.

In the course of their duties, officers may encounter cases of sexual exploitation and abuse and should be prepared to take appropriate action. In order to do so, there is a need for officers to develop the skills and acquire the knowledge necessary to recognize these situations where they exist and to conduct a thorough investigation.

THE LAW

All jurisdictions will have several laws that define and prohibit conduct that may subject children to sexual exploitation and abuse. Usually these laws grant law enforcement agencies specific authority to deal with situations that involve these offenses. Law enforcement personnel investigating these cases should be thoroughly familiar with all pertinent local statutes. The statutes will usually include the following:

Physical abuse
Sexual molestation
Unfit home
Endangering
Unlawful sexual intercourse
Pandering
Contributing to the delinquency of a minor
Willful cruelty toward child; endangering life, limb, or health
Sodomy with a minor
Crimes against children
Oral copulation with a minor
Sale or distribution of obscene matter
Hiring, employing etc., a minor for sale or distribution of obscene matter
Annoying or molesting children

Of course, other laws may be applicable.

RECOGNITION OF VICTIMS AND SUSPECTS

Officers should become familiar with the people who frequent locations where juveniles congregate. The frequent appearance of adults may indicate that the location is a meeting place or a pickup point.

Officers should also be familiar with the terms that are used to refer to victims and suspects, which will aid in recognition:

1. *Pedophile*: One with a sex perversion in which children are the preferred sexual object.
2. *Child Molester*: An adult male or female who seeks sexual gratification from young girls.
3. *Chickenhawk*: An adult male or female who seeks gratification from young boys.
4. *Chicken*: A young boy under the age of eighteen years.

A chickenhawk has a sexual preference limited to boys of a certain age range, which may not span more than three years, i.e. boys who are either nine, ten, and eleven years old. A twelve-year-old boy would not be sexually stimulating to a particular chickenhawk

The child molester, though, has a broader sexual preference age range and may cover as much as a ten-year span.

Child molesters and chickenhawks have a genuine interest in children. Most of these individuals have no children of their own. Because of their sexual preference, they must continually seek out new children. Officers should be aware that the chickenhawk or child molester is often the child's best friend. The sexually exploited child is seduced through attention and affection. The relationship between the victim and suspect may be so close as to give the impression of a parent-child relationship. The victim may, in fact, believe that nothing is wrong with what the chickenhawk or child molester does. Officers should also be aware that there are usually numerous victims involved.

There are several factors that can aid officers in identifying victims and suspects. Some of these factors may be readily apparent and others may become known only after an interview. The victims of child molesters and chickenhawks usually are

- in the 8–16-year age bracket
- unsupervised and may be runaways
- from an unstable home environment with poor family ties and perhaps one parent absent
- underachievers at home and at school
- from low- or average-income families
- subject to abrupt changes in moods, attitude, and behaviors
- without strong moral or religious values
- not necessarily delinquent
- seeking attention, affection, praise, rewards, and approval
- in possession of more money than normal, new toys, new clothes, etc. (rewards from the child molester or chickenhawk)
- found at recreation areas, theaters, and other juvenile hangouts where they may spend more than the normal amount of time
- in the company of adults with whom they spend inordinate amounts of time
- withdrawn from family and peer groups and may form new peer groups

The profile of a child molester/chickenhawk suspect would generally include the following:

- more often a middle-aged male

- relates far better to children than to adults
- usually unmarried but may have a "protective marriage"
- associated with few adults except other pedophiles
- usually has an identifiable sexual preference in regard to children and will frequent locations that cater to them
- may seek employment and/or volunteer programs involving children or his sexual preference
- sexually pursues children by eye contact, furtive glances, or staring at the genital area of a prospective victim
- pays more than a normal amount of attention to a child in his company (doting)
- usually photographs the victims
- collects child pornography and uses it for self-gratification as well as for lowering the inhibition of victims
- may possess and use narcotics to lower the inhibitions of victims
- may have a genuine interest in children
- is usually intelligent enough to recognize his personal problem and to understand the severity of it
- may go to great lengths to conceal the illicit activity
- often rationalizes any involvement, emphasizing the positive impact upon the victim and repressing the harm committed
- often portrays the child as the sexual aggressor
- talks about the child in the same manner as one would talk about an adult lover or spouse
- often was molested at an early age, is usually nonviolent, and has few problems with the law

THE USE OF PORNOGRAPHY BY THE CHICKENHAWK AND THE CHILD MOLESTER

The use of pornographic material by the chickenhawks and child molesters is extensive, as evidenced by the ever-increasing volume of such material seized in investigations of sexual exploitation. Corroborating this physical evidence are the statements of the victims who in practically all cases were exposed to pornographic literature. It can be concluded that pornography in many forms is extensively used by those who engage in sexual crimes against children.

Pornography serves as a method by which the suspect can turn a normal conversation with a juvenile toward a sexual theme. As an example, a suspect who picks up a victim in a vehicle and leaves a pornographic magazine on the vehicle seat solely to stimulate conversation about sex.

Pornography is also frequently used to sexually stimulate both the suspect and victim as well as to break down inhibitions a victim may have regarding the acts that he or she is expected to commit. The nature of the literature used will correspond to the suspect's sexual inclinations. If the victim displays reluctance to engage in such conduct, the suspect will use the literature as an element of persuasion. He will show the victim the publication and present the argument that if the young boy in the magazine is willing to remove his clothing or orally copulate the penis of another boy, why should not the victim be willing to also do so? If the suspect observes that the victim is not responsive to homosexual literature, he may also use literature depicting young girls. Viewing the young girls may cause the victim to achieve an erection. The chickenhawk will then offer to copulate the victim to fulfill the victim's growing need for sexual gratification. Like the chickenhawk, the child molester directs the victim's attention to the fact that the young girl in the magazine is posing nude and suggests that it is all right for the victim to act similarly.

Photographs as Used by the Child Molester and Chickenhawk

Often, personal photographs are taken by or of the suspect, which are generally not intended for commercial sale or profit, but rather for the private use and stimulation of the suspect. The act of taking the photographs may be so stimulating to the suspect that it causes him to reach a climax. In most cases involving the taking of photographs, the suspect has molested the victim either before, during, or after the process. In a few cases, photographs have been used to threaten exposure of victims who have indicated they may leave the suspect or go to the authorities for help.

Professionally Produced Pornographic Publications

The production of professional pornographic publications depicting youths exposes a minor to hazards as great as those presented by the chickenhawk or child molester who "keeps" a minor for his personal gratification. In almost all cases, the professional photographer of such publications will himself be a child molester or chickenhawk.

Models for pornographic publications are obtained in various ways. The runaway juvenile, alone and without support in a strange city, is a particularly attractive target for these publications. Ads soliciting "kids who have just hit town" appear frequently in underground newspapers. As in the case of the private chickenhawk or child-molesting photographer, the professional pornographic photographer will probably molest his victim before, during, or after the photographic process.

In addition to sexual gratification, the photographer will reap a handsome profit. A pornographic publication that retails for between eight and fifteen dollars per copy costs between forty and sixty cents to produce.

REPORTING THE OFFENSE

Most officers are conscientious about including in their reports the elements of the crime and chronologically relating all those events that contributed to probable cause leading to a good arrest. In sexually exploitative/abusive crimes against children there is often much evidence not collected and consequently, not reported. This evidence is often essential to show intent. Pornography, both that which is legal as well as that which is illicit, is often used by suspects in these crimes to lower a victim's inhibition and to persuade a victim to participate in the desired sexual act. Investigators have discovered through their investigations and through interviews with child molesters, chickenhawks, and their victims that pornography and drugs are commonly used to gain a victim's compliance.

When officers receive information for a crime report or any related report that narcotics or pornography was present at the scene of or used in the commission of any sex crime, this information should be included in the narrative section of the report. When collecting evidence at the scene of sex crime or in any other place in which an officer has a legal right to collect evidence, all pornographic material, even that which is legitimately sold at newsstands, should be booked into evidence and noted on the appropriate reports.

SEARCH WARRANTS AND INFORMANTS

The use of search warrants and informants with regard to exploitation/molestation cases is generally beyond any investigative action that a field officer may take. However, for the benefit of those officers who may become involved in a follow-up investigation, certain general guidelines will be presented.

The preparation of a search warrant will require reliable information that such activity is taking place. The statement of victims should be corroborated. Other victims and suspects should be identified. Locations, circumstances, and evidence to be found should be identified and described. When executing a search warrant, extensive photographs should be taken of the location, interior furnishings, and, particularly anything that may corroborate the victim's statements.

When an officer uses an informant, the reliability of the informant should be established. Victims and suspects should be identified. Locations at which chickenhawks and child molesters and their victims meet and, if possible, the locations where the sexual activity takes place should be identified. An informant can be used to verify the statements of victims, suspects, and witnesses. When dealing with an informant, the nature of information should be as detailed and explicit as possible. Subsequent confirmation of this information will lend greater weight to the testimony of the informant. Even in the event that an informant does not testify in court, confirming the information by the officers strengthens the informant's reliability for future cases. Informants may or may not be involved in the type of activity under investigation. Thought should be given to an informant's motivation, as well as how the informant came to possess the information provided to the officers. A good informant cannot only provide particulars on a given case, but can also help officers learn of and monitor the level of sexual exploitation activity at a particular location or in the community at large.

INTERVIEWING SUSPECTS*

The interrogation of adult suspects should be handled tactfully to elicit their cooperation. Child molesters and chickenhawks are well

---

*See Chapter 12 for details on conducting interviews with suspects.

aware of the low esteem in which society holds them. They are also aware of the consequences of going to prison under a child-molesting conviction. For this reason, they fear going to prison and generally react to the hard approach by total withdrawal, completely denying all allegations. However, when these suspects are approached with the understanding that they have an emotional problem that can be treated, they become more cooperative in interview situations. Remember that many child molesters/chickenhawks are individuals who had similar experiences in their youth. Once an officer gains their confidence, they may open up and talk about the incident.

Chickenhawks/child molesters usually associate with other pedophiles and, consequently, can provide information on other sexual exploitation activity.

INTERVIEWING THE CHILD SEX-CRIME VICTIM

Although it has been estimated that more than one million American children are sexually assaulted each year, very few of these cases are brought to the attention of law enforcement. The reason why sexual abuse is underreported is that more than likely the victim and offender are related. Family members fail to report these crimes due to

- Personal shame
- Misguided loyalty
- Personal embarrassment
- Public exposure
- Fear of prosecution
- Complicity
- Guilty knowledge
- Naivety and obedience of child victim
- Fear of retaliation
- Destruction of family unit
- An awareness that a crime has been committed

Sexual assault upon children committed by strangers is more likely to be reported to law enforcement agencies. However, under-reporting is still prevalent due to the fact that children have difficulty in comprehending and relating unusual experiences. The sexual assault complaint is usually registered by the parents. It becomes obvious that they must first understand and believe the child's account of the sexual episode.

A secondary problem to underreporting the sexual abuse is usually a delay in reporting, caused by a child's limitations in recollecting and communicating the experience. Children may not mention an incident to a parent until some environmental factor triggers their memories. During a bath or caress the child may spontaneously remember the incident of sexual abuse and communicate details to a parent. Of course, this delay in reporting adds immeasurably to the difficulty in investigating the complaint.

After the incident of sexual abuse is officially reported, the victim is interviewed. Interviewing a child is quite different from interviewing an adult. The officer must use special skills in conducting a successful interview of a juvenile sexual abuse victim. The officer must have a basic knowledge of physiology and psychology, in order to have an understanding of how children perceive and relate events, and the emotional reactions of the child victim and the parents to the incident.

An officer who has occasion to interview a victim should keep in mind the fact that this particular victim is an emotionally confused individual. Most victims are "willing victims" in spite of the fact that they have known lies, misuse, and abuse at the hands of the molester or chickenhawk. Nevertheless, the chickenhawk and molester are generally the only individuals who have ever given a victim affection and attention. Consequently, the victim has no reason to expect any better treatment from a police officer than that received from any other adult. An officer must establish and maintain rapport with the victim. Only then will the victim trust an officer.

An officer can acquire the trust of a victim by exhibiting the following characteristics:

- Be attentive (really listen to the victim)
- Be honest
- Be patient (it may take hours to establish the trust necessary to reveal the details of sexual activities)
- Be understanding (particularly of the underlying factors of a victim's involvement in sexual exploitation)
- Show genuine concern

During any interview at least two officers should be present. This is particularly the case when interviewing a child who has been the victim of a sex crime. In some events, depending on the age and sex of the victim, a female officer should also be involved in the interview. This affords investigating officers protection against false allegations of sexual misconduct by a victim who subsequently becomes uncooperative.

As soon as the officer has established the rapport necessary, the course of the interview should be directed to include the specifics of the case under investigation. Have the victim identify the suspect(s) as accurate as possible. Anything unique or unusual about the suspect's personal clothing, vehicle, or residence should be noted. Even seemingly trivial information can strengthen a case when it is later corroborated. Following this, questions should be asked about the specific acts committed by the suspect upon the victim and those which the victim was induced to commit upon the suspect. Officers should determine what inducement or persuasion the suspect employed to gain the victim's compliance and pinpoint the date and times these acts took place, including details which facilitate the victim's recall. Why the victim clearly recalls one aspect of involvement as opposed to another is a question that will arise in court and may be pertinent to the prosecution. This should be brought out and covered in the officer's report.

Many child molesters/chickenhawks employ pornography and/or narcotics not only for their self-gratification, but also to lower the inhibitions of their victims. If the suspect did use one or both of these, have the victim describe the manner in which it was used and where on the premise or in the vehicle it (pornography/narcotics) was kept. Victims should be asked whether or not they were photographed and whether they had seen photos of other children who might be victims. Include this information in all reports to describe the suspects' or arrestees' *modus operandi*.

Child Development Considerations

It is mandatory that law enforcement officers have some knowledge of child development for a successful interview. Children usually progress towards adulthood in a very predictable model, mastering a certain skill level before moving on to the next. However, no two children will develop at exactly the same rate. Two children of the same age may vary greatly in physical, psychological, personal, intellectual, and social maturity.

A general knowledge of child development stages will aid the interviewer in choosing appropriate interview techniques in order to illicit information and to evaluate the child's responses.

The following child development generalities focus on characteristics that are relevant to the official law enforcement interview process:

The Pre-School Child

- Language is developed as a primary mode of communication between the ages of two and four.
- Does not understand abstract concepts; therefore individual verbal skills may imply more comprehension than actually exists.
- Memorizes without comprehension of text.
- Does not comprehend metaphors, analogies, irony.
- Narrative accounts are rambling and disjointed with no distinction between relevant and irrelevant details.
- Does not understand cause and effect.
- Capable of focusing on only one thought at a time; cannot combine thoughts into a pattern or integrated whole.
- Memories are spotty and lacking in any continuity and organization.
- Comprehension of such concepts as time, space, and distance are not yet logical.
- Is emotionally spontaneous with few internalized inhibitors.
- Is able to distinguish fact from fantasy.
- Is capable of lying to solve problem, but believes authoritarian figures would perceive any lie.
- Is dependent on parents for all physical and psychological needs
- Has self-centered perception of environment.

The School-Age Child

- Gradually shifts from total reliance on family to peer group involvement.
- Identifies new role for themselves, i.e. student, child, peer.
- Develops peer group loyalty, usually with members of their own sex.

- Capable of deception with adults as a part of establishing their own separateness.
- Seldom will lie about a major issue, particularly in relation to justice and equality. They are extremely sensitive to unfairness.
- Develops increasing understanding and use of language skills.
- Understands symbols, but most thought patterns are concrete rather than abstract
- Understands concepts of time, space, and others.
- Intensively interested in understanding how all things work.

The Adolescent

- Undergoes profound physical and psychological changes as body matures.
- Relates to peer group; has minimal outward rapport with adults.
- Desires self-identity separate from family.
- May question values and beliefs that they have been taught.
- May be shy in some environmental settings but very outgoing and responsive in others.
- Is capable of deception and manipulation.
- Outward manifestations of bravado or hostility often cover feeling of shyness, insecurity, and inferiority.
- Capable of thinking abstractly with an understanding of metaphors, analogies, and irony.[3]

Psychological Reactions

In child abuse investigations, the interviewer must understand the emotional condition of the victim, parents, and possible parental perpetrator of the crime. This knowledge of the possible psychological reactions of these persons assists the officer to avoid causing unnecessary anguish and further trauma and helps to create an atmosphere of mutual trust and support in which the investigative process, especially the all important initial interview, can be successfully conducted.

Reaction of Parents

The sexual abuse of a child is a crime where the emotions of the parents or guardians may be more complex and explosive than the psychological reactions of the victim. The victim's emotional condition will tend to reflect that of the parents. Therefore it is often necessary for the interviewer to deal with the emotional reaction of the parents, if they are not involved in the offense, prior to concentrating on the victim.

The emotional reaction of parents may vary, but the officer can be prepared for the more typical responses. Perhaps the most common is grief reaction, a combination of fear, anger, and sorrow. In this response the officer must be considerate and very patient, allowing the parents to express or "ventilate" their emotions. After they have relieved some of their emotional tension, the officer should try to further calm the parents, assuring them that the child is safe and everything during the investigation will be carried out in the best interest of the sexually abused victim.

Frequently the parents of child sex victims will be overwhelmed with feelings of guilt. They blame themselves in some way for allowing the sexual offense. Where appropriate, the interviewer should assure them that they have been responsible parents and that the only guilty party is the offender.

Occasionally, the parents will direct their guilt toward the victim in the form of verbal abuse. The parents blame the crime on the victim. The officer should tactfully separate the child from the parents and try to explain to them that their behavior will adversely affect the child's present condition and future recovery.

The officer must be extremely sensitive to these emotional reactions on the part of parents and victim, for the success of the interview and the well-being of the victim depend greatly on the rapport established between the law enforcement officer and the parents.

If one parent is the offender and the other parent's guilt is justified, the officer should acknowledge the nonguilty parent's emotions but not be critical of their behavior. Antagonizing or criticizing the nonguilty parent, usually the mother, will only increase the difficulty in interviewing the child victim.

Reaction of the Child

A number of factors influence the emotional reactions that child sex victims experience, including

- The age
- The level of physical and emotional development
- The understanding of sex
- The stability of the family unit
- The brutality of the attack
- The relationship between the victim and the offender

The immediate goal of the officer is to calm and protect the victim from any further emotional trauma while carrying out the investigative responsibilities. The sexual abuse victim will frequently exhibit complete emotional shock, manifested by crying, shaking, and restlessness. In such cases, the officer and parents must comfort and support the child until his sense of well-being is restored.

Some children with more sophisticated emotional development may protect their shattered self-image by utilizing one or more of the more common defense mechanisms.

With certain older children, there may be extreme guilt feelings associated with the sexual assault. The child may feel that somehow he provoked the sexual assault by his behavior. For example, the child may feel guilty for accepting candy and a ride from a stranger although warned against such activity by parents.

The victim's guilt may take on a more mature form, such as wondering whether his/her own sexuality somehow enticed the offender. In these cases the law enforcement officer must make it completely clear that the child was not at fault and should not in any way hold him/herself responsible for the sexual offense.

Most young victims may be genuinely confused about the sexual attack. They know that something unusual occurred, but not that a criminal offense took place. The concept of "protection through innocence" should be recognized by the interviewer. The premise of the concept is that the young child, because of his/her lack of awareness of the social taboos violated, will not suffer a serious emotional disturbance from a sexual assault. Although all child sex victims will probably experience some degree of short-term psychological stress, most will not suffer any long-term emotional problems unless they are adversely affected by the reactions of adults. Here the officer must obtain the facts of the case without alerting the victim to the serious nature of the criminal sexual assault.

Timing the Interview

The interview should take place as soon as possible after the incident is reported. The longer the time interval between the assault and the interview, the less able the child is to recall the attack and relate details. The welfare of the child cannot, however, be sacrificed for investigative expediency. Since extensive questioning by more than one officer can cause the victim emotional trauma, it should be avoided when possible. However, detailed questioning by the officer responsible for the initial interview is, however, necessary to establish whether a crime was committed and to obtain the identity or description of the suspect. The following procedures should, therefore, be appplied during both the preliminary and following interviews.

Setting

The in-depth interview of the victim should not take place until after the child has been medically examined and treated and other physical needs have been met.

The interview should take place in a comfortable setting where the child feels secure. The setting should provide privacy. Places that are not free from interruptions, distractions, and noise are inappropriate for effective interviewing. A preferred location is the child's home, so long as it is not the site of the attack. It is familiar to the child and will provide the needed privacy.

It is often desirable that a female police officer conduct the interview of a child sex victim. This will depend on the age, sex, and feelings of the victim. In many cases, though, a policewoman will not be available. In this event, the officer should consider using the presence of a female nurse or social worker to facilitate the interview process. Although the nurse or social worker will not participate in the actual interview, her mere presence may be comforting to the child.

Parents as Observers

When one of the victim's parents is the suspected offender, it is usually most productive to interview the child without either parent being present. In these cases the child probably will be hesitant to discuss the attack if family members participate in or observe the interview.

Where a parent is not the perpetrator, the police officer should explain to the child's parents the purpose and structure of the questioning before the interview begins. The officer's attitude must convey a sympathetic understanding of the parents' position, and their cooperation should be openly solicited. Experience has shown that a child's initial reaction to an interview is influenced greatly by the attitude of the parents. When the parents feel secure and display cooperativeness, the child will likely behave in the same way. This will help to establish good rapport.

Whether the parents should be present during the interview depends entirely on the specific circumstances of the case. Some children will be frightened and uncommunicative if their parents are not present; others will be reluctant to discuss the matter in front of their family. Generally, if children request that their parents be present, their wish should be complied with. The parents can be seated behind the child so as not to interfere with the questioning. When the child does not want their parents present, they may be seated outside the room where they can observe but not overhear the victim. An interview room equipped with a two-way mirror can fulfill this requirement. In all cases, the interviewing officer will have to judge what arrangement is best, keeping the welfare of the victim uppermost in his mind.

Rapport

One of the most important elements of the interview is the officer's ability to establish a good rapport with the victim. An effective means of accomplishing this is for the officer to question the child about himself. Questions concerning the child's hobbies, school friends, and activities will show the child that the officer is interested in him as a person. In this way, an informal and friendly relationship between the two can be developed, and, in addition, the child will become accustomed to answering personal questions. Once rapport is established, the officer should be able to smoothly lead into discussion of the assault.

Obtaining the Statement

As when interviewing an adult victim, the police officer should let the child describe the incident in his own words and should not ask detailed questions until the victim's statement is complete. The officer should listen attentively and encourage conversation with supporting gestures and comments. By nodding their heads, the officers let the child know that they are listening and understanding what is being said. Another way to encourage conversation is to repeat key words and the last word or statement that the child has made.

The language that the officer uses must suit the age and level of development of the child being interviewed. It is important that the officer stay on the child's level and phrase his questions in a language that the victim understands. Young children usually do not know the correct words for various parts of the body, especially sexual organs. When referring to some parts of the body, for example, children often use nicknames. The officer should ask the parents for the meaning of these nicknames, and his report should reflect the terms used by the child and include the meaning attached to them by the victim. With older children, the officer's choice and manner of language will often be that of an adult. When talking to adults about sexual relationships, adolescents typically use formal terms. Adolescent girls, for instance, prefer formal language to child or street talk when discussing the topic of sex because it is less likely to embarrass them.

Because the purpose of the interview is to determine the facts of the crime, the police officer must question the victim about the details of the assault. Some details are not common knowledge among children, and they frequently cannot describe sexual activities in a vivid way. In addition, children sometimes find it difficult to distinguish between what actually happened and what they imagined to have occurred. This is especially true when the experience is a very emotional one. In overcoming these interview obstacles, the police officer relies on past experience, exercises patience, and seeks the advice of the victim's parents.

Victim Evaluation

During the interview, the police officer has to establish the potential of the child as a credible witness as well as to determine the truthfulness of the child's statement. This evaluation is aimed at two characteristics of the victim: the child's ability to accurately relate the event and to distinguish between fantasy and truth.

The child's capacity to recall and relate information can be tested by asking him/her personal questions. Information should be solicited about family, friends, school, and other interests. General questions about the community in which he/she lives, such as church and recreational activities, also help to determine their level of intellectual development.

The victim's ability to tell time is often a crucial factor in establishing when the attack occurred. Questions about what hours and days of the week that the child attends school will aid in this evaluation. There are other routine functions in the child's life that the officer can use to determine the time of the offense, including television schedule, eating habits, and daylight and nighttime activities.

Whether the child can differentiate between the truth and a lie needs to be assessed by the interviewing officer. The officer should ask the victim if he/she knows the difference between the two and what happens when he/she tells a lie. The victim's answer may be expressed in child terms, but the important thing is their attitude. The child should consider telling the truth as being positive and telling a lie as being negative. If there is a need, the police officer can verify the child's reputation for honesty by talking with the parents, teachers, friends, and parents of friends.

The child's ability to distinguish between fantasy and reality must also be established. If the victim's account seems improbable, overly imaginative, or exaggerated, the police officer may have to probe into the child's background to determine whether he/she often confuses real events with those imagined.

Ending the Interview

The police officer should never end an interview abruptly. When all the facts have been obtained about the incident, the officer should ask the child whether there is anything else he/she wishes to say. The child should be told that, if he/she remembers anything else about the assault, he/she should tell the parents. If the child is old enough to understand, the officer can explain the investigative steps to be followed.

The police officer should explain to the parents that the child may have to repeat the story to others, including the prosecutor, as well as testify in court. The parent should also be told that, if the case goes to trial, the police will help prepare the child for the courtroom hearing so that the experience will not be too emotionally traumatic.

The parents should be cautioned against questioning the child about the incident. The less the child has to think about the assault, the faster the emotional recovery will probably take place. If the child wants to discuss the matter, however, the parents should be advised to talk about it frankly and without embarrassment.

Sometimes child sex victims and their families experience long-term emotional difficulties. Depending on the circumstances, the police officer may suggest that they seek the help of an appropriate social service agency, family physician, psychologist, or clergyman.

PREPARING THE CHILD FOR COURT

When the investigation of a child sex offense ends successfully and a trial is scheduled, the police should begin to prepare the child for court. The officer should explain to the child courtroom procedures and the roles of the judge, jury, prosecutor, and defense attorney. This explanation must be in such a manner that the child understands it. Where possible, the officer and the prosecutor should familiarize the child with the courtroom. The child should be taken to the courtroom and allowed to sit in the judge's chair, at the attorney's table, and in the witness chair. The victim should also be familiar with where he/she and his/her parents will be sitting. By acquainting the victim with the legal proceedings, the officer accomplishes two goals: he makes the child a better witness by reinforcing the child's self-confidence and makes the courtroom experience less mysterious and frightening.

SUMMARY

When investigators attempt to define the nature and scope of the sexual exploitation of children in this country, they are frustrated by the lack of research and prior investigation in this area. They are operating on the "tip of the iceberg" premise, because as the extent of the problem unfolds, they are constantly finding themselves at junctures that present new opportunities for investigation. Of this they may be certain: the problem of the sexual exploitation of children manifests itself in various forms and is national in scope.

REFERENCES

1. National Advisory Commission on Criminal Justice Standards and Goals: *Corrections*. Washington, D.C., U.S. Government Printing Office, 1973. p. 264.
2. Frank L. Manella, Nerrud, Duane R., and Taylor, Charles R.: *The Illinois Youth Officers Manual*. Champaign, Illinois, Police Training Institute, Division of University Extension, University of Illinois, 1972, pp. 24-28.
3. Thomas Taglianetti: "Child Development Considerations." Lectures, Delinquency Control Institute, University of Southern California, Los Angeles, California, 1980-81.
4. Lloyd Martin: Investigator, Sexual Exploitation Unit (SEC), Juvenile Division, Los Angeles Police Department, Los Angeles, California. Lectures at Delinquency Control Institute (DCI), University of Southern California, Los Angeles, California, 1980-1981.

Chapter 19

PLANNING

P LANNING connotes selecting optimal measures to achieve desired objectives or goals. For the most part, planning in the criminal justice system has depended upon the availability of external funds. It can, however, occur without additional dollar expenditures but rather with more efficient or effective allocation of existing resources. While that may occur in the 1980s, the 1970s were marked by an expansion of criminal justice programming through external funding.

During the 1970s, planning in the criminal justice system was virtually an invention of the Law Enforcement Assistance Administration. Components of the system (i.e. law enforcement, courts, and corrections) were urged to experiment with new approaches to the solution of crime problems. Agencies were forbidden from utilizing funds for existing programs. Existing programs were to remain the responsibility of local government. New, federal funds were to be used in exploring new programs, thus expanding the nationwide attack on crime while systematically testing hypotheses and action research programs, which, hitherto, had not materialized. Accordingly, planning evolved as a method for comparing the new techniques with existing programming. Juveniles, for example, were compared with respect to such measures as recidivism by separating them into a group enjoying the benefits of the new program while comparing this result with a group undergoing the typical criminal justice response. More specifically, of 100 first-time burglary offenders, 50 might be referred to juvenile court, while 50 might be diverted to a community diversion program. In due course, each would be compared for the number of offenses as well as offenders recurring in each group. Presumably the court group received the "average" treatment afforded all other like offenders similarly referred to the court.

The results of LEAA's ten years in criminal justice "planning" are mixed by anyone's definition. Funds were occasionally misspent, misallocated, lost, and often wasted. As we commence the 1980s, many argue that money alone will not solve the problem. Selective expenditure is necessary. Those programs presenting the greatest potential for system impact deserve the greatest attention. Naturally, one would need to determine on what basis such a selection would be made. Fortunately, at least a few programs survived the LEAA era as "productive" programs. These remain as the "exemplary" programs which, in all likelihood, will continue to receive federal support.

The efforts of LEAA brought attention to the planning process. Planning in an expanding economy or with fusions of outside income stimulates innovative approaches and mobilizes interdisciplinary experimentation. Interestingly enough, the LEAA era may have achieved a side effect of longer-lasting significance. Planning implies the coordination of internal components in order to pursue a common objective. In the criminal justice system the parts interact and influence each other out of necessity, rather than by design. The American system of jurisprudence is an adversary process designed on the basis of "separation of powers." Planning, if it is to be planning, thus creates a framework within which the courts, law enforcement, and corrections need to participate in programs collectively if the *system* is to address its problems. Planning typically responds to problems — either real or perceived. Perhaps for the first time in recent memory the LEAA era witnessed law enforcement, courts, and corrections acting in parallel rather than in series. Law enforcement still provided the intake of juvenile offenders, but now, at least in some cases, it was confident of the outcome if certain offenders were referred to certain programs. Some law enforcement officers occasionally preferred to refer a youth to a diversion project *knowing* that the program would intervene through counseling, education, and work programs rather than to deliver the youth to court in which the outcome might be more uncertain. In certain instances, similar linkages were accomplished with courts that resulted in viable police-to-court programs. As a result of these transactions, at least a few law enforcement, court, and correctional officers became aware of the power that could be galvanized when the system parts pursued a common objective through prior planning. The analysis and categorization of youthful offenders permitted the development of strategies that provided reasonable certainty while maintaining needed case-by-case flexibility. This attempt at "systematizing" juvenile processing struck some as co-optation of law enforcement, courts, and corrections. For others, it introduced an element of consistency and predictability that contributed toward legitimacy in the system. No system can operate effectively if its component parts act completely out of synchronization with each other. A police officer reads *Miranda* and *Gault* in order to recognize circumstances in which to apply the law appropriately. If he acts on his best reading of the law, the advice of department counsel, and department policy and he still errs, the system has created unnecessary uncertainty and slack, which acts counterproductively toward the pursuit of system goals. The system members should expend most of their energy on *marginal* cases in which system policy is least clear. A system that is characterized by adversariness at each stage of *most* cases will be unable to mount significant strategies for dealing with crime problems.

PLANNING APPLICATIONS

Planning typically applies the allocation of scarce resources to attain a general goal or particular objective. Goals and objectives are normally prompted by the existence of a problem requiring the making of a decision. Planning decisions inevitably involve *efficiency* and *effectiveness*. Methods of reaching particular objectives are *efficient* when the benefit of using the particular method is greater than the *cost*. A method is *effective* when the method used does not violate one's norms or values or some other objective. It might be efficient to monitor the movement of parolees by implanting a miniature locating device under the skin of each parolee. Parolees' whereabouts could be ascertained at all times. But the method would not be effective, since the loss of privacy would not be acceptable to society.

Planners concern themselves not only with what "ought to be," which postulates solutions to existing problems, but in their analyses they concentrate on what "is." Planners seek to carefully identify processes with particular interest toward prediction. If planners are able to observe that a particular phenomenon occurs more often, given certain circumstances, it is possible to postulate changing the circumstances or applying additional resources in anticipation of the event. Crime, for example, may be more prevalent in poorly lighted neighborhoods, particularly those characterized by high-rise apartments. A plan to deal with this situation might be to raise the level of street lighting substantially, thus altering the conditions. A second plan might be to increase law enforcement patrols during darkness, particularly during peak hours for criminal activity.

A careful study of the process may reveal helpful clues that suggest solutions. By analyzing police response times, analysts observed that apprehensions increased substantially as the response time decreased. Planners determined that to increase apprehensions, either patrols would need to be drastically increased or citizens would need call boxes or some other communications device with which to report the crime. Similarly, the helicopter was considered in view of its rapid response time. In each case, costs and benefits were weighed, both from the perspectives of efficiency and effectiveness. Naturally, as the communications networks expand, their use increases. As law enforcement increases its ability to respond, it finds itself in a reactive posture continually dashing from one call for service to the next. With the continual rise in criminal activity, planners remain perplexed about methods for *responding* to calls rather than adopting a proactive stance toward anticipating crime. Attempts at "sting" operations or "decoy" strategies seek to attract the criminal to law enforcement rather than disperse one's forces in hopes of observing a criminal act or positioning oneself to respond.

Further study of the response phenomenon has shown the need for categorizing crimes and responses. Certain crimes suggest longer response times since apprehension is impossible, such as the typical report of a residential burglary. Response becomes a matter of investigation as well as an expected procedure by the victims. The facts surrounding the incident are not affected by a delay of sixty minutes or more. To the extent that other categories of crime can be released from immediate response, law enforcement increases its ability to remain on patrol and respond to other incidents. Some even suggest that nonsworn officers might be utilized to a greater extent in interviewing victims and witnesses and in providing official crime reports. Such a use would further release the sworn officer for response to serious crimes.

Strategic planning might suggest various alternatives toward altering outcomes in a positive way. Such strategies hinge less on the process of a phenomenon than upon its incidence in planning to reduce the incidence of crime, for example, planners would consider geographic and temporal factors particularly pinpointing those locations and times of day or night generating the highest incidence of criminal acts. Alternatives might include special foot patrols, special scooter or motor-bike patrols, special unmarked vehicles manned by experts in gang violence, saturation patrols, team policing, random deployment of patrols or location and time critical patrols. Again, each strategy would be measured against benefits versus costs, paying direct attention to the rate of reduction in criminal acts once a measure was adopted. In this particular example, attention would need to be shown for possible displacement of crime from one locality to another or from one time period to another.

CONTINGENCY PLANNING

Contingency planning postulates alternative actions in the event of certain occurring events. Contingency plans seek to anticipate as many potential outcomes, which are then matched by a response strategy. Such plans are devised for bomb threats, natural disasters, fires, riots, barricaded suspects, and other events for which a programmed response can be devised. To some extent, such plans depend on a certain predictability of the unfolding of the event *when* it happens. One cannot usually predict the locus and time of the event, but the scenario may typically be analyzed for identifiable and similar patterns. Contingent plans may then be tested in a training mode as well as during actual occurrences. Naturally, variations may occur in actuality causing contingent plans to possess some flexibility for on-site modifications. The patience and skill of the SWAT team, for example, often receives critical support from a negotiator removed from the immediate scene, thus permitting some response flexibility as requests from the scene are not immediately affected by the tension surrounding the hostage scene.

Criminal justice planning traces flows of activities among the components in the system. It then relates these flows to outcomes. Thus, systems analysis demonstrates the actual existence of a criminal justice system despite protestations that such a system does not exist. Many point to the defensible boundaries erected by the courts, corrections, and law enforcement. Lack of cooperation, hostile relationships, independence, autonomy, and the absence of a system head all fail to coalesce the parts into a system, so it is said. But as components interact, a system exists despite its frail structure. These interactions are apparent when we trace flows among the components and observe outcomes. Plea bargaining, for example, subsists on understandings that exist among law enforcement, prosecutor, defense attorney, judge, and defendant. Few deals are struck in which one party is totally unaware of the outcome. Each actor perceives, on the basis of past experience or system data, how the other will act within a particular range of tolerance, and an outcome can be predicted with reasonable accuracy. Change one actor and new data will flow among the components causing new assessments and influencing future deals. Placing plea bargains on the record would simply formalize an informal process that is already based upon strong expectations.

To illustrate system flows that transcend the individual perceptions of system actors we find more dramatic evidence of movement occurring seemingly in the absence of cognitive understanding. Saturation patrols, for example, often displace criminal offenders from one part of the city to another. Thus, elimination of crime in one part of the system does not eliminate the *offender* who pops up in a suburb to ply his trade. The problem is not eradicated, but merely suppressed or displaced. If a juvenile needs to extract $100.00 per day to support a particular need, you cannot eliminate the need with increased patrols or prevention. He must either be incapacitated in a closed, correctional facility, where, if his problem is drugs, he will still seek the drug, place him in a drug rehabilitation program, or eliminate access to the drug. Systems analysis showed us the futility of simply passing a law or arresting an individual without matching these measures that deal with the offender and the particular problem. The Santa Clara County, California, incest program is successful not only because of strong leadership by the chief of the rehabilitation program, but because law enforcement and the courts understand the strategy for dealing with incestuous fathers and their families. The strategy is to invoke the power of arrest, followed by an adjudication of probation, which directs the defendant and the family to cooperate in a therapeutic program. Thus, the criminal justice system observes a drop in recidivism, an outcome measure that is directly affected by the interactive participation of the system components: law enforcement, courts and corrections, and in this case, a social serving, rehabilitative agency. Systems analysis often develops pathways for tentative strategies that can be tested. It does not depend on removing the original cause or causes affecting the outcome. It tends to concentrate on methods for controlling symptomatic behavior while seeking alternatives for displacing the *behavior* rather than simply displacing the act to another time and location. Obviously, successes are difficult to achieve and complex in implementation. Few veterans of juvenile justice would believe otherwise. Panaceas for removing juvenile or adult crime may often be espoused, but are seldom rewarding.

SELECTED BIBLIOGRAPHY

Abrams, S.: *A Polygraph Handbook for Attorneys.* Lexington, Massachusetts: Lexington Books, D.C. Heath and Co., 1977.

Adams, G.B. et al. (Ed.): *Juvenile Justice Management.* Springfield: Thomas, 1973.

Akers, R.L., and Sagarin, E.: *Crime Prevention and Social Control.* New York: Praeger, 1974.

Amir, M.: *Patterns in Forcible Rape.* Chicago: University of Chicago Press, 1971.

Armstrong, L.: *Kiss Daddy Goodnight.* New York: Pocket Books, 1978.

Arnold, M.B.: Neural mediation of the emotional components of action. In Arnold, M.B. (Ed.): *The Nature of Emotion.* Penguin Books, 1968.

Arons, H.: *Hypnosis in Criminal Investigation.* Springfield: Thomas, 1967.

Arther, R.O., and Caputo, R.R.: *Interrogation for Investigators.* New York: W.C. Coppard and Associates, 1959.

Banton, M.: *Police-Community Relations.* London: Collins, 1973.

Barefoot, J.K. (Ed.): *The Polygraph Technique.* American Polygraph Association, 1972.

Barefoot, J.K. (Ed.): *The Polygraph Story.* American Polygraph Association, 1974.

Barry, K.: *Female Sexual Slavery.* Englewood Cliffs, New Jersey: Prentice-Hall, 1979.

Bell, A.P., and Hall, C.S.: *The Personality of a Child Molester.* Chicago: Aldine, 1971.

Belson, W.A.: *Juvenile Theft: The Casual Factors.* New York: Harper and Row, 1975.

Berliner, L., and Stevens, D.: Special techniques for child witnesses. In Schultz, L. (Ed.): *The Sexual Victimology of Youth.* Springfield: Thomas, 1980.

Block, E.: *Hypnosis: A New Tool in Crime Detection.* New York: David McKay Publishing Co., forthcoming.

Bolton, F.G., Reich, J., and Guiterres, S.E.: Delinquency patterns in maltreated children and siblings. *Victimology, 2*(Summer):349-359, 1977.

Bopp, W.J.: *Police-Community Relationships.* Springfield: Thomas, 1972.

Brecher, E.M. et al.: *Licit and Illicit Drugs: The Consumers Union Report.* Boston: Little, Brown and Co., 1972.

Brown, H.F.: *Interim Report: Exploratory Study of the Impact of Child Abuse and Neglect Laws on the Justice System in Cook County.* Chicago: Jane Addams College of Social Work, University of Illinois, Chicago Circle, September 1976.

Burges, A.W., Groth, A.N., Holmstrom, L.L., and Sgroi, S.M.: *Sexual Assault of Children and Adolescents.* Lexington, Massachusetts: Lexington Books, D.C. Heath and Co., 1978.

Burgess, A.W., and Holmstrom, L.L.: *Rape: Victims of Crises.* Bowie, Maryland: Brady, 1974.

Butler, S.: *Conspiracy of Silence: The Trauma of Incest.* San Francisco: New Glide Publications, Inc., 1978.

Carter, A.: *The Sadian Woman: An Ideology of Pornography.* New York: Pantheon Books, 1978.

Carter, R.M., and Klein, M.W.: *Diversion of Offenders.* Englewood Cliffs, New Jersey: Prentice-Hall, 1974.

Carter, R.M., and Wilkins, L.: *Probation and Parole: Selected Readings.* New York: John Wiley, 1970.

Carter, R.M., Glaser, D., and Wilkins, L.: *Correctional Institutions.* Philadelphia: Lippincott, 1972.

Carter, R.M., McGee, R., and Nelson, E.K.: *Introduction to Corrections.* Philadelphia: Lippincott, 1974.

Cartwright, D.S. et al. (Eds.): *Gang Delinquency.* Belmont, California: Brooks-Cole, 1975.

Chein, I., Gerard, D.L., Lee, R.S., and Rosenfeld, E.: *The Road to H: Narcotics, Delinquency and Social Policy.* New York: Basic Books, 1964.

Cloward, R.A., and Ohlin, L.E.: *A Theory of Delinquent Gangs: Delinquency and Opportunity.* Glencoe, Illinois: Free Press, 1960.

Cohen, A.K.: *Delinquent Boys — The Culture of the Gang.* Glencoe, Illinois: Free Press, 1955.

Colbach, E.M., and Fosterling, C.D.: *Police Social Work.* Springfield: Thomas, 1976.

Cornacchia, H.J., Smith, D.E., and Bentel, D.J.: *Drugs in the Classroom: A Conceptual Model for School Programs,* 2nd ed. St. Louis: C.V. Mosby, 1978.

Cox, S.M., and Conrad, J.J.: *Juvenile Justice: A Guide to Practice and Theory.* Dubuque, Iowa: William C. Brown, 1978.

Davis, S.M.: *Rights of Juveniles: The Juvenile Justice System,* 2nd ed. New York: Clark Boardman, 1980.

Deutsch, M. et al.: *The Disadvantaged Child.* New York: Basic Books, 1967.

Drew, D., and Drake, J.: *Boys for Sale.* New York: Brown, 1964.

Empey, L.T.: *American Delinquency.* Homewood, Illinois: Dorsey, 1978.

Eisenberg, A.M.: *Living Communication.* Englewood Cliffs, New Jersey: Prentice-Hall, 1975.

Eisenberg, A.M., and Smith, R.R.: *Nonverbal Communication.* Indianapolis: Bobbs-Merrill, 1971.

Fast, J.: *Body Language.* New York: Pocket Books, 1970.

Finkelhor, D.: *Sexually Victimized Children.* New York: Free Press, 1979.

Friedman, A.S.: *Therapy With Families of Sexually Acting-Out Girls.* New York: Springer, 1971.

Friedman, R.M.: Child abuse: A review of the psychosocial research. In *Four Perspectives on the Status of Child Abuse and Neglect Research.* Washington, D.C.: U.S. Department of Health, Education, and Welfare, National Center on Child Abuse and Neglect, 1976.

Fromm, E., and Shor, R.: *Hypnosis: Research Developments and Perspectives.* Chicago: Aldine-Atherton, 1972.

Geary, D.P.: *Community Relations and the Administration of Justice.* New York: Wiley, 1975.

Geis, G.: *Juvenile Gangs*. Washington, D.C.: President's Committee on Juvenile Delinquency and Youth Crime, U.S. Government Printing Office, 1965.

Geiser, R.L.: *Hidden Victims: The Sexual Abuse of Children*. Boston: Beacon Press, 1979.

Giaretto, H.: Humanistic treatment of father–daughter incest. In Helfer, R., and Kempe, C. (Eds.): *Child Abuse and Neglect: The Family and the Community*. Cambridge, Massachusetts: Ballinger, 1976.

Gibbons, D.C.: *Delinquent Behavior*. Englewood Cliffs, New Jersey: Prentice-Hall, 1970.

Gil, D.G.: *Violence Against Children*. Cambridge, Massachusetts: Harvard University Press, 1970.

Glueck, S., and Glueck, E.: *Unraveling Juvenile Delinquency*. Cambridge, Massachusetts: Harvard University Press, 1950.

Goldstein, H.: *Policing in a Free Society*. Cambridge, Massachusetts: Ballinger, 1977.

Goldstein, M.J., and Kant, H.S.: *Pornography and Sexual Deviance*. Berkeley: University of California Press, 1973.

Goshen, C.E.: *Society and the Youthful Offender*. Springfield: Thomas, 1974.

Grealy, J.: *School Crime and Violence*. Fort Lauderdale: Ferguson E. Peters Co., 1980.

Greller, J.: *Young Hookers*. New York: Dell, 1976.

Groth, A.N., and Birnbaum, H.J.: *Men Who Rape: The Psychology of the Offender*. New York: Plenum, 1979.

Hardy, R.E., and Cull, J.G.: *Fundamentals of Juvenile Criminal Behavior and Drug Abuse*. Springfield: Thomas, 1975.

Harral, S.: *Key to Successful Interviewing*. Norman: University of Oklahoma Press, 1954.

Haskings, J.: *Street Gangs: Yesterday and Today*. New York: Hastings House, 1974.

Helfer, R.E., and Kempe, C.H. (Eds.): *The Battered Child*, 2nd ed. Chicago: University of Chicago Press, 1974.

Humphreys, L.: *Out of the Closets: The Sociology of Homosexual Liberation*. Englewood Cliffs, New Jersey: Prentice-Hall, 1972.

Kalant, O.J.: *The Amphetamines: Toxicity and Addiction*, 2nd ed. Springfield: Thomas, 1973.

Kempe, C.H., and Helfer, R.E.: *Helping the Battered Child and His Family*. Philadelphia: Lippincott, 1972.

Kenney, J.P.: *Police Administration*, 2nd ed. Springfield: Thomas, 1975.

Kenney, J.P., and More, H.W. Jr.: *Principles of Investigation*. St. Paul: West, 1979.

Klein, M.W. (Ed.): *Juvenile Gangs in Context*. Englewood Cliffs, New Jersey: Prentice-Hall, 1971.

Klonoff, H., and Low, M.D.: Psychological and neurophysiological effects of marihuana in man: An interaction model. In Miller, L.L. (Ed.): *Marijuana: Effects on Human Behavior*. New York: Academic Press, 1974.

Kobetz, R.W. (Ed.): *Crisis Intervention and the Police — Selected Readings*. Gaithersburg, Maryland: International Association of Chiefs of Police, 1974.

Kobetz, R.W.: *The Police Role and Juvenile Delinquency*. Gaithersburg, Maryland: International Association of Chiefs of Police, 1971.

Kobetz, R.W., and Bosarge, B.: *Juvenile Justice Administration*. Gaithersburg, Maryland: International Association of Chiefs of Police, 1973.

Leonard, V.A.: *Fundamentals of Law Enforcement*. St. Paul: West, 1980.

Leonard, V.A.: *Police Crime Prevention*. Springfield: Thomas, 1972.

Lerner, J.W.: *Children With Learning Disabilities*, 2nd ed. New York: Houghton Mifflin, 1976.

Lester, D., and Brockopp, G.W.: *Crisis Intervention and Counseling by Telephone*. Springfield: Thomas, 1973.

Levin, M.M., and Sarri, R.C.: *Juvenile Delinquency: A Comparative Analysis of Legal Codes in the United States*. Ann Arbor: University of Michigan, 1974.

Libai, D.: The protection of the child victim in the criminal justice system. In Schultz, L.G. (Ed.): *Rape Victimology*. Springfield: Thomas, 1975.

MacDonald, J.M.: Rape: *Offenders and Their Victims*. Springfield: Thomas, 1971.

MacNamara, D.E.J., and Sagarin, E.: *Sex, Crime, and the Law*. New York: The Free Press, 1977.

Matte, J.A.: *The Art and Science of the Polygraph Technique*. Springfield: Thomas, 1980.

Matza, D.: *Delinquency and Drift*. New York: Wiley, 1964.

Mays, J.B.: *Juvenile Delinquency, the Family and the Social Group—A Reader*. Harlow, Essex, England: Longman Group, 1972.

McGree, R.K.: *Crisis Intervention in the Community*. Baltimore: University Park, 1974.

McLean, R.J.: *Education for Crime Prevention and Control*. Springfield: Thomas, 1975.

Mendelson, J.H., Rossi, A.M., and Meyer, R.E.(Eds.): *The Use of Marijuana: A Psychological and Physiological Inquiry*. New York: Plenum, 1975.

Mercer, J.R.: *Labeling the Mentally Retarded*. Berkeley: University of California Press,

Miller, W.: *Violence by Youth Gangs and Youth Groups as a Crime Problem in Major American Cities*. Washington, D.C.: Law Enforcement Assistance Administration, U.S. Department of Justice, 1975.

Milner, C., and Milner, R.: *Black Players: The Secret World of Black Pimps*. New York: Little, Brown, 1972.

Mohr, J.W., Turner, R.E., and Jerry, M.B.: *Pedophilia and Exhibitionism*. Toronto: University of Toronto Press, 1965.

Morneau, R.H., and Rockwell, R.R.: *Sex, Motivation, and the Criminal Offender*. Springfield: Thomas, 1980.

Mule, S.J. (Ed.): *Cocaine: Chemical, Biological, Social and Treatment Aspects*. Cleveland: CRC Press, 1976.

Musto, D.F.: *The American Disease: Origins of Narcotic Control*. New Haven, Connecticutt: Yale University Press, 1973.

Niederhoffer, A., and Smith, A.B.: *New Directions in Police–Community Relations*. Corte Madera, California: Rinehart, 1974.

Nierenberg, G.I., and Calero, H.H.: *How to Read a Person Like A Book*. New York: Hawthorne Books, Inc., 1971.

Norman, S.: *The Youth Service Bureau: A Key to Delinquency Prevention*. Paramus, New Jersey: The National Council on Crime and Delinquency, 1972.

Olsen, J.: *The Man With the Candy*. New York: Simon and Schuster, 1974.

Packard, V.: *The Naked Society*. New York: David McKay Co., 1964.

Portune, R.: *Changing Adolescent Attitudes Toward Police*. Cincinnati: Anderson, 1971.

Poston, R.W.: *The Gang and the Establishment*. New York: Harper and Row, 1971.

Pursuit, D.G., Gerletti, J.D., Brown, R.M. Jr., and Ward, S.M.: *Police Programs for Preventing Crime and Delinquency*. Springfield: Thomas, 1972.

Quinney, R.: *Critique of Legal Order: Crime Control in Capitalist Society*. Boston: Little, Brown, 1973.

Ray, O.: *Drugs, Society and Human Behavior*, 2nd ed. St. Louis: The C.V. Mosby Co., 1978.

Reckless, W.C., and Dinitz, S.: *Prevention of Juvenile Delinquency: An Experiment*. Columbus: Ohio State University Press, 1972.

Regional Institute of Social Welfare Research: *Child Abuse in the Southeast: Analysis of 1,172 Reported Cases*. By Clara L. Johnson. Athens, Georgia: Regional Institute of Social Welfare Research, University of Georgia, 1974.

Reid, J.E., and Inbau, F.E.: *Truth and Deception: The Polygraph ("Lie Detector") Technique*. Baltimore: Williams & Wilkins, 1966.

Reiser, M.: *Handbook of Investigative Hypnosis*. Los Angeles: LEHI Publishing Company, 1980.

Reiser, M.: *Practical Psychology for Police Officers*. Springfield: Thomas, 1973.

Reiss, A.J. Jr.: *The Police and the Public*. New Haven, Connecticutt: Yale University Press, 1971.

Rosenkrantz, H., and Fleischman, R.W.: Effects of cannabis on lungs. In Nahas, G., and Paton, W. (Eds.): *Marijuana: Biological Effects, Analysis, Metabolism, Cellular Responses, Reproduction and Brain. Proceedings of the Second Satellite Symposium on Marijuana, Seventh International Pharmacological Congress*. New York: Pergamon Press, 1979.

Rosenkrantz, H.: The immune response and marihuana. In Nahas, G.G. (Ed.): *Marijuana: Chemistry, Biochemistry and Cellular Effects*. New York: Springer-Verlag, 1976.

Rossman, G.: *Sexual Experiences Between Men and Boys*. New York: Association Press, 1976.

Royal, R.F., and Schutt, S.R.: *The Gentle Art of Interviewing and Interrogation*. Englewood Cliffs, New Jersey: Prentice-Hall, 1976.

Rubin, H.T.: *Juvenile Justice: Policy, Practice and Law*. Santa Monica, California: Goodyear, 1979.

Rubin, V., and Comitas, L.: *Ganja in Jamaica: The Effects of Marihuana*. New York: Anchor/Doubleday, 1976.

Rush, F.: *The Best Kept Secret: Sexual Abuse of Children*: Englewood Cliffs, New Jersey: Prentice-Hall, 1980.

Russell, H.E., and Beigel, Al: *Understanding Human Behavior for Effective Police Work*. New York: Basic, 1975.

Sanders, W.B. (Ed.): *Juvenile Offenders for a Thousand Years: Selected Readings from Anglo-Saxon Times to 1900*. Chapel Hill: University of North Carolina Press, 1970.

Sanford, L.: *The Silent Children: A Book for Parents About the Prevention of Child Sexual Abuse*. Garden City, New York: Anchor Press, 1980.

Sassenrath, E., Chapman, L.I., and Goo, G.P.: Reproduction in Rhesus monkeys chronically exposed to delta-9-THC. In Nahas, G., and Paton, W. (Eds.): *Marihuana: Biological Effects.* New York: Pergamon Press, 1979.

Sattin, D.B., and Miller, J.K.: The ecology of child abuse within a military community. *American Journal of Orthopsychiatry, 41*(4):675-678, 1971.

Scheffen, A.E.: *Body Language and the Social Order.* Englewood Cliffs, New Jersey: Prentice-Hall, 1973.

Schofield, M.: *The Sexual Behavior of Young People.* Boston: Little, Brown, 1967.

Schultes, R.E., and Hoffman, A.: *The Botany and Chemistry of Hallucinogens.* Springfield: Thomas, 1973.

Schultz, L. (Ed.): *Rape Victimology.* Springfield: Thomas, 1975.

Shaw, C.R., and McKay, H.D.: *Juvenile Delinquency and Urban Areas—A Study of Rates of Delinquency in Relation of Differential Characteristics of Local Communities in American Cities,* Rev. ed. Chicago: University of Chicago Press, 1972.

Short, J.F. Jr., and Strodtbeck, F.L.: *Group Process and Gang Delinquency.* Chicago: University of Chicago Press, 1965.

Smith, D.E. (Ed.): *Proceedings from the 1977 San Francisco National Drug Abuse Conference: A Multicultural View of Drug Abuse.* Cambridge, Massachusetts: Schenkman, 1978.

Stearns, F.: Anger: *Psychology, Physiology, Pathology.* Springfield: Thomas, 1972.

Stefanis, C., Dornbush, R., and Fox, M. (Eds.): *Hashish: Studies of Long-Term Use.* New York: Raven Press, 1977.

Stumphauzer, J.S.: *Behavior Therapy With Delinquents.* Springfield: Thomas, 1973.

Tinterow, M.: *Foundations of Hypnosis.* Springfield: Thomas, 1970.

Trojanowicz, R.C.: *Juvenile Delinquency: Concepts and Control.* Englewood Cliffs, New Jersey: Prentice-Hall, 1973.

Torjanowicz, R.C., Trojanowicz, J.M., and Moss, F.M.: *Community Based Crime Prevention.* Pacific Palisades, California: Goodyear, 1975.

Treger, H. et al.: Police-social work team model: Some preliminary findings and implications for system change. *Crime and Delinquency, 20*:3(July):281-290, 1974.

Vedder, C.B., and King, P.G.: *Problems of Homosexuality in Corrections.* Springfield: Thomas, 1967.

Violante, R., and Ross, S.A.: *Research on Interrogation Procedures.* Contract NONR-4129 (00). Stanford Research Institute, October 1964.

Voss, H.L. (Ed.): *Society, Delinquency and Delinquent Behavior.* Waltham, Massachusetts: Little, Brown, 1970.

Walker, R.N.: *Psychology of the Youthful Offender.* Springfield: Thomas, 1973.

Walters, D.R.: *Physical and Sexual Abuse of Children.* Bloomington: Indiana University Press, 1975.

Wesson, D.R., and Smith, D.E.: *Barbiturates, Their Use, Misuse and Abuse.* New York: Human Sciences Press, 1977.

Whitehouse, J.E.: *A Police Bibliography.* New York: AMS Press, 1980.

Wicks, R.J., and Josephs, E.H.: *Techniques in Interviewing for Law Enforcement and Corrections Personnel: A Programmed Text.* Springfield: Thomas, 1972.

Willette, R.E. (Ed.): *Drugs and Driving.* National Institute on Drug Abuse Research

Monograph 11. DHEW Pub. No. (ADM) 77-432. National Institute on Drug Abuse, 1977.

Wilson, J.Q.: *Varieties of Police Behavior.* Cambridge, Massachusetts: Harvard University Press, 1968.

Wilson, O.W., and McLaren, R.C.: *Police Administration.* New York: McGraw-Hill, 1972.

Wolberg, L.: *Hypnosis: Is It For You?* New York: Harcourt, Brace and Jovanovich, 1972.

Wooden, K.: *Weeping in the Playtime of Others: America's Incarcerated Children.* New York: McGraw-Hill, 1976.

Yablonsky, L.: *The Violent Gang.* New York, Macmillan, 1962.

Zimmerman, C.H.: *The Polygraph in Court.* Auburndale, Massachusetts: B.H.B. Printing, 1972.

United States Government Reports

Commission on Obscenity and Pornography: *The Report of the Commission on Obscenity and Pornography.* New York: Bantam Books, 1970.

Department of Health, Education and Welfare. American Human Association. *National Analysis of Official Child Neglect and Abuse Reporting.* Denver: American Humane Association, 1978.

Department of Health, Education and Welfare. National Institute of Mental Health. *Child Abuse and Neglect Programs: Practice and Theory.* Washington, D.C.: U.S. Government Printing Office, 1977.

Department of Health, Education and Welfare: *Youth Development and Delinquency Prevention Administration. State Responsibility for Juvenile Detention Care.* Washington, D.C.: U.S. Government Printing Office, 1970.

Department of Health and Human Services. Office of Human Development Services. Administration for Children, Youth and Families. *The Status of Children, Youth and Families.* Washington, D.C.: U.S. Government Printing Office, 1980.

Department of Justice. Law Enforcement Assistance Administration. National Institute for Law Enforcement and Criminal Justice. *Child Abuse Intervention: Prescriptive Package.* By A. Schuchter. Washington, D.C.: U.S. Government Printing Office, December 1976.

Department of Justice. Office of Juvenile Justice and Delinquency Prevention. *Juvenile Justice: Before and After the Onset of Delinquency: United States Discussion Paper for the Sixth United Nations Congress on the Prevention of Crime and Treatment of Offenders.* Washington, D.C.: Superintendent of Documents, 1980.

National Advisory Commission on Civil Disorders: *Report of the National Advisory Commission on Civil Disorders.* Washington, D.C.: U.S. Government Printing Office, 1968, Bantam, 1968.

National Advisory Commission on Criminal Justice Standards and Goals: *A National Strategy to Reduce Crime., Criminal Justice System., Police., Courts., Corrections., Community Crime Prevention., Proceedings of the National Conference on Criminal Justice.* Washington, D.C.: U.S. Government Printing Office, 1973.

National Advisory Committee for Juvenile Justice and Delinquency Prevention. *Standards for the Administration of Juvenile Justice*. Washington, D.C.: U.S. Government Printing Office, 1980.

National Commission of the Causes and Prevention of Violence Report. Washington, D.C.: U.S. Government Printing Office, 1969.

National Commission on Marihuana and Drug Abuse: *Drug Abuse in America: Problem in Perspective*. Washington, D.C.: U.S. Government Printing Office, 1973.

President's Commission on Law Enforcement and Administration of Justice: *The Challenge of Crime in a Free Society (Commission's General Report). Task Force Reports: The Police., The Courts., Organized Crime., Corrections., Science and Technology., Drunkenness., Juvenile Delinquency and Youth Crime., Narcotics and Drug Abuse., Crime and Its Impact—An Assessment*. Washington, D.C.: U.S. Government Printing Office, 1967.

National Juvenile Justice System Assessment Center

Cardarelli, A.P., and Smith, C.P.: Delinquency prevention and control programs: The need for a conceptual framework and evaluation strategies. In *How Well Does It Work? Review of Criminal Justice Evaluation*. Washington, D.C.: U.S. Department of Justice, Law Enforcement Assistance Administration, U.S. Government Printing Office, 1979.

National Institute on Drug Abuse: *Criminal Justice Alternatives for Disposition of Drug Abusing Offender Cases—Judge*. Washington, D.C.: U.S. Government Printing Office, 1978.

National Institute on Drug Abuse: *Criminal Justice Alternatives for Disposition of Drug Abusing Offender Cases—Prosecutor*. Washington, D.C.: U.S. Government Printing Office, 1978.

National Institute on Drug Abuse, Research Monograph 13: *Cocaine*. Washington, D.C.: U.S. Government Printing Office, 1977.

National Institute on Drug Abuse: *Diagnosis and Treatment of Adverse Reactions to Sedative-Hypnotics*. Washington, D.C.: U.S. Government Printing Office, 1974.

National Institute on Drug Abuse: *Drug Abuse Treatment and the Criminal Justice System—Three Reports*. Washington, D.C.: Department of Health, Education and Welfare, 1977.

National Institute on Drug Abuse: *Drug Dependence in Pregnancy: Clinical Management of Mother and Child*. Washington, D.C.: U.S. Government Printing Office, 1979.

National Institute on Drug Abuse: *Handbook on Drug Abuse*. Washington, D.C.: U.S. Government Printing Office, 1979.

National Institute on Drug Abuse: *Highlights from Drug Use Among American High School Students*. Washington, D.C.: U.S. Government Printing Office, 1975/1977.

National Institute on Drug Abuse, Research Monograph 21: *Phencyclidine (PCP) Abuse: An Appraisal*. Washington, D.C.: U.S. Government Printing Office, 1978.

National Institute on Drug Abuse: *Review of Inhalants: Euphoria to Dysfunction*. Washington, D.C.: U.S. Government Printing Office, 1977.

Smith, C.P., and Alexander, P.S.: *A National Assessment of Serious Juvenile Crime and the Juvenile Justice System: The Need for a Rational Response — Volume I: Summary.* Washington, D.C.: U.S. Government Printing Office, 1980.

Smith, C.P., Alexander, P.S., Halatyn, T.V., and Roberts, C.F.: *A National Assessment of Serious Juvenile Crime and the Juvenile Justice System: The Need for a Rational Response — Volume II: Definition; Characteristics of Incidents and Individuals; and Relationship to Substance Abuse.* Washington, D.C.: U.S. Government Printing Office, 1980.

Smith, C.P., Alexander, P.S., Kemp, G.L., and Lemert, E.M.: *A National Assessment of Serious Juvenile Crime and the Juvenile Justice System: The Need for a Rational Response — Volume III: Legislation; Jurisdiction; Program Interventions; and Confidentiality of Juvenile Records.* Washington, D.C.: U.S. Government Printing Office, 1980.

Smith, C.P., Alexander, P.S., and Thalheimer, D.J.: *A National Assessment of Serious Juvenile Crime and the Juvenile Justice System: The Need for a Rational Response — Volume IV: Economic Impact.* Washington, D.C.: U.S. Government Printing Office, 1980.

Smith, C.P., Berkman, D.J., and Fraser, W.M.: *A Preliminary National Assessment of Child Abuse and Neglect and the Juvenile Justice System: The Shadows of Distress.* Washington, D.C.: U.S. Government Printing Office, 1980.

Smith, C.P., Berkman, D.J., Fraser, W.M., and Sutton, J.R.: *A Preliminary National Assessment of the Status Offender and the Juvenile Justice System: Role Conflicts, Constraints, and Information Gaps.* Washington, D.C.: U.S. Government Printing Office, 1980.

Smith, C.P., Black, T.E., and Campbell, F.R.: *A National Assessment of Case Disposition and Classification in the Juvenile Justice System: Inconsistent Labeling — Volume I: Process Description and Summary.* Washington, D.C., U.S. Government Printing Office, 1979.

Smith, C.P., Black, T.E., and Campbell, F.R.: *A National Assessment of Case Disposition and Classification in the Juvenile Justice System: Inconsistent Labelling — Volume III: Results of a Survey.* Washington, D.C.: U.S. Government Printing Office, 1980.

Smith, C.P., Black, T.E., and Weir, A.W.: *A National Assessment of Case Disposition and Classification in the Juvenile Justice System: Inconsistent Labeling — Volume II: Results of a Literature Search.* Washington, D.C.: U.S. Government Printing Office, 1980.

Usdin, E., and Efron, D.H.: *Psychotropic Drugs and Related Compounds.* Washington, D.C.: U.S. Government Printing Office, 1972.

INDEX

A

Absconder, 217
Abused children, 307, 326
Abusers, drug and narcotic, 96
Access, control for records, 285
Accuracy of records, 281
Adjudication of juveniles, 25, 38, 41
Administrative functions, 162, 200
Admissions, 50
Adolescents, 337
Adversary proceedings, 25
Alcohol, 96
American Bar Association, 32
Amphetamines, 95
Arrests, 12, 210
  guidelines, 213
  rates, 6
  taken into custody, 215
Artist-hypnosis composites, 261

B

Bail, 22
Barbiturates, 94
Battering child syndrome, 309
Becker, Howard, 61
Bicycle programs, 223
Burden of proof, 42, 54

C

California juvenile law, 39
California Dental Identification System, 222
California Youth Authority wards, 8
Cases, 199, 283
Central Registry, abuse and neglect cases, 312
"Chicken," 327
"Chickenhawk," 327

Child abuse, 307
  parent reaction, 337
  police procedures, 319
  psychological factors, 337
  victim reaction, 338
Child development, 335
Child molester, 325
  interviewing, 332
  reporting, 331
Child neglect, 307
Children
  protection of, 43
  sex offenses against, 110
Civil actions of juvenile court, 45, 47
Civil liberties, police protection of, 168, 171
Cocaine, 95
Coercive activities, police, 169
Commissioners, 42
Communications, nonverbal, 242
Community agencies, 163
Community coordination, 200
Complaints, 289, 300
Confessions, 50
Confidentiality of records, 279
Confinement, institutional, 42
Consent decree, 19
Constitutional rights, 19, 48
Control of juveniles, 37
Coordination, interagency, 35
Correctional agencies, sex offender control, 116
Counsel, legal, 24, 53
Counselling, police role, 170
Court
  preparation of victims for, 344
  jurisdiction, 268
  police relations, 167
  policy influence on police, 163
  sex offender procedures, 116
Crime, violent, 166

Crime control, 152
Criminal court
jurisdiction, 4, 268
juvenile processing, 40
transfer due process, 41
Criminal justice planning, 351
Criminal law, 37
Criminal responsibility of children, 44
Custodial interrogation, 234

D

Defense counsel, 23
Delinquency
abused child, 316
defined, 64
Delinquency Control Institute, 197
Delinquent, stigmatized, 71
Depressants, 94, 100
Destruction of records, 281, 287
Detention, 6, 21
categories, 207
comingling juveniles and adults, 276
hearing, 23
police role, 13, 160
Deterrence, 84
Deviance theory, 58
Discretion
circumscribed, 153
exercise of, 13, 35, 147
labeling impact, 70
police, 47, 165
Dispositions, 25, 34, 202
hearings, 26
by juvenile unit, 150, 189, 206
police, 171
prejudicial, 17
types, 208
Diversion, 6, 81, 272
juvenile court, 75
labeling effect, 73
police, 151
Drug abuse prevention, 103
Drug Enforcement Administration, 93
Drugs, 85
abusers, 96
abuse symptoms, 99
history of, 91
Drug unit, 158
Due process, 45

parole hearing, 57
Durkheim, Emile, 60

E

Emotional symptoms, 246
Environment
police maintenance, 168
security and stability of, 171
Escapees, 217
Executive branch of government, 272
Exhibitionism, 107
Exploitation, sexual, 326

F

Family court, 269
Family violence, 317
Faust, Frederic, 66
Feedback, 30
Fetishism, 110
Field operation, police, 147, 155, 200
Fingerprints, 292
Force, police exercise of, 166

G

Gangs, 71, 88, 133
Gault decision, 22, 31, 51
General information reports, 288
Gluecks, 5
Glue sniffer, 100

H

Hallucinogens, 94, 102
Hashish, 95
Harrison Narcotics Act, 93
Heroin, 95
Homosexuality, 108
Hypnosis, 256

I

Incorrigibility, 216
Informal case processing, 17
Informants, 332
Institute of Judicial Administration, 32
Institutional confinement, 8, 42, 271
Intake, 16

police role, 160
investigations, 299
records and reports, 299
Interstate Compact on Juveniles, 217
Intervention, police strategies, 88
Interviewer qualifications, 235
Interviewing, 229, 340
parents involved, 239
procedures, 246
sex offenses, 332
skills, 249
techniques, 236
Investigation, 33, 49, 157, 200
child molester, 326
hypnosis use in, 256
legal complications of, 48
reports, 290

J

Jails, 21
Judges, 265, 274
Judiciary impact, 273
Jurisdiction
age set by legislatures, 276
juvenile court trends, 268
Jury trial, 55
Juvenile
adjudication process, 38
control functions, 173, 201
gangs, 133
index, 297
labeling, 151, 264
police role, 172
records and reports, 278
rights, 41
suicides, 119
Juvenile court
civil process, 47
diversion, 75
founded, 38
jurisdiction, 4, 43, 268
labeling role, 66
nature of, 46
philosophy, 14
police referral to, 81
privacy protection act, 285
proceedings, 12, 15, 20
records, 299
transfer to criminal court, 42

Juvenile Justice and Delinquency Prevention Act, 276
Juvenile justice philosophy, 39
Juvenile justice system, 10, 74
Juvenile officers
selection, 32, 190
specialists, 188
training, 193
Juvenile teams, police, 186
Juvenile unit, police, 149, 159, 177, 203

K

Kidnapping, 221

L

Labeling, 5, 58, 62, 73, 82
Law enforcement, 12, 88
Law Enforcement Assistance Administration, 7, 83, 270, 346
Laws, 37, 40, 326
Legal action, abuse and neglect cases, 312
Legal aspects of hypnosis, 226
Legal rights, interviewing, 231
Legislatures, 275
Lemert, Edwin, 60
LSD, 95

M

McKeiver decision, 55
Marijuana, 93, 103
Mental abuse of children, 310
Methaqualone, 95
Minors in need of supervision (MINS), 17
Miranda decision, 19, 50, 233
"Missing Child Act of 1981," 222
Missing juveniles, 221
Mommy Dearest, 310
Morphine, 95
Morrissey decision, 56
Murder, sex related, 112

N

Narcotics, 93, 101
National Advisory Commission, 32
Neglect, child, 307
New York juvenile laws, 40
Noncoercive police activities, 169

O

Offenders, 264
    criminal, 268
    sex, 106
    status, 268
Offenses, 39, 136
Office of Juvenile Justice Delinquency and
    Prevention, 270
Organizations, police, 32, 175, 181, 186,
    203

P

"Parens patriae doctrine, 5
Parents
    child abuse cases, 318, 337
    interviewing, 239
    investigation participation, 9
    rights, 45
    sex offense prevention, 118
Parole, 29, 55
Patrol, 155, 203
Pedophile, 327
Persons in need of supervision (PINS), 17
Petitions, 41, 300
Peyote, 95
Phencyclidine, 96
Philosophy, police, 153
Photographs
    juvenile offenders, 292
    use by child molesters, 330
Planning, 346
Police
    abuse and neglect processing, 307, 319
    civil liberties protection, 168
    court relationships, 167
    discretion, 47
    dispositions, 81, 171, 322
    exercise of force, 166
    gang relations, 144
    juvenile specialist, 188
    labeling role, 66
    prevention, 167, 173
    reports and records, 282, 298
    role and functions, 43, 147, 151, 165,
        172, 199
    sex offense procedures, 115
    vandalism, 129
Policy, 31, 145, 154

    abuse and neglect cases, 314
    external influences, 163
    jurisdiction age, 4
    police, 32
    rights of juveniles, 279
    trends, 4
Polygraph, 252
Pornography, 329
Predisposition reports, 301
Preschool child, 336
Prevention, 35, 83, 152
    organization for, 159
    police role, 167
    sex offenses, 114
Privacy requirements, 279, 285
Probation, 7, 264
    officers, 266
    policy influence on police, 163
    procedures, 266
    records, 299, 303
    supervision, 26, 41
Procedures, juvenile court, 39, 46
Prosecuting attorneys, 23, 40
Protection of minors, 210
Protective custody doctrine, 46
Protective services, 320
Proxemics, 246
Psychological abuse of children, 310, 337
Punishment, 38
Purging records, 284

Q

Questioning juveniles, 232

R

Rapport, interviewing, 235
Recividism, 6, 271
Records, 278
Referees, 42
Rehabilitation, 38
Reports, 278
Research, 279
Rights, 39, 41, 45
Runaways, 217

S

Sanctions, labeling effect, 66, 85

Schools
 ages, 336
 safety patrols, 226
 sex offense prevention, 117
 vandalism, 130
Schur, Edwin, 64
Screening, 16
Sealing of records, 287
Security of records, 279
Services of police, 171
Sex offenses, 106, 110, 311, 326
Sheriff departments, 187
Social norms, 67
Social service, 167
Society, protection of, 5, 39
Specialist, juvenile officer, 188, 196
Specialization, police juvenile, 177, 201
State
 court role in programs, 174
 institutional care, 27
 police, 187
 programs, 270
Status offenders, 4, 265, 268
Status offenses, 39
Stimulants, 94, 101
Strategies, police intervention, 87
Sudden infant death syndrome, 315
Suicides, 119
Suspects, sexual abusers, 327
Sustaining police activities, 161, 200
Symbolic interactionism, 59
System analysis, 351

T

Taking into custody, 33, 51, 215

legal complications of, 48
procedures, 49
reports, 291
Tannenbaum, Frank, 59
Team policing, 181
Toch, Hans, 63
Traffic
 control, 156
 education, 227
 juvenile offender, 268
 safety, 222
Training, police, 33, 193, 196
Treatment
 for parents in abuse cases, 310
 sex offenders, 112
Truancy, 215

U

Ungovernability, 216

V

Vandalism, 128
Vice unit, 158
Victims of sexual abuse, 327
Violence, family, 317
Virginia juvenile law, 40
Vollmer, August, 167, 181

W

Warrants, 332
Washington juvenile law, 40
Winship decision, 23, 54